Using
Peachtree Complete
FOR ACCOUNTING
2007

Glenn Owen

Allan Hancock College

*University of California
at Santa Barbara*

THOMSON
SOUTH-WESTERN

Australia · Brazil · Canada · Mexico · Singapore · Spain · United Kingdom · United States

THOMSON

SOUTH-WESTERN

Using Peachtree Complete 2007 for Accounting
Glenn Owen

VP/Editorial Director:
Jack W. Calhoun

Publisher:
Rob Dewey

Acquisitions Editor:
Matt Filimonov

Developmental Editor:
Allison Rolfes

Marketing Manager:
Kristen Hurd

Content Project Manager:
Elycia Arendt

Manager of Technology, Editorial:
John Barans

Technology Project Editor:
Robin Browning

Manufacturing Coordinator:
Doug Wilke

Project Management:
LEAP Publishing Services, Inc.

Compositor:
International Typesetting
and Composition

Art Director:
Linda Helcher

Cover and Internal Designer:
C Miller Design

Cover Images:
© Getty Images

Printer:
West
Eagan, MN

Library of Congress Control Number:
0324378033

ISBN 13: 978-0-324-37797-2 (package)
ISBN 10: 0-324-37797-5 (package)

ISBN 13: 978-0-324-37803-0 (book)
ISBN 10: 0-324-37803-3 (book)

ISBN 13: 978-0-324-37799-6 (cd)
ISBN 10: 0-324-37799-1 (cd)

ISBN 13: 978-0-324-65172-0 (software)
ISBN 10: 0-324-65172-4 (software)

Thomson Higher Education
5191 Natorp Boulevard
Mason, OH 45040
USA

For more information about our products, contact us at:
Thomson Learning Academic
Resource Center
1-800-423-0563

For permission to use material from
this text or product, submit a request
online at **http://**
www.thomsonrights.com.

Brief Contents

Contents

Preface

What If?

What if you could integrate the leading computerized accounting program into your classroom without using a confusing and complicated manual? What if your book helped your students go beyond data entry and actually learn how a computer system works? *Using Peachtree Complete 2007 for Accounting* is your answer.

Go Beyond Data Entry

Instructors often want to incorporate Peachtree into their program but are reluctant to invest the time and effort necessary to accomplish this laudable goal. The existing books are often all too "preparer" driven. They focus on teaching students how to enter information into the accounting system. While important, students are often discouraged because of the complicated and confusing books that concentrate on accounting mechanics.

Using Peachtree Complete 2007 for Accounting teaches students how to use Peachtree; it also develops their skills in using and interpreting accounting information. Using a self-paced, step-by-step approach helps students understand how to use the software, to create financial statements and other financial reports, to reinforce the concepts they learn in their first course, and to see how computer software can be used to make business decisions.

What Are the Goals of This Textbook?

The text's first and foremost goal is to help students learn or review fundamental accounting concepts and principles through the use of Peachtree and the analysis of business events. The content complements the first course in accounting and, therefore, may be used in conjunction with a core text on accounting.

A second goal is to enable students to build a foundation for understanding financial statements. After an initial tour of Peachtree, students learn how to use Peachtree to understand and interpret financial statements.

A third goal of the text is to provide students a means to investigate the underlying source documents that generate most financial accounting information, such as purchase orders, sales invoices, and so on. Students will experience this process by entering a few business events for later inclusion in financial reports.

A fourth goal is to provide students a means of exploring some managerial aspects of accounting by performing financial analysis and comparisons. Budgets are created and compared to actual operating results, and receivables and payables are aged for analysis of cash management and cash flow projections.

A fifth goal of this text is to reduce the administrative burdens of accounting faculty by providing a self-paced environment, data sets, cases, and a correlation table describing how this text might be used with a variety of popular accounting texts.

Finally, this textbook takes a user perspective by illustrating how accounting information is both used and created. Peachtree is extremely user friendly and provides point and click simplicity with excellent, sophisticated accounting reporting and analysis tools. The textbook uses a proven and successful pedagogy to demonstrate the software's features and elicit student interaction.

How Is This Textbook Organized?

Using Peachtree Complete 2007 for Accounting is organized into two parts. Part 1 introduces the student to the "use" of the Peachtree software in five chapters using a case (Century Kitchens). Ideally, a student using Part 1 will be familiar with most aspects of the software. Part 2, covering Chapters 6 through 11, explains how Peachtree is used to record business transactions for later reporting.

Part 2 also contains a case, Wild Water Sports, Inc. This new case will help students create a new company, record cash and noncash transactions, make adjustments for accrual accounting, create and manage budgets, generate useful reports for decision making, and more. It also starts off with beginning balances which students include in their creation of the original file.

A service-only company, Aloha Property Management, is included as a comprehensive case at the end of Chapters 6 through 11. This case contains no product-related transactions, instead focusing on service-based accounting issues.

Finally, a payroll appendix has been added to help students understand where payroll deductions originate. Throughout this text, you will be provided with information for employee payroll tax withholding and employer payroll tax expenses. Peachtree has the ability to calculate each of these for you; however, it charges you an annual fee to do so. Some businesses will find this service very valuable and worth the cost, and some will not. Payroll tax computations are not straightforward. They are, in fact, quite convoluted and dependent on all sorts of exceptions and rules. For example, federal income tax withholding is dependent on an employee's income; whether they are being paid weekly, biweekly, semimonthly, monthly, etc.; the number of exemptions they claim; and their filing status: married, single, head of household, etc. This appendix is designed to provide you with a basic overview of the payroll tax conundrum and is focused on federal taxes only, as each state has its own rules for income tax withholding, unemployment, etc.

What Are the Key Features of This Textbook?

Using Peachtree Complete 2007 for Accounting uses a proven pedagogy to teach both how to use Peachtree, but also to develop students' skills in using and interpreting accounting information. The hallmarks of this approach are the narrative framework and the step-by-step format.

The narrative approach presents the use of Peachtree software in context for students. Each chapter focuses on a small business and the managers who are making decisions and using the software. When the book guides students through setting up vendors, for example, the student understands why. This approach helps students understand not just how, but why—and students always perform better when they know why.

The step-by-step approach of this book presents key tasks such as completing weekly timesheets or creating jobs for existing customers in a simple, straight forward manner. Using ample screen captures, students are guided through each step in the process. Students have hands-on, no-nonsense guidance for using and mastering Peachtree.

Other key features of this book include:

- A tested, proven, step-by-step methodology keeps students on track. Students enter data, analyze information, and make decisions all within the context of the case. The text constantly guides students, letting them know where they are in the course of completing their accounting tasks.

- Numerous screen shots include callouts that direct students' attention to what they should look at on the screen. On almost every page in the book, you will find examples of how steps, screen shots, and callouts work together.

- *Trouble?* paragraphs anticipate the mistakes that students are likely to make or problems they are likely to encounter, and then help students recover and continue with the chapter. This feature facilitates independent learning and frees you to focus on accounting concepts rather than on computer skills.

- Questions begin the end-of-chapter material. They are intended to test students' recall of what they learned in the chapter.

- Chapter Assignments follow the Questions and provide students additional hands-on practice with Peachtree skills.

- A continuing Case Problem—Kelly Jennings Advertising, an advertising firm—concludes Chapters 2 through 5. This case has approximately the same scope as the Century Kitchens chapter case.

- A continuing Case Problem—Ocean View Flowers, a wholesale flower distributor—is included in Chapters 6 through 11. This is a series case which needs to be completed for each chapter before the following chapter's case can be performed. Unlike the Kelly Jennings Advertising Case (to follow), there are no data files for this case. This initial file, created in Chapter 6, is used in each successive chapter. The Case Problems ask the students to apply the same Peachtree skills they learned in the chapter to this entirely new case.

- A continuing assignment—Central Coast Cellular, a retail cellular phone sales and consulting service—is included in Chapters 6 through 11. Like Ocean View, there are no data files in this case. The original Peachtree file created in Chapter 2 is used in each successive chapter, once again asking the students to apply the same skills they learned in the chapter to this new case.

- Chapters 6 through 11 incorporate a continuing, interesting, realistic case—Wild Water Sports, Inc.—that helps students apply Peachtree's features and key accounting concepts.

- Comprehensive problems appear at the end of Chapters 7 and 11. These problems provide an opportunity for students to demonstrate their comprehensive understanding of Peachtree procedures.

- The Instructor's Package contains an *Instructor's Manual*, which includes solutions to end-of-chapter materials and troubleshooting tips.

What Are the Features in This Version of Peachtree?

Use the new home page to start your key tasks with just one click. The home page gives you one-click access to all of your most important Peachtree activities, all in one place—from invoicing and writing checks to making deposits and reconciling bank accounts. It presents a big picture view of how everything fits together, with arrows to guide you from one task to the next. Peachtree previously showed these activities in multiple navigators, but the new home page consolidates key activities in one place. The home page also lets you see account balances that are updated automatically as you work. If you want to hide these balances for privacy, just click the minus button next to the Account Balances list.

The Customer Center, Vendor Center, and Employee Center let you access your lists, contact information, notes, and transactions all on one simple screen. The Peachtree Centers consolidate all the key information about your customers, vendors, and employees.

From the Centers, you can:

- Click on a name to get immediate access to contact information for customers, vendors, or employees.

- View and edit transaction information in the same window, such as open invoices, unpaid bills, or paychecks.

- See a summary list of customers, vendors, or employees, or click the maximize button to see more columns.

- View and edit notes about the customer, vendor, or employee while you are viewing other relevant information.

Do all this and more in a single location, rather than having to run separate reports to get the information.

If you need help managing your inventory and its associated costs, you'll find a number of new and improved features to help you manage your product-based business more effectively. You can:

- Store an unlimited number of ship-to addresses per customer.

- Include the manufacturer's part number as part of your item definition, making reordering faster and easier.

- Set prices that end in .99, .49, or whatever you choose with Peachtree's improved price rounding options.

Dates

Peachtree, as all accounting programs, is extremely date sensitive. This follows from the accounting periodicity concept, which requires accounting information to be organized by accounting periods such as months, quarters, or years. It is very important that while using this text you be aware of entering the proper dates to record business transactions or to view business reports. For example, if you are using this book in 2007 (and thus your computer has a system date of 10/1/07, for example), you will need to adjust the date references. In the Employee Center, for example, the concept of "The Calender Year" means 2007, and thus to view Century Kitchens data, you need to change the date reference to "Next Calender Year" since all of Century Kitchens' transactions are recorded in 2008. However, if you are using this book in 2008 (and thus your computer has a system date of 2/1/08, for example), the reference to "The Calender Year" now refers to 2008 and you wouldn't need to change the date reference.

About the Author

Glenn Owen is a tenured member of Allan Hancock College's Accounting and Business faculty, where he has lectured on accounting and information systems since 1995. In addition, he is a lecturer at the University of California at Santa Barbara, where he has been teaching accounting and information systems courses since 1980 and a lecturer at the Orfala College of Business at Cal Poly San Luis Obispo teaching financial and managerial accounting courses. His professional experience includes five years at Deloitte & Touche, vice-president of finance positions at Westpac Resources, Inc., and Expertelligence, Inc. He has authored many Internet-related books and accounting course supplements and is currently developing online accounting instruction modules for his Internet-based financial accounting courses. Mr. Owen has recently published another text, *Excel and Access in Accounting*, which gives accounting students specific, self-paced instruction on the use of spreadsheets (Excel) and database applications (Access) in accounting. His innovative teaching style emphasizes the decision maker's perspective and encourages students to think creatively. His graduate studies in educational psychology and his 31 years of business experience combine for a balanced blend of theory and practice.

Acknowledgments

I am grateful to the many adopters and colleagues who provided substantial and meaningful advice and suggestions. Their many comments shaped this book and made me a better author and educator. In particular, I would like to thank those who served as reviewers on this edition and who provided comments and valuable suggestions in the planning and writing of this book:

Linda Bressler — University of Houston — Downtown
Josephine M. Mathias — Mercer County Community College
Jeanne Miller — Cypress College
P.N. Saksena — Indiana University South Bend
Howard Smith — Texas State University — San Marcos
Larry Stoffel — Taylor University
Bob Urell — Irvine Valley College

Note to Student and Instructor

Peachtree Version and Payroll Tax Tables

The text and related data files created for this text were constructed using *Peachtree® Pro 2007* release R_3. To check your release number, open *Peachtree® Pro 2007* and type **Ctrl 1**. If your release is less than number R_3, use the Peachtree Update Service under the Online menu to update your version. This is a free service to version 2007 Pro users and requires an Internet connection. The files accompanying this text can be used in any *Peachtree® Pro 2007* release R_3 or higher.

In this version of Peachtree, Intuit continues its use of a basic payroll service. This is a requirement in order to use the Peachtree payroll features that automatically calculate taxes due to federal or state agencies. Initially, Peachtree comes with the current tax tables; however, they become out of date, which can occur within a month of purchase, and the payroll feature is disabled unless the user subscribes to the payroll service.

Some previous versions of this text utilized whatever tax tables were in effect at the time of publication. Users who had different tax tables often noted differences in solutions as a result. This new requirement solves that problem. The author decided to utilize the manual payroll tax feature, which requires that students manually enter the tax deductions. This alleviates the discrepancies between the solutions manual and the students' data entry and lifts the burden of having to purchase the tax table service for each copy of Peachtree installed in a lab environment. Instructions on how to set up payroll for manual calculation of payroll taxes are provided in the text. For more information, see your Peachtree documentation.

All reports have a default feature which identifies the basis in which the report was created, such as accrual or cash, and the date and time the report was printed. The date and time shown on your report will, of course, be different from that shown in this text.

Getting Started with Peachtree

In this part, you will:

- **Take an interactive tour of Peachtree.**
- **Create a balance sheet and modify its presentation.**
- **Create an income statement and modify its presentation.**
- **Create a statement of cash flows and modify its presentation.**
- **Create supporting reports and modify their presentation.**

P art 1 is designed to help you navigate through Peachtree. It provides a foundation for Part 2, which will show you how to create a new Peachtree file and record a variety of operating, investing, and financing transactions.

This part is divided into five chapters—each with its own set of questions, assignments, and case problems. Chapter 1 gives you a quick interactive tour of Peachtree, in which you will create your Working Disk and become familiar with Peachtree's essential features. Chapters 2, 3, 4, and 5 introduce you to creating and preparing the balance sheet, the income statement, the statement of cash flows, and supporting reports.

An Interactive Tour of Peachtree

1

Case: **Century Kitchens**

You've been working in a part-time job at a restaurant, and today you decide that you've served your last hamburger. You want a new part-time job—one that's more directly related to your future career in business. As you skim the want ads, you see an ad for an administrative assistant at Century Kitchens, a remodeling contractor. Century specializes in remodeling existing homes and is well known in town for its quality construction and timely completion of projects. The ad says that job candidates must have earned or be earning a business degree, have some computer skills, and be willing to learn on the job. This looks promising. And then you see the line "Send a résumé to Scott Montalvo." You know Scott! He was in one of your marketing classes two years ago; he graduated last year with a degree in business. You decide to send your résumé to Scott right away.

A few days later, you're delighted to hear Scott's voice on the phone. He remembers you well. He explains that he wants to hire someone to help him with clerical and other administrative tasks in support of his new company, Century Kitchens. He asks if you could start right away. When you say yes, he offers you the job on the spot! You start next Monday.

When you arrive Monday morning, Scott explains that the first thing he needs you to learn is how to use a software package called Peachtree. You quickly remind Scott that you're not an accounting major. Scott laughs as he assures you you'll have no problem with Peachtree because it is so user oriented. He chose Peachtree exactly for that reason and has been using it for about three months. Scott wants accurate, useful, and timely financial information to help him make sound business decisions, and he's not an accountant.

Scott explains that the company incorporated on January 1, 2007, and he's been using Peachtree since then. Since January 1, 2007, he's been entering each transaction, but he's become so busy at Century that he needs someone else in the office who can enter transactions, generate reports for the managers, and so on. So he says that today he will give you a tour of Peachtree and teach you some of the basic features and functions of this package. You tell him that you're familiar with Windows and you're ready to start.

Using This Text Effectively

Before you begin the tour of Peachtree, note that this textbook assumes you are familiar with the basics of Windows: how to control windows, how to choose menu commands, how to complete dialog boxes, and how to select directories, drives, and files. If you do not understand these concepts, please consult your instructor. Also note that this book is designed to be used with your instructor's and/or another textbook's discussion of essential accounting concepts.

The best way to work through this textbook is to carefully read the text and complete the numbered steps, which appear on a shaded background, as you work at your computer. Read each step carefully and completely before you try it.

As you work, compare your screen with the figures in the chapter to verify your results. You can use Peachtree with any Windows operating system. The screen shots you will see in this book were captured in a Windows XP Professional environment. So if you are using Windows 98, 2000, ME, or XP, you may see some minor differences between your screens and the screens in this book. Any significant differences that result from using the different operating systems with Peachtree will be explained.

Don't worry about making mistakes—that's part of the learning process. The *Trouble?* paragraphs identify common problems and explain how to correct them or get back on track. Follow the suggestions *only* if you are having the specific problem described.

After you complete a chapter, you can do the questions, assignments, and case problems found at the end of each chapter. They are carefully structured so that you will review what you have learned and then apply your knowledge to new situations.

Restoring Peachtree Backup Files from Your CD

To complete the chapters and exercises in this book, you must have access to data files. The CD located inside the back cover of this book contains backups of all the practice files you need for the chapters, the assignments, and the case problems.

You will need to restore the backup files to their original format in new folders.

To restore a backup file (file with a .ptb extension):

1 Insert your Data Files CD into your CD drive.

2 Launch Peachtree.

3 Click **File**, and then click **Restore**.

4 Click the **Browse** button. Select a file, Century Kitchens, for example, and then click **Open**.

5 Click the **Next** button and then choose to have your backup restored to a New Company folder. See the example in Figure 1.1. *Note:* Your location will be different than that shown in the figure.

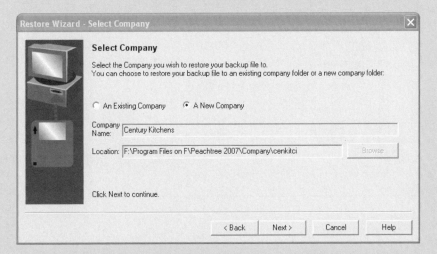

Figure 1.1

Restore Company Backup Window

6 Click **Next**. Check the Company Data check box and then click **Next**.

7 Click **Finish** in the Peachtree Confirmation window. Your restored company will appear in a few minutes.

8 Continue this process for all the backup files on your Data Files CD as you need them.

Working from your computer's hard drive is the most efficient way to use the Peachtree program. However, if you are in a lab environment and want to take your file with you when you leave, you'll need to make a backup copy of the file and save it to a removable disk (ideally a portable USB drive).

To create a backup file (file labeled with a .ptb extension):

1 Attach your portable USB drive (in this case labeled F:\).

2 Launch Peachtree (if not already running).

3 Open the file you want to back up (once again, only if it is not already open).

4 Click **File**, and then click **Back Up**.

5 Place a check in the Include company name check box and then click **Back Up**.

6 Change the backup location to your disk. See the example in Figure 1.2. The file name provided should be Century Kitchens—followed by the date you're making the backup, in this case 070607, meaning July 6, 2007.

Figure 1.2

Peachtree Backup Window

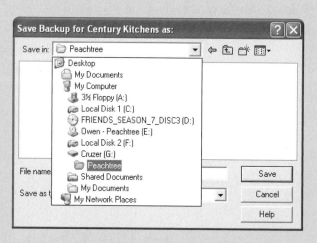

7 Click **Save** to begin the backup process.

8 Click **OK** two times to begin the process. After a few seconds, your file has been backed up.

To restore the .ptb file you just created to a different computer, follow the restore procedures described above but instead of restoring from the Data CD you'll be restoring from your USB drive.

Peachtree Lists, Maintain, Tasks, Analysis, and Reports Menus/Functions

Scott is excited about using Peachtree since it is the best selling small business accounting software on the market today. He explains that **Peachtree** is an automated accounting information system that describes an entity's financial position and operating results and that helps managers make more effective business decisions. He also likes Peachtree's reports and graphs, which quickly and easily organize and summarize all the data he enters.

Scott says he especially likes Peachtree because it can handle all of Century Kitchens' needs to invoice customers and maintain receivables, as well as pay bills and maintain payables. It can track inventory and create purchase orders using Century Kitchens' on-screen forms—all without calculating, posting, or closing. Scott can correct all transactions he's recorded at any time, while an audit trail feature automatically keeps a record of any changes he makes.

Scott explains further that Peachtree has five key menus/functions that, when combined, help manage the financial activity of a company. The five menus/functions—Lists, Maintain, Tasks, Analysis, and Reports—work together to create an accounting information system. He decides to explain these without yet opening the Peachtree software.

Lists

The Lists menu/function gives you access to current information on customers and sales, vendors and purchases, employees and payroll, inventory and services, and accounts, to name a few. Lists are created and edited either from a list window or while completing a form, such as an invoice, bill, or time sheet. Figure 1.3 shows a list of Century Kitchens' customer names and balances owed.

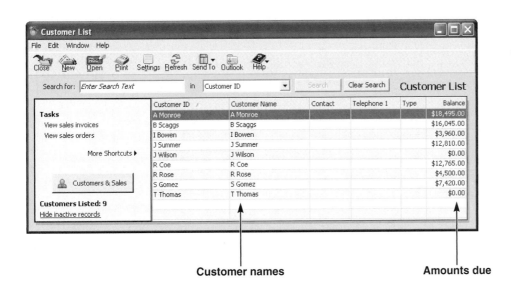

Customer names   **Amounts due**

Figure 1.3

A Customer List from Century Kitchens

Maintain

The Maintain menu/function gives you the ability to add, delete, and edit customers, vendors, employees, inventory, etc. You access an existing vendor by selecting their Vendor ID. From there you can add, edit, or delete existing information. A typical vendor record is shown in Figure 1.4. The address, city, state, zip, and phone number fields provide unique information for this vendor. Additional tabs provide you access to purchase defaults, custom fields, and history. More on the specifics of record windows will be discussed later.

Tasks

The Tasks menu/function is where you access the various accounting functions of Peachtree for your business. This is where you would access invoices to bill your customers, bills to recognize a liability to your vendors and record receipt of inventory, payroll records to account for your employees' time and effort, cash receipts records to account for payments received from your customers, and checks to pay your vendors and employees.

Figure 1.5 illustrates one of those tasks—invoicing your customer. The invoice requires a Customer ID, date, invoice number, terms, quantity of items sold, and an Item ID, which specifies what was sold to the customer. The Customer ID links to the customer list referred to above so that the Bill To: information is automatically provided. Terms are also linked to the customer file and are input automatically. Upon entering the Item ID, the item description, unit price, tax code, and amount are automatically provided as well. More on the specifics of this task window will be discussed later.

Figure 1.4

A Maintain Vendor Window from Century Kitchens

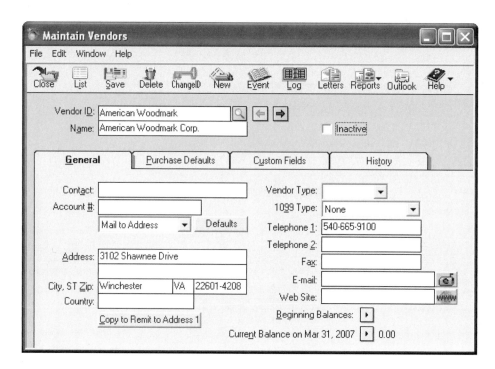

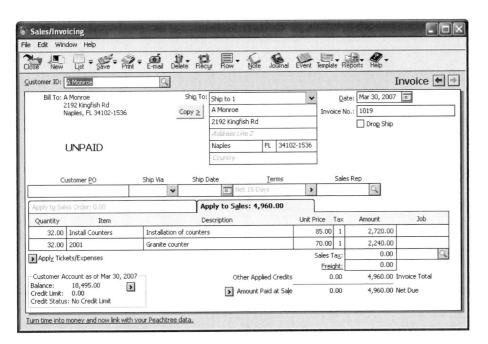

Figure 1.5

A Sales/Invoicing Window from Century Kitchens

Analysis

The Analysis menu/function helps you analyze the state of your business from four different facets. Each allows you to view information in either a graphic or numeric perspective. The cash manager analyzes your projected cash flows, the collections manager analyzes your accounts receivable, the payment manager analyzes your accounts payable, and the financial manager provides a business summary of key ratios and amounts as shown in Figure 1.6.

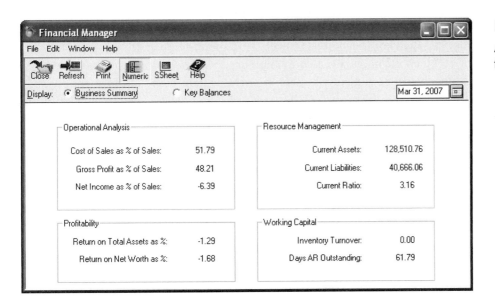

Figure 1.6

A Financial Manager Window from Century Kitchens

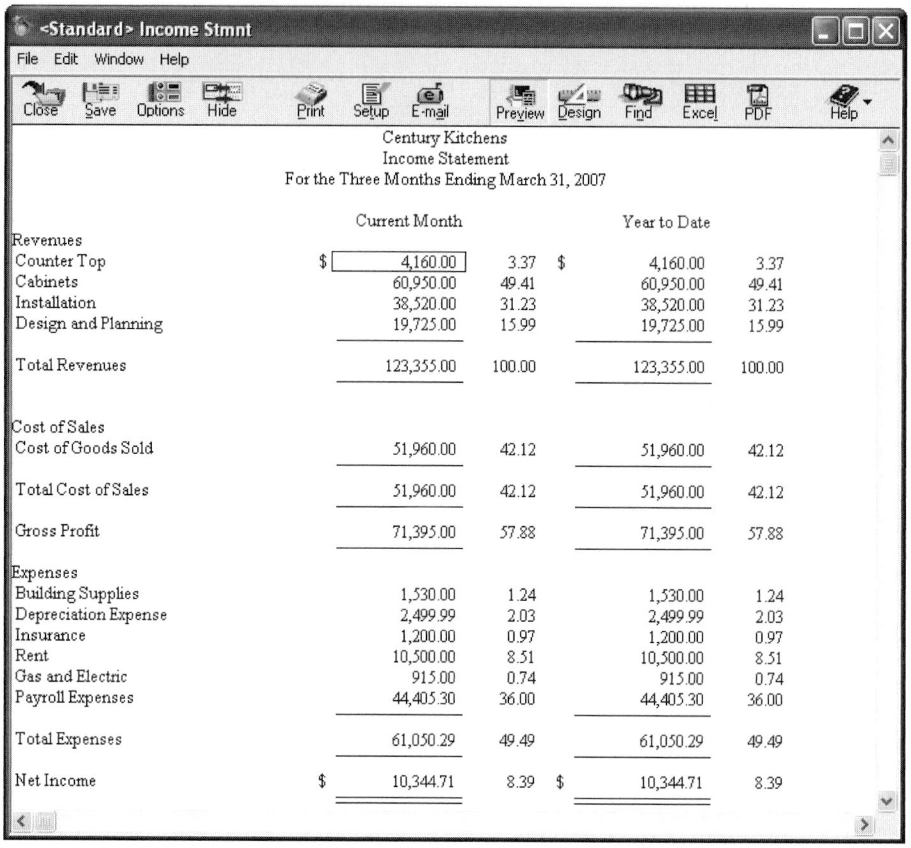

Century Kitchens
Income Statement
For the Three Months Ending March 31, 2007

	Current Month			Year to Date	
Revenues					
Counter Top	$ 4,160.00	3.37	$	4,160.00	3.37
Cabinets	60,950.00	49.41		60,950.00	49.41
Installation	38,520.00	31.23		38,520.00	31.23
Design and Planning	19,725.00	15.99		19,725.00	15.99
Total Revenues	123,355.00	100.00		123,355.00	100.00
Cost of Sales					
Cost of Goods Sold	51,960.00	42.12		51,960.00	42.12
Total Cost of Sales	51,960.00	42.12		51,960.00	42.12
Gross Profit	71,395.00	57.88		71,395.00	57.88
Expenses					
Building Supplies	1,530.00	1.24		1,530.00	1.24
Depreciation Expense	2,499.99	2.03		2,499.99	2.03
Insurance	1,200.00	0.97		1,200.00	0.97
Rent	10,500.00	8.51		10,500.00	8.51
Gas and Electric	915.00	0.74		915.00	0.74
Payroll Expenses	44,405.30	36.00		44,405.30	36.00
Total Expenses	61,050.29	49.49		61,050.29	49.49
Net Income	$ 10,344.71	8.39	$	10,344.71	8.39

Figure 1.7

A Profit and Loss Report (Income Statement) from Century Kitchens

Reports

The Reports menu/function presents the financial position and the operating results of a company in a way that makes business decision making easier. The income statement report in Figure 1.7 shows the revenues and expenses of Century Kitchens for a specific period of time. You can modify reports in many ways, such as by comparing monthly periods, comparing this year with prior years, or examining year-to-date activity. Other standard financial reports such as the balance sheet, statement of cash flows, and statement of retained earnings are also available.

Peachtree can also produce reports which help support the business decision-making process in the areas of accounts receivable, accounts payable, payroll, and inventory. Sample reports include a customer sales history for the period 3/1/07 to 3/31/07 (shown in Figure 1.8), an aging of accounts payable, payroll tax report, and inventory valuation report to name a few.

The Peachtree Desktop

Scott explains that Peachtree operates like most other Windows programs, so most of the Peachtree window controls will be familiar to you if you have used other Windows programs. He reaches for the mouse and quickly clicks a few times until his screen looks like Figure 1.9, the Peachtree desktop. The desktop

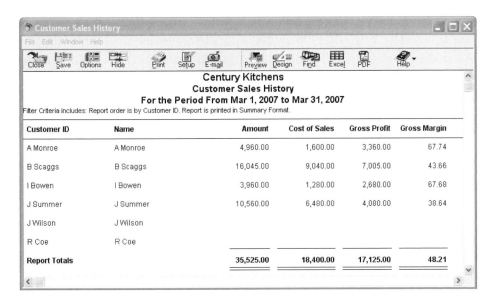

Figure 1.8

A Customer Sales History from Century Kitchens

is the starting point for accessing all of Peachtree's key features. The main components of the Peachtree desktop are shown in this figure. Let's take a look at these components so you are familiar with their location and use.

The **title bar** at the top of the window tells you that you are in the Peachtree program and identifies the company file currently open.

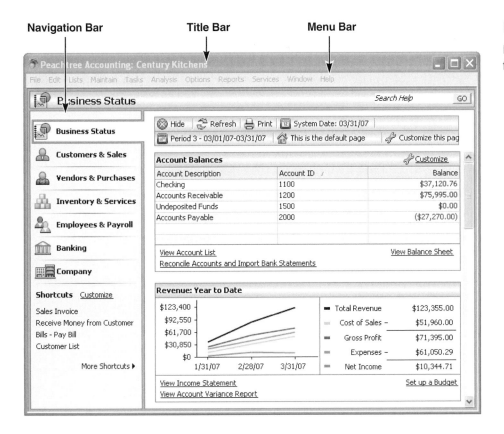

Figure 1.9

Peachtree's Opening Screen from Century Kitchens

The **menu bar** contains the **command menus**, which open windows within Peachtree. The File, Edit, Window, and Help menus are similar to other Windows programs in that they allow you to perform such common tasks as open, save, copy, paste, find, and get help.

The Lists menu gives you access to all lists, including the chart of accounts, customers, vendors, employees, and inventory items, to name a few. The Lists, Maintain, Tasks, and Reports menus provide easy access to the previously mentioned functions as well as common tasks unique to that menu. Remember, in the Lists menu, you can access lists of customers, vendors, employees, and inventory items. The Maintain menu will allow you to add new customers, vendors, employees, and inventory items. The Tasks menu will allow you to create invoices, enter cash sales, create credit memos, receive payments, etc. The Reports menu will give you quick access to common reports for easy creation. Finally, the Help menu will give you immediate access to an index of help topics.

The navigation bar on the left, gives you one-click access to the Navigation Centers and shortcuts to common business tasks. The Navigation Centers themselves provide useful access to tasks unique to whichever center you've opened. Figure 1.10 illustrates a partial view of the Customers & Sales Navigation Center. At the top, you have quick icon access to customers, jobs, and sales taxes. Below those icons are more icons simulating the flow of business events in the sales process: providing a customer a quote, then sales order, sales invoice, cash collection, etc.

Figure 1.10

Peachtree's Customers & Sales Navigation Center from Century Kitchens

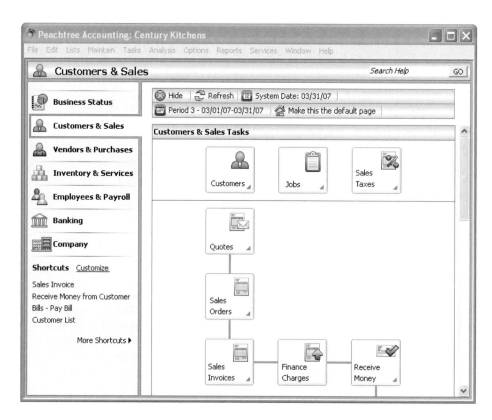

Figure 1.11

Changing Peachtree's System Date

At the top of all Navigation Centers is the Button Control Bar. Two critical components of the button control bar are the System Date and Accounting Period buttons. Clicking the **System Date** button allows you to change the system date for all Peachtree applications. See Figure 1.11. It does not change the system date of your computer or other applications you may be running. If the system date falls within the current accounting period, that date is used as the default date for entering business transactions like invoices, cash receipts, and checks, for example. Setting the System Date is critical to your success in this course. Since many of you will be entering Peachtree information on dates other than that specified by the assignment or case problem you're working on, *it's critical that you specify a system date within a particular assignment or case's date range.* Otherwise, you may accidentally enter a business event on a date outside the range of dates for the assignment of a case which will make it appear that an event you know you recorded has disappeared.

Clicking the **Accounting Period** button allows you to change accounting period. This informs the user of the current fiscal year and allows them to move between accounting periods to enter or view business events occurring in that period. Figure 1.12 illustrates the various accounting period options open to the user for Century Kitchens.

Peachtree Records and Tasks Windows

Scott explains that you'll spend most of your time in Peachtree working with Records and Tasks. Records are lists of information such as the customer list referred to previously. Remember you'll use the Maintain menu/function to add, delete, and access these records. A typical record is shown in Figure 1.13. The toolbar provides access to common processes unique to a record such as New for adding a new record, Save for saving the record, and Delete for deleting the record. Clicking the arrows next to the Customer ID moves between records, and clicking the different tabs provides access to unique information for each customer such as their terms and credit, sales defaults such as the general ledger account most often affected when entering a transaction for this customer, etc. The current balance owed by this customer is also displayed based on the system date you've specified.

Tasks include transactions such as sales invoices, cash receipts, purchase orders, etc. Remember you'll use the Tasks menu/function to

Figure 1.12

Changing Peachtree's Accounting Period

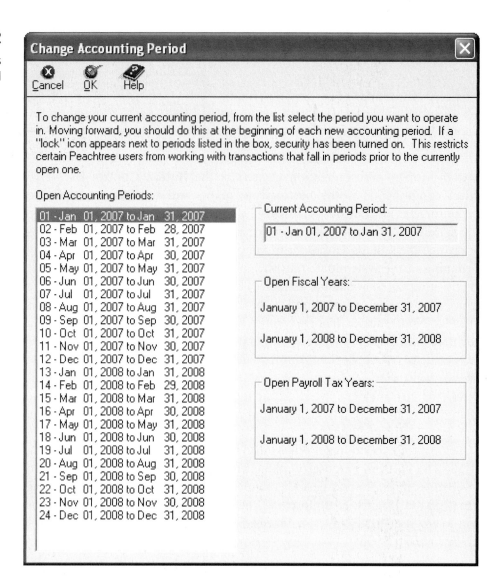

record new business transactions. A typical task, recording a cash receipt transaction, is shown in Figure 1.14. The toolbar provides access to common processes unique to a record such as New for adding a new cash receipt, Save for saving the transaction, and Delete for deleting the transaction. Clicking the arrows next to Receipt moves the user between various cash receipt transactions. Clicking the Apply to Revenues tab is appropriate when the cash receipt if from a cash sale. The receipt shown was used to pay an existing invoice.

Launching Peachtree

Now that you know about the lists, maintain, tasks, analysis, and reports functions, you are ready to launch Peachtree. Scott invites you to join him in

Figure 1.13

Customer Record Window from Century Kitchens

Scroll to view different customers | Toolbar | Tabs contain specific information on each customer

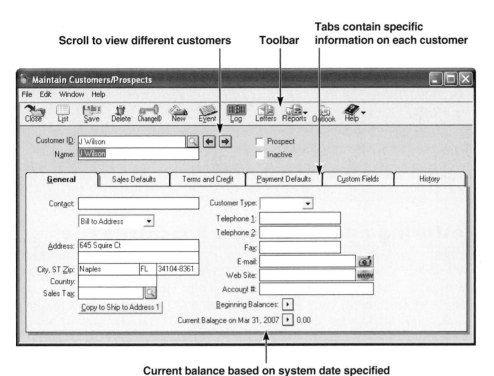

Current balance based on system date specified

Figure 1.14

Cash Receipts Task Window from Century Kitchens

Toolbar | Scroll to view different cash receipts

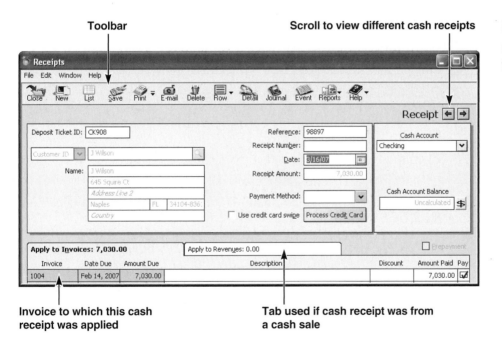

Invoice to which this cash receipt was applied

Tab used if cash receipt was from a cash sale

his office and use his large-screen monitor to start your tour. You open Windows, and Scott tells you how to launch Peachtree.

Now that you have launched Peachtree, you can begin to learn how to use it.

To launch Peachtree in Windows:

1 Click the **Start** button.

2 Select the **Programs** menu and look down the list for Peachtree.

3 Once you've located the Peachtree program, click and release the Peachtree Complete Accounting 2007 icon or name.

Restoring and Opening a Peachtree File

Scott hands you a CD and tells you to restore the backup file he made last night at home called Century Kitchens.ptb. He took the file home last night to get it ready for your discussion today. The file on the office computer has the data before his effort last night and he wants to restore it onto the office computer today. (You will find this file included on your Data Files CD.)

To restore and open the Century Kitchens Company file:

1 Insert your Data Files CD into your CD ROM drive.

2 Launch Peachtree.

3 Click **File**, and then click **Restore**.

4 Click the **Browse** button. Select Century Kitchens and then click **Open**.

5 Click the **Next** button and then choose to have your backup restored to a New Company folder.

6 Click **Next**. Check the Company Data check box and then click **Next**.

7 Click **Finish** in the Peachtree Confirmation window. Your restored company will appear in a few minutes.

Trouble? If your Peachtree Application window does not already fill the desktop, click the Application window **Maximize** button, located next to the **Close** button.

Closing a Peachtree File

Now that you have seen the components of the Peachtree screen, Scott wants to show you how to close a file, so that you will always be able to save your

work and exit Peachtree. He explains that to close a Peachtree file, you can
do one of three things:

- Exit Peachtree using the Exit command on the File menu.
- Open another company file using the Open Company command.
- Close the file using the Close Company command on the File menu.

To close the Century Kitchens Company file:

1 Click **File**.

2 Click **Exit**.

Then Scott tells you something very unusual. He says that unlike other
Windows programs, Peachtree *does not have a Save command*. In other
words, in Peachtree you cannot save a file whenever you want. You stare
at Scott in disbelief and ask how that can be possible. Scott explains
that *Peachtree automatically saves all of the data you input and the
changes you make as soon as you make them and click OK*. Scott
admits that when he first used Peachtree, he was uneasy about exiting
the program until he could find a way to save his work. But he discovered
that there are no Save or Save As commands on the Peachtree File menu
as there are on most other Windows programs. He reassures you that as
unsettling as this is, you'll get used to it when you become more familiar
with Peachtree.

Peachtree's Menus, Navigation Centers, and Shortcuts

Scott explains that to enter sales receipts, create invoices, pay bills, receive
payments, and so on, you can use Peachtree menu commands. Some of these
functions are also available from buttons in the Peachtree Navigation Centers
or the Shortcuts list. While having multiple ways of accomplishing the same
thing is often confusing, what matters is that you get the business transaction
or event recorded accurately.

Some Peachtree menus are dynamic; in other words, the options
on the menu change depending upon what form, list, register, or report
with which you are working. For instance, when you enter sales receipts
information, the File and Edit menus change to include menu commands
to print the sales receipts, or to edit, delete, memorize, or void the sales
receipts.

Because this is all new to you, Scott suggests that first you become familiar
with how managers at Century Kitchens use Peachtree to make business
decisions.

Using Peachtree to Help Make Business Decisions: An Example at Century Kitchens

Once transactions are entered into the Peachtree accounting information system, they can be accessed, revised, organized, and reported in many ways to aid business decision making. This ability is what makes a computerized accounting information system so valuable to managers.

While you're sitting with Scott, he receives a phone call from Laurie McConnell. Laurie needs some information on whether any accounts are past due. You know from your accounting course that Laurie is really asking for information about Century Kitchens' **accounts receivable**, or amounts due from customers from previously recorded sales. Laurie wants to know how much is due from customers and how current those receivables are, specifically, she wants to know which customers owe Century Kitchens and when their payments were due. Scott tells Laurie he'll look into this immediately and call her right back.

Be aware that dates are critical to retrieving relevant information in Peachtree. In most cases when you ask for a report, Peachtree will give you that report as of the system date (today's date, whatever that might be). For example, if you are working on this assignment on January 5, 2007, and you request a report on receivables, Peachtree will give you a report of receivables as of January 5, 2007. If you want a report as of March 31, 2007, you will need to change the date on the report and then refresh the report to see that information. Alternatively, you can set Peachtree's system date to a date within the accounting period you're working with as explained above.

To identify the customers who owe Century Kitchens money and the total amount of receivables due from these customers:

1 Launch the Peachtree 2007 application.

2 Click the system date.

3 Type **3/31/2007** into the Date text box, and then click **OK**.

4 Click the accounting period.

5 Select accounting period **03-Mar 01, 2007** to **Mar 31, 2007**, and then click **OK**.

6 Click **No** when asked if you would like to print reports.

7 Click **Analysis**, and then click **Collection Manager**.

8 Select the **Graph** option button.

9 Select **Pie** from the drop-down edit box. Your window should look like Figure 1.15.

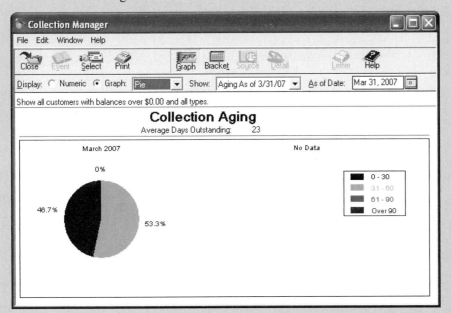

Figure 1.15

Graphic Collection Analysis from Century Kitchens

10 Select the **Numeric** option button. Your window should look like Figure 1.16.

Click here to print

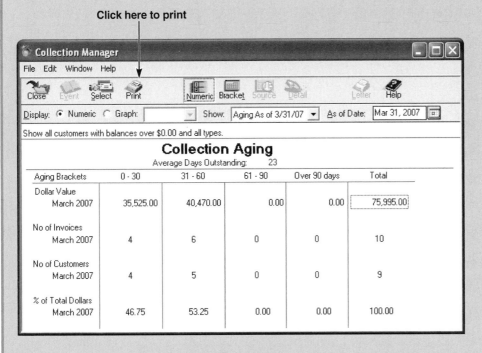

Figure 1.16

Numeric Collection Analysis from Century Kitchens

11 Double-click the **40,470.00** balance in the 31–60 day column to view the detail of what makes up that balance. See Figure 1.17.

Figure 1.17

Detail of Balances 31–60 Days Old

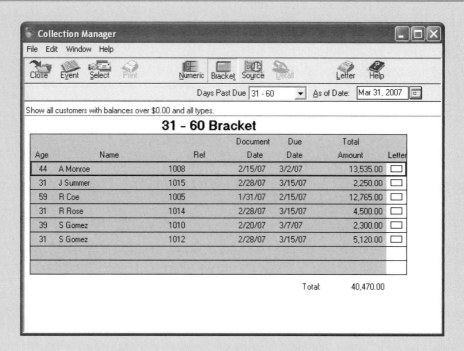

12 Double-click the oldest invoice **1005** due from R Coe.

13 Double-click invoice **1005** again in the following customer detail window to view invoice 1005.

14 Maximize the invoice window, and then use the scroll bar to move down through the invoice detail. (*Note:* Depending on the size of your screen, some of the invoice detail may be hidden from view, as shown in Figure 1.18.)

Figure 1.18

Invoice 1005 from Century Kitchens

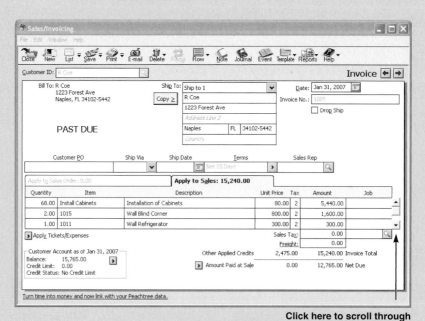

Scott calls Laurie back and tells her that $75,995.00 is due from customers. He explains that $40,470.00 of that amount is 31 to 60 days old and that the oldest invoice is 1005 from **R Coe**. Laurie would like to know specifically when payments were made if any, and in what amounts. Scott knows he can easily get this information from the windows he just reviewed.

He tells her that the invoice date was 1/31/2007 for $15,240 and that a credit of $2,475 was applied to that invoice. He has quickly and easily accessed financial information from the company's Peachtree data and Laurie thanks him. She is grateful for his quick response so she can make her decision. She asks if, before the end of the day, he would print out a copy of the numeric collection aging and leave it on her desk. Scott is happy to oblige.

Printing in Peachtree

Scott suddenly remembers a meeting he must attend. But before exiting Peachtree, you remind him that he promised to print a numeric collection aging report for Laurie.

To print a numeric Collection Aging report:

1 If you have closed the numeric collection aging report, click **Analysis**, and then click **Collection Manager**.

2 Select the **Numeric** option button.

3 Click the **Print** button located on the button bar to print this window.

4 You've opened several windows and not closed them. Close all open windows and return to the Peachtree Desktop.

Scott asks you to drop off this report at Laurie's desk sometime after lunch.

Using Peachtree Help

Scott suggests you explore Peachtree's Help features while he is at his meeting. He tells you that Peachtree Help has the standard features and functions of Windows Help, and, in addition, has other help features specific to Peachtree. These other features are listed in the main Help menu shown in Figure 1.19.

Figure 1.19

Help Menu

As with other Windows programs, you can access Help by clicking on the Help menu or pressing F1. Peachtree Help is context sensitive—that is, different help screens appear depending on where you are in the program. You can get help for a specific topic by choosing the Help Index menu item.

You decide to follow up on Scott's suggestion to look at a help feature he finds very useful, the Help Index. You are specifically interested in how Peachtree uses accounts.

To use the Help Index:

1 Click **Help** from the menu bar.

2 Click **Contents and Index** on the menu (see Figure 1.19) and then click the **Index** tab.

3 Type the word **accounts** as a keyword.

4 Double-click **adding new** to view the Peachtree Help window. You should see the window as shown in Figure 1.20.

5 Click the **Print** button, and then click **Print** to print this screen.

6 Close this window.

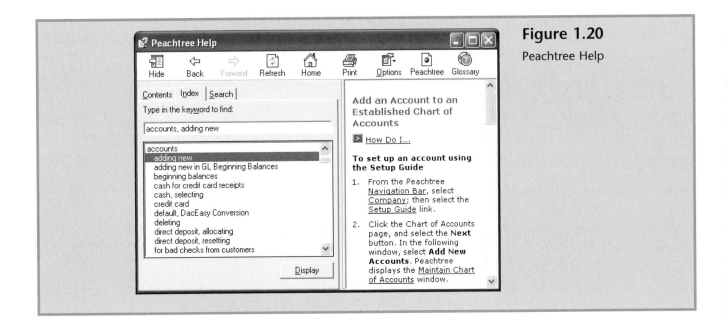

Figure 1.20

Peachtree Help

You will have an opportunity to use most of these options in this and later chapters. Scott had also mentioned something about Peachtree's Guided Tour which leads you through basic transactions in Peachtree Accounting. It also provides overviews of new features in the current release.

Peachtree Guided Tour

The Peachtree Guided Tour is accessed via the Help menu. You are particularly interested in how reports and forms work in Peachtree and decide to explore that section of the Guided Tour.

To view the Guided Tour on Reports and Forms:

1 Click the **Help** menu and then click **Peachtree Accounting Guided Tour** to open the Peachtree Guided Tour window.

2 Click **Reports and Forms** and then use the arrows at the bottom of the screen to step through the guided tour. Your window should look like Figure 1.21.

3 Close the guided tour when you are done.

Figure 1.21

Guided Tour

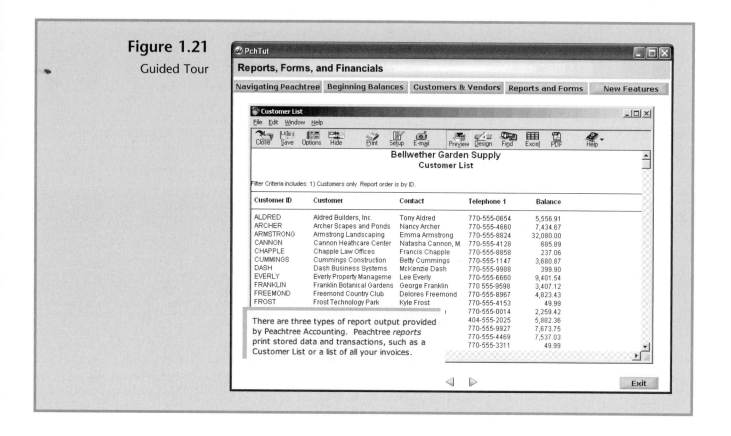

What's This

Scott returns from his meeting. He asks if you've used the What's This feature in Peachtree. He's found this an effective way to quickly access information anywhere in Peachtree. The What's This feature is accessed by right-clicking most anywhere in a Peachtree window. Right-clicking an area in a window gives you quick access to a description of what that area of the window is asking for or expecting.

To see how the What's This feature can help you use Peachtree:

1 Click **Vendors & Purchases** to open the Vendors & Purchases Navigation Center.

2 Click **Write Checks** and then click **New Check** to open the Write Checks window.

3 Right-click inside the Check Number text edit box and then click **What's This**. The What's This answer should pop up as shown in Figure 1.22.

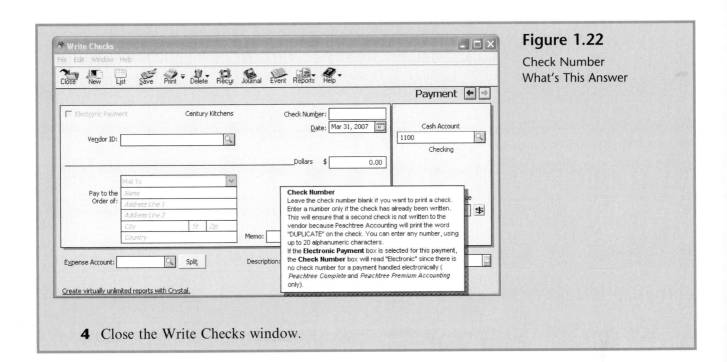

Figure 1.22

Check Number
What's This Answer

4 Close the Write Checks window.

How Do I

Scott then asks if you've discovered the How Do I feature of Peachtree. He finds all of Peachtree's features very useful, but he particularly recommends that you use the How Do I feature as you begin to work with Peachtree. The How Do I feature provides a list of common procedures to accomplish various tasks in the context of where you activate the How Do I menu. Scott offers to demonstrate this feature of Peachtree.

The How Do I menu item appears in the Help menu of every window in Peachtree. The resulting list provides access to various sections of Peachtree Help including step-by-step procedures and other context-sensitive help.

To see how the How Do I feature can help you use Peachtree:

1 Open the **Customers & Sales** Navigation Center, and then click the **Sales Invoices** button and then click **New Sales Invoice**.

2 Click **Help** and then click **How Do I...** to reveal the How Do I: Customers, Sales, and Receipts section of Peachtree Help as shown in Figure 1.23.

Figure 1.23

How Do I Feature

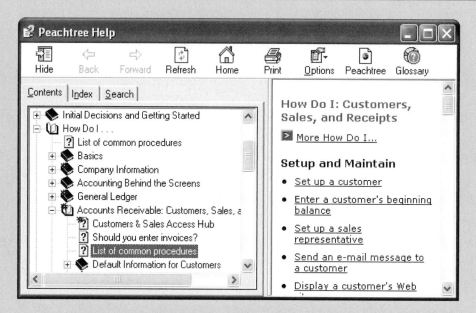

3 Scroll down the help listing shown on the right side of the window until you find the Receipts section. Click **Receive a payment from a customer** to reveal Peachtree's description of how to apply a customer payment to an invoice as shown in Figure 1.24.

Figure 1.24

Partial View of How Do I
Apply a Customer Payment
to an Invoice

Apply a Customer Payment to an Invoice

▶ How Do I...

When a customer pays an invoice, enter the amount in the Receipts window.

To enter customer payment on an invoice

1. From the **Tasks** menu, select **Receipts**. Peachtree displays the Receipts window.

2. Enter a deposit ticket ID that can easily represent the type and source of payment. This will make account reconciliation easier to manage.

   Peachtree automatically enters the deposit ticket ID as a numeric representation of the current date. All receipts that use the same deposit ticket ID will appear as one lump sum in Account Reconciliation. If you want this transaction to be reconciled as a separate item, enter a unique deposit ticket ID.

3. Enter or select the customer ID. To display a list of existing customers, type **?** in this field, or select the Lookup button.

   If there are unpaid invoices for this customer, Peachtree lists them on the **Apply to Invoices** tab. If there are no unpaid invoices, Peachtree displays the **Apply to Revenue** tab.

4 Close all open windows to return to the Navigation Center.

Peachtree Demos

The demos in Peachtree will help you get started right away. You will get a "big picture" overview of important concepts in Peachtree, as well as step-by-step instructions for key tasks.

Scott offers to demonstrate these demos by examining one on how to quickly add an item to a list.

To access Peachtree demos:

1 Click **Help**, and then click **Show Me How To**, and then click **All Demos**.

2 Click the drop-down list of demos available and select **Fast Add a List Item**, then click the **Start** button to view the demo. The starting page should look like Figure 1.25. The demo should start automatically.

Figure 1.25

Peachtree Demo

Click here to start demo. When it's running you click in this space to pause the demo.

3 Close all windows when you are done watching the demo.

"Wow!" you exclaim, "That was pretty easy."

Scott explains that all of these help features are yours for the taking as you explore how to use Peachtree.

Exiting Peachtree

You thank Scott for taking the time to introduce you to Peachtree as he rushes off to yet another meeting. You know you can probably exit Peachtree on your own, using standard Windows commands. You choose to use the Exit command on the File menu.

To exit Peachtree:

1 Click **File** on the Peachtree menu bar to display the File menu.

2 Click **Exit**. Good accounting practice encourages backing up data files, but backup is not necessary now with these sample files.

End Note

Scott has shown you some of the features of Peachtree, how to navigate these features, and how business decisions can be aided by the reporting and analysis of accounting information afforded by Peachtree. You are impressed by the speed at which information is made available and are anxious to learn more.

Chapter 1 Questions

1 Describe, in your own words, the various uses of Peachtree.

2 List the five important menus/functions in Peachtree.

3 Describe the Lists menu/function.

4 Describe the Maintain menu/function.

5 Describe the Tasks menu/function.

6 Describe the Analysis menu/function.

7 Describe the Reports menu/function.

8 Describe the Peachtree desktop and Peachtree Navigation Centers.

9 Describe the importance of setting the System Date.

10 Describe the What's This, How Do I, and Show Me How To help features available in Peachtree.

Chapter 1 Assignments

1 *Working with Files and Printing a List*

Use the Century Kitchens file to practice opening, closing, and printing. Be sure to set the System Date to 1/31/07. Change the accounting period to Period 1. Open the Customers & Sales Navigation Center. Click **Print** next to Customer Ledgers in the Recently Used Customer Reports section and accept the defaults provided.

merchandising

2 *Practice Using Peachtree Help Features*

Use the Peachtree Help menu to learn more about Peachtree.

   a. From the Help menu, select **Peachtree Accounting Help**. Type Customer List as the keyword to find, then double-click Customer List, and print this topic.

   b. Go to the Inventory & Services Navigation Center. Click the **Purchase Order** button and then click **New Purchase Order**. Right-click the **Quantity** section and select **What's This**. Right-click the window that appears and then click **Print Topic...**

   c. Open the **Employees & Payroll** Navigation Center, click the **Employee** button, and then click **New Employee**. Click **Help** and then click **How Do I...** to reveal the How Do I: Employees and Payroll section of Peachtree Help. Click **Print** to print this topic.

3   *Using the Peachtree Demos and Guided Tour*

a. Open the Business Status Navigation Center. From the Help menu, select **Show Me How To**. Click **Drill Down on a Report**, and then watch the demo. When you're done, exit the demo. What does the cursor do when the mouse hovers over an eligible transaction?

b. From the Help menu, select **Peachtree Accounting Guided Tour**. Click **Beginning Balances** and then watch the tour. When you're done, exit the tour. What is the first step to establishing beginning balances?

4   *Accessing Inventory Data*

Scott Montalvo wants to know the amount and nature of inventory on hand as of January 31, 2007. Remember to set the system date to 1/31/07 and the accounting period to Period 1. Open the Inventory & Services Navigation Center. View the Inventory listing on the right-hand side of the window.

a. What is Item 1003?

b. How many of this item were on hand on that date?

c. How many of these units were sold as of that date?

5   *Accessing Sales Data*

Scott also wants to know the company's sales for the period February 1 through February 28, 2007. Remember to set the system date to 2/28/07 and the accounting period to Period 2. Open the Customers & Sales Navigation Center. View the Customers listing on the right-hand side of the window.

a. How much did J Wilson owe Century Kitchens?

b. What is I Bowen's street address?

c. Use the Collections Manager in the Analysis section to determine how much was owed to Century Kitchens in the 31–60 days outstanding category.

Preparing a Balance Sheet Using Peachtree

2

In this chapter, you will:

- Create and print a standard balance sheet.
- Create a balance sheet with ratios using the Financial Statement Wizard.
- Create a comparative balance sheet using the Design feature.
- Investigate detail supporting balance sheet items.

Case: **Century Kitchens**

It's your second day at your new job, and you arrive early. Scott is already hard at work at the computer. He tells you he is preparing for Century Kitchens' quarter year ending on March 31, 2007. Since this is the first time he will prepare financial statements using Peachtree, he's a little nervous.

You recall from your accounting course that a balance sheet reports the assets, liabilities, and owners' equity of a company at a specific point in time. As part of your continued training on Peachtree, Scott asks you to watch what he does as he prepares the balance sheet. He explains that his immediate goals are to familiarize himself with how to prepare a balance sheet using Peachtree and to examine some of the valuable features Peachtree provides to help managers analyze and interpret financial information.

Creating and Printing a Balance Sheet

You know from your business courses that the information on a balance sheet can be presented in many ways. Scott tells you that Peachtree provides one preset way to present a balance sheet. However, Peachtree also allows him to customize the way he presents the information. He decides to examine the preset balance sheet first. He chooses what Peachtree calls the Standard Balance Sheet report.

> **To create and print a Standard Balance Sheet report:**
>
> **1** Open Century Kitchens.

2 Set the System Date to **3/31/07** and the accounting period to **Period 3**.

3 Click **Reports** and then click **Financial Statements**.

4 Double-click **< Standard > Balance Sheet** as shown in Figure 2.1.

Figure 2.1

Select a Report Window

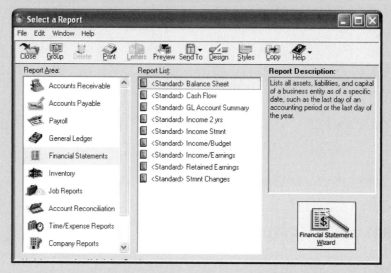

5 Be sure the Print Page Numbers and Show Zero Amounts check boxes are unchecked.

6 Click **OK**. The resulting standard balance sheet's Assets section is shown in Figure 2.2.

Figure 2.2

Assets Section of Peachtree's Standard Balance Sheet for Century Kitchens

Century Kitchens
Balance Sheet
March 31, 2007

ASSETS

Current Assets		
Checking	$ 37,120.76	
Accounts Receivable	75,995.00	
Inventory Asset	11,795.00	
Prepaid Insurance	3,600.00	
Total Current Assets		128,510.76
Property and Equipment		
Cost	50,000.00	
Accumulated Depreciation	(2,499.99)	
Total Property and Equipment		47,500.01
Other Assets		
Total Other Assets		0.00
Total Assets		$ 176,010.77

7 Click the **Print** button on the report button bar.

8 Click **OK** to print your report.

"Why did Peachtree create the March balance sheet and not the January or February balance sheet?" you ask.

"Peachtree initially creates a balance sheet for the period you've specified." Scott answers. "Remember one of our first steps was to specify the accounting period as Period 3 (March 7). If you wanted to create a balance sheet for the end of February, you would have selected Period 2."

Scott is amazed at how rapidly Peachtree created this balance sheet compared to how long it's taken him to create one manually in the past. As you both look over this balance sheet, Scott comments that because he generated this information so quickly with so little effort he might now be able to add information to balance sheets that he didn't have time to include before. For example, he has always wanted to include ratio information on balance sheets to help him make better business decisions.

Creating Balance Sheets with Ratios Using the Financial Statement Wizard

By using the Help function of Peachtree, Scott discovered how easy it is to create a balance sheet which shows a ratio column. He learns that he can either use Peachtree's Financial Statement Wizard or modify the existing balance sheet with Peachtree's Design feature. He decides to use the Wizard this time to add a ratio column. The ratio column will divide each line item on the balance sheet like cash, accounts receivable, inventory, etc., by total assets. This ratio column on a balance sheet is commonly referred to as a common-sized balance sheet.

To create a balance sheet with a ratio column using the Financial Statement Wizard:

1 Click **Reports** and then click **Financial Statements**.

2 Click the **Financial Statement Wizard** button and then click **Next**.

3 Select **< Standard > Balance Sheet** from the drop-down list of Financial Statement Templates.

4 Type **Common-Sized Balance Sheet** as the name of the newly created financial statement. Your screen should look like Figure 2.3.

Figure 2.3

Financial Statement Wizard

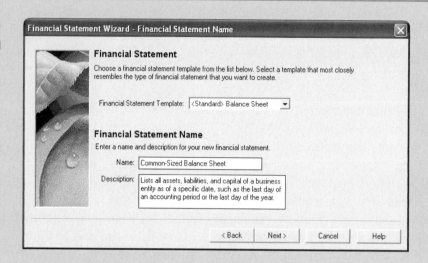

5 Click **Next** three times to accept the default information.

6 Select **Ratio** from the Contents column #3 section drop-down list.

7 Select **Column 2** from the Use Column drop-down list. Your screen should look like Figure 2.4.

Figure 2.4

Financial Statement Wizard Column Properties

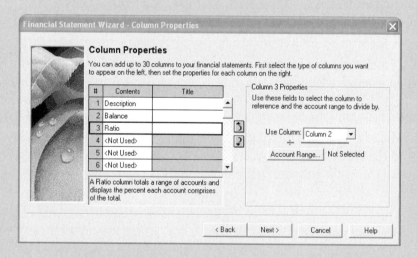

"What is meant by the term *balance* when it appears in the contents section of a column properties window?" you ask.

"This type of column displays the balance amount—net, budget, credit, or debit—of the accounts appearing on the statement," Scott responds. "Peachtree used net since it wanted the net debit/credit balance shown for each balance sheet account."

8 Click the **Account Range** button. Choose from account **1100** to account **1890** as the range of accounts in the ratio as shown in Figure 2.5 since you want to include the total of all asset accounts.

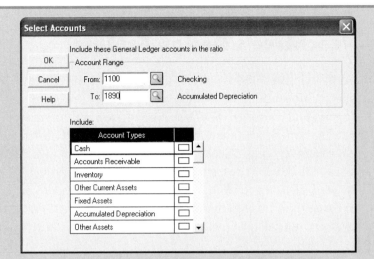

Figure 2.5

Financial Statement Wizard Select Accounts

9 Click **OK** to accept this range of accounts for the denominator of the ratio.

10 Click **Next** four more times to select the defaults provided.

11 Choose the **Display your new financial statement** option button and then click **Finish**.

12 Make sure the Print Page Numbers and Show Zero Amounts check boxes are unchecked and then click **OK**. The assets portion of the resulting balance sheet is shown in Figure 2.6.

Century Kitchens
Balance Sheet
March 31, 2007

ASSETS

Current Assets		
Checking	$ 37,120.76	21.09
Accounts Receivable	75,995.00	43.18
Inventory Asset	11,795.00	6.70
Prepaid Insurance	3,600.00	2.05
Total Current Assets	128,510.76	73.01
Property and Equipment		
Cost	50,000.00	28.41
Accumulated Depreciation	(2,499.99)	(1.42)
Total Property and Equipment	47,500.01	26.99
Other Assets		
Total Other Assets	0.00	0.00
Total Assets	$ 176,010.77	100.00

Figure 2.6

Balance Sheet with a Ratio Column

Creating a Balance Sheet with Peachtree's Design Feature

Scott wonders if Peachtree has a preset report that compares balance sheet information—in other words, one that provides ending balances for several months. Such a comparison in annual reports is useful to external financial statement users who are usually interested in how accounts change over time. Scott again consults Help and learns that Peachtree does not have a preset report like that. Alternatively, he has learned that instead of using the Financial Statement Report Wizard, he can modify an existing report using the Design feature of Peachtree and customize his report even more.

To create a comparative balance sheet report using the Design feature of Peachtree:

1 Click **Reports** and then click **Financial Statements**.

2 Double-click **< Standard > Balance Sheet** from the drop-down list of Financial Statement Templates.

3 Select **Current 3 Periods** from the Time Frame drop-down list and then click **OK**.

4 Click **Design** from the Report button bar.

5 The Design view of the standard balance sheet, as shown in Figure 2.7, shows the top of the report.

6 Double-click the second Text — Header button and type **Comparative Balance Sheets** as the name of your new financial statement instead of Balance Sheet as shown in Figure 2.8, and then click **OK**.

7 Double-click the third Text - Header button and replace the current text with **As of** and then click **OK**.

8 Double-click the **Column Desc.** button.

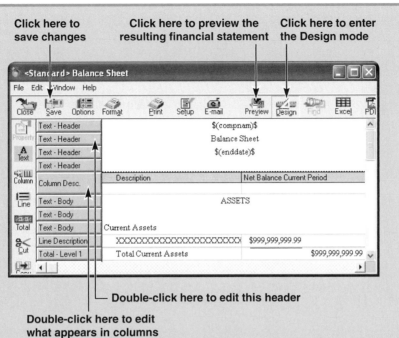

Figure 2.7

Design View of a Report

Click here to save changes

Click here to preview the resulting financial statement

Click here to enter the Design mode

Double-click here to edit this header

Double-click here to edit what appears in columns

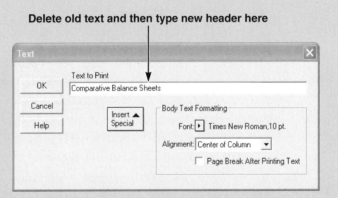

Figure 2.8

Modifying a Text Header

Delete old text and then type new header here

9 Add column #3 by clicking on the third line below the "Column" heading; then enter the boldface information where indicated: Contents = **Balance**, Title = **$(EndDate 2)$**, Width = **18**, Format/$ = ✓ (checked), Align Title = **Center of Column**, Qualifier = **Net**, Time Frame = **Current Period − 2**, Round = **Whole Dollars**, Alignment Options: **Data and Totals aligned**, and finally make sure the **Print** check boxes to the left of the column numbers are checked. The resulting window is shown in Figure 2.9.

Figure 2.9

Modifying Column
Descriptions

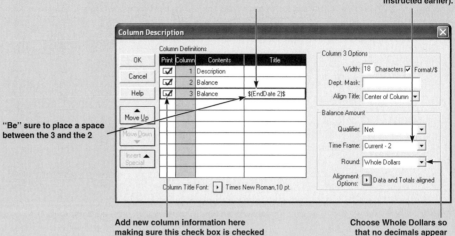

This is a special code reflecting the end of the period date – 2 months prior to the current period

Select Current – 2 which means back 2 months from the current period (Make sure you have already set the current period = Period 3 on the navigation (desktop) page, as instructed earlier).

"Be" sure to place a space between the 3 and the 2

Add new column information here making sure this check box is checked

Choose Whole Dollars so that no decimals appear

"What did you mean by selecting Current - 2 in the Time Frame section of the Balance Amount section of the Column Properties window?" you ask.

"The Time Frame section specifies what accounting period data you want in this column relative to the current period," Scott comments. "For example, since we specified Period 3 before we started this exercise, Peachtree knows that is our current period, in this case March 07. Thus, in a separate column, we told Peachtree to place balances in one column two periods before Period 3, or Period 1 (January 07). Thus, Current − 2 means two periods before the current period."

10 Add column #4 with Contents = **Balance**, Title = **$(EndDate 1)$**, Width = **18**, Format/$ = **Yes** (checked) Align Title = **Center of Column**, Qualifier = **Net**, Time Frame = **Current Period − 1**, Round = **Whole Dollars**, Alignment Options: **Data and Totals aligned**, and finally make sure the **Print** check box is checked.

11 Set Title = **$(EndDate)$**, as the Title of column #2, set Width = **18**, set Round = **Whole Dollars**, Alignment Options: **Data and Totals aligned**.

12 Select column #2 and then click the **Move Down** button twice so that it ends up as column #4 below February. Your screen should now look like Figure 2.10.

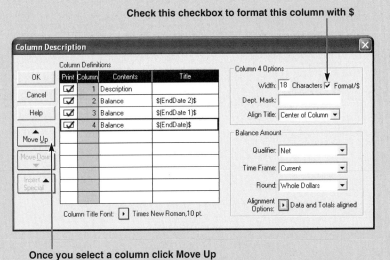

Check this checkbox to format this column with $

Figure 2.10

Further Modification of
Column Descriptions

Once you select a column click Move Up
or Move Down to reorient the columns

"What does $(EndDate)$ and $(EndDate 1)$ mean?" you ask. "$(EndDate)$ and $(EndDate 1)$ are special codes which can be inserted in Peachtree reports," Scott answers. "The $ signs bookend special data fields which are used to put information on reports depending on the accounting period selected. In this case, the special data field EndDate means the last day of the current accounting period. In our current case, that would be March 31, 2007, since we've selected to be in accounting period 3. The data field EndDate 1 means the last day of the previous accounting period. In our current case, that would be February 28, 2007."

"Would EndDate 2 translate to January 31, 2007?" you ask.

"Exactly" Scott responds.

13 Click **OK**.

14 Double-click the text body button for ASSETS (which is just below the Column Desc. button) and change the alignment to **Left of Column** and then click **OK**.

15 Double-click the text body button for LIABILITIES AND CAPITAL and change the alignment to **Left of Column** and then click **OK**.

16 Click the **Preview** button from the button bar and then after making sure the Print Page Numbers and Show Zero Amounts check boxes are unchecked, click **OK**. The asset portion of the new balance sheet should look like Figure 2.11. (*Note:* The statement heading position moves when the screen is resized so your heading may not be in the same position as that shown in the figures.)

Figure 2.11

Partial View of the
New Balance Sheet for
Century Kitchens

		January 31, 2007	February 28, 2007	March 31, 2007
ASSETS				
Current Assets				
Checking	$	48,189 $	42,924 $	34,121
Accounts Receivable		36,795	65,630	78,995
Inventory Asset		6,980	0	11,795
Prepaid Insurance		0	4,000	3,600
Total Current Assets		91,964	112,554	128,511
Property and Equipment				
Equipment		50,000	50,000	50,000
Accumulated Depreciation		(833)	(1,667)	(2,500)
Total Property and Equipment		49,167	48,333	47,500
Other Assets				
Total Other Assets		0	0	0
Total Assets	$	141,131 $	160,887 $	176,011

Century Kitchens
Comparative Balance Sheets
For the Month Ended

17 Click **Save** to save your changes.

18 Type **Comparative Balance Sheets** as the name of your newly created financial statement. Replace the existing description with the one shown in Figure 2.12.

Figure 2.12

Saving Your New Financial
Statement Design

Type new name here

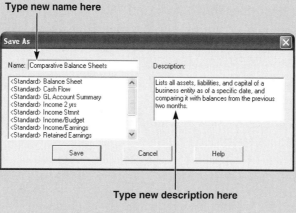

Type new description here

19 Click the **Save** button.

20 Close all windows.

Investigating the Balance Sheet

Now that Scott knows he can generate the type of reports he wants, he decides to drill down to the underlying general ledger report which supports each financial statement he creates. You know that this is a helpful feature because managers often need to be able to quickly explain report balances; thus, knowledge of the underlying detailed transactions is essential. Scott decides to practice drilling down by analyzing the transactions that make up the accounts receivable balance.

To investigate accounts receivable:

1 Click **Reports** and then click **Financial Statements**.

2 Double-click < **Standard** > **Balance Sheet** from the drop-down list of Financial Statement Templates.

3 Select **Current 3 Periods** from the Time Frame drop-down list and then click **OK**.

4 Place the cursor over the Accounts Receivable balance of 75,995.00. A cursor shaped like a magnifying glass and containing a "Z" appears. This cursor indicates that a drilling down is available for this amount. See Figure 2.13.

When you click on this amount a box surrounds the amount. This indicates it is available for the drill down process.

Figure 2.13

Drilling Down

Double-click to view the general ledger report which supports this amount.

	ASSETS
Current Assets	
Checking	$ 37,120.76
Accounts Receivable	Ⓩ 75,995.00
Inventory Asset	11,795.00
Prepaid Insurance	3,600.00

5 Double-click the amount **75,995.00**. The general ledger report for account 1200 (Accounts Receivable) appears but lists only one month's transactions. That's because this report is showing only the events that took place during Period 3 (March). See Figure 2.14.

Figure 2.14

General Ledger Report for Account 1200

Double-click to view the invoice which supports this transaction.

Century Kitchens
General Ledger
For the Period From Mar 1, 2007 to Mar 31, 2007
Filter Criteria includes: 1) IDs from 1200 to 1200. Report order is by ID. Report is printed with Truncated Transaction Descriptions and in Detail Format.

Account ID Account Description	Date	Reference	Jrnl	Trans Description	Debit Amt	Credit Amt	Balance
1200	3/1/07			Beginning Balance			65,630.00
Accounts Receivable	3/12/07	887654	CRJ	B Scaggs - Invoice:		1,425.00	
	3/15/07	9656	CRJ	I Bowen - Invoice:		8,425.00	
	3/15/07	9656	CRJ	I Bowen - Invoice:		5,280.00	
	3/16/07	98897	CRJ	J Wilson - Invoice:		7,030.00	
	3/30/07	1016	SJ	B Scaggs	Ⓩ 16,045.00		
	3/30/07	1017	SJ	I Bowen	3,960.00		
	3/30/07	1018	SJ	J Summer	10,560.00		
	3/30/07	1019	SJ	A Monroe	4,960.00		
	3/31/07	65412	CRJ	R Coe - Invoice: 10		2,475.00	
	3/31/07	65412	CRJ	R Coe - Invoice: 10		525.00	
				Current Period Ch	35,525.00	25,160.00	10,365.00
	3/31/07			**Ending Balance**			**75,995.00**

When you click on this transaction a box surrounds the transaction. This indicates it is available for the drill down process.

6 Double-click invoice **1016** to examine one of the actual invoices which increased accounts receivable during March. This is referred to in general as a support document. See Figure 2.15.

Figure 2.15

Invoice 1016

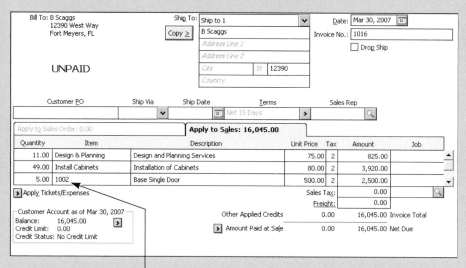

Note that you will see the entire invoice by opening the screen to full size (and the same is true for many of the images you will be viewing throughout the text)

7 Close the Sales/Invoicing window. The general ledger report, which was hidden while you examined invoice 1016, reappears.

8 Double-click anywhere on the row containing the payment made by R Coe posted 3/31/2007 for **$2,475**. A Receipts window appears. See Figure 2.16. Note that this payment was a payment on account for $3,000 and was applied to invoices 1002 and 1005.

Figure 2.16

Customer Payment Received from R Coe on 3/31/2007

Deposit Ticket ID: CK909			Reference: 65412		Cash Account
			Receipt Number:		Checking
Customer ID R Coe			Date: 3/31/07		
Name: R Coe			Receipt Amount: 3,000.00		Cash Account Balance
1223 Forest Ave					Uncalculated
Address Line 2			Payment Method:		
Naples FL 34102-544;					
Country			Use credit card swipe Process Credit Card		

Apply to Invoices: 3,000.00			Apply to Revenues: 0.00			Prepayment
Invoice	Date Due	Amount Due	Description		Discount	Amount Paid Pay
1002	Jan 19, 2007	525.00				525.00 ☑
1005	Feb 15, 2007	15,240.00				2,475.00 ☑

9 Close all windows.

End Note

Scott is pleased with the drill down capability of Peachtree because it allows him to quickly and easily investigate any of the balances reported. He's seen that accounts receivable is supported by the general ledger report for that account and that accounts receivable are affected by the sales journal (SJ) and related sales invoice source documents and by the cash receipts journal (CRJ) and related cash receipts source documents. He explains to you that only those items shown with a box around them are available for the drill down process. He feels much more confident about using Peachtree. You are quickly becoming more comfortable with Peachtree as well.

In the next chapter, you will expand your Peachtree knowledge to include the creation, modification, and printing of another useful financial statement—the income statement.

Chapter 2 Questions

1 How many preset ways does Peachtree provide for a balance sheet?

2 What alternatives exist for creating a customized balance sheet or any other financial statement for that matter?

3 List the steps you would take to create a balance sheet for a different accounting period than currently indicated.

4 What does *balance* mean when defining the contents of a column?

5 How do you enter the Design mode to modify a current financial statement?

6 How do you edit what appears in the columns for any financial statement?

7 How do you force amounts in a column to be rounded to whole dollars?

8 What is meant by Current - 2 in the column properties Balance Amount section? Explain.

9 What is meant by *drill down*?

10 Identify two source documents which might be found when drilling down accounts receivable.

Chapter 2 Assignments

1 *Prepare and print the following reports using the Century Kitchens Peachtree files. Set the current accounting period to* **Period 2.** *(Place your name in the footer of each report. To do so, scroll to the bottom of any report in Design mode, double-click the* **Text − Footer,** *type your name, and click* **OK.** *This will help you locate your report as opposed to any other students' reports when using computer labs.)*

   a. A standard balance sheet as of the current period.

   b. Modify the standard balance sheet using Peachtree's Design feature to create a balance sheet comparing balances for the previous period and the current period exactly as you did in the chapter except with just two months. Save it as **Comparative Balance Sheets 2.** The asset portion of the new balance sheet should look like Figure 2.17:

Figure 2.17

Comparative Balance Sheet

Century Kitchens
Comparative Balance Sheets
For the Month Ended

ASSETS	January 31, 2007	February 28, 2007
Current Assets		
Checking	$ 48,189	$ 42,924
Accounts Receivable	36,795	65,630
Inventory Asset	6,980	0
Prepaid Insurance	0	4,000
Total Current Assets	91,964	112,554
Property and Equipment		
Cost	50,000	50,000
Accumulated Depreciation	(833)	(1,667)
Total Property and Equipment	49,167	48,333
Other Assets		
Total Other Assets	0	0
Total Assets	$ 141,131	$ 160,887

c. Modify the standard balance sheet you just created in (b) above using Peachtree's Design feature to create a balance sheet comparing balances at 1/31/07 and 2/28/07 with a ratio column for each month. Save it as **Comparative Balance Sheets 3**. The asset portion of the new balance sheet should look like Figure 2.18.

Figure 2.18

Comparative Balance Sheet with Ratios

Century Kitchens
Comparative Balance Sheets
For the Month Ended

ASSETS	January 31, 2007		February 28, 2007	
Current Assets				
Checking	$ 48,189	34.14	$ 42,924	26.68
Accounts Receivable	36,795	26.07	65,630	40.79
Inventory Asset	6,980	4.95	0	0.00
Prepaid Insurance	0	0.00	4,000	2.49
Total Current Assets	91,964	65.16	112,554	69.96
Property and Equipment				
Cost	50,000	35.43	50,000	31.08
Accumulated Depreciation	(833)	(0.59)	(1,667)	(1.04)
Total Property and Equipment	49,167	34.84	48,333	30.04
Other Assets				
Total Other Assets	0	0.00	0	0.00
Total Assets	$ 141,131	100.00	$ 160,887	100.00

    d. A general ledger report of those transactions recorded in February 2007 that affected accounts receivable.

    e. A general ledger report of those transactions recorded in February 2007 that affected accounts payable.

2   *Answer the following questions using the Century Kitchens Peachtree files.*

    a. Drill down from the accounts receivable balance owed at 2/28/07. Locate invoice 1008. What did Century Kitchens sell on the first line of this invoice? Who is it billing? What was the total invoice amount?

    b. Drill down from the accounts receivable balance owed at 2/28/07. Locate the $4,050 payment received on 2/05/07. Who was the payment received from? What was the total payment?

    c. Drill down from the accounts payable balance owed at 2/28/07. Locate a bill dated 2/16/07 from Thomasville Cabin (shortened from Cabinets). What is the first item listed on the bill? What was the total cost for this item?

    d. Drill down from the accounts payable payments made on 2/28/07. Who was the payee? What invoice of theirs is being paid?

Chapter 2 Case Problem
KELLY JENNINGS ADVERTISING

Kelly Jennings has just started working full time in her new business—an advertising agency named Kelly Jennings Advertising located in San Martin, California. Like many eager entrepreneurs, she started her business while working full time for another firm. At first, her billings were quite small. But as her client base and billings grew, she decided to leave her job and set out on her own. Two of her colleagues and friends—Cheryl Boudreau and Diane Murphy—see Kelly's eagerness and dedication and decide the time is right for them, too. Kelly agrees to have them join her sole proprietorship as employees, and so together they leave the traditional corporate agency environment.

    Kelly set up an accounting system for her business using Peachtree and has recorded beginning balances as of 12/31/07 and transactions for the months of January and February with help from an accounting friend. She has just received a request from her banker to submit a balance sheet as documentation for a business loan.

1   Prepare and print the following reports using Kelly Jennings Advertising Peachtree files. Set the period to **Period 2** and the system date to 2/29/08. (Remember, you'll need to restore this file from your Data Files CD. Also be sure to place your name in the footer of each report. To do so, scroll to the bottom of any report in Design mode, double-click the **Text – Footer** and then type your name. This will help you locate your report as opposed to any other student's report when using computer labs.)

a. A standard balance sheet as of the current period.

b. Use the Financial Statement Wizard to create a balance sheet with ratios as you did in the chapter as of the current period. Save it as **Balance Sheet** with Ratios.

c. Modify the standard balance sheet using Peachtree's Design feature to create a balance sheet comparing balances at the current and previous month exactly as you did in the chapter except with just two months. Save it as **Comparative Balance Sheets.**

d. A general ledger report of those transactions recorded in January 2008 that affected accounts receivable. (*Hint:* You need to be in Period 1.)

e. A general ledger report of those transactions recorded in February 2008 that affected accounts payable. (*Hint:* You need to be in Period 2.)

2 Answer the following questions:

a. Drill down from the accounts receivable balance owed at 1/31/08. Locate invoice 3. What did Kelly Jennings Advertising sell on this invoice? Who is it billing? What was the total invoice amount?

b. Drill down from the accounts receivable balance owed at 1/31/08. Locate the $600 payment received on 1/29/08. The payment was applied to what invoice?

c. Drill down from the accounts payable balance owed at 2/29/08. Locate a bill dated 2/19/08 from Rex's Film Supply. What did Kelly Jennings Advertising purchase on this bill? What was the total cost?

d. Drill down from the accounts payable balance owed at 2/29/08. Locate a payment made on check 1003 for $150. The payment was applied to what invoice?

Preparing an Income Statement and Statement of Retained Earnings Using Peachtree

Learning Objectives

In this chapter, you will:

- Create and print a standard income statement and statement of retained earnings.
- Create an income statement without ratios and year-to-date information using the Financial Statement Wizard.
- Create a comparative income statement using Design.
- Investigate details supporting income statement items.

Case: Century Kitchens

Now that Scott has created a balance sheet, he is ready to create an income statement and a statement of retained earnings for the period January 1, 2007, through March 31, 2007. You may recall from your accounting course that the income statement reports revenues and expenses for a specific period and that the statement of retained earnings reports beginning retained earnings plus net income less dividends equaling ending retained earnings for a period.

Again, as part of your training with Peachtree, Scott asks you to watch how he prepares the income statement. He expects to use many of the same functions and features to prepare an income statement that he used to prepare the balance sheet.

Creating an Income Statement and a Statement of Retained Earnings

The income statement can be presented in four preset ways and can be customized. Scott decides to examine one of the preset income statement formats first—the format called Standard Income Stmnt (Statement).

To create a standard income statement:

1 Open Century Kitchens.

2 Set the System Date to **3/31/07** and the accounting period to **Period 3**.

3 Click **Reports** and then click **Financial Statements**.

4 Double-click **< Standard > Income Stmnt**.

5 Be sure the Print Page Numbers and Show Zero Amounts check boxes are unchecked.

6 Click **OK**. The resulting standard income statement is shown in Figure 3.1.

Figure 3.1

Income Statement for the Three Months Ended March 31, 2007

Century Kitchens
Income Statement
For the Three Months Ending March 31, 2007

	Current Month		Year to Date	
Revenues				
Counter Top	$ 4,160.00	11.71	$ 4,160.00	3.37
Cabinets	19,300.00	54.33	60,950.00	49.41
Installation	11,240.00	31.64	38,520.00	31.23
Design and Planning	825.00	2.32	19,725.00	15.99
Total Revenues	35,525.00	100.00	123,355.00	100.00
Cost of Sales				
Cost of Goods Sold	18,400.00	51.79	51,960.00	42.12
Total Cost of Sales	18,400.00	51.79	51,960.00	42.12
Gross Profit	17,125.00	48.21	71,395.00	57.88
Expenses				
Building Supplies	690.00	1.94	1,530.00	1.24
Depreciation Expense	833.33	2.35	2,499.99	2.03
Insurance	400.00	1.13	1,200.00	0.97
Rent	3,500.00	9.85	10,500.00	8.51
Gas and Electric	375.00	1.06	915.00	0.74
Payroll Expenses	13,598.00	38.28	44,405.30	36.00
Total Expenses	19,396.33	54.60	61,050.29	49.49
Net Income	$ (2,271.33)	(6.39)	$ 10,344.71	8.39

Scott comments that this version of the standard income statement presents the current period, which he defined as Period 3 (March 07), and a year-to-date column showing income statement data from January 1, 2007, through March 31, 2007. It also shows ratio information commonly referred to as a common-sized income statement. Each ratio item is that line item divided by sales.

"What are the other preset income statements?" you ask.

"Well, there is the income 2 yrs. (years) statement which shows comparative information between the current month and the same month in the previous fiscal year," he answers. "Then there is the income/budget statement which compares actual income statement data for the current month and year to date with budget amounts and computes a variance, Finally, the income/earnings statement adds retained earnings information to the standard income statement we just prepared."

Scott explains that since we don't yet have budget information entered into Peachtree and we don't have prior year data to compare to, it makes no sense to prepare those statements right now. Instead, he suggests you create the income/earnings preset income statement.

To create and print a standard income/earnings income statement:

1 Open Century Kitchens.

2 Set the System Date to **3/31/07** and the accounting period to **Period 3**.

3 Click **Reports** and then click **Financial Statements**.

4 Double-click **< Standard > Income/Earnings**.

5 Be sure the Print Page Numbers and Show Zero Amounts check boxes are unchecked.

6 Click **OK**. The resulting combined income and retained earnings statement is shown in Figure 3.2.

Figure 3.2

Income and Retained Earnings Statement for the Three Months Ended March 31, 2007

Century Kitchens
Statement of Income and Retained Earnings
For the Three Months Ending March 31, 2007

	Current Month		Year to Date	
Revenues				
Counter Top	4,160.00	11.71	4,160.00	3.37
Cabinets	19,300.00	54.33	60,950.00	49.41
Installation	11,240.00	31.64	38,520.00	31.23
Design and Planning	825.00	2.32	19,725.00	15.99
Total Revenues	35,525.00	100.00	123,355.00	100.00
Cost of Sales				
Cost of Goods Sold	18,400.00	51.79	51,960.00	42.12
Total Cost of Sales	18,400.00	51.79	51,960.00	42.12
Gross Profit	17,125.00	48.21	71,395.00	57.88
Expenses				
Building Supplies	690.00	1.94	1,530.00	1.24
Depreciation Expense	833.33	2.35	2,499.99	2.03
Insurance	400.00	1.13	1,200.00	0.97
Rent	3,500.00	9.85	10,500.00	8.51
Gas and Electric	375.00	1.06	915.00	0.74
Payroll Expenses	13,598.00	38.28	44,405.30	36.00
Total Expenses	19,396.33	54.60	61,050.29	49.49
Net Income	(2,271.33)	(6.39)	10,344.71	8.39
Beginning Retained Earnings	12,616.04		0.00	
Adjustments to Date	0.00		0.00	
Ending Ratained Earnings	$ 10,344.71		10,344.71	

7 Click **Print** from the button bar and then click **OK** to print this report.

Scott comments that preparing a statement of retained earnings by itself is just as easy.

To create a standard retained earnings statement:

1 Open Century Kitchens.

2 Set the System Date to **3/31/07** and the accounting period to **Period 3**.

3 Click **Reports** and then click **Financial Statements**.

4 Double-click **< Standard > Retained Earnings**.

5 Be sure the Print Page Numbers and Show Zero Amounts check boxes are unchecked.

6 Click **OK**. The resulting retained earnings statement is shown in Figure 3.3.

Figure 3.3

Retained Earnings Statement for the Three Months Ended March 31, 2007

Century Kitchens
Statement of Retained Earnings
For the Three Months Ending March 31, 2007

Beginning Retained Earnings	$	0.00
Adjustments to Date		0.00
Net Income		10,344.71
Subtotal		10,344.71
Ending Retained Earnings	$	10,344.71

7 Click **Print** from the button bar and then click **OK** to print this report.

"What if we wanted an income statement without those ratios and year-to-date information?" you ask.

"We would have to create one using Peachtree's Financial Statement Wizard or Design feature. I'll have you create a basic income statement like that using Peachtree's Financial Statement Wizard," Scott answers.

Creating a Basic Income Statement Using the Financial Statement Wizard

Previously, Scott had discovered how easy it was to create a balance sheet which showed a ratio column. He learned that he could either use Peachtree's Financial Statement Wizard or modify the existing balance sheet with Peachtree's Design feature. He decides to use the Wizard this time to create an income statement without ratios and without a year-to-date column.

To create and print a basic income statement using the Financial Statement Wizard:

1 Open Century Kitchens.

2 Set the System Date to **3/31/07** and the accounting period to **Period 3**.

3 Click **Reports** and then click **Financial Statements**.

4 Click the **Financial Statement Wizard** button and then click **Next**.

5 Select **<Standard> Income Stmnt** from the drop-down list of Financial Statement Templates.

6 Type **Basic Income Statement** as the name of the newly created financial statement and change the description, as shown in Figure 3.4.

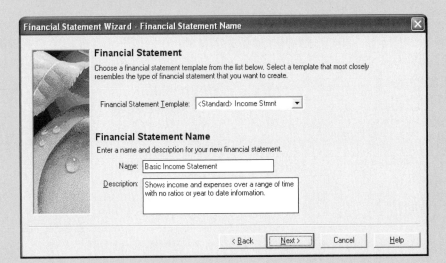

Figure 3.4

Financial Statement Wizard

7 Click **Next**, delete the existing header 3, and type **For the Month Ending $(enddate)$** as header 3 instead. (The $ tell Peachtree that the text in between them is a special data field. Be sure to type this exactly. More on special date fields later.)

8 Click **Next** two times to accept the default information.

9 Delete all titles except Current Month for column #2.

10 Select **<Not Used>** from the Contents column #3, #4, and #5 section drop-down lists. Your screen should look like Figure 3.5.

Figure 3.5

Column Properties

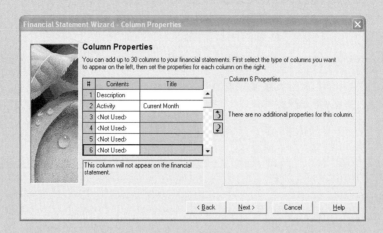

11 Click **Next** three times to accept the defaults provided.

12 Uncheck the Print Page Numbers and Show Zero Amounts check boxes.

13 Click **Next**, click **Finish**, and then click **OK** to view your new income statement as shown in Figure 3.6.

Figure 3.6

Basic Income Statement

Century Kitchens
Income Statement
For the Month Ending March 31, 2007

	Current Month
Revenues	
Counter Top	$ 4,160.00
Cabinets	19,300.00
Installation	11,240.00
Design and Planning	825.00
Total Revenues	35,525.00
Cost of Sales	
Cost of Goods Sold	18,400.00
Total Cost of Sales	18,400.00
Gross Profit	17,125.00
Expenses	
Building Supplies	690.00
Depreciation Expense	833.33
Insurance	400.00
Rent	3,500.00
Gas and Electric	375.00
Payroll Expenses	13,598.00
Total Expenses	19,396.33
Net Income	$ (2,271.33)

14 Click **Print** from the button bar and then click **OK** to print this report.

Creating an Income Statement with Peachtree's Design Feature

Scott decides to revise the previously created income statement to make it a month-by-month income statement for the periods February and March of 2007. In fact, what he will create is an income statement that will display the current and previous months' amounts depending on the accounting period selected.

To create and print a comparative income statement report using the Design feature of Peachtree:

1 Open Century Kitchens.

2 Set the System Date to **3/31/07** and the accounting period to **Period 3**.

3 Click **Reports** and then click **Financial Statements**.

4 Double-click **Basic Income Statement** from the drop-down list of Financial Statement Templates. (If you didn't save it last time, you'll need to recreate it!)

5 Select **Current Period** from the Time Frame drop-down list and make sure the Print Page Numbers and Show Zero Amounts check boxes are unchecked and then click **OK**.

6 Click **Design** from the Report button bar.

7 Figure 3.7 shows the top of the report. Each line or column of the report can be edited by double-clicking the buttons on the left like Text - Header, Column Desc., etc.

8 Double-click the third **Text - Header**. Remove the existing text and then type **For the Months Ended**. Click **OK** to accept changes and close the Text window.

9 Double-click **Column Desc.**

Figure 3.7
Design View

Click here to save changes

Click here to preview the resulting financial statement

Click here to enter the Design mode

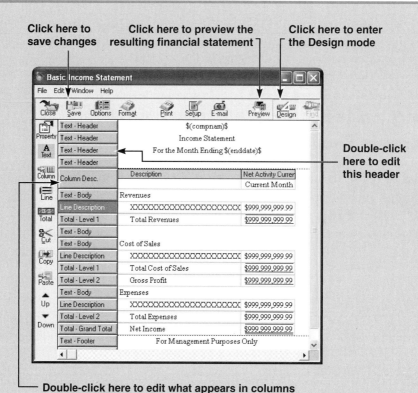

Double-click here to edit this header

Double-click here to edit what appears in columns

10 In column #3, select **Activity** from the Contents section and type **$(EndDate 1)$** as the title. (*Hint:* Be sure to place a space after EndDate and before 1.)

11 Set Width = **18** and select **Right of Column** from the Align Title drop-down list.

12 Check the **Format/$** check box.

13 Select **Current − 1** from the Time Frame drop-down list and **Whole Dollars** from the Round drop-down list.

14 Set the Alignment Options to **Data and Totals Aligned**. Your screen should look like Figure 3.8. Be sure the **Print** check box is checked for all three columns.

Figure 3.8
Column Description

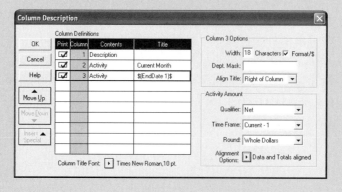

15 Select column #2 and then change the title from Current Month to **$(EndDate)$**.

16 Select **Whole Dollars** from the Round drop-down list, set Width = **18**. The Format/$ check box should already be checked, the Time Frame text box should indicate Current, and the Alignment Options should indicate Data and Totals Aligned. Now click **OK** to close the window.

17 Click **Preview** and then click **OK** to view your new income statement as shown in Figure 3.9.

Figure 3.9

Comparative Income Statement

Century Kitchens
Income Statement
For the Months Ended

	March 31, 2007	February 28, 2007
Revenues		
Counter Top	$ 4,160	$ 0
Cabinets	19,300	26,300
Installation	11,240	15,360
Design and Planning	825	8,175
Total Revenues	35,525	49,835
Cost of Sales		
Cost of Goods Sold	18,400	21,200
Total Cost of Sales	18,400	21,200
Gross Profit	17,125	28,635
Expenses		
Building Supplies	690	675
Depreciation Expense	833	833
Insurance	400	800
Rent	3,500	3,500
Gas and Electric	375	375
Payroll Expenses	13,598	14,216
Total Expenses	19,396	20,399
Net Income	$ (2,271)	$ 8,236

18 Click **Save** from the button bar and then type **2 Mo. Comparative Income Stmt** as the name of the newly created statement.

19 Click **Save**.

20 Click **Print** from the button bar and then click **OK** to print this report.

21 Close all windows.

"What does $(EndDate)$ and $(EndDate 1)$ mean?" you ask.

"$(EndDate)$ and $(EndDate 1)$ are special codes which can be inserted in Peachtree reports," Scott answers. "The $ signs bookend special data fields which are used to put information on reports depending on the accounting period selected. In this case, the special data field EndDate means the last day of the current accounting period. In our current case, that would be March 31, 2007, since we've selected to be in accounting period 3. The data field EndDate 1 means the last day of the previous accounting period. In our current case, that would be February 28, 2007."

"Would EndDate 2 translate to January 31, 2007?" you ask.

"Exactly" Scott responds.

Scott suggests you add one more column to your new income statement that computes the percentage of the current month compared to the prior month. You offer to read through the Help function of Peachtree to figure it out.

To add a percentage column to your income statement:

1 Open Century Kitchens.

2 Set the System Date to **3/31/07** and the accounting period to **Period 3**.

3 Click **Reports** and then click **Financial Statements**.

4 Double-click **2 Mo. Comparative Income Stmt** from the drop-down list of Financial Statement Templates. (If you didn't save it last time, you'll need to recreate it!)

5 Select **Current Period** from the Time Frame drop-down list and make sure the Print Page Numbers and Show Zero Amounts check boxes are unchecked and then click **OK**.

6 Click **Design** from the Report button bar.

7 Double-click **Column Desc.**

8 Add a 4th column with Contents = **Percentage**, Title = **Pct. of Prior Mo.**, Width = **20**, and Align Title = **Right of Column**.

9 Select **2** as the numerator of the percentage and then select **3** as the denominator of the percentage. Your column descriptor window should look like Figure 3.10.

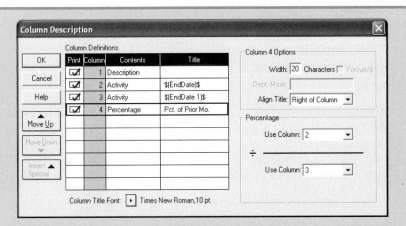

Figure 3.10

Adding a Percentage

10 Click **OK** and then click **Preview** on the button bar and then **OK** to view your new statement as shown in Figure 3.11.

Figure 3.11

Income Statement with Percentage

	Century Kitchens Income Statement For the Months Ended		
	March 31, 2007	February 28, 2007	Pct. of Prior Mo.
Revenues			
Counter Top	$ 4,160	$ 0	0.00
Cabinets	19,300	26,300	73.38
Installation	11,240	15,360	73.18
Design and Planning	825	8,175	10.09
Total Revenues	35,525	49,835	71.29
Cost of Sales			
Cost of Goods Sold	18,400	21,200	86.79
Total Cost of Sales	18,400	21,200	86.79
Gross Profit	17,125	28,635	59.80
Expenses			
Building Supplies	690	675	102.22
Depreciation Expense	833	833	100.00
Insurance	400	800	50.00
Rent	3,500	3,500	100.00
Gas and Electric	375	375	100.00
Payroll Expenses	13,598	14,216	95.65
Total Expenses	19,396	20,399	95.08
Net Income	$ (2,271)	$ 8,236	(27.57)

11 Click **Save**, type **2 Mo. Comp. Income Stmt w Pct** as the name of your new statement, and then click **Save**. Don't close the statement window as you're going to do some more work!

"I thought the percentage column added would show increases or decreases but instead the percentage column showed what percentage a line item was compared to the same item the previous month," you comment.

"You're right," Scott says. "I prefer a statement that shows whether a line item increased or decreased from the previous month. I'll try that next by adding a column showing the amount changes from the previous period to the current period and then a percentage change column as well."

To add an increase or decrease column to your income statement and remove the percentage column:

1 Click **Design** (assuming you kept the 2 Mo. Comp. Income Stmt w Pct report open from above. If not, you'll have to open it now.).

2 Double-click **Column Desc.**

3 Change column #4 so that Contents = **Formula**, Title = **Inc./Dec.**, Width = **16**, Round = **Whole Dollars**, and Align Title = **Right of Column**.

4 Set the Formula Activity as shown in Figure 3.12.

Figure 3.12

Column Description for Column #4

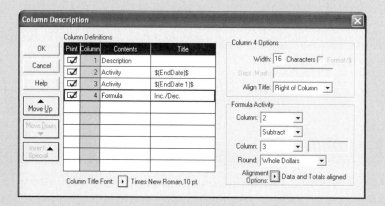

5 Add a new column 5 with Contents = **Formula**, Title = **Pct. Change**, Width = **16**, Align Title = **Right of Column**, and Round = **None**.

6 Set the Formula Activity as shown in Figure 3.13.

Figure 3.13

Column Description for Column #5

7 Click **OK** to close the Column Description window.

8 Click **OK**, click **Preview** on the button bar, and then click **OK** to view your new statement as shown in Figure 3.14

		Century Kitchens Income Statement For the Months Ended			
		March 31, 2007	February 28, 2007	Inc./Dec.	Pct. Change
Revenues					
Counter Top	$	4,160 $	0	4,160	0.00
Cabinets		19,300	26,300	(7,000)	0.27
Installation		11,240	15,360	(4,120)	0.27
Design and Planning		825	8,175	(7,350)	0.90
Total Revenues		35,525	49,835	(14,310)	0.29
Cost of Sales					
Cost of Goods Sold		18,400	21,200	(2,800)	(0.13)
Total Cost of Sales		18,400	21,200	(2,800)	(0.13)
Gross Profit		17,125	28,635	(11,510)	0.40
Expenses					
Building Supplies		690	675	15	0.02
Depreciation Expense		833	833	0	0.00
Insurance		400	800	(400)	(0.50)
Rent		3,500	3,500	0	0.00
Gas and Electric		375	375	0	0.00
Payroll Expenses		13,598	14,216	(618)	(0.04)
Total Expenses		19,396	20,399	(1,003)	(0.05)
Net Income	$	(2,271) $	8,236	(10,507)	1.28

Figure 3.14

Income Statement with Increases and Decreases

9 Click **Save**, type **2 Mo. Comp. Income Stmt IncDec** as the name of your new statement, and then click **Save**.

10 Close all windows.

Investigating the Income Statement

Scott had been concerned about the company's performance in March and now he can see how things differed between March and February. His most immediate concern is the drop-off in design and planning revenues since he knows that will correlate to future reductions in revenues for cabinet and counter purchases and installations. Further, he sees that his expenses seem fairly consistent between periods, making his biggest concern the decrease in revenues. He is, however, a bit curious about payroll expenses and decides to use Peachtree's drill down capabilities to investigate like he did previously with the balance sheet.

To investigate payroll expenses for March, Scott uses the drill down capabilities of Peachtree to examine the underlying general ledger report and paycheck details. He explains that the paycheck in this example is referred to as a source document and will prove helpful in his analysis.

To investigate payroll expenses:

1 Open Century Kitchens.

2 Set the System Date to **3/31/07** and the accounting period to **Period 3**.

3 Click **Reports** and then click **Financial Statements**.

4 Double-click **2 Mo. Comparative Income Stmt** from the drop-down list of Financial Statement Templates. (If you didn't save it last time, you'll need to recreate it!)

5 Select **Current Period** from the Time Frame drop-down list, make sure the Print Page Numbers and Show Zero Amounts check boxes are unchecked, and then click **OK**.

6 Click once on the March Payroll Expenses amount of **13,598**. Note how a box appears around the amount indicating you can drill down from this number.

7 Double-click the **13,598** amount to reveal a general ledger report for March payroll expenses as shown in Figure 3.15.

Figure 3.15

General Ledger Report for Account 6560 for March 2007

Century Kitchens
General Ledger
For the Period From Mar 1, 2007 to Mar 31, 2007
Filter Criteria includes: 1) IDs from 6560 to 6560. Report order is by ID. Report is printed with Truncated Transaction Descriptions and in Detail Format.

Account ID Account Description	Date	Reference	Jrnl	Trans Description	Debit Amt	Credit Amt	Balance
6560	3/1/07			Beginning Balance			30,807.30
Payroll Expenses	3/15/07	127	PRJ	Jessie Landon	10.47		
	3/15/07	127	PRJ	Jessie Landon	3.27		
	3/15/07	127	PRJ	Jessie Landon	81.16		
	3/15/07	127	PRJ	Jessie Landon	18.98		
	3/15/07	127	PRJ	Jessie Landon	1,309.00		
	3/15/07	128	PRJ	Juan Gomez	4.17		
	3/15/07	128	PRJ	Juan Gomez	103.35		
	3/15/07	128	PRJ	Juan Gomez	24.17		
	3/15/07	128	PRJ	Juan Gomez	1,666.67		
	3/15/07	128	PRJ	Juan Gomez	13.34		
	3/15/07	129	PRJ	Laurie McConnell	810.00		
	3/15/07	129	PRJ	Laurie McConnell	2.03		
	3/15/07	129	PRJ	Laurie McConnell	6.48		
	3/15/07	129	PRJ	Laurie McConnell	50.22		
	3/15/07	129	PRJ	Laurie McConnell	11.75		
	3/15/07	130	PRJ	Scott Montalvo	193.75		
	3/15/07	130	PRJ	Scott Montalvo	45.31		
	3/15/07	130	PRJ	Scott Montalvo	3,125.00		
	3/31/07	137	PRJ	Jessie Landon	544.00		
	3/31/07	137	PRJ	Jessie Landon	7.89		
	3/31/07	137	PRJ	Jessie Landon	33.73		
	3/31/07	138	PRJ	Juan Gomez	103.35		
	3/31/07	138	PRJ	Juan Gomez	24.17		
	3/31/07	138	PRJ	Juan Gomez	1,666.67		
	3/31/07	139	PRJ	Laurie McConnell	0.86		
	3/31/07	139	PRJ	Laurie McConnell	5.00		
	3/31/07	139	PRJ	Laurie McConnell	21.39		
	3/31/07	139	PRJ	Laurie McConnell	345.00		
	3/31/07	139	PRJ	Laurie McConnell	2.76		
	3/31/07	140	PRJ	Scott Montalvo	193.75		
	3/31/07	140	PRJ	Scott Montalvo	3,125.00		
	3/31/07	140	PRJ	Scott Montalvo	45.31		
				Current Period Ch	13,598.00		13,598.00
	3/31/07			**Ending Balance**			**44,405.30**

8 Double-click any of the 3/15/07 entries for Jessie Landon. For example, double-click the **10.47** entry shown in Figure 3.15.

9 Check number 127 should appear. This is the source
document for this payroll entry as shown in Figure 3.16.

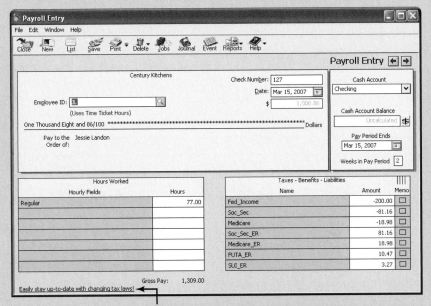

Figure 3.16

Payroll Check for Jessie
Landon

Text in this location may be different in your window

10 Note that the 10.47 payroll expense is the employer's cost for
FUTA (federal unemployment).

11 Close all windows.

Scott is satisfied that payroll entries for March are reasonable. However,
he's still curious about the drop-off in revenues. He decides to investigate
February revenues.

To investigate February revenues:

1 Open Century Kitchens.

2 Set the System Date to **3/31/07** and the accounting period to
Period 3.

3 Click **Reports** and then click **Financial Statements**.

4 Double-click **2 Mo. Comparative Income Stmt** from the drop-
down list of Financial Statement Templates.

5 Select **Current Period** from the Time Frame drop-down list,
make sure the Print Page Numbers and Show Zero Amounts
check boxes are unchecked, and then click **OK**.

6 Click once on the February Design and Planning revenue amount of **8,175**. Note how a box appears around the amount indicating you can drill down from this number. Note that all of the transactions affecting this revenue account are invoices.

7 Double-click the **8,175** amount to reveal a general ledger report for Design and Planning revenues as shown in Figure 3.17.

Figure 3.17

General Ledger Report

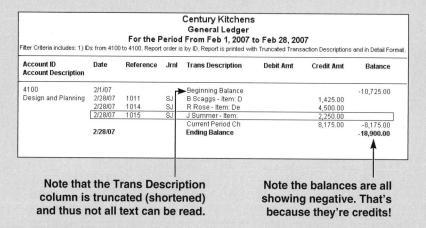

Note that the Trans Description column is truncated (shortened) and thus not all text can be read.

Note the balances are all showing negative. That's because they're credits!

8 Note how the Trans (Transaction) Description column of the report cuts off some of the information. To fix this, click **Design** from the button bar.

9 To increase the column size click and drag the blue arrows to the right of Trans Description until the column is wide enough to show all of the text. (You would click and drag to the left to reduce the column size.) Note that the report won't fit on one page as evidenced by the blue dotted line showing the page break. See Figure 3.18.

Figure 3.18

Modifying Column Widths in a Report

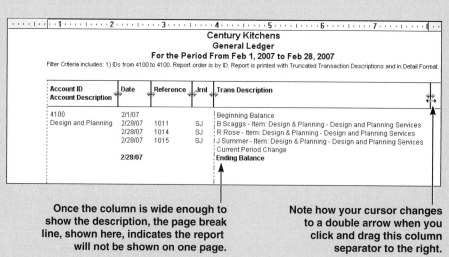

Once the column is wide enough to show the description, the page break line, shown here, indicates the report will not be shown on one page.

Note how your cursor changes to a double arrow when you click and drag this column separator to the right.

10 Click **Setup** from the button bar, choose **Landscape** Orientation, and then click **OK**. (This is the most common and easiest way to make your reports print one page wide.)

11 Note that the report still won't fit on one page. Change the column size of the Ref column, the Debit Amt, and the Credit Amt columns until the dotted blue vertical line on the right side of the screen disappears indicating the report will fit on one page.

12 Click **Print** on the button bar and then click **OK** in the print window to print this resized report.

13 Click **Close** to close this window but don't save the changes.

14 Alternatively, Peachtree lets you turn off the truncating feature for this report thereby wrapping text around a column. Reopen the general ledger report for revenue account 4100 (Design and Planning), click **Options** from the button bar.

15 Uncheck the **Truncate Transaction Description** check box and then click **OK**.

16 Click **Print** on the button bar to print this reconfigured report. Note how this makes the report longer but no wider.

17 Click **Close** to close this window but don't save the changes.

18 Scott notices three different invoices on the printed report all of which were recorded on 2/28/07. He's almost certain the J Summer invoice actually was done in March, not February. Reopen the general ledger report for revenue account 4100 and then double-click invoice **1015** to view the actual invoice shown in Figure 3.19.

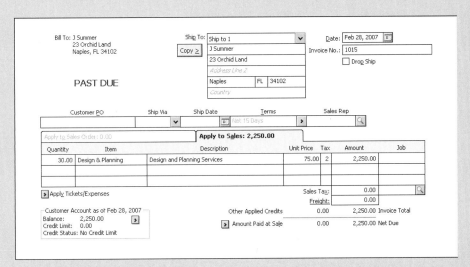

Figure 3.19

Invoice 1015

19 Close all windows.

Scott's certain that the work shown on invoice 1015 was performed in March and not in February as reported. He chooses to leave it recorded as is, but that does explain some of the drop-off in revenues.

End Note

Now that you have completed Chapters 2 and 3, you can see how easily Peachtree creates the two financial reports most commonly used to communicate accounting information to external users—the balance sheet and the income statement. In Chapter 4 you will continue your quick overview of Peachtree by creating a statement of cash flows.

Chapter 3 Questions

1 What information is included in the Standard Income Stmnt report option?

2 How is the ratio included in the Standard Income Stmnt calculated?

3 How do you access Peachtree's Design feature to modify or create reports?

4 What does $(EndDate)$ and $(EndDate 1)$ mean?

5 How do you know if a report amount can use the drill down capability of Peachtree?

6 What happens when you double-click a number on a report that can use the drill down capability?

7 What happens when you double-click a particular transaction in a general ledger report?

8 How do you modify the column width of a general ledger report?

9 What is the most common and easiest way to make your reports print one page wide?

10 What source document would you expect to see when you drill down from a revenue general ledger report?

Chapter 3 Assignments

1 *Prepare and print the following reports using the Century Kitchens Peachtree files. Set the accounting period to* **Period 1.** *(Place your name in the footer of each report. To do so, scroll to the bottom of any report in Design mode, double-click the* Text – Footer, *then type your name, and click* OK. *This will help you locate your report as opposed to any other student's report when using computer labs.)*

merchandising

   a. A standard income statement for the current period (with the accounting period set to **Period 1**).

   b. Modify a standard income statement using Peachtree's Design feature to create an income statement comparing three accounting periods (with the accounting period set to **Period 3**). For example, 1/31/07, 2/28/07, and 3/31/07, exactly as you did in the chapter except with three months instead of two. Save it as **3 Mo. Comparative Income Stmt.** The new statement should look like Figure 3.20.

Figure 3.20

3 Month Comparative
Income Statement

Century Kitchens Income Statement For the Months Ended			
	March 31, 2007	February 28, 2007	January 31, 2007
Revenues			
Counter Top	$ 4,160	$ 0	$ 0
Cabinets	19,300	26,300	15,350
Installation	11,240	15,360	11,920
Design and Planning	825	8,175	10,725
Total Revenues	35,525	49,835	37,995
Cost of Sales			
Cost of Goods Sold	18,400	21,200	12,360
Total Cost of Sales	18,400	21,200	12,360
Gross Profit	17,125	28,635	25,635
Expenses			
Building Supplies	690	675	165
Depreciation Expense	833	833	833
Insurance	400	800	0
Rent	3,500	3,500	3,500
Gas and Electric	375	375	165
Payroll Expenses	13,598	14,216	16,591
Total Expenses	19,396	20,399	21,254
Net Income	$ (2,271)	$ 8,236	$ 4,381

c. Modify the income statement you just created in (b) above using Peachtree's Design feature to create an income statement showing increases/decreases for each month. Save it as **3 Mo. Comp Income Stmt IncDec**. It should look like Figure 3.21.

Figure 3.21

Comparative Income
Statement with
Increases/Decreases

Century Kitchens Income Statement For the Months Ended					
	March 31, 2007	Inc./Dec.	February 28, 2007	Inc./Dec.	January 31, 2007
Revenues					
Counter Top	$ 4,160	4,160	$ 0	0	$ 0
Cabinets	19,300	(7,00)	26,300	10,950	15,350
Installation	11,240	(4,120)	15,360	3,440	11,920
Design and Planning	825	(7,350)	8,175	(2,550)	10,725
Total Revenues	35,525	(14,310)	49,835	11,840	37,995
Cost of Sales					
Cost of Goods Sold	18,400	(2,800)	21,200	8,840	12,360
Total Cost of Sales	18,400	(2,800)	21,200	8,840	12,360
Gross Profit	17,125	(11,510)	28,635	3,000	25,635
Expenses					
Building Supplies	690	15	675	510	165
Depreciation Expense	833	0	833	0	833
Insurance	400	(400)	800	800	0
Rent	3,500	0	3,500	0	3,500
Gas and Electric	375	0	375	210	165
Payroll Expenses	13,598	(618)	14,216	(2,375)	16,591
Total Expenses	19,396	(1,003)	20,399	(855)	21,254
Net Income	$ (2,271)	(10,507)	$ 8,236	3,855	$ 4,381

d. A general ledger report of those transactions recorded in January 2007 that affected revenue account 4060 Installation. (Make sure it fits on one page and that all items are visible by adjusting the width of each column and printing in landscape view. Don't save changes!)

e. A general ledger report of those transactions recorded in January, February, and March 2007 that affected expense account 6150 Depreciation Expense. (Make sure it fits on one page and that all items are visible by turning off the truncating feature. Don't save changes!)

2 *Answer the following questions using the Century Kitchens Peachtree files after opening a standard income statement for the three-month period:*

a. Drill down from the Counter Top revenue account. Locate invoice 1019. What did Century Kitchens sell on the first line of this invoice? Who is it billing? What was the total invoice amount?

b. Drill down from the Rent expense account. What check numbers were used to pay rent for the three months? To whom was rent paid?

c. Drill down from the Building Supplies expense account. What check numbers were used to pay for this expense during the three months? To whom were these checks written?

Chapter 3 Case Problem
KELLY JENNINGS ADVERTISING

service

1 Prepare and print the following reports using Kelly Jennings Advertising Peachtree files. (Remember, you'll need to restore this file from your Data Files CD. Also, be sure to place your name in the footer of each report. To do so, scroll to the bottom of any report in Design mode, double-click the **Text — Footer**, and then type your name. This will help you locate your report as opposed to any other student's report when using computer labs. Set the system date to **2/29/08** and the accounting period to **Period 2**.)

a. A standard income/earnings statement as of 2/29/08 with no page numbers and no zero amounts.

b. Modify the income statement you just created in (a) using Peachtree's Design feature to create an income/earnings statement comparing two accounting periods with no ratios rounded to whole dollars in $ format and a column width of 18 for all numbers. For example, 1/31/08 and 2/29/08 exactly as you did in the chapter. Save it as **2 Mo. Comparative Income Stmt**.

c. Modify the income statement you just created in (b) using Peachtree's Design feature to create an income/earnings statement comparing two accounting periods with a column showing increases/decreases and a column showing percentage increases/decreases rounded to whole dollars. Save it as **2 Mo. Comp Income Stmt. IncDec**.

    d. A general ledger report of those transactions recorded in January 2008 that affected the Radio revenue account. (Make sure it fits on one page and that all items are visible by adjusting the width of each column and printing in landscape view. Don't save changes!)

    e. A general ledger report of those transactions recorded in January 2008 that affected expense account 6172 Film expenses. (Make sure it fits on one page and that all items are visible by turning off the truncating feature. Don't save changes!)

2   Answer the following questions:

    a. Drill down from account 4523 Television revenue account in January 2008. Locate invoice 7. What did Jennings sell on the first line of this invoice? Who is it billing? What was the total invoice amount?

    b. Drill down from the TV Commercial Spots expense account in January 2008. What is the amount owed and to whom is the payment due? What invoice did the vendor use to bill them?

    c. Drill down from the Depreciation expense account in January 2008. What is the amount owed and to whom is the payment due? What source document was used to create this expense? What is the expense for?

Preparing a Statement of Cash Flows Using Peachtree

Learning Objectives

In this chapter, you will:

- Create and print a standard cash flow statement.
- Create a comparative cash flows statement using the Design feature.
- Investigate details supporting cash flow items.

Case: **Century Kitchens**

One of the main financial statements used by businesses is the statement of cash flows. Your previous experience with this statement has not always been good so the thought of the computer preparing this one for you is quite enticing. You recall that this statement reports cash flows from operating, investing, and financing activities for a specific period.

Once again, as a part of your training with Peachtree, Scott asks you to work with him as he prepares a statement of cash flows for the period January 1, 2007 through March 31, 2007.

Creating a Statement of Cash Flows

The statement of cash flows in Peachtree is presented in only one format, although it can be modified after it is created. There is another report for cash flows, called Stmnt Changes, which creates a statement of changes in financial position and is not addressed in this text. Scott decides to create the statement of cash flows and modify it later.

To create a standard cash flows statement:

1 Open Century Kitchens.

2 Set the System Date to **3/31/07** and the accounting period to **Period 3**.

3 Click **Reports** and then click **Financial Statements**.

4 Double-click **< Standard > Cash Flow**.

5 Be sure the Print Page Numbers and Show Zero Amounts check boxes are unchecked.

6 Click **OK**. The resulting standard cash flow statement is shown in Figure 4.1.

Figure 4.1

Standard Statement of Cash Flows

	Century Kitchens		
	Statement of Cash Flow		
	For the three Months Ended March 31, 2007		
		Current Month	Year to Date
Cash Flows from operating activities			
Net Income	$	(2,271.33) $	10,344.71
Adjustments to reconcile net			
income to net cash provided			
by operating activities			
Accumulated Depreciation		833.33	2,499.99
Accounts Receivable		(10,365.00)	(75,995.00)
Inventory Asset		(11,795.00)	(11,795.00)
Prepaid Insurance		400.00	(3,600.00)
Accounts Payable		13,050.00	27,270.00
Payroll Liabilities		4,344.94	13,396.06
Total Adjustments		(3,531.73)	(48,223.95)
Net Cash provided by Operations		(5,803.06)	(37,879.24)
Cash Flows from investing activities			
Used For			
Equipment		0.00	(50,000.00)
Net cash used in investing		0.00	(50,000.00)
Cash Flows from financing activities			
Proceeds From			
Common Stock		0.00	125,000.00
Used For			
Net cash used in financing		0.00	125,000.00
Net increase <decrease> in cash	$	(5,803.06) $	37,120.76

7 Scroll down this report as shown in Figure 4.1 and notice the three sections: operating activities, investing activities, and financing activities. Notice at the bottom of the statement the net cash increase for the period is reported. It is then added to the cash at the beginning of the period to yield cash at the end of the period. Do not close this window.

In your examination of the statement of cash flows, you notice in the operating activities section that several adjustments are made to reconcile net income to net cash provided by operations. Scott points out that one of the more common adjustments is depreciation, since it reduces income but does not use cash. In the Peachtree report, this is derived from the changes in the accumulated depreciation type accounts. From your accounting classes, you remember this as usually being described as depreciation expense, not accumulated depreciation. Scott decides not to bother with semantics and just leave it as is.

"How about modifying the statement of cash flows to reflect comparative amounts like prior months? Is there a preset previous month comparative report available?" you ask.

"Well, no," Scott explains. "Not only is there no present comparative report in Peachtree, but there is no Financial Statement Wizard to create one. Maybe Peachtree will have one in the next version."

Creating a Statement of Cash Flows with Peachtree's Design Feature

Scott decides to revise the previously created statement of cash flows to make it a month-by-month statement of cash flows for three periods—January, February, and March—with no Year-to-Date column. In fact, what he will create is a statement of cash flows that will display the current and previous two months' amounts depending on the accounting period selected. Creating this comparative statement of cash flows will give the company some insight into how cash flows change over several months.

To create and print a comparative statement of cash flows report using the Design feature of Peachtree:

1 Continuing from the previous section.

2 Click **Design** from the Report button bar.

3 The following design view of the standard statement of cash flows (Figure 4.2) shows the top of the report. Each line or column of the report can be edited by double-clicking the buttons on the left like **Text – Header**, **Column Desc.**, etc.

4 Double-click the third **Text – Header**. Remove the existing text and then type **For the Months Ended**. Click **OK** to accept changes and close the Text window.

Figure 4.2

Design View

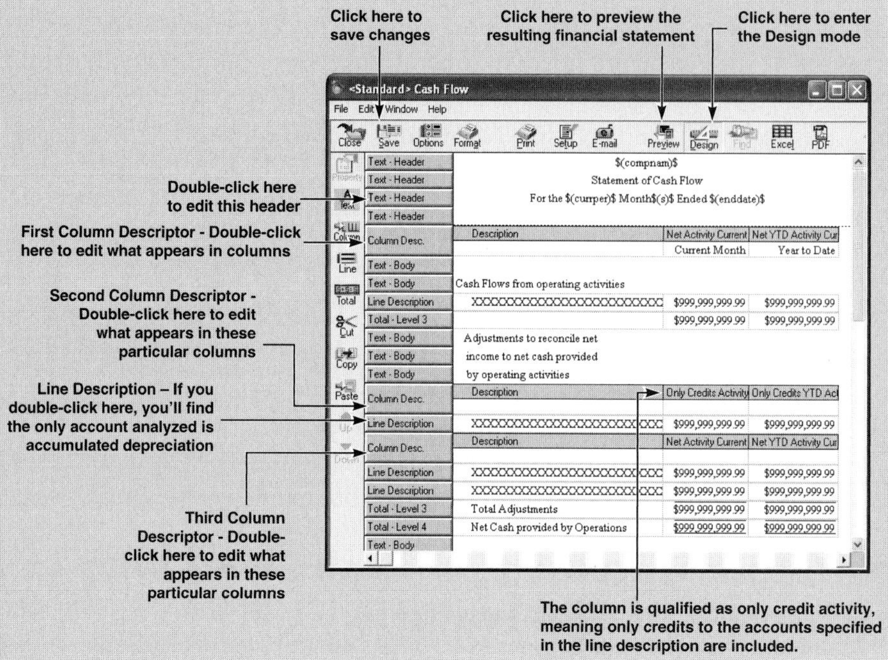

Click here to save changes

Click here to preview the resulting financial statement

Click here to enter the Design mode

Double-click here to edit this header

First Column Descriptor - Double-click here to edit what appears in columns

Second Column Descriptor - Double-click here to edit what appears in these particular columns

Line Description – If you double-click here, you'll find the only account analyzed is accumulated depreciation

Third Column Descriptor - Double-click here to edit what appears in these particular columns

The column is qualified as only credit activity, meaning only credits to the accounts specified in the line description are included.

5 Double-click the first **Column Desc.** button from the top.

6 Select column #3 (Year to Date), set Contents = **Activity**, type **$(EndDate 1)$** as the Title, set Width = **18**, select **Center of Column** from the Align Title drop-down list, check the **Format/$** check box, select **Current – 1** from the Time Frame drop-down list and **Whole Dollars** from the Round drop-down list, and set the Alignment Options to **Data and Totals Aligned**. Be sure the **Print** check box is checked for all three columns.

7 Select column #4 and check the Print check box, then set Contents = **Activity**, type **$(EndDate 2)$** as the Title, set Width = **18**, select **Center of Column** from the Align Title drop-down list, check the **Format/$** check box, select **Current – 2** from the Time Frame drop-down list and **Whole Dollars** from the Round drop-down list, and set the Alignment Options to **Data and Totals Aligned**.

8 Select column #2 and make sure the Print check box is checked, then change the title from Current Month to **$(EndDate)$**. Select **Whole Dollars** from the Round drop-down list, set Width = **18**, select **Center of Column** from the Align Title drop-down list. Your screen should look like Figure 4.3.

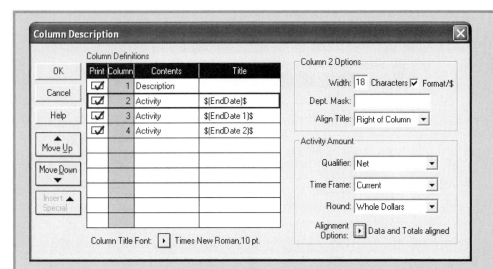

Figure 4.3
Column Description

9 Click **OK** to close the Column Description window.

10 Double-click the second **Column Desc.** button from the top.

11 Select column #3 (Year to Date), set Contents = **Activity**, set Width = **18**, select **Center of Column** from the Align Title drop-down list, select **Only Credits** from the drop-down list of Qualifiers, check the **Format/$** check box, select **Current − 1** from the Time Frame drop-down list and **Whole Dollars** from the Round drop-down list, and set the Alignment Options to **Data and Totals Aligned**. Be sure the **Print** check box is checked for all three columns.

12 Select column #4 and check the Print check box, set Contents = **Activity**, select **Only Credits** from the drop-down list of Qualifiers, set Width = **18**, select **Center of Column** from the Align Title drop-down list, check the **Format/$** check box, select **Current − 2** from the Time Frame drop-down list and **Whole Dollars** from the Round drop-down list, and set the Alignment Options to **Data and Totals Aligned**.

13 Select column #2 and then select **Whole Dollars** from the Round drop-down list and set Width = **18**. Your screen should look like Figure 4.4.

14 Click **OK** to close the Column Description window.

15 Double-click the third **Column Desc.** button from the top.

Figure 4.4

Column Description

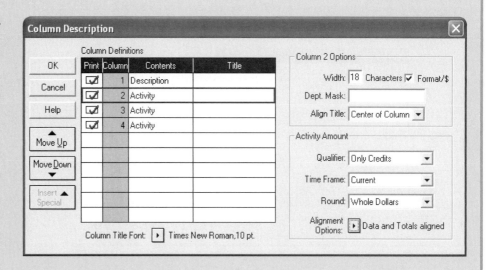

16 Select column #3 (Year to Date), set Contents = **Activity**, set Width = **18**, select **Center of Column** from the Align Title drop-down list, select **Net** from the drop-down list of Qualifiers, check the **Format/$** check box, select **Current − 1** from the Time Frame drop-down list and **Whole Dollars** from the Round drop-down list, and set the Alignment Options to **Data and Totals Aligned**. Be sure the **Print** check box is checked for all three columns.

17 Select column #4 and check the Print check box, set Contents = **Activity**, select **Net** from the drop-down list of Qualifiers, set Width = **18**, select **Center of Column** from the Align Title drop-down list, check the **Format/$** check box, select **Current − 2** from the Time Frame drop-down list and **Whole Dollars** from the Round drop-down list, and set the Alignment Options to **Data and Totals Aligned**.

18 Select column #2, select **Whole Dollars** from the Round drop-down list, set Width = **18**, and make sure the Qualifier is Net.

19 Double-click the fourth **Column Desc.** button from the top. (This one is for the top of the investing section.)

20 Select column #3 (Year to Date), set Contents = **Activity**, set Width = **18**, select **Center of Column** from the Align Title drop-down list, select **Only Debits** from the drop-down list of Qualifiers, check the **Format/$** check box, select **Current − 1** from the Time Frame drop-down list and **Whole Dollars** from the Round drop-down list, and set the Alignment Options to **Data and Totals Aligned**. Be sure the **Print** check box is checked for all three columns.

21 Select column #4, check the Print check box, set Contents = **Activity**, select **Only Debits** from the drop-down list of Qualifiers, set Width = **18**, select **Center of Column** from the Align Title drop-down list, check the **Format/$** check box, select **Current − 2** from the Time Frame drop-down list and **Whole Dollars** from the Round drop-down list, set the Alignment Options to **Data and Totals Aligned**, and make sure the Print box is checked.

22 Select column #2, select **Whole Dollars** from the Round drop-down list, and set Width = **18**.

23 Continue the same process down the statement of cash flows, being sure to keep the Qualifier the same for the current and previous periods. When you get to the last two columns, notice that you switch from the contents being an activity to the contents being a balance. Also, note that the last column, which represents cash at the beginning of the period (which is actually the cash balance at the end of the previous period), has a bit different time frame than the previous columns. Column 2's time frame should be **Current − 1**, column 3's time frame should be **Current − 2**, and column 4's time frame should be **Total Last Year** as shown in Figure 4.5.

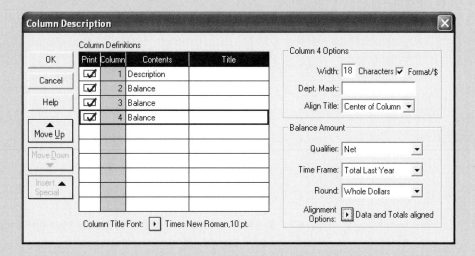

Figure 4.5

Column Descriptions for the Net Increase <Decrease> in Cash

24 Click **OK** to close the Column Descriptions window.

25 Click **Preview** and then click **OK** to view your new statement of cash flows. The top portion is shown in Figure 4.6, while the balance portion is shown in Figure 4.7.

Figure 4.6

Comparative Statement of
Cash Flows

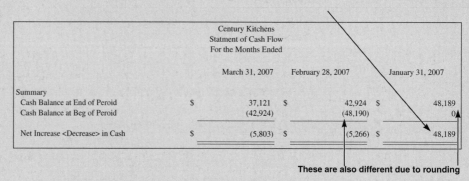

Figure 4.6

Comparative Statement of
Cash Flows

Century Kitchens
Statement of Cash Flow
For the Months Ended

	March 31, 2007	February 28, 2007	January 31, 2007
Cash Flows from operating activities			
Net Income	$ (2,271)	$ 8,236	$ 4,381
Adjustments to reconcile net income to net cash provided by operating activties			
Accumulated Depreciation	833	833	833
Accounts Receivable	(10,365)	(28,835)	(36,795)
Inventroy Asset	(11,795)	6,980	(6,980)
Prepaid Insurance	400	(4,000)	0
Acconts Payable	13,050	7,240	6,980
Payroll Liabilities	4,345	4,280	4,771
Total Adjustments	(3,532)	(13,502)	(31,191)
Net Cash Provided by Operations	(5,803)	(5,266)	(26,810)
Cash Flows from investing activites			
Used For			
Equipment	0	0	(50,000)
Net cash used in investing	0	0	(50,000)
Cash Flows from financing activities			
Proceeds from			
Common Stock	0	0	125,000
Used For			
Net cash used in financing	0	0	125,000
Net increase <decrease> in cash	$ (5,803)	$ (5,266)	$ 48,190

Note that these two balances don't agree. Rounding to whole dollars is at fault!

Figure 4.7

Comparative Statement of
Cash Flows

Century Kitchens
Statment of Cash Flow
For the Months Ended

	March 31, 2007	February 28, 2007	January 31, 2007
Summary			
Cash Balance at End of Peroid	$ 37,121	$ 42,924	$ 48,189
Cash Balance at Beg of Peroid	(42,924)	(48,190)	0
Net Increase <Decrease> in Cash	$ (5,803)	$ (5,266)	$ 48,189

These are also different due to rounding

26 Click **Save** from the button bar and then type **3 Mo. Comparative Cash Flows** as the name of the newly created statement.

27 Click **Save**.

28 Click **Print** from the button bar and then click **OK** to print this report.

29 Close all windows.

"That was a lot of work!" you comment.

"Right you are," Scott answers, "but once complete you can use this for any accounting period you'd like, and it will always show a comparison between the current and prior two months of cash flow."

Scott reminds you that typing **$(EndDate)$** as a title inserts the end of the period date of the period selected which makes the report flexible and dependent on the period selected. Selecting **Current − 2** as the time frame inserts data requested two periods before the current accounting period selected. This also makes the report flexible and dependent on the period selected.

Upon further inspection of his newly created comparative statement of cash flows, Scott notices that the two net increases in cash for January don't agree. He realizes that this is the consequence of rounding to whole dollars.

Investigating the Statement of Cash Flows

Scott had been concerned about the company's performance in March and now he can see how cash flow differed each month by looking at his newly created comparative cash flow statement. His most immediate concern is the cash used by operations. He notes that the loss generated in March certainly didn't help his cash flow and that increases in accounts receivable and inventory seem to be exacerbating the problem.

You remember from your accounting classes that changes in accounts receivable are one of the adjustments to net income to arrive at operating cash flow. You also remember that accounts receivable increases are subtracted from net income to arrive at operating cash flow since the revenues from some sales aren't collected in cash immediately. Thus, as accounts receivable increase, the revenue (reflected in net income under accrual accounting) is not realized (i.e., not received in cash yet). He decides to use Peachtree's drill down capabilities to investigate the changes in accounts receivable for the last three months.

To investigate the adjustment to the statement of cash flows from changes in accounts receivable:

1 Open Century Kitchens.

2 Set the System Date to **3/31/07** and the accounting period to **Period 3**.

3 Click **Reports** and then click **Financial Statements**.

4 Double-click **3 Mo. Comparative Cash Flows** from the drop-down list of Financial Statement Templates. (If you didn't save it last time, you'll need to recreate it!)

5 Select **Current Period** from the Time Frame drop-down list, make sure the Print Page Numbers and Show Zero Amounts check boxes are unchecked, and then click **OK**.

6 Click **(36,795)** from the January column. Note the box which surrounds this amount indicates a drill down value.

7 Double-click the **(36,795)** value to reveal a general ledger report for accounts receivable explaining the net increase in accounts receivable for the month of January. See Figure 4.8.

Figure 4.8

Change in Accounts Receivable for January

			Century Kitchens				
			General Ledger				
			For the Period From Jan 1, 2007 to Jan 31, 2007				

Filter Criteria includes: 1) IDs from 1200 to 1200. Report order is by ID. Report is printed with Truncated Transaction Descriptions and in Detail Format.

Account ID Account Description	Date	Reference	Jrnl	Trans Description	Debit Amt	Credit Amt	Balance
1200	1/1/07			Beginning Balance			
Accounts Receivable	1/2/07	1001	SJ	J Wilson	450.00		
	1/4/07	1002	SJ	R Coe	525.00		
	1/9/07	1003	SJ	A Monroe	750.00		
	1/29/07	23987	CRJ	J Wilson - Invoice:		450.00	
	1/29/07	283	CRJ	A Monroe - Invoice:		750.00	
	1/30/07	1004	SJ	J Wilson	12,030.00		
	1/31/07	1005	SJ	R Coe Ⓩ	15,240.00		
	1/31/07	1006	SJ	I Bowen	4,950.00		
	1/31/07	1007	SJ	S Gomez	4,050.00		
				Current Period Ch	37,995.00	1,200.00	36,795.00
	1/31/07			Ending Balance			36,795.00

8 Note the magnifying glass looking cursor next to the R Coe invoice. Double-click anywhere on the **R Coe invoice** from the sales journal (SJ) to reveal this source document (an invoice) explaining that particular increase in accounts receivable.

9 Look over the invoice and then close that window.

10 Double-click the **750.00** amount from the cash receipts journal (CRJ) to reveal this source document (a cash receipt) explaining that particular decrease in accounts receivable.

11 Look over the cash receipt and then close that window and the general ledger report window.

12 Double-click **(11,795)** in the March column of the statement of cash flows to reveal a general ledger report explaining the increase in inventory during March.

13 Scroll to the bottom of that report noting the total debits to the account of 30,195 and the net credits to the account of 18,400 resulting in the 11,795 net increases as shown in Figure 4.9.

Figure 4.9

Change in Inventory for March

14 Double-click the 3/30/07 credit of **1,600.00** to reveal the underlying source document (invoice) supporting this credit. (The invoice does not actually show the $1,600 since that is the cost of the goods sold, but the invoice does reflect 32 units sold × $50 cost per unit = $1,600 cost of goods sold.)

15 Look over this invoice and then close the invoice window.

16 Scroll back up the general ledger report and double-click the **2,250.00** amount recorded on 3/12.

17 This action reveals a source document (purchase receipt of granite counter) from a vendor (i.e., an inventory purchase).

18 Close all open windows.

"After looking over this general ledger report on inventory in March, can you explain the reason for the increase?" Scott asks.

"Yes," you retort. "Inventory is increased by purchases as shown by the purchase receipt and decreased by the cost of goods sold as shown by the sales invoice. We must have purchased more inventory than we sold."

"Exactly," Scott responds.

End Note

You've now seen how all three of the key financial statements, the balance sheet, income statement, and statement of cash flows, can be easily created, modified, and printed from within Peachtree. In Chapter 5, you will complete your overview of Peachtree by creating supporting reports for accounts receivable, inventory, and accounts payable.

Chapter 4 Questions

1 What accounting periods are included in the standard statement of cash flows?

2 What are the three sections called in the standard statement of cash flows?

3 Why is depreciation an adjustment to net income in the operating activities section of the standard statement of cash flows?

4 Why would you create a comparative statement of cash flows for several months?

5 Why type **$(EndDate)$** as a title for a new statement of cash flows?

6 Why select **Current − 2** as the time frame when creating a new statement of cash flows?

7 What's the risk of using Whole Dollars as your choice for rounding?

8 What report appears when you double-click the change in accounts receivable in the statement of cash flows?

9 What source documents are typically shown in the accounts receivable general ledger report?

10 What causes inventory to show a net increase?

Chapter 4 Assignments

1 *Prepare and print the following reports using the Century Kitchens Peachtree files. (Place your name in the footer of each report. To do so, scroll to the bottom of any report in Design mode, double-click the* **Text − Footer**, *and then type your name. This will help you locate your report as opposed to any other student's report when using computer labs.)*

    a. A standard cash flows for the current period (with the accounting period set to **Period 2**).

    b. Modify the cash flow statement you created in (a) using Peachtree's Design feature to create a comparative cash flow statement comparing two accounting periods. For example, 1/31/07and 2/28/07, exactly as you did in the chapter except with two months. Save it as **2 Mo. Comparative Cash Flows**. The new statement, without the report header, should look like Figure 4.10.

	February 28, 2007	January 31, 2007
Cash Flows from operating activities		
Net Income	$ 8,236	$ 4,381
Adjustments to reconcile net income to net cash provided by operating activties		
Accumulated Depreciation	833	833
Accounts Receivable	(28,835)	(36,795)
Inventroy Asset	6,980	(6,980)
Prepaid Insurance	(4,000)	0
Accounts Payable	7,240	6,980
Payroll Liabilities	4,280	4,771
Total Adjustments	(13,502)	(31,191)
Net Cash Provided by Operations	(5,266)	(26,810)
Cash Flows from investing activities		
Used For		
Equipment	0	(50,000)
Net cash used in investing	0	(50,000)
Cash Flows from financing activities		
Proceeds From		
Common Stock	0	125,000
Used For		
Net cash used in financing	0	125,000
Net increase <decrease> in cash	$ (5,266)	$ 48,190
Summary		
Cash Balance at End of Period	$ 42,924	$ 48,189
Cash Balance at Beg of Period	(48,190)	0
Net Increase <Decrease> in Cash	$ (5,266)	$ 48,189

Figure 4.10

2 Month Comparative Cash Flows

    c. A general ledger report of those transactions recorded in February that affected prepaid insurance.

    d. A general ledger report of those transactions recorded in February that affected accounts payable.

2   *Answer the following questions using the Century Kitchens Peachtree files after opening a standard cash flow statement (with accounting period set to Period 3).*

    a. Drill down from the year-to-date accounts payable account. Locate check 135. What did Century Kitchens pay for with this check? What was the date of the purchase?

    b. Drill down from the year-to-date accounts payable account. What was purchased on 3/12/07? Who invoiced Century? What was their invoice number?

    c. Drill down from the year-to-date accounts receivable account. What happened on 3/16/07?

3   *Using the South-Western Home Page for More Assignments or Cases*

Go to the home page for this textbook at http://www.thomsonedu.com/accounting/owen. Click **Additional Problem Sets**, select the Chapter 4 section, and complete the problem(s) your instructor assigns.

Chapter 4 Case Problem
KELLY JENNINGS ADVERTISING

1   Prepare and print the following reports using Kelly Jennings Advertising Peachtree files. (Remember, you'll need to restore this file from your Data Files CD. Also be sure to place your name in the footer of each report. To do so, scroll to the bottom of any report in Design mode, double-click the **Text – Footer**, and then type your name. This will help you locate your report as opposed to any other student's report when using computer labs. Set the accounting period to **Period 2** and set system date to Feb. 29, 2008.)

    a. A standard cash flows statement as of 2/29/08 with no page numbers and no zero amounts.

    b. Modify the cash flows statement you just created in (a) using Peachtree's Design feature to create a cash flows statement comparing two accounting periods with no rounding, 18 character widths, and aligned to the right column. Save it as **2 Mo. Comparative Cash Flows**.

    c. A general ledger report of those transactions recorded in January 2008 that affected the accounts receivable account. (Make sure it fits on one page and that all items are visible by turning off the truncating feature. Don't save changes!)

    d. A general ledger report of those transactions recorded in January 2008 that affected the inventory account. (Make sure it fits on one page and that all items are visible by turning off the truncating feature. Don't save changes!)

2   Answer the following questions:

    a. Drill down from the year-to-date accounts payable account. Locate check 1253. What did Jennings pay for with this check?

    b. Drill down from the year-to-date accounts payable account. What was purchased on 1/28/08? Who invoiced Jennings? What was their invoice number?

    c. Drill down from the year-to-date accounts receivable account. What happened on 2/26/08?

Creating Supporting Reports to Help Make Business Decisions

5

Learning Objectives

In this chapter, you will:

- Review the Business Status Center.
- Create, print, and analyze a detailed and summary aged receivables report.
- Create, print, and analyze an inventory valuation report.
- Create, print, and analyze a detailed and summary aged payables report.

Case: **Century Kitchens**

You arrive at work, and two phones are ringing. As Scott hangs up from one call and is about to answer another, he quickly explains what's happening—he's thinking about expanding the business and needs to borrow from the bank, and they are requesting up-to-the-minute information. You quickly answer a phone and write down the banker's request for some information on inventory. As you hang up from the call, Scott asks you to come into his office. You compare notes—he has requests for information on accounts receivable and accounts payable. You show him your note requesting information on Century Kitchens' inventory.

Scott has shown you that Peachtree can easily generate transaction reports, but you can see that the banker's requests require more detailed information. You remember from your accounting course that accountants frequently use what are called supporting schedules—reports that provide the underlying details of an account. You ask Scott if Peachtree can help. He smiles and says, "You bet. Peachtree calls these schedules 'reports,' but they are the same thing. Let's get to work."

Scott reminds you that usually when you start Peachtree and open the Century Kitchens data file, the first screen you see is the Business Status Center. He suggests you start with a review of what's available in the Business Status Center.

Reviewing the Business Status Center

The Peachtree Business Status Center displays a variety of general business information, including account balances, revenue figures, receivables and

Figure 5.1

Account Balances

Account Balances		Customize
Account Description	Account ID /	Balance
Checking	1100	$37,120.76
Accounts Receivable	1200	$75,995.00
Undeposited Funds	1500	$0.00
Accounts Payable	2000	($27,270.00)
View Account List		View Balance Sheet
Reconcile Accounts and Import Bank Statements		

payables data, and action items. It also includes a feature that lets you find, display, and/or print a Peachtree report.

Some of the information that appears in the Business Status Center can be drilled down on to investigate the underlying source documents which created that information.

The default settings in Peachtree reveal an Account Balances section first. This section provides account balances as of the end of the accounting period you've specified. For system date 3/31/07 and accounting period 3, the Account Balances section looks like Figure 5.1. Note that if you change the system date and accounting period, the information displayed in the Business Status Center changes. The blue text indicates the ability to drill down for further information. In this case, you can drill down on Account ID to reveal a specific account register which shows transactions for the day, month, period, quarter, year, or week to date, month to date, period to date, quarter to date, year to date, or all. The blue text also indicates reports or lists you might want to see related to this section. For Century Kitchens, that would include an account list or balance sheet. Lastly, common tasks are also provided, in this case reconciling accounts or importing bank statements can be activated quickly and easily.

The second section, on the right, reveals Revenue: Year to Date. This section reveals a chart of revenues by period and a quick income statement as well as drill down ability to view a full income statement, budget, or account variance report as shown in Figure 5.2.

The next section titled Customers Who Owe Money reveals a list of—you guessed it—customers who owe the company money. By default, this list is in order of due dates as shown in Figure 5.3. This list will prove helpful to Scott when he investigates accounts receivable balances. The red dates indicate a past due amount and when double-clicked reveal the underlying course document creating that receivable. The same document can also be found by single clicking the Customer ID. You remember that the due dates are determined by the invoice date and the terms afforded each customer. Once again, the blue text reveals access to common lists or tasks. As you can see, not all balances are shown in Figure 5.3. Depending on the size of your monitor, you may need to use the scroll bar to scroll down the list. When you do, you'll notice that the current receivable due dates are in black, not red.

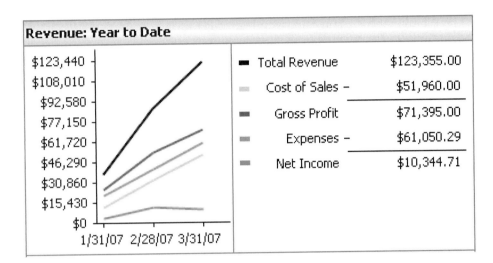

Figure 5.2

Revenue Year to Date

Click here to display customer balances sorted in ascending order by amount due. Click again here to display customer balances sorted in descending order by amount due.

By default, this section displays customer balances sorted in ascending order by due date.

Figure 5.3

Customers Who Owe Money

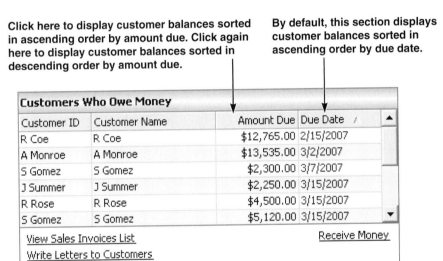

The section below, also related to the amounts customers owe, is titled Aged Receivables. It shows a graph of accounts receivable as of the end of the accounting period and a table of amounts by days overdue as seen in Figure 5.4. This blue text again indicates common lists, reports, and tasks you can access from this section.

Figure 5.4

Aged Receivables

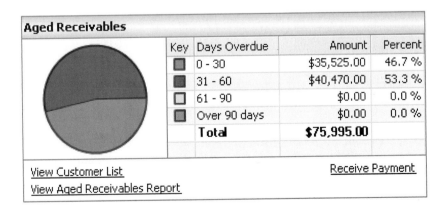

To the right is a section titled Vendors to Pay, which reveals amounts owed to vendors sorted by due date, as shown in Figure 5.5. Again, in this case, the red due dates indicate past due amounts, and the black due dates indicate current payments due. Again, you remember that the due dates are determined by the purchase date and the terms afforded you by each vendor. Individual source documents are accessed by double-clicking on specific due dates or a click on the Vendor ID.

The next section, titled Aged Payables, stratifies accounts payable like the Aged Receivables section above. A graph and table of accounts payable amounts by days overdue are shown as seen in Figure 5.6. Access to common lists, reports, and tasks is also provided.

The last section in the Business Status Center provides the user the ability to find a report based on specific categories. Knowing Scott

Figure 5.5

Vendors to Pay

Double-clicking here reveals the underlying
source document creating this liability.

Vendors to Pay

Vendor ID	Vendor Name	Amount Due	Due Date
Dupont	Dupont Surfaces	$1,000.00	3/19/2007
Thomasville Cabinets	Thomasville Cabinets	$9,040.00	3/19/2007
Dupont	Dupont Surfaces	$1,280.00	3/23/2007
Ameron	Ameron Industries Inc.	$2,250.00	3/27/2007
Ameron	Ameron Industries Inc.	$1,600.00	4/4/2007
Kraft Maid	Kraft Maid	$5,620.00	4/14/2007
Kraft Maid	Kraft Maid	$6,480.00	4/14/2007

View Purchases List   Make a Payment
Make Multiple Payments

Figure 5.6

Aged Payables

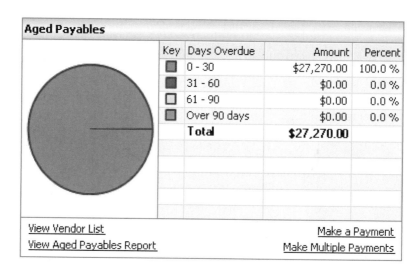

Aged Payables

Key	Days Overdue	Amount	Percent
■	0 - 30	$27,270.00	100.0 %
■	31 - 60	$0.00	0.0 %
□	61 - 90	$0.00	0.0 %
■	Over 90 days	$0.00	0.0 %
	Total	**$27,270.00**	

View Vendor List   Make a Payment
View Aged Payables Report   Make Multiple Payments

Click here to reveal a list of categories available.

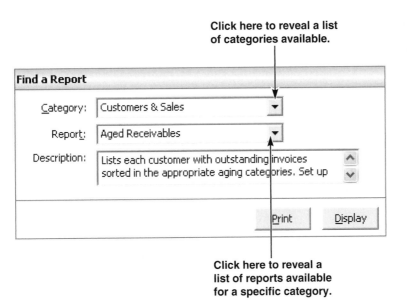

Click here to reveal a list of reports available for a specific category.

Figure 5.7

Find a Report

was interested in a report which provided information on receivables from customers, you searched for a report under the category of Customers & Sales and found an Aged Receivables report along with a description of what that report provides. See Figure 5.7.

This section gives the user the ability to print or display the report.

"The Business Status Center looks like it can be very helpful to us as we try and answer the bank's questions," you comment.

"Quite true" Scott responds. "Let's investigate this aged receivables report."

Create, Print, and Analyze an Aged Receivables Report

You know from your accounting course that accounts receivable represent amounts due from customers for goods or services they have received but for which they have not yet been paid. Peachtree provides several preset accounts receivable reports that anticipate the information managers most often need.

The banker wants information on a particular customer's past due account balance, and she wants to know the total amount due from customers as of today.

Scott tells you that the best way to get information on past due accounts is to create a schedule that Peachtree calls an "Accounts Receivable Aging report"—but what you learned in your accounting course is usually called an "accounts receivable aging schedule." You remember that an aging schedule is a listing of how long each receivable has been uncollected. He wants it short and to the point.

To create an aged receivables report:

1 Open Century Kitchens.

2 Set the System Date to **3/31/07** and the accounting period to **Period 3**.

3 Click **Reports** and then click **Accounts Receivable**.

4 Double-click **Aged Receivables** from the Report List. (Alternatively, you could access this report from the Aged Receivables section of the Business Status Center or by searching for reports as described earlier.)

5 Click **Design**.

6 Click the **Fields** icon on the left of the design page.

7 Uncheck the Show check boxes for Customer ID, Contact, and Telephone 1 fields as shown in Figure 5.8.

Figure 5.8

Aged Receivables Fields

Click here to uncheck or check a field. Removing the check causes the report to not show a field.

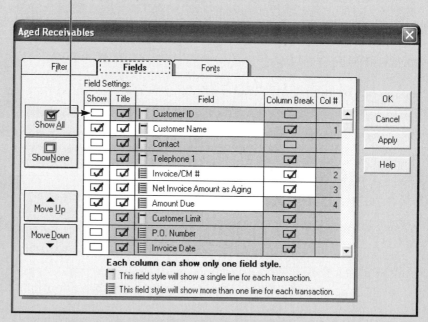

8 Click **OK** to accept changes.

9 Click **Preview** to look at the modified report.

10 Click **Print** and then click **OK** in the Print window to print it. Your printed version should look like Figure 5.9.

Figure 5.9
Aged Receivables Report

Century Kitchens
Aged Receivables
As of Mar 31, 2007

Filter Criteria includes: Report order is by ID. Report is printed in Detail Format.

Customer	Invoice/CM #	0–30	31–60	61–90	Over 90 days	Amount Due
A Monroe	1008		13,535.00			13,535.00
	1019	4,960.00				4,960.00
A Monroe		4,960.00	13,535.00			18,495.00
B Scaggs	1016	16,045.00				16,045.00
B Scaggs		16,045.00				16,045.00
I Bowen	1017	3,960.00				3,960.00
I Bowen		3,960.00				3,960.00
J Summer	1015		2,250.00			2,250.00
	1018	10,560.00				10,560.00
J Summer		10,560.00	2,250.00			12,810.00
R Coe	1005		12,765.00			12,765.00
R Coe			12,765.00			12,765.00
R Rose	1014		4,500.00			4,500.00
R Rose			4,500.00			4,500.00
S Gomez	1010		2,300.00			2,300.00
	1012		5,120.00			5,120.00
S Gomez			7,420.00			7,420.00
		35,525.00	40,470.00			75,995.00

11 Click **Save** on the button bar, type **Aged Receivables 1** as the name of this report, and then click the **Save** button.

You can see that this report gives Scott an up-to-date listing of customers and their balances. It tells him how long each receivable has been uncollected so he can take appropriate action.

You ask Scott the name of the customer about whom the banker requested information. He says the customer's name is R Coe and that the banker wants to know the status of his account and his payment history. He says that, as you have done with other reports, you can drill down to gather this information.

To investigate a particular receivable on an aged receivables report:

1 Double-click the **12,765.00** balance owed by R Coe.

2 Invoice 1005 appears as shown in Figure 5.10.

Figure 5.10

Invoice 1005

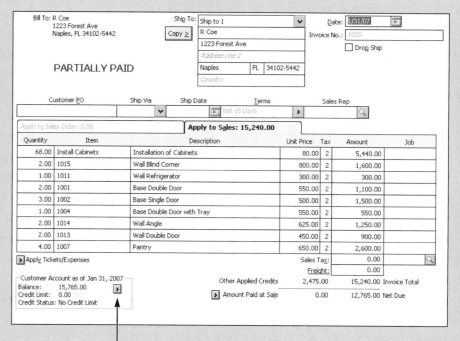

Click here to reveal this customer's ledger.

3 Expand the invoice if necessary to view all items including the Net Due of $12,765, which matches the aging balance.

4 Click the **right arrow** button in the lower left-hand corner of the invoice in the box labeled Customer Account as of Jan 31, 2007. A customer ledger appears for the month of January.

5 Click **Options** from the button bar, change the range by changing the To: date to Mar 31, 2007, and then click **OK**. A revised customer ledger for R Coe appears as shown in Figure 5.11.

Figure 5.11

R Coe Customer Ledger For the Period Jan 1, 2007 to Mar 31, 2007

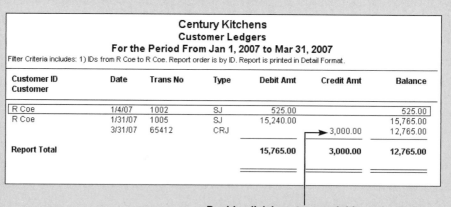

Double-click here to reveal this cash receipt.

6 Note that the ending receivable balance due is 12,765.00, which is made up of two invoices and one payment on account.

7 Double-click the **3,000.00** payment received on 3/31/07. A receipt source document should appear as shown in Figure 5.12.

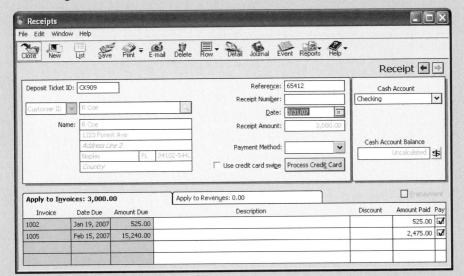

Figure 5.12
Receipt Source Document

8 Notice that the $3,000.00 check was received from R Coe on 3/31/07. Of this payment, $525.00 was applied to pay off invoice 1002. The balance of the $3,000.00—$2,475.00—was applied to invoice 1005. This explains why the balance due and the invoice amount were different. (See Figure 5.10, bottom right.)

Scott has copied down the information the banker requested—R Coe is 44 days past due on invoice 1005, he owes $12,765.00 on that invoice, and invoice 1002 was paid off on 3/31/07. He is now ready to fulfill the banker's other requests for a summary report for all receivables.

To create and print a summary aged receivables report:

1 Click **Report** and then click **Accounts Receivable**.

2 Double-click **Aged Receivables 1** from the Report List. (This, of course, is the report you just created and saved.)

3 Click **Options** from the button bar and then check the check box **Print Report in Summary Format**.

4 Click **OK** to reveal the newly modified Aged Receivables report as shown in Figure 5.13.

Figure 5.13

Summary Aged Receivables Report

Century Kitchens
Aged Receivables
As of Mar 31, 2007
Filter Criteria includes: Report order is by ID. Report is printed in Summary Format.

Customer ID	0–30	31–60	61–90	Over 90 days	Amount Due
A Monroe	4,960.00	13,535.00			18,495.00
B Scaggs	16,045.00				16,045.00
I Bowen	3,960.00				3,960.00
J Summer	10,560.00	2,250.00			12,810.00
R Coe		12,765.00			12,765.00
R Rose		4,500.00			4,500.00
S Gomez		7,420.00			7,420.00
Report Total	35,525.00	40,470.00			75,995.00

5   Click **Save** on the button bar, type **Aged Receivables 2** as the name of this report, and then click the **Save** button.

Create, Print, and Analyze an Inventory Valuation Report

Scott asks you about the request you took over the phone. You show him your notes; you spoke to Kim Hui, one of the company's investors. He stopped by the other day and noticed a lot of cabinet inventory in the shop and wondered why we had so much.

Scott explains that in his business he never places a purchase order to a cabinet or counter top manufacturer unless it's been signed off by a customer. "We hold the inventory until we can schedule it for installation. Once installed, we then bill the customer and the inventory becomes cost of goods sold."

He suggests that you use Peachtree to show, via an inventory valuation report, just exactly what inventory you have as of 3/31/07.

To create an inventory valuation report:

1   Click **Reports** and then click **Inventory**.

2   Double-click **Inventory Valuation Report**. You note that the report is quite long and has truncated (shortened) item descriptions and lots of items for which there is no quantity on hand.

3 Click **Design** from the button bar.

4 Click the **Filter** icon on the left of the report. (Alternatively, you could have clicked the **Options** button on the button bar.)

5 Uncheck the check boxes Truncate Long Description and Include items with no quantity on hand.

6 Click **OK** to close the window and then click **Preview** from the button bar to view the Inventory Valuation Summary below in Figure 5.14.

Century Kitchens Inventory
Valuation Report
As of Mar 31, 2007

Filter Criteria includes: 1) Stock/Assembly. Report order is by ID.

Item ID Item Class	Item Description	Stocking U/M	Cost Method	Qty on Hand	Item Value	Avg Cost	% of Inv Value
1002 Stock item	Base Single Door	EACH	Average	3.00	1,200.00	400.00	10.17
1003 Stock item	Base Double Door Double Drawer	EACH	Average	2.00	960.00	480.00	8.14
1006 Stock item	Base Lattice	EACH	Average	3.00	960.00	320.00	8.14
1008 Stock item	Chopping Block Table	EACH	Average	1.00	360.00	360.00	3.05
1012 Stock item	Wall Double Door	EACH	Average	5.00	1,600.00	320.00	13.57
1014 Stock item	Wall Angle	EACH	Average	1.00	540.00	540.00	4.58
2001 Stock item	Granite counter	EACH	Average	45.00	2,250.00	50.00	19.08
2002 Stock item	Silestone	EACH	Average	65.00	2,925.00	45.00	24.80
2003 Stock item	Corian	EACH	Average	25.00	1,000.00	40.00	8.48
					11,795.00		100.00

Figure 5.14

Inventory Valuation Summary

7 Scroll around this report to familiarize yourself with its contents. It describes the inventory on hand as of 3/31/07.

8 Click **Print** on the button bar to print this report.

9 Click **Save** on the button bar, type **Inventory Valuation Report 1** as the name of this report, and then click the **Save** button.

10 Close the newly saved **Inventory Valuation Report** and **Select a Report** windows.

Create, Print, and Analyze an Aged Payables Report

The last request to which you and Scott need to respond is from Juan Gomez, who handles all inventory purchase orders, pays bills, and monitors accounts payable. He wants two reports so he can plan next month's cash flow.

You quickly ask if Peachtree handles accounts payable aging the same way it handles accounts receivable aging. Scott smiles, "You catch on fast," he says. "Let's start with an aged payables report. It provides the detail Juan needs."

To create an aged receivables report:

1 Click **Reports** and then click **Accounts Payable**.

2 Double-click **Aged Payables** from the Report List. (Alternatively you could access this report from the Aged Payables section of the Business Status Center or by searching for reports as described earlier.)

3 Click **Design**.

4 Click the **Fields** icon on the left of the design page.

5 Uncheck the Show check boxes for Vendor ID, Contact, and Telephone 1 fields as shown in Figure 5.15.

Figure 5.15

Aged Payables Fields

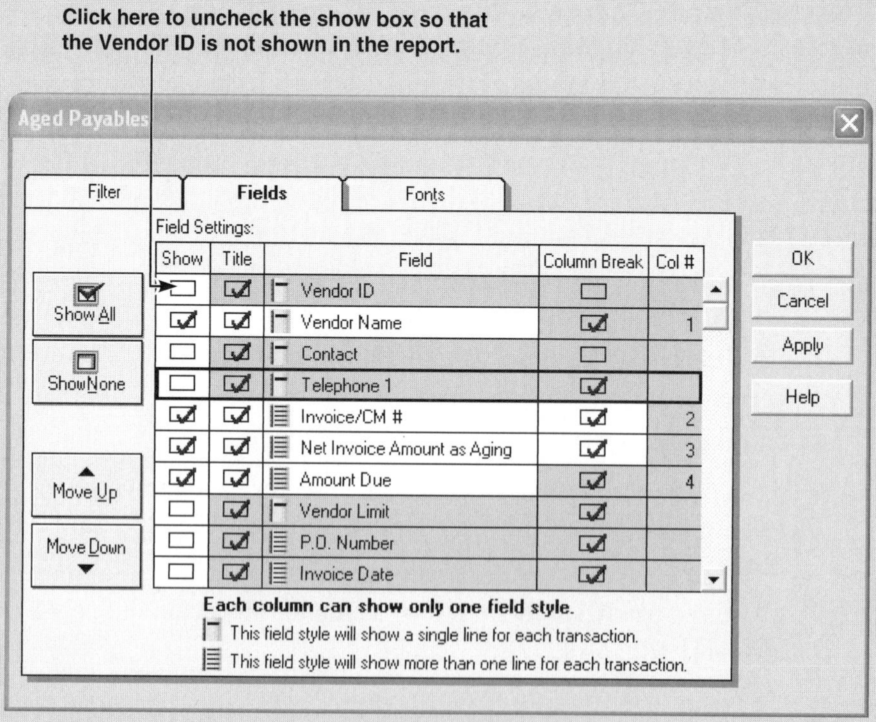

Click here to uncheck the show box so that the Vendor ID is not shown in the report.

6 Click **OK** to accept changes.

7 Click **Preview** to look at the modified report. Your report should look like Figure 5.16.

Note that in Detail Format each invoice creating a vendor balance is shown.

Figure 5.16

Aged Payables Report

Century Kitchens
Aged Payables
As of Mar 31, 2007

Filter Criteria includes: Report order is by ID. Report is printed in Detail Format.

Vendor	Invoice/CM #	0 - 30	31 - 60	61 - 90	Over 90 days	Amount Due
Ameron Industries Inc.	AI09000	2,250.00				2,250.00
	AI029830	1,600.00				1,600.00
Ameron Industries Inc.		**3,850.00**				**3,850.00**
Dupont Surfaces	DS87444	1,000.00				1,000.00
	DS74452	1,280.00				1,280.00
Dupont Surfaces		**2,280.00**				**2,280.00**
Kraft Maid	KM98445	6,480.00				6,480.00
	KM89787	5,620.00				5,620.00
Kraft Maid		**12,100.00**				**12,100.00**
Thomasville Cabinets	TC14899	9,040.00				9,040.00
Thomasville Cabinets		**9,040.00**				**9,040.00**
		27,270.00				**27,270.00**

8 Click **Print** and then click **OK** in the Print window to print it.

9 Click **Save** on the button bar, type **Aged Payables 1** as the name of this report, and then click the **Save** button.

After Scott prints this report for Juan, you look it over. You notice a large outstanding balance to Thomasville Cabinets, and you suggest using drill down to investigate it further. Scott and you both decide to investigate this liability for which Century Kitchens owes $9,040.00.

To investigate a particular payable on an aged payables report:

1 Double-click the **9,040.00** balance owed to Thomasville Cabinets.

2 Invoice TC14899 appears as shown in Figure 5.17.

Figure 5.17

Purchase/Receipt from Thomasville Cabinets

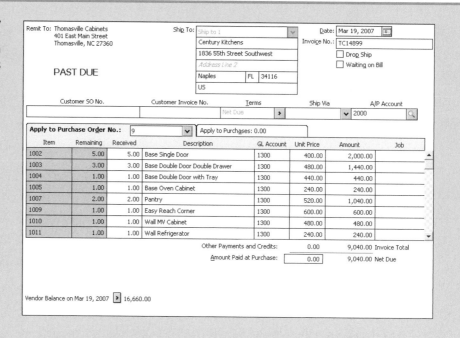

3 Expand the invoice if necessary to view all items including the Net Due of $9,040.00 which matches the aging balance.

4 Click the **right arrow** button in the lower left-hand corner of the invoice in the box labeled Vendor Balance on Mar 19, 2007. A customer ledger appears for part of the month of March.

5 Click **Options** from the button bar, change the range by changing the To: date to Mar 31, 2007 and the From: date to Jan 1, 2007, and then click **OK**. A revised vendor ledger for Thomasville Cabinets appears as shown in Figure 5.18.

Figure 5.18

Thomasville Cabinets Vendor Ledger for the Period Jan 1, 2007 to Mar 31, 2007

Century Kitchens
Vendor Ledgers
For the Period From Jan 1, 2007 to Mar 31, 2007
Filter Criteria includes: 1) IDs from Thomasville Cabinets to Thomasville Cabinets. Report order is by ID.

Vendor ID Vendor	Date	Trans No	Type	Paid	Debit Amt	Credit Amt	Balance
Thomasville Cabinets	1/19/07	TC87256	PJ	*		7,920.00	7,920.00
Thomasville Cabinets	1/31/07	109	CDJ		7,920.00		0.00
	2/16/07	TC98745	PJ	*		7,620.00	7,620.00
	3/19/07	TC14899	PJ			9,040.00	16,660.00
	3/21/07	135	CDJ		7,620.00		9,040.00
Report Total					**15,540.00**	**24,580.00**	**9,040.00**

The types here are PJ(purchases journal)
and CDJ (cash disbursements journal).

6 Note that the ending receivables balance due is $9,040.00 which is made up of three invoices and two payments on account.

Scott has copied down the information Juan requested. He is now ready to fulfill Juan's other request for a summary report for all payables.

To create and print a summary aged payables report:

1 Click **Report** and then click **Accounts Payable**.

2 Double-click **Aged Payables 1** from the Report List. (This, of course, is the report you just created and saved.)

3 Click **Options** from the button bar and then check the check box **Print Report in Summary Format**.

4 Click **OK** to reveal the newly modified aged receivables report as shown in Figure 5.19.

Note that in Summary Format, no invoices are shown.

Figure 5.19

Summary Aged Payables Report

Century Kitchens
Aged Payables
As of Mar 31, 2007

Filter Criteria includes: Report order is by ID Report is printed in Summary Format.

Vendor	0 - 30	31 - 60	61 - 90	Over 90 days	Amount Due
Ameron Industries Inc.	3,850.00				3,850.00
Dupont Surfaces	2,280.00				2,280.00
Kraft Maid	12,100.00				12,100.00
Thomasville Cabinets	9,040.00				9,040.00
	27,270.00				27,270.00

5 Click **Save** on the button bar, type **Aged Payables 2** as the name of this report, and then click the **Save** button.

6 Close all windows.

End Note

As you gather the reports and set out to deliver them, you are struck by how easily and quickly Scott has been able to respond to the managers' requests. Within a short time, Peachtree has generated accurate, up-to-the-minute financial information to help Scott and his staff make important business decisions. The many preset reports—summaries, details, and supporting documentation—anticipate the information that owners often need to make sound business decisions.

Chapter 5 Questions

1 What does the Business Status Center display?

2 What does the blue text indicate in the Business Status Center?

3 What happens to the information displayed in the Business Status Center when you change the system date and/or accounting period?

4 What is the default order for the Customers Who Owe Money section?

5 How do you sort the Customers Who Owe Money section by amount due in ascending or descending order?

6 What three ways can you access an aged receivables report?

7 From an invoice to a customer, how do you access that particular customer's ledger?

8 What happens if you don't uncheck the box **Include items with no quantity on hand** in the **Options** section of the Inventory Valuation Report?

9 What's the difference between an aged payables report in detail vs. summary format?

10 What do PJ and CDJ stand for in the Type column of the Vendor Ledger?

Chapter 5 Assignments

1 *Set the system date to 1/31/07 and the accounting period to Period 1—1/1/07–1/31/07. Then use the Business Status Center to answer the following questions:*

a. What is the balance in accounts receivable?

b. How much does A Monroe owe, and what is the due date?

c. What was the cost of sales?

d. How much does the company owe Dupont that was due 3/19/07?

e. How much of the company's receivables are 31–60 days overdue?

f. How much of the company's payables are 31–60 days overdue?

2 *Set the system date to 2/28/07 and the accounting period to* **Period 2—2/1/07–2/28/07.** *Prepare and print the following reports (using the same parameters used in the chapter) using the Century Kitchens Peachtree files. (Place your name in the footer of each report. To do so,* *scroll to the bottom of any report in Design mode, double-click the Text – Footer and then type your name. This will help you locate your report as opposed to any other student's report when using computer labs.)*

    a. Create and print a summary aged receivables report as of 2/28/07.

    b. Create and print a detailed aged receivables report as of 2/28/07.

    c. Create and print a summary aged payables report as of 2/28/07.

    d. Create and print a detailed aged payables report as of 2/28/07.

    e. Create and print an inventory valuation report as of 2/28/07.

3   *Set the system date to **3/31/07** and the accounting period to* **Period 3—3/1/07–3/31/07.** *Answer the following questions:*

    a. What is the amount of the largest customer receivable, and what is the customer's name? What invoice(s) support that receivable?

    b. What is the largest past due invoice? When is it due? Which customer owes us that amount?

    c. Which vendor is owed the second largest total amount, and what is that total? What invoice(s) support that payable?

    d. What is the second largest past due payable? When is it due? Which vendor do we owe?

    e. What is the largest dollar value inventory item in stock at 3/31/07? How much did we pay for it?

Chapter 5 Case Problem
KELLY JENNINGS ADVERTISING

1   Set the system date to **1/31/08** and the accounting period to **Period 1—1/1/08–1/31/08**. Then use the Business Status Center to answer the following questions:

    a. What was the balance in accounts receivable?

    b. How much did Paulson's Nursery owe, and what is the due date?

    c. What was the total of expenses for the period?

    d. How much did the company owe KCOY that was due 1/10/08?

    e. How much of the company's receivables were 31–60 days overdue?

    f. How much of the company's payables were 0–30 days overdue?

2   Set the system date to **2/29/08** and the accounting period to **Period 2—2/1/08–2/29/08**. Prepare, print, and save (just add 1 to the standard name of each report modified like you did in the chapter) the following reports (do not show the ID, Contact, or Telephone 1 fields) using the Kelly Jennings Advertising Peachtree files. (Place your name in the footer of each report. To do so, scroll to the bottom of any report in Design mode, double-click the **Text – Footer**, and then type your name. This will help you locate your report as opposed to any other student's report when using computer labs.)

a. Create and print a summary aged receivables report as of 2/29/08.

b. Create and print a summary aged payables report as of 2/29/08.

c. Create and print an inventory valuation report as of 2/29/08.

3 Answer the following questions as of 2/29/08:

a. What is the amount of the second largest customer receivable, and what is the customer's name? What invoice(s) support that receivable?

b. What is the second largest past due invoice? When is it due? Which customer owes us that amount?

c. What is the amount of the smallest vendor payable, and what is the vendor's name? What invoice(s) support that payable?

d. What is the second largest past due payable? When is it due? Which vendor do we owe?

e. What is the largest total dollar value inventory item in stock? How much did we pay for it?

Creating a Peachtree File to Record and Analyze Business Events

part

2

In this part, you will:

- **Set Up Your Business's Accounting System**
- **Enter Cash-Oriented Business Activities**
- **Enter Additional Business Activities**
- **Enter Adjusting Entries**
- **Perform Budgeting Activities**
- **Generate Reports of Business Activities**

Part 2 is designed to teach you how to use Peachtree and the accounting methods and concepts you've learned in your introductory accounting course. This part is divided into six chapters, each with its own set of questions, assignments, and case problems. You'll follow the adventures of Donna and Karen at Wild Water Sports who have hired you to help them set up their business in Peachtree, capture various business transactions, make adjusting entries, set up and use budgets, and generate key business reports. You'll utilize Peachtree to establish accounts, customers, vendors, items, and employees and then record business transactions using key source documents like sales receipts, invoices, bills, deposit forms, and checks. You will learn how to create journal entries in Peachtree to accrue revenues and expenses, adjust deferred assets and liabilities, and record depreciation of long-lived assets. Finally, you'll learn how Peachtree's budgeting and reporting process can help Wild Water Sports plan and control its business activities.

Setting Up Your Business's Accounting System

6

Learning Objectives

In this chapter, you will:

- Create a new company file.
- Set up customers.
- Set up vendors.
- Set up inventory and service items.
- Set up employees.
- Set up beginning balances and new accounts.
- Create a backup file.

Case: **Wild Water Sports, Inc.**

Donna Chandler and her best friend Karen Wilson have been water sports enthusiasts since they were six years old. They would spend a good portion of each summer vacation wake boarding and skiing the lakes and reservoirs of Central Florida. After high school, both went their separate ways. Donna went off to a four-year college and then began a career in real estate, while Karen attended a local community college and started her career in small business accounting.

At their 10-year high school reunion, they became reacquainted and reminisced about their fun-filled weekends and summers with boats and boys. They pondered how they could mix their careers and their love of boating into a business. Both vowed to keep in touch. Later that year, Donna called with a plan. She had run into a business investor, Ernesto Martinez, who had opened a retail boat dealership in Orlando, Florida, but didn't have the time to mind the details. Donna felt she could handle the marketing and sales if Karen could handle the day-to-day business operations. From that plan, Wild Water Sports, Inc., was born. The company had some existing cash, receivables, inventory, equipment, and liabilities. Karen and Donna have decided to make an investment by purchasing common stock in the existing company; each will gain a one-third interest in the corporation, and the remaining one-third will belong to Ernesto.

Karen knows she will need some help with the daily accounting records and has chosen Peachtree as her accounting program to replace the manual accounting system that currently exists. When she contacted an employment agency to find a part-time accountant, you answered her call. Since you are a student who can use some spending money and have completed a basic accounting course, you were hired the same day.

Your job will be to work with Karen and establish and maintain accounting records for Wild Water Sports using Peachtree. The company will open its doors for business under new ownership in January but needs to set up accounts, items, customers, vendors, employees, etc. The company rents its show room and service bays from a former auto dealership. It plans to offer top-of-the-line ski-boats, personal water craft, accessories, skis, and boats. It also plans to service boats and equipment and offer training. The company has leased a man-made lake that will be used as a training site and also be available for rent to groups.

You agree to meet with Karen the next day to get started.

Creating a New Company File

When you return to Karen's office, she's already purchased a new computer, the Peachtree software, Microsoft's Office suite, and supplies. The software is loaded and ready to go. Karen explains that you have two choices to begin setting up your company. Peachtree has a built-in Setup Guide, which can guide you through the company setup process, or you can skip the guide and set the company up yourself. Since this is your first time setting up a company in Peachtree, you opt for the Setup Guide.

"Starting with the Setup Guide is probably a good idea," Karen says. "Besides, no matter which method you start with, you can always change the decisions you make during setup later."

Karen explains that this process will accomplish various tasks. First, you will provide company information like an address, phone number, name, etc. Then you'll be asked to establish a chart of accounts (standard accounts and numbers to store your business event information). You'll want to use the accrual vs. cash method of accounting and the standard calendar months for reporting your financial information. Since this company has existing transactions and account balances, you will need to eventually establish those beginning balances and enter new transactions beginning in January 2007, the first month of business under new ownership.

To create a new company file:

1 Before you begin, close any previously created company files.

2 Start Peachtree. Click **Create a New Company** and the Create a New Company – Introduction window should appear as shown in Figure 6.1.

Figure 6.1

The New Company Setup Window

3 Click **Next** and then enter the information as specified in Figure 6.2.

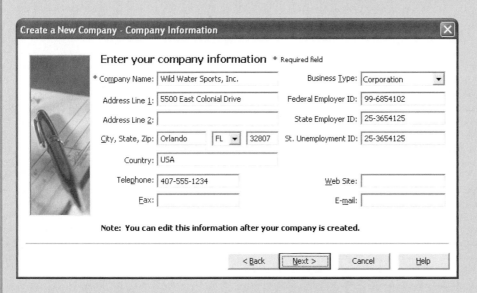

Figure 6.2

Company Information

4 Click **Next** and a window appears asking you to select a method to create your company.

5 Choose the first option to use a sample business type, and then click **Next**.

6 Select **Retail Company** from the list of simplified business types. This will establish your basic chart of accounts as shown in Figure 6.3.

Figure 6.3

Selecting a Business Type

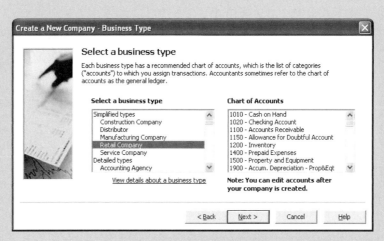

7   Click **Next** and then select **Accrual accounting**.

8   Click **Next** and then select **Real Time** as your posting method.

9   Click **Next** and then select **12 monthly accounting periods** as your period structure.

10 Click **Next** and then select your starting month as **January 2007**.

11 Click **Next** and then click **Finish** to complete your new company setup.

12 After a few minutes of setup, Peachtree will reveal the Setup Guide as shown in Figure 6.4. Close this window, click **File**, and then click **Close Company**.

Figure 6.4

Peachtree's Setup Guide

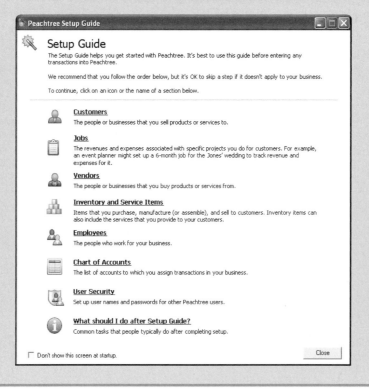

Donna has met with Ernesto and determined his business did have some outstanding balances from a few customers and owed some vendors for purchases made in the previous months. His business has an existing bank account and a MasterCard business credit card account. It also owned some equipment and had a related note payable.

Karen has also decided to use Peachtree's job tracking feature to follow service-related efforts for customers. The firm plans to market its service program to existing customers and will need to track costs for each job as well as bill customers based on hours worked and materials used for each job. You decide to begin with setting up the customer information.

Set Up Customers

The customer setup process includes creating existing customers, establishing beginning balances, creating default conditions for all customers, determining sales tax issues, and establishing defaults for statements and invoices.

"We will run credit checks on all new customers before giving them credit," Karen explains. "Our default credit amount will be $65,000 and net 30 days with no discount."

"How do you indicate whether customers are subject to sales tax or not?" you ask.

"First things first," Karen answers. "Before we can specify a sales tax condition for a customer, we must first establish a sales tax authority and establish a sales tax code. The company is located in Orange County, Florida, which collects ½% surtax in addition to the state sales tax rate of 6%. We'll set that up after we establish customers and their beginning balances and then go back to each customer to specify each as being subject to this sales tax."

To set up customers:

1 Open the Wild Water Sports, Inc., file by clicking **File**, click **Open Previous Company**, and then select **Wild Water Sports, Inc.** Note that the Setup Guide should open automatically. If not, click **Company** from the Navigation Bar. From the Company Center, click the **Setup Guide** button. Alternatively, click the **File** menu and then click **Setup Guide**.

2 Move the Setup Guide window down slightly so that you can access the System Date and accounting period buttons.

3 Change the system date to **12/31/06** and the accounting period to **Period 1 — 01/01/07 — 01/31/07**.

4 Click **Customers** from the Setup Guide.

5 The Peachtree Setup Guide – Customers window opens as shown in Figure 6.5. Note that in this section you will enter customers, then beginning balances, defaults, sales tax, and statement and invoice defaults.

Figure 6.5

Setting Up Customers

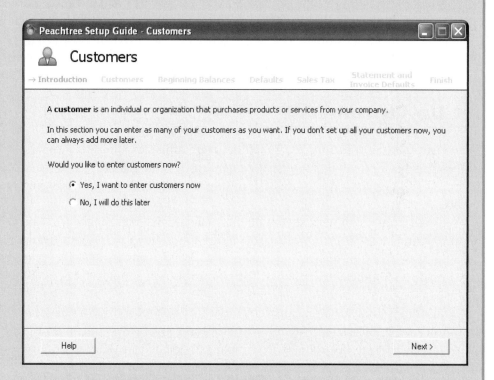

6 Select the **Yes, I want to enter customers now** option and then click **Next**.

7 Click the **Add New Customer** button.

8 Type **50001** as the Customer ID and then type **Orlando Water Sports** as the customer name.

9 Click the **Beginning Balances** button and then click **Yes** to save this customer.

10 Type the information specified in Figure 6.6 to establish $48,300, the beginning balance owed by Orlando Water Sports. (*Note:* To enter dates, you'll have to right-click the date field and select the appropriate date from the calendar provided.)

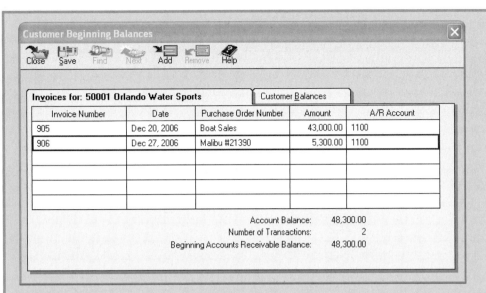

Figure 6.6

Sales to Orlando Water Sports

11 Click **Save** to save the customer beginning balance and then click **Close** to close the window.

12 Click **New** and then enter two additional customers (50002 and 50003) and their related beginning balances as shown below.

Customer ID	Customer Name	Invoice #	Date	Purchase Order	Amount
50002	Buena Vista Water Sports	910	12/10/06	P23423	$30,000
50002	Buena Vista Water Sports	915	12/15/06	P23435	$3,000
50003	Walking on Water	920	12/28/06	WW5258	$15,000

13 To close the Maintain Customers/Prospects screen, click **Close** after you have entered the above information and saved the new customers and balances.

14 Click **Next** and then select **Yes, but I already entered balances**, or **I want to skip this for now** since you already entered beginning balances.

15 Click **Next** to view the default payment, credit, and finance charge terms.

16 Click the **Change Customer Defaults** button.

17 Change the Credit Limit to 65,000.00 so that your window looks like Figure 6.7.

Figure 6.7

Changing Customer
Defaults

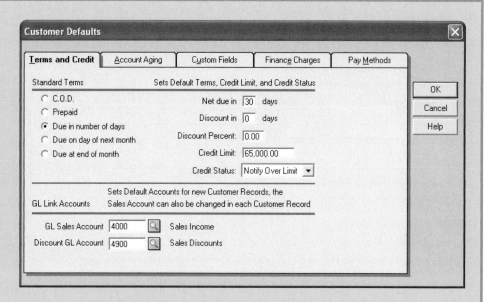

18 Click **OK** to close the Customer Defaults window. Your Setup Guide window should look like Figure 6.8.

Figure 6.8

Customer Defaults

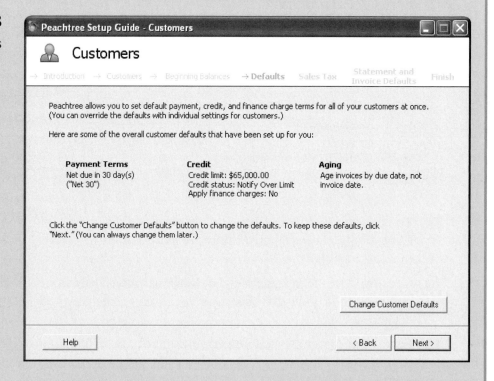

19 Click **Next** and then select **Yes, I collect sales tax from my customers**.

20 Click **Next** and then click the **Set up Sales Tax Vendor** button.

21 Type **12000** as the Vendor ID and then type **Florida Department of Revenue** as the vendor name.

22 Type **6854102** as the account number.

23 Type **1379 Blountstown Hwy** in the Address text box and then type **Tallahassee FL 32304-2716** as the city, state, and zip code.

24 Click the **Purchase Default** tab and then type **2310** in the Expense Acct: text edit box. (*Note:* This is the sales tax payable account.)

25 Click **Save** to save this new vendor and then click **Close**.

26 Click **Next** and then click the **Set up Sales Tax Authorities** button.

27 Enter the information from Figure 6.9.

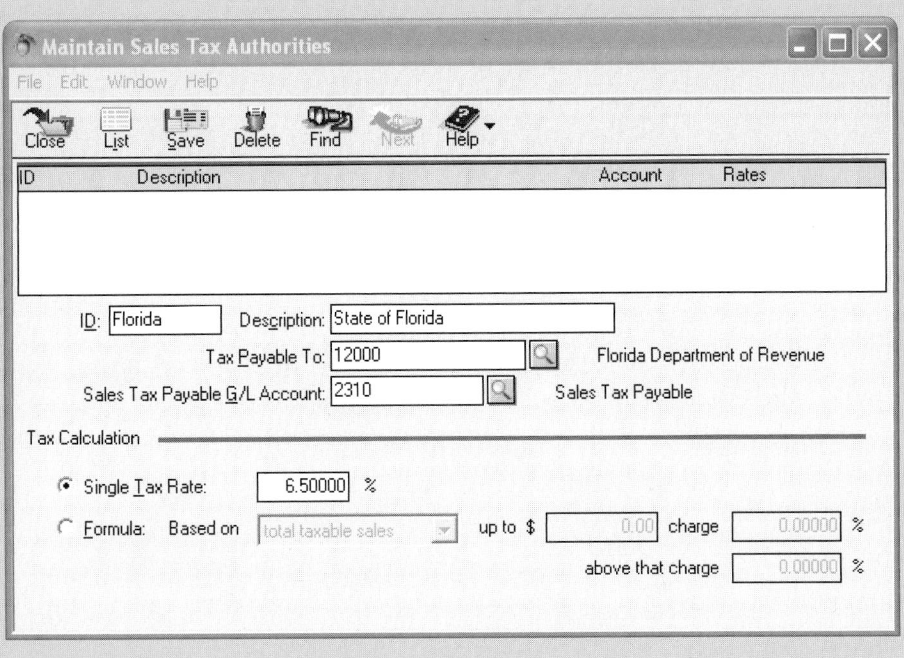

Figure 6.9

Creating a Sales Tax Authority

28 Click **Save** to save this new Sales Tax Authority and then click **Close**.

29 Click **Next** and then click the **Set up Sales Tax Codes** button.

30 Enter the information from Figure 6.10.

Figure 6.10

Creating a Sales Tax Code

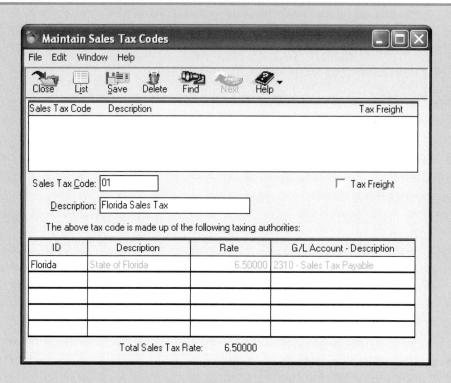

31 Click **Save** to save this new Sales Tax Code and then click **Close**.

32 Click **Next** and then click the **Assign Sales Tax to Customer** button.

33 For all existing customers, select **01** as the Sales Tax as shown in Figure 6.11 for customer 50001. (*Hint:* For each customer, once you enter **01** for the sales tax code, you must click **Save** before entering information for the text customer.)

Figure 6.11

Assigning Sales Tax Codes to Customer 50001

34 When you've entered the sales tax code for all customers, click **Close** to close the Maintain Customers/Prospects window.

35 Click **Next**. Accept the Statement and Invoice Defaults by clicking **Next** again.

36 Select **Return to the main Setup Guide** screen and then click **Next**.

37 Reduce the Setup Guide screen and click the **Reports** menu on the Business Status screen; then click **Accounts Receivable**.

38 Double-click **Customer Ledgers** from the Select a Report window.

39 Click the **Print** button and then click **OK** to print. Your printed document should look like Figure 6.12. Be sure to save this and all future printed ledgers, lists, etc., for use later in this chapter.

Wild Water Sports, Inc.
Customer Ledgers
For the Period From Jan 1, 2007 to Jan 31, 2007
Filter Criteria includes: Report order is by ID. Report is printed in Detail Format.

Customer ID Customer	Date	Trans No	Tipe	Debit Amt	Credit Amt	Balance
50001 Orlando Water Sports	1/1/07	Balance Fwd				48,300.00
50002 Buena Vista Water Sport	1/1/07	Balance Fwd				33,000.00
50003 Walking on Water	1/1/07	Balance Fwd				15,000.00
Report Total						96,300.00

Figure 6.12
Customer Ledgers

40 Click **Close** to close the Customer Ledgers window.

41 Double-click **Customer List** from the Select a Report window. You may have to resize the columns so that the whole customer name appears on your report.

42 Click the **Print** button and then click **OK** to print. Your printed document should look like Figure 6.13.

Wild Water Sports, Inc.
Customer List

Filter Criteria includes: 1) Customers only. Report order is by ID.

Customer ID	Customer	Contact	Telephone 1	Resale No
50001	Orlando Water Sports			
50002	Buena Vista Water Sports			
50003	Walking on Water			

Figure 6.13
Customer List

43 Click **Close** to close the Customer List window and then click **Close** to close the Select a Report window.

44 Close the Setup Guide window as well.

"Why did we print a customer list and a customer ledger?" you ask. "What's the difference?"

"In its default form, the customer list displays the customer's ID, name, contact information, phone number, type, and balance only," Karen responds. "The customer ledger lists detail transaction information as well as outstanding balances per customer. I wanted to show you both because, depending on the situation, you may need to print one or both."

You've decided since you have no current jobs pending, you will create new jobs as they occur. Thus, the next step in the Setup Guide is to set up vendors.

Set Up Vendors

Now that Karen's customers are established, you'll need to set up vendors, which includes setting up vendor defaults, creating vendors, and inputting beginning balances. Most of your vendors will be supplying inventory for you to sell and will give you 30 days credit with no discount available and $150,000 in credit.

"When do we establish accounts payable in the general ledger?" you ask.

"You will later," Karen responds. "However, the general ledger only reflects the balance owed, not to whom you owe it! The following process will establish the two vendors we owe at the beginning of the period and specifically identify the amounts and invoices relating to the overall accounts payable balances which we'll input into the general ledger later."

To set up vendors:

1 Open the Setup Guide.

2 Click **Vendors**.

Trouble? If you close the Peachtree accounting program and then return at a later time, the system date of the computer, and thus the system date for Peachtree, reverts to the date your are working with the information (i.e., today's date). You will need to reset the system date to **12/31/06**.

3 Select **Yes, I want to enter vendors now** and then click **Next**.

4 Click the **Add New Vendor** button.

5 Type **10000** as the Vendor ID and then type **Malibu Boats** as the vendor name.

6 Click the **Purchase Defaults** tab and type **1200** as the Expense Acct.

7 Click **Save**.

8 Click the **General** tab and then click the **Beginning Balances** button.

9 Type the information specified in Figure 6.14 to establish $76,000, the beginning balance owed to Malibu Boats.

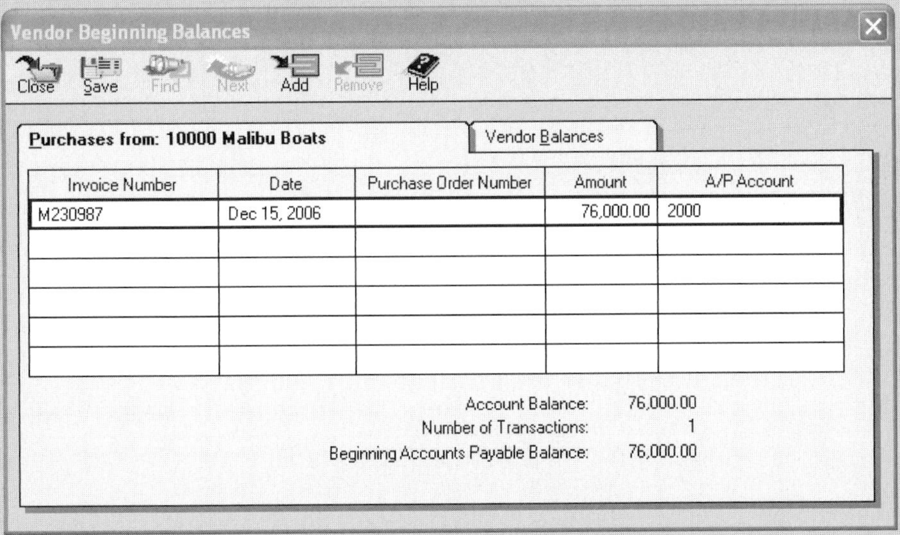

Figure 6.14

Purchases from Malibu Boats

10 Click **Save** to save the vendor beginning balance and then click **Close** to close the window.

11 Click **New** to enter a new vendor for your credit card.

12 Type **11000** as the Vendor ID and **MasterCard** as the vendor name.

13 Click the **Purchase Defaults** tab and enter **6450** as the expense account most often charged when the credit card is used.

14 Click the **General** tab and then click **Save** to save this vendor information.

15 Click the **Beginning Balance** button and enter invoice **MC0909238** on **12/12/06** for **$1,000** in the Beginning Balance window, click **Save**, and then click **Close**. Click **Close** again to close the Maintain Vendor window; then, close the two Setup Guide windows.

16 On the Business Status screen, click the **Reports** menu item and then click **Accounts Payable**.

17 Double-click **Vendor Ledgers** from the Select a Report window.

18 Click the **Print** button and then click **OK** to print. Your printed document should look like Figure 6.15.

Figure 6.15

Vendor Ledger

Wild Water Sports, Inc.
Vendor Ledgers
For the Period From Jan 1, 2007 to Jan 31, 2007
Filter Criteria includes: Report order is by ID.

Vendor ID Vender	Date	Trans No	Type Paid	Debit Amt	Credit Amt	Balance
10000 Malibu Boats	1/1/07	Balance Fwd				76,000.00
11000 MasterCard	1/1/07	Balance Fwd				1,000.00
12000 Florida Department of Re						0.00
Report Total						77,000.00

19 Close the Vendor Ledger window.

20 Double-click **Vendor List** from the Select a Report window.

21 Click the **Print** button and then click **OK** to print. Your printed document should look like Figure 6.16.

Figure 6.16

Vendor List

Wild Water Sports, Inc.
Vender List
Filter Criteria includes: Report order is by ID.

Vendor ID	Vendor	Contact	Telephone 1	Tax Id No.
10000	Malibu Boats			
11000	MasterCard			
12000	Florida Department of Rev			

22 Close the Vendor List window and then click **Close** to close the Select a Report window.

"That was painless," you admit.

"True, but we have much more work to do so let's keep going," Karen suggests.

Set Up Inventory and Service Items

"Now it's time to establish information about our inventory in Peachtree." Karen says. "Peachtree has some very nice inventory features which will help us track inventory cost and quantities."

She suggests that you set up some new activity items and inventory part items. Items show up on a company's invoice as a description of work performed or product delivered. For Wild Water Sports, activity items would be things like changing engine oil and filter, engine tune ups, and 20-hour service checks, for example. Inventory part items would include boats, accessories, and parts for repairs.

To set up items, Karen and Donna had to agree on prices for common service items, hourly service rates for nonstandard repairs, and pricing for products to be sold. They also had to set up item names and descriptions. They agreed to charge customers for actual hours worked by their employees at a predetermined rate per hour as opposed to a flat amount for certain types of work. As a result, they'll be setting up activity items, not service items. There is a big difference in Peachtree. Again, service items would charge a flat amount for work, whereas activity items involve an employee charging a job for hours worked for a specific activity. Stock items, on the other hand, are inventory items that the company purchases for resale. In this company's case, that would include the various boats it purchases from the manufacturer for resale to the consumer. Karen provides you the pertinent information and suggests you establish activity items and stock items now.

To set up activity items:

1 Select **Inventory and Service Items** from the Setup Guide to begin.

2 Select **Yes, I want to enter inventory items or service items now** and then click **Next**.

3 Click the **Add New Item or Service** button.

4 Type **101** in the Item ID text box and type **Engine Service** in the Description text box.

5 Type **Labor for changing engine oil and filter** in the General Description edit box.

6 Type **125** in the Price Level 1 edit box.

7 Select **Activity** as the Item Class from the drop-down edit list.

8 Click the **magnify glass** icon next to the GL Income Acct edit box to view a list of accounts from which to choose.

9 Click **New** to add a new account.

10 Type **4010** as the new Account ID, type **Service Income** as the Description, and then choose **Income** as the account type from the Account Type drop-down edit list. (This final step is critical to the proper placement and treatment of transactions in this account.)

11 Click **Save** and **Close**.

12 Make sure **4010** is selected as the GL Income Acct: and then Type **1** in the Item Tax Type edit box. Click **Save**. Your completed inventory item should look like Figure 6.17.

Figure 6.17

Adding a New Inventory Activity Item

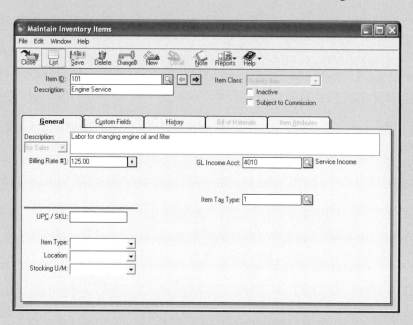

13 Continue this process for the remaining activity items listed below by clicking the **New** button and saving your changes.

Item ID/	Description	General Description	Item Class	Billing Rate	Item Tax Type	Income A/C
101	Engine Service	Labor for changing engine oil and filter	Activity	$125.00	01	4010 Service Income
102	Engine Tune Up	Labor for engine tune up	Activity	$250.00	01	4010 Service Income
103	20 Hour Service	Labor for 20 hour service check	Activity	$175.00	01	4010 Service Income
104	Service	Hourly service rate	Activity	$85.00	01	4010 Service Income

14 Now, on the same screen (Maintain Inventory Items), enter the following inventory part item shown. Type **201** in the Item ID text box and then type **Malibu Sunsetter LXi** in both Description text boxes.

15 Select **Stock item** as the Item Class and type **Malibu Sunsetter LXi** in both Description boxes.

16 Type **60000** in the Price Level 1 edit box.

17 Accept **4000** as the GL Sales Account and **1** as the Item Tax Type.

18 Type **48000** in the Last Unit Cost box. (*Note:* All merchandise is marked up 25% of cost; thus, all merchandise cost is 80% of the sales price.)

19 Select **Average** as the Cost Method.

20 Click **Save** to save your work. Your window should look like Figure 6.18.

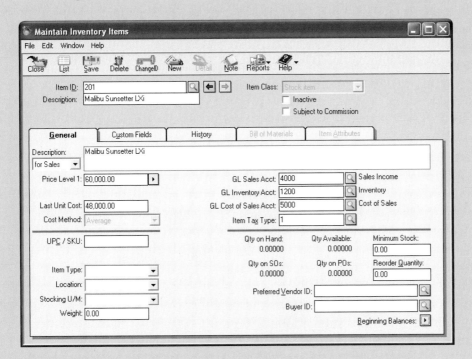

Figure 6.18
Item ID 201

21 Click the **Beginning Balances arrow** in the lower right-hand corner of the Maintain Inventory Items window.

22 Choose the **201** Item ID and then type **1** as the Quantity and **48000** as the Unit Cost. Click **Enter**. The Inventory Beginning Balances window should look like Figure 6.19.

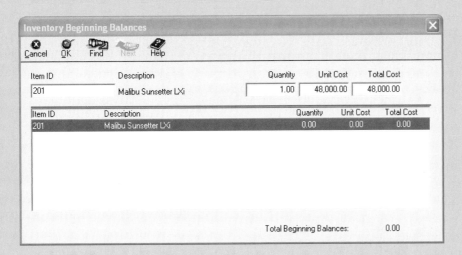

Figure 6.19
Entering Beginning Inventory Balances

23 Click **OK** in the Inventory Beginning Balances window to save your work.

24 Click **New** to add a new stock item.

25 Continue this process for the remaining inventory part items listed below. Remember all of these items are Item Class: Stock item, Item Tax Type 01, use the average cost method, and are recorded to the 4000 Sales Income account.

Item ID	Description	Price Level 1	Last Unit Cost	Qty
201	Malibu Sunsetter LXi	$ 60,000	$ 48,000	1
202	Malibu Sportster LX	$ 52,000	$ 41,600	1
203	Malibu Sunscape LSV	$ 65,000	$ 52,000	2
204	Malibu Vride	$ 48,000	$ 38,400	2
205	Malibu WakeSetter VLX	$ 57,000	$ 45,600	1
206	Malibu WakeSetter XTI	$ 70,000	$ 56,000	1

26 Close the **Maintain Inventory Items** window and the two **Setup Guide** windows.

27 Click the **Reports** menu item and then click **Inventory**.

28 Double-click **Item List** from the Select a Report window.

29 Click the **Print** button and then click **OK** to print. Your printed document should look like Figure 6.20.

Figure 6.20

Item List

Wild Water Sports, Inc.
Item List

Filter Criteria includes: Report order is by ID.

Item ID	Item Description	Item Class	Active?	Item Type	Qty on Hand
101	Engine Service	Activity item	Active		
102	Engine Tune Up	Activity item	Active		
103	20 Hour Service	Activity item	Active		
104	Service	Activity item	Active		
201	Malibu Sunsetter LXi	Stock item	Active		1.00
202	Malibu Sportster LX	Stock item	Active		1.00
203	Malibu Sunscape LSV	Stock item	Active		2.00
204	Malibu Vride	Stock item	Active		2.00
205	Malibu WakeSetter VLX	Stock item	Active		1.00
206	Malibu WakeSetter XTI	Stock item	Active		1.00

30 Close the **Item List**.

31 Double-click **Inventory Valuation Report** from the Select a Report window.

32 Click the **Design** button to edit the report so it can fit on one page by removing a field.

33 Click the **Options** button and then click the **Fields** tab.

34 Uncheck the Show check box for the **Stocking U/M** field and then click **OK**.

35 Click the **Print** button and then click **OK** to print. Your printed document should look like Figure 6.21.

Figure 6.21

Inventory Valuation Report

Wild Water Sports, Inc.
Inventory Valuation Report
As of Jan 31, 2007

Filter Criteria includes: 1) Stock/Assembly. Report order is by ID. Report is printed with Truncated Long Descriptions

Item ID Item Class	Item Description	Cost Method	Qty on Hand	Item Value	Avg Cos	% of Inv Val
201 Stock item	Malibu Sunsetter LXi	Average	1.00	48,000.00	48000.00	12.90
202 Stock item	Malibu Sportster LX	Average	1.00	41,600.00	41600.00	11.18
203 Stock item	Malibu Sunscape LSV	Average	2.00	104,000.00	52000.00	27.96
204 Stock item	Malibu Vride	Average	2.00	76,800.00	38400.00	20.65
205 Stock item	Malibu WakeSetter VLX	Average	1.00	45,600.00	45600.00	12.26
206 Stock item	Malibu WakeSetter XTI	Average	1.00	56,000.00	56000.00	15.05
				372,000.00		100.00

36 Close the **Inventory Valuation Report** without saving it and then close the **Select a Report** window.

Karen reminds you that you're just in the setup mode and are not actually entering any business transactions for the current period. Next up is payroll setup.

Set Up Payroll

"Now it's time to establish information about our employees in Peachtree," Karen says. "Peachtree has some very nice payroll features which will help us track employee information, prepare payroll tax reports, and account for our employee cost."

"Will it calculate payroll withholding for federal and state taxes?" you ask.

"It will if we purchase a payroll tax table service," Karen answers, "but we haven't decided whether we want to pay for that or not. We'll decide later. For the time being, we'll do our payroll in-house and maintain our own payroll tax tables."

The company employs five people: Donna and Karen as managers, and Raul, Peggy, and Ryder as sales staff and service technicians. For each employee, you'll need to add personal address, contact, and tax information. In doing so, Karen points out that you will also be setting up payroll tax items like salary and hourly as well as identifying how often your employees are paid (monthly in this case). You'll also be identifying each employee's salary or hourly rate, taxes to be withheld, state worked, filing status, tax rates (like unemployment), and tax payees (like the Florida Department of Revenue) to whom state taxes are paid. Karen then explains the actual process of entering employees into Peachtree for Wild Water Sports by using Donna as an example, but first she must set up employee defaults for payroll.

To set up payroll:

1 Select **Employees** from the Setup Guide to begin.

2 Click **In-house payroll, where I do everything myself** and then click **Next**.

3 Click the **Run Payroll Setup Wizard** button.

4 Select the **Payroll Tax Table Information Will Be Manually Maintained** option and then click **Next**.

5 Select **FL** for the state from the drop-down menu. Type **2.7** as the Unemployment Percent for Your Company and accept the remaining default accounts as shown in Figure 6.22.

Figure 6.22

Initial Payroll Setup

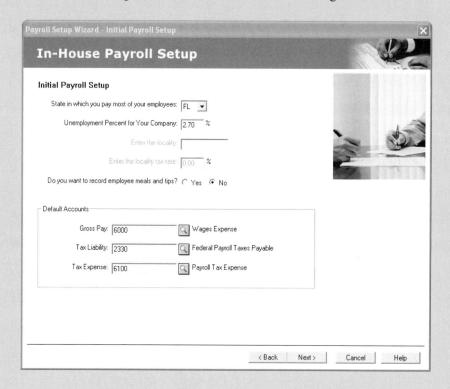

6 Click **Not offered** when asked about a 401(k) plan and then click **Next**.

7 Accept the default responses regarding vacation and sick pay by clicking **Next**.

8 Click **Finish** to end the payroll setup process.

9 Continue with the Setup Guide for employees by clicking **Next**.

10 Select **Yes, I want to enter employees now** and then click **Next**.

11 Click the **Add New Employee or Sales Rep** button.

1   Type **001** as Donna's employee number.

2   Then fill in the blank spaces on the General tab using the information in Figure 6.23. Then, click **Save**.

Click this tab to enter more employee information

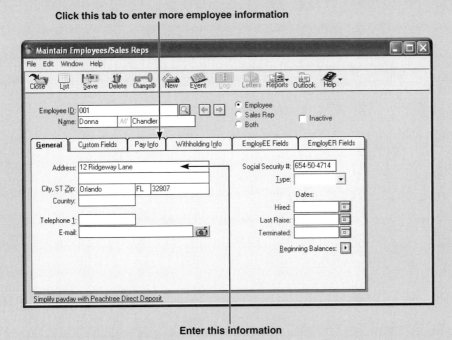

Figure 6.23

Adding Information for a New Employee in the General Tab

Enter this information

3   Select the **Pay Info** tab.

4   Select **Salary** from the Pay Method drop-down edit box, select **Monthly** from the Frequency drop-down edit box, and then type **4166.67** as her monthly salary rate as shown in Figure 6.24.

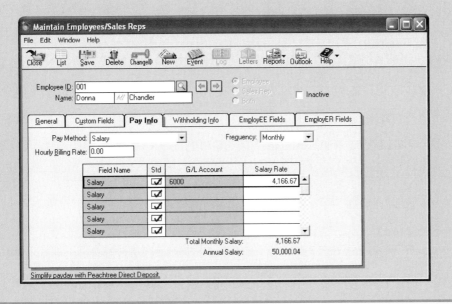

Figure 6.24

Pay Info Tab Information

5 Select the **Withholding Info** tab.

6 Select **Married** as Donna's Filing Status for Federal, State and Local boxes and leave her Allowances (Allow) at 0. Then, click **Save**.

7 Select the **EmployEE Fields** tab, noting the various fields and accounts where payroll transactions will be allocated as shown in Figure 6.25.

Figure 6.25

Employee Fields

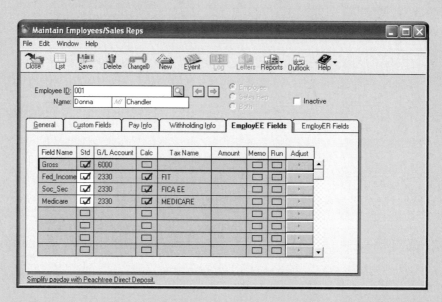

8 Select the **EmployER Fields** tab, noting the various fields and accounts where payroll transactions will be allocated as shown in Figure 6.26.

Figure 6.26

Employer Fields

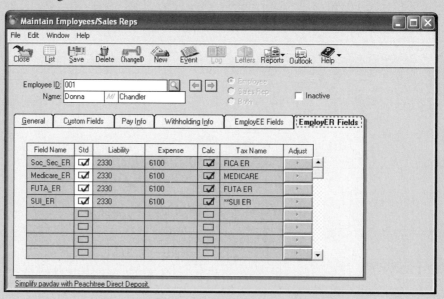

9 Click **Save** to save this employee, but don't close this window.

You note that Donna Chandler is now set up as an employee for the company but you still have more employees to go. Karen suggests you add one employee for now, perhaps Ryder Zacovic, an hourly employee. You respond that you're up to the task.

To enter Ryder as an employee into Peachtree:

1 Click **New** in the Maintain Employees/Sales Reps window.

2 Be certain that the General tab is selected. Then fill in the form with the following information:
Employee ID: 003
Name: Ryder Zacovic
Social security number: 556-74-6585
Address: 1554 Rose Avenue Apt. #4, Orlando, FL 32804
Country: USA

3 Select the appropriate tabs to enter the following additional information:
Pay Method: Hourly – Time Ticket Hours
Frequency: Monthly
Hourly Rate: 15
Filing Status: Single
Allowances (Allow): 0

4 Click **Save** and then click **Close**.

You have now entered two employees into Peachtree's payroll system and decide to enter the remaining employees later. If you were starting Peachtree midyear, it would be appropriate to enter beginning balances for withholdings and payroll taxes now. Since you are starting to use Peachtree at the beginning of the fiscal/calendar year, this is not necessary.

To finish the employee setup process:

1 Click **Next** and then select **No** when asked if you have any employees that you need to enter salary history for; then click **Next**.

2 Click the **Change Employee Defaults** button.

3 Click the **EmployEE Fields** tab.

4 Uncheck all of the Calc check boxes as shown in Figure 6.27.

Figure 6.27

Turning Off Automatic
Calculation of Payroll Taxes
for the Employee

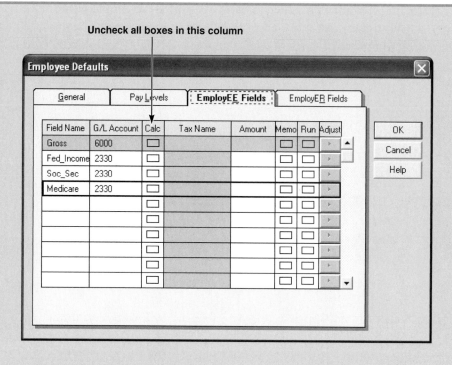

Uncheck all boxes in this column

5 Click the **EmployER Fields** tab.

6 Type **2340** as the default liability account for FUTA_ER.

7 Type **2350** as the default liability account for SUI_ER.

8 Uncheck all of the Calc check boxes as shown in Figure 6.28.

Figure 6.28

Turning Off Automatic
Calculation of Payroll Taxes
for the Employer

Uncheck all boxes in this column

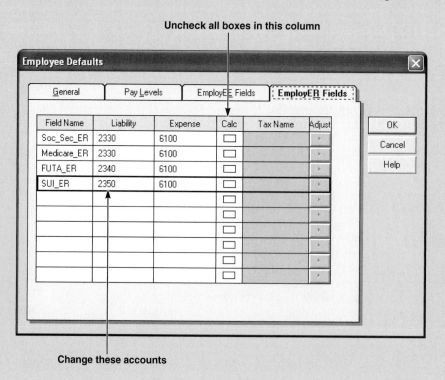

Change these accounts

9 Click **OK** to save and close the Employee Defaults window. Close the two Setup Guide windows.

10 Click the **Reports** menu item and then click **Payroll**.

11 Double-click **Employee List**.

12 Click the **Print** button and then click **OK** to print. Your printed document should look like Figure 6.29.

Wild Water Sports, Inc. Employee List				
Filter Criteria includes: Report order is by ID.				
Employee ID Employee	Address line 1 Address line 2 City ST ZIP	SS No	Fed Filing Status	Pay Type
001 Donna Chandler	12 Ridgeway Lane Orlando, FL 32807	654-50-4714	Married	Salaried
003 Ryder Zacovic	1554 Rose Avenue Apt. #4 Orlando, FL 32804 USA	556-74-6585	Single	Hourly

Figure 6.29
Employee List

13 Close the Employee List and Select a Report windows.

"We're almost done with the initial company setup," Karen explains. "All that is left is for us to establish our beginning account balances."

Set Up Beginning Balances and New Accounts

"The general ledger is where all accounts reside," says Karen. "This includes all asset, liability, equity, revenue, and expense accounts. Each business event which impacts a company's accounting records will affect at least two of these accounts."

She then explains that the next step in setting up a company in Peachtree is to review the chart of accounts, add any additional accounts you want, and then set up general ledger beginning balances.

To set up general ledger beginning balances:

1 Click **Chart of Accounts** from the Setup Guide.

2 Click **Next** and then click the **Add New Accounts** button.

3 Enter the information from Figure 6.30 to create a new account.

Figure 6.30

Adding a New Account

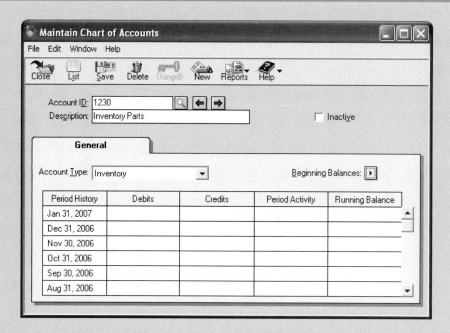

4 Click **Save** and then click **Close** to close the Maintain Chart of Accounts window.

5 Click **Next** in the Setup Guide, choose **Yes** to the question **Do any of your accounts have balances**, and then click **Next**.

6 Click the **Enter Account Beginning Balances** button.

7 Scroll down the window, select **From 12/1/06 through 12/31/06**, and then click **OK**.

8 Enter the following balances for each account:

Account	Description		
1020	Checking Account	25,000	
1100	Accounts Receivable	96,300	
1200	Inventory	372,000	
1500	Property and Equipment	75,000	
1900	Accumulated Depreciation		7,500
2000	Accounts Payable		77,000
2700	Long-Term Debt-Noncurrent		383,800
3930	Common Stock		100,000

9 After entering the above information, your screen should look like Figure 6.31.

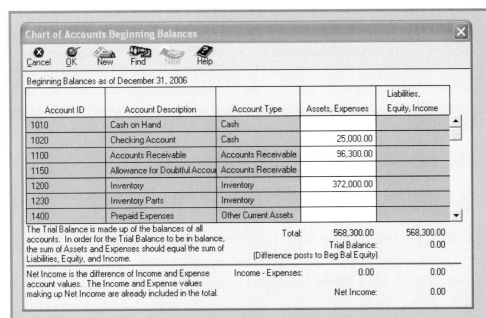

Figure 6.31

Chart of Accounts Beginning Balances

10 Make sure that the total of your Assets, Expenses column equals the total of your Liabilities, Equity, Income column. If they are equal, click the **OK** button to indicate you've entered all the beginning balances. If not, recheck your entries.

11 Click **Next** two more times. Click **Return** to main Setup Guide screen, click **Next**, and then close the Setup Guide.

12 Click the **Lists** menu item at the top of the Business Status screen and then click **Chart of Accounts**.

13 Click **Print** and then click **OK** to print. The first part of your printed document should look like Figure 6.32.

Figure 6.32

Partial View of the Printed Account List

Wild Water Sports, Inc.

Account List

Account ID	Description	Type	Running Balance
1010	Cash on Hand	Cash	$0.00
1020	Checking Account	Cash	$25,000.00
1100	Accounts Receivable	Accounts Receivable	$96,300.00
1150	Allowance for Doubtful Account	Accounts Receivable	$0.00
1200	Inventory	Inventory	$372,000.00
1230	Inventory Parts	Inventory	$0.00
1400	Prepaid Expenses	Other Current Assets	$0.00
1500	Property and Equipment	Fixed Assets	$75,000.00
1900	Accum. Depreciation - Prop&Eqt	Accumulated Depreciation	($7,500.00)
2000	Accounts Payable	Accounts Payable	($77,000.00)

14 Click **Close** to close the Accounts List window.

You have now entered your beginning balances and have set up the subsidiary ledgers for accounts payable, accounts receivable, and inventory which identify vendors, customers, and inventory items that support those balances. Now you will need to verify that the details you established for each of these accounts are the same as for the general ledger accounts you just established. Karen explains that once again this is a critical step in setting up the company.

To verify that accounts payable, accounts receivable, and inventory details match your general ledger balances:

1 Click **General Ledger** from the Reports menu.

2 Double-click **General Ledger Trial Balance** to view the trial balance at 1/31/07 as shown below in Figure 6.33.

Figure 6.33

General Ledger
Trial Balance at 1/31/07

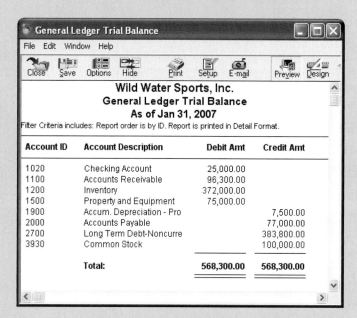

3 Click **Print** and then click **OK** to print.

4 Gather up your Customer Ledgers, Vendor Ledgers, and Inventory Valuation Report you previously printed.

5 Compare the report total in the Customer Ledgers report and make sure it equals the Accounts Receivable balance above of 96,300.00. If it doesn't, go back and figure out what you did wrong.

6 Compare the report total in the Vendor Ledgers report and make sure it equals the Accounts Payable balance above of 77,000.00. If it doesn't, go back and figure out what you did wrong.

7 Compare the report total in the Inventory Valuation report and make sure it equals the Inventory balance above of 372,000.00. If it doesn't, go back and figure out what you did wrong.

You are both somewhat relieved that the detail amounts you entered in the subsidiary ledgers for customers, vendors, and inventory items equal the general ledger balances you entered as of the beginning of the year.

Karen then enlightens you as to the arrangement that she and Donna have with Ernesto. The three agreed that the opening balance equity (assets - liabilities) was $100,000 as was shown above in the trial balance. Donna and Karen will each be purchasing stock in the company for $100,000 on 1/1/07. This will give the company a total value of $300,000 and thereby give each stockholder (Ernesto, Donna, and Karen) a one-third interest in the company.

"We are well on our way to getting this company set up," Karen explains.

"Should we save our work?" you ask.

"Funny you should mention that," Karen responds. "Peachtree automatically saves every event you record. In fact, Peachtree doesn't even have a save or save as feature like most other software."

"Shouldn't we at least make a copy of the file in case something happens to this one?" you inquire.

"Good point," Karen says. "Once we're set up, we can use Peachtree's backup procedure to save a copy."

Your final task is to back up your data file for safe keeping.

Backing Up Your Company File

"It is very important to keep a backup of your company file just in case your computer hard drive crashes or your data file gets corrupted or destroyed," Karen explains. She goes on to explain that some business users save their files to USB drives, CD ROMs, Zip disks, or floppy disks. Floppy disks do not have enough room to hold the typical data file and are too slow to work from. Zip drives are also too slow to work from and CD ROMs are often read only and thus can't be used to work from but can be used to store a backup.

"USB drives are ideal if you can afford one," you point out.

Karen suggests that the two of you try it out.

To back up and restore a file using Peachtree's backup procedure to an external disk:

1 Open the Wild Water Sports file if by chance you closed it after the last lesson.

2 Connect your USB drive.

3 Click **Back Up** from the File menu.

4 Click in the check box to indicate you want to include the company name in the backup file name.

5 Click the **Backup** button.

6 Choose a location you'd like to back your file up to. In Figure 6.34, we chose to back the file up to an external disk located in Drive F in a folder we called Peachtree. Choose a location from the **Save in** drop-down list.

Figure 6.34

Backing Up to an External Drive

Your data file location will be different than that shown here.

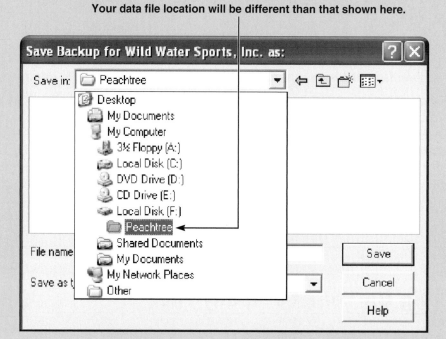

7 Click **Save** to begin the backup process.

8 Click **OK** when Peachtree informs you of the size of the file to be backed up and then click **OK** again to begin. When the backup is finished, you'll be returned to the main Peachtree window.

9 To restore that same file from the external drive to your hard drive, choose **Restore** from the Peachtree file menu.

10 Click **Browse** to identify the location of your backup file as shown in Figure 6.35. (Once again your location may be different than shown.)

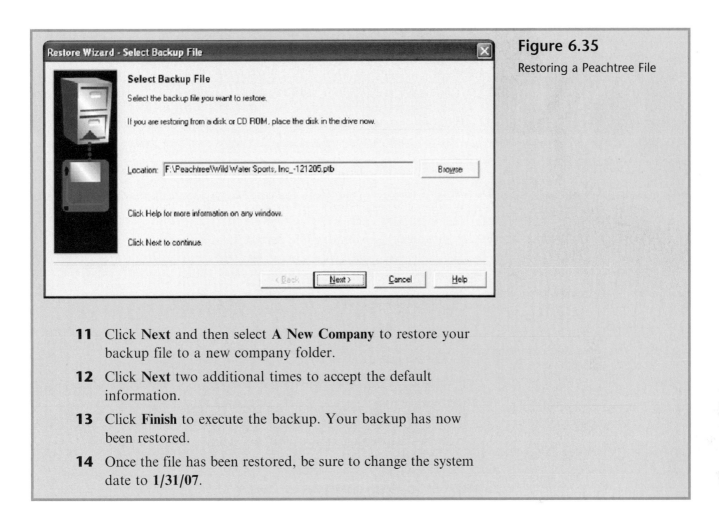

Figure 6.35

Restoring a Peachtree File

11 Click **Next** and then select **A New Company** to restore your backup file to a new company folder.

12 Click **Next** two additional times to accept the default information.

13 Click **Finish** to execute the backup. Your backup has now been restored.

14 Once the file has been restored, be sure to change the system date to **1/31/07**.

"Why did you restore your files to a new company folder?" you ask.

"Good question," Karen answers. "I do that to start fresh and to have a full version backup on my computer. It's not really necessary as long as we continue to make backups on a regular basis."

"What about the User Security section of the Setup Guide?" you ask. "We didn't complete that section."

"You only need to set up user names and passwords if more than one user will use Peachtree at the same time or if you need to restrict the information some users can access," Karen answers. "Since we only have the one computer with Peachtree and we don't desire any restricted access, we can skip that part."

End Note

Karen thanks you for your patience in helping create a Peachtree file for Wild Water Sports. You've created a new company, set up company preferences, company items, customers, vendors, accounts, and employees. Next up you'll begin recording business transactions.

Chapter 6 Questions

1 What information should you have handy when setting up a new company using the new company wizard?

2 What key parts of the Setup Guide were illustrated in this text for Wild Water Sports, Inc.?

3 What does the customer setup process include?

4 What does the vendor setup process include?

5 What does the inventory and service item setup process include?

6 What does the employee setup process include?

7 What does the chart of accounts setup process include?

8 What is the difference between an activity item, a service item, and a stock item?

9 Does the act of entering beginning balances for customers, vendors, and inventory items create balances in the general ledger?

10 Why is it important to back up your company information?

Chapter 6 Assignments

merchandising

1 *Using the Setup Guide to Add More Information to Wild Water Sports*

Restore the file Wild Water Sports, Inc. 6A file found on the text CD or download it from the text Web site. Use the Setup Guide to add additional accounts, items, customers, vendors, and employees.

a. Create a new account with Account ID = 4030, Description = Parts Income, Account Type = Income.

b. Add the following <u>activity</u> items:

Item ID	Description	Item Class	General Description	Billing Rate	GL Income Acct:	Item Tax Type
105	Cleaning	Activity item	Labor for cleaning boats	75.00	4010	1
106	Painting & Body Repairs	Activity item	Labor for painting and body repairs	80.00	4010	1

c. Add the following inventory items (all use the average cost method, are item class stock items, and are item tax type 1) and use GL Sales Acct = 4030, GL Inventory Acct = 1230, and GL Cost of Sales Acct = 5000.

Item ID	Description/ General Description	Price Level 1	Last Unit Cost
901	Engine Oil	5.00	4.00
902	Oil Filter	15.00	12.00
903	Tune-up Parts	250.00	200.00
904	Air Filter	35.00	28.00

d. Add the following customers:

Customer ID	Customer Name	Balance Due
50004	Freebirds	$0
50005	Florida Sports Camp	$0

e. Add the following vendors:

Vendor ID	Vendor Name	Address	Phone	Default Acct	Balance Owed
10100	MB Sports	280 Air Park Road Atwater, CA 95301	209-357-4153	1200	$0
10200	Tige Boats	6803 US Hwy 83 N., Abilene, TX 79601	325-676-7777	1200	$0

f. Add the following employees:

Employee Name	Karen Wilson	Pat Ng
Employee ID	002	004
Address	16 Ocean Dr. Orlando, FL 32807	432 West Hwy 3 Orlando, FL 32807
Social security number	654-85-7844	125-95-4123
Salary	$4,166.67 per month	n/a
Hourly wage	n/a	$18 per hour using time tickets
Filing status	Single	Single
Taxes	Subject to Medicare, Social Security FUTA, and all applicable State taxes	Subject to Medicare, Social Security FUTA, and all applicable State taxes
Filing state	Florida	Florida
Pay period	Monthly	Monthly

g. Print the following as of 1/1/07 (similar to what you did in the chapter):

1 Customer Ledgers report

2 Customer List

3   Vendor Ledger report

4   Vendor List

5   Employee List

6   Item List

7   Inventory Valuation report

8   Account Listing

2   *Creating a New Company: Central Coast Cellular*

Van Morrison would like to use Peachtree for his new company, Central Coast Cellular. (Use company name: Central Coast Cellular Ch 6.) The company's address is 950 Higuera St., San Luis Obispo, CA 93401. The company's phone number is 805-555-9874. It uses the accrual method of accounting, posts in real time, and uses 12 monthly accounting periods. The company's main business is cellular phone sales and rentals, but it also earns revenue by consulting with customers on alternative cellular phone plans. Choose a retail company chart of accounts for this case. Central Coastal Cellular's fiscal and tax year begins January 1, 2009. The company's federal employer ID is 77-9418745 and state employer ID is 65-8588. Payroll is done manually. Federal taxes are accrued to the federal payroll taxes payable account. State taxes are accrued to the state payroll taxes payable account. California collects a training tax (CA_Train) from employers as a percentage of employee income. The company collects an 8% sales tax payable to the State Board of Equalization (SBOE). Create a sales tax ID = T and a sales tax code = 01.

Change the following defaults in Peachtree. Default terms for customers are net 30 with no discount and a credit limit of $10,000. Default terms for vendors are net 30 with no discount and a credit limit of $15,000 and a standard expense account 1200 (Inventory). Employee withholding and employer payroll taxes will be manually calculated. The company uses the average inventory costing method. Set up the following vendors, customers, employees, and inventory items. Each ID is noted within the ( ).

Set up the following vendors:

- Verizon Communications (VZ), 1255 Corporate Drive, Irving, TX 75038, 972-507-5000, Terms: Net 30, Contact: Francisco Rojas

- Nokia Mobile Phones (NK), 23621 Park Sorrento Road, Suite 101, Calabasas, CA 91302, 818-876-6000, Terms: Net 30, Contact: Brandy Parker

- Ericsson, Inc. (EK), 740 East Campbell Road, Richardson, TX 75081, 972-583-0000, Terms: Net 30, Contact: Monty Python

Set up the following customers:

- Tribune (T), 3825 S. Higuera St., San Luis Obispo, CA 93401, 805-781-7800, Terms: Net 30, Contact: Sara Miles, Sales Tax Code: 01

- City of San Luis Obispo (SLO), 990 Palm Street, San Luis Obispo, CA 93401, 805-781-7100, Terms: Net 30, Contact: Robert Preston, Sales Tax Code: 01

- Sterling Hotels Corporation (ST), 4115 Broad Street, Suite B-1, San Luis Obispo, CA 93401, 805-546-9388, Terms: Net 30, Contact: Monica Flowers, Sales Tax Code: 01

Set up the following employees. All employees are paid semimonthly and are subject to Social Security, FUTA, Medicare, SUI, SDI, and California's Employment Training taxes. Federal taxes are payable to the U.S. Treasury. State taxes are payable to the Employment Development Department (EDD).

- Name: Mr. Jay Bruner (JB), Address: 552 Olive St., San Luis Obispo, CA 93401, Phone: 805-555-7894, SS#: 578-94-3154, Start date: 1/1/09, Salary: $1,500 paid semimonthly, single

- Name: Mr. Alex Rodriguez (AR), Address: 1480 Monterey St., San Luis Obispo, CA 93401, Phone: 805-555-1579, SS#: 487-98-1374, Start date: 1/1/09, Salary: $2,000 paid semimonthly, married

- Name: Ms. Megan Paulson (MP), Address: 400 Beach St., San Luis Obispo, CA 93401, Phone: 805-555-4489, SS#: 547-31-5974, Start date: 1/1/09, Hourly: $12 per hour married

Set up the following inventory items:

- Consulting Services (CON) Item Class: Service, Rate: $95, Taxable, and using income account: Consulting

- Nokia 8290 (N8290) Item Class: Stock item, Cost: $150, Preferred vendor: Nokia, Sales price: $225

- Nokia 8890 (N8890) Item Class: Stock item, Cost: $175, Preferred vendor: Nokia, Sales price: $250

- Nokia 3285 (N3285) Item Class: Stock item, Cost: $200, Preferred vendor: Nokia, Sales price: $300

- Ericsson LX588 (ELX588) Item Class: Stock item, Cost: $50, Preferred vendor: Ericsson, Sales price: $85

- Ericsson T19LX (ET19LX) Item Class: Stock item, Cost: $75, Preferred vendor: Ericsson, Sales price: $100

This is a continuous assignment in that the next chapter will use the work you've accomplished here as the basis for recording additional business events. After you've printed the following reports, create a backup of this file and store it on some type of external medium (flash drive, Internet site, CD, disk, etc.). The backup file should be named Central Coast Cellular Ch 6 for easy identification later. You'll be restoring this file in the next chapter.

a. Customer List

b. Vendor List

c. Employee List

d. Item List

3   *Using the South-Western Home Page for More Assignments or Cases*

Go to the home page for this textbook at **http://www.thomsonedu.com/ accounting/owen**. Click **Additional Problem Sets**, select the **Chapter 6** section, and complete the problem(s) your instructor assigns.

Chapter 6 Case Problem 1
ALOHA PROPERTY MANAGEMENT

Aloha Property Management, Inc., a property manager, is located at 4-356 Kuhio Highway, Suite A-1, Kapaa Kauai, HI 96746. (Use company name: Aloha Property Management Ch 6.) The phone number is 808-823-8375. The company specializes in Hawaii Vacation Rentals. The federal tax ID number is 72-6914707, and it plans to start using Peachtree as its accounting program on January 1, 2008. The firm has been in business for two years using a manual accounting system but wishes to have you help it migrate to Peachtree. It is a property management corporation filing Form 1120 each year and collecting a 4% general excise tax (Tax ID: HI Tax, description: HI Sales Tax) on all rental income which must be paid to the State of Hawaii Department of Taxation (DOT) located at P.O. Box 1425 Honolulu, HI 96806-1425. The company chose to use 23100 (Sales Tax Payable) as the default account. Create a sales tax code with ID = Tax, Description = Excise Tax which is made up of one tax authority ID = HI Tax. Choose Property Management Company as the business type for this case.

   Aloha plans to use Peachtree's service invoice format and use sales receipts to record cash sales. It also plans to use Peachtree's payroll features but will plan to calculate payroll manually as it currently has only two W-2 employees. Aloha doesn't prepare estimates or track employee time or segments. It does, however, plan to enter bills as received and then enter payments later. Reports are to be accrual based, and Aloha plans to use the income and expense accounts created in Peachtree for a property management company and will be providing services only, no products. Most revenue comes from renting properties located on the island of Kauai to individual and corporate accounts. The company's policy is to collect a 50% deposit upon reservation, with the balance due upon arrival. Some customers (those that have prior credit approval) are invoiced upon arrival, and the remaining payment is due 30 days thereafter. Deposits are recorded as prepayments on account even though revenue is not recorded until customers arrive. Other customers (those that don't have prior credit approval) must pay upon arrival, at which time a sales receipt is generated and the remaining payment is collected. Default payment terms for customers are due on receipt (i.e., net due in 0 days) with no discounts available. Default payment terms for vendors are net due in 30 days with a credit limit of $5,000. Service items are used, but no inventory is maintained. Existing service items, customers, vendors, and employee information is provided below. (*Note:* Deposits for rentals not yet provided are shown as negative numbers.) The default income account for all items is 40000. All customers are subject to the excise tax.

Item ID	Service Item Name	Description	Rate
M1	Moana Unit #1	Weekly rent for Moana Unit #1	$2,000
M1	Moana Unit #2	Weekly rent for Moana Unit #2	$2,500
M1	Moana Unit #3	Weekly rent for Moana Unit #3	$4,000
M1	Moana Unit #4	Weekly rent for Moana Unit #4	$12.000
V1	Villa Kailani Unit #1	Weekly rent for Villa Unit #1	$3,000
V2	Villa Kailani Unit #2	Weekly rent for Villa Unit #2	$4,500
V3	Villa Kailani Unit #3	Weekly rent for Villa Unit #3	$4,200
V4	Villa Kailani Unit #4	Weekly rent for Villa Unit #4	$6,000

Customer ID	Customer Name	Balance Due (Deposits)	Invoice #
B	Boeing	$10,000	7505
GM	General Motors	$75,000	7506
BM	Brice Montoya	($3,000)	999
SR	Sara Rice	($6,000)	999
AC	Apple Computer	$25,000	7507

Vendor ID	Vendor Name	Balance Owed
RC	Reilly Custodial	$4,500
BS	Blue Sky Pools	$1,800

Employee Name	Fran Aki	Danièle Castillo
Employee ID	FA	DC
Social Security number	128-85-7413	984-74-1235
Salary	$75,000 per year	n/a
Hourly wage	n/a	$20 per hour
Filing status	Married	Single
Taxes	Subject to Medicare, Social Security, FUT, and all applicable state taxes	Subject to Medicare, Social Security, FUT, and all applicable state taxes
Filing state	Hawaii	Hawaii

The company owns two buildings: Moana Lani Kai located in Princeville and Villa Kailani located in Poipu. It owed $3,875,000 (a 25-year note payable) on the two properties for which it paid $2,000,000 and $3,000,000, respectively, several years ago. Accumulated depreciation on the two assets as of 12/31/07 was $500,000 and $700,000, respectively. The land on which the buildings sit is leased from the state of Hawaii for 100 years at a nominal amount per year.

The company has one checking account with the Bank of Hawaii, which had a balance of $15,000 as of 12/31/07. The Hawaii withholding, unemployment, and disability identification number is 84325184. The unemployment rate is 2.4%, and disability rate is 0.01%. Federal taxes are paid to the U.S. Treasury (Use Vendor ID UST and default account 23400) and state taxes are paid to the State of Hawaii Department of Taxation (Use Vendor ID HI DOT). All employees are paid monthly. Use the default accounts provided by Peachtree for in-house payroll setup. The company does not offer a 401(k) plan and does not track vacation. The company will manually calculate payroll taxes rather than have Peachtree calculate them. You will need to set up one additional employer payroll tax field: HI_E& T_ER. Both this and the SUI_ER payroll tax fields accrue to payroll tax expenses (a/c 72000) and to State Payroll Taxes Payable (a/c 23600). On the employee side, be sure to change the G/L account for state withholding and SDI to State Payroll Taxes Payable (a/c 23600).

Use the information provided above to create a new Peachtree file for Aloha. (*Hint:* Read the entire case before you begin, establish the new company files accepting the default name provided, and modify preferences like you did in the main chapter. Enter all beginning asset, liability, and equity account balances as of 12/31/07. Your trial balance at 12/31/07 should look like this:

Account ID	Account Description	Debit Amt	Credit Amt
10200	Regular Checking Account	15,000.00	
11000	Accounts Receivable	101,000.00	
15500	Building	5,000,000.00	
17500	Accum. Depreciation – Building		1,200,000.00
20000	Accounts Payable		6,300.00
27000	Notes Payable-Noncurrent		3,875,000.00
39003	Common Stock		10,000.00
39005	Retained Earnings		24,700.00
	Total:	**5,116,000.00**	**5,116,000.00**

This is a continuous case in that the next chapter will use the work you've accomplished here as the basis for recording additional business events. After you've printed the following reports, create a backup of this file and store it on some type of external medium (flash drive, Internet site, CD, disk, etc.). The backup file should be named **Aloha Property Management Ch 6** for easy identification later. You'll be restoring this file in the next chapter.

    a. Customer Ledgers

    b. Vendor Ledgers

    c. Employee List

    d. Item List

    e. General Ledger Trial Balance

Chapter 6 Case Problem 2
OCEAN VIEW FLOWERS

merchandising

Ocean View Flowers, a wholesale flower distributor, is located at 100 Ocean Ave., Lompoc, CA 93436. Since the company sells to retailers, it does not collect sales tax. Use the Distributor Company chart of accounts, under accrual accounting, with real time posting and with a 12-month accounting period. Ocean View started business January 1, 2008, and the owners would like you to use Peachtree to keep track of their business transactions. Ocean View is a calendar year company (for both fiscal and tax purposes) and will need to use the inventory and manual payroll features of Peachtree. In addition, the company filed for federal (91–3492370) and state (23–432) employer ID numbers. All employees are single and paid semimonthly but do not earn sick or vacation pay. Hourly employees payroll is charged to general ledger account 77500, while salaried employees payroll is charged to general ledger account 77000. All state payroll taxes are paid to the Employment Development Department and are accrued to a state payroll tax payable account, while all federal payroll taxes are paid to the U.S. Treasury and are accrued to a federal payroll tax payable account. All payroll tax amounts will be hand calculated without the use of Peachtree's built-in tables. Default credit terms for customers should be net 30 and a credit limit of $12,000. Default credit terms for vendors should be net 30 and a credit limit of $20,000 and a default expense account = inventory. The company has elected to track inventory cost using the average method. The company's expected customers and vendors are shown below.

Customer ID	Name	Address	Contact
VF	Valley Florists	101 Main St., Los Angeles, CA 90113	Sam Davies
FTD	FTD	2033 Lakewood Dr., Chicago, IL 60601	Beverly Rose
CB	California Beauties	239 Hyde Street, San Francisco, CA 95114	Farrah Faucet
ES	Eastern Scents	938 42nd Street, New York, NY 10054	Nick Giovanni
LL	Latin Ladies	209 Zona Rosa, Mexico City, DF 06600 Mexico	Juan Valdez

Vendor ID	Name	Address	Contact
HF	Hawaiian Farms	2893 1st Street, Honolulu, HI 05412	Mahalo Baise
BB	Brophy Bros. Farms	90 East Hwy 246, Santa Barbara, CA 93101	Tim Beach
PF	Princess Flowers	92 West Way, Medford, OR 39282	Bonnie Sobieski
KP	Keenan's Pride	10 East Betteravia, Santa Maria, CA 93454	Kelly Keenan
VF	Vordale Farms	62383 Lido Isle, Newport, CA 90247	Donna Vordale

Ocean View Flowers employees were hired on 1/4/08 and are subject to federal and state taxes and withholdings, state unemployment, state disability, and state employee training taxes. This last tax needs to be set up in employee defaults as Train_ER. All other tax fields are a part of Peachtree's default setup. A list of employees is shown below. Be sure to set up each employee's GL account properly (i.e., account 77500 for hourly employees and 77000 for salaried employees).

Employee ID	Name	Address	SS#	Compensation
MC	Margie Conner	2322 Courtney, Buellton, CA 93246	654-85-1254	$12/hour
KG	Kelly Gusland	203 B St., Lompoc, CA 93436	567-78-1334	$15/hour
SC	Stan Comstock	383 Lemon St., Lompoc, CA 93436	126-85-7843	$2,083.34/period
MM	Marie McAninch	1299 College Ave., Santa Maria, CA 93454	668-41-9578	$2,500/period
ET	Edward Thomas	1234 St. Andrews Way, Lompoc, CA 93436	556-98-4125	$2,916.67/period

Assignment

This is a continuous case in that the next chapter will use the work you've accomplished here as the basis for recording additional business events. After you've printed the following reports, create a backup of this file and store it on some type of external medium (flash drive, Internet site, CD, disk, etc.). The backup file should be named **Ocean View Flowers Ch 6** for easy identification later. You'll be restoring this file in the next chapter.

    a. Customer List

    b. Vendor List

    c. Employee List

Cash-Oriented Business Activities

7

Learning Objectives

In this chapter, you will:

- Record cash-oriented business transactions classified as financing activities, such as owner contributions.
- Record cash-oriented business transactions classified as investing activities, such as equipment purchases.
- Record cash-oriented business transactions classified as operating activities, such as sales orders, inventory purchases, sales invoicing, expense disbursements, and payroll.
- Evaluate a firm's performance and financial position.

Case: **Wild Water Sports, Inc.**

You and Karen completed the initial setup of the Peachtree program at the beginning of January and are ready to begin recording business transactions for the month. The new company has completed its first month of business, and Ernesto is pleased with the new business relationship he established with Karen and Donna. However, no one knows the extent of their profitability or financial position since none of the accounting events have yet been recorded into Peachtree. You had to start the spring semester, and Karen has been busy just keeping the business going.

"I'm brand new to Peachtree," you explain. "I know a little about financial accounting and I'm taking a managerial class right now, but I haven't had a course in Peachtree or any other computerized accounting program for that matter."

"No problem," Karen says, trying to reassure you. "Peachtree is very easy for first-time users to learn, and you'll be pleased with how much it will help the company understand its performance and financial position."

The two of you agree to meet today to review the business transactions which took place in January. Karen agrees to explain the nature of each transaction and how it should be recorded in Peachtree. She suggests that the best way to accomplish this is to view each transaction by the three fundamental business activities: financing, investing, and operating.

"I remember studying those concepts in my first accounting course," you comment. "If I remember correctly, financing activities are initiated when money or other resources are obtained from short-term nontrade creditors, long-term creditors, and/or owners. Financing activities are completed when amounts owed are repaid to or otherwise settled with these same creditors and/or owners. Investing activities are initiated when the money obtained from financing activities is applied to nonoperating uses, such as buying investment securities and/or productive assets like equipment, buildings, land, or furniture and fixtures. Investing activities are completed when the investment securities and/or productive assets are sold. Finally, operating activities occur when the money obtained from financing activities and the productive assets obtained from investing activities are applied to either purchase or produce goods and services for sale. These operating activities are substantially completed when goods are delivered or when services are performed."

"Wow, they taught you well!" Karen exclaims. "Let's begin with a few cash-oriented financing activities."

Recording Cash-Oriented Financing Activities

You begin with two financing activities. The first occurred on January 3 when the company received $200,000 from Karen and Donna ($100,000 each) as their purchase of stock in the company. The second deposit was made on January 4 when the company borrowed $250,000 from their bank (Bank of Florida) at 5% payable in five years. Karen reminds you to make sure the system date is set to 1/1/07 and the Period is set to Period 1.

To record the cash received from the sale of stock and borrowing:

1   Start the Peachtree program.

2   Restore the Wild Water Sports, Inc 7 file from your Data Files CD or download from the Internet. See "Data Files CD" in Chapter 1 if you need more information.

3   Set the system date to **1/1/07** and the accounting period to **Period 1**.

4   Open the **Company** center from the Navigation bar and then click **General Journal Entry**.

5   Enter the information for Karen and Donna's stock purchase as shown in Figure 7.1. Be sure to enter the correct date.

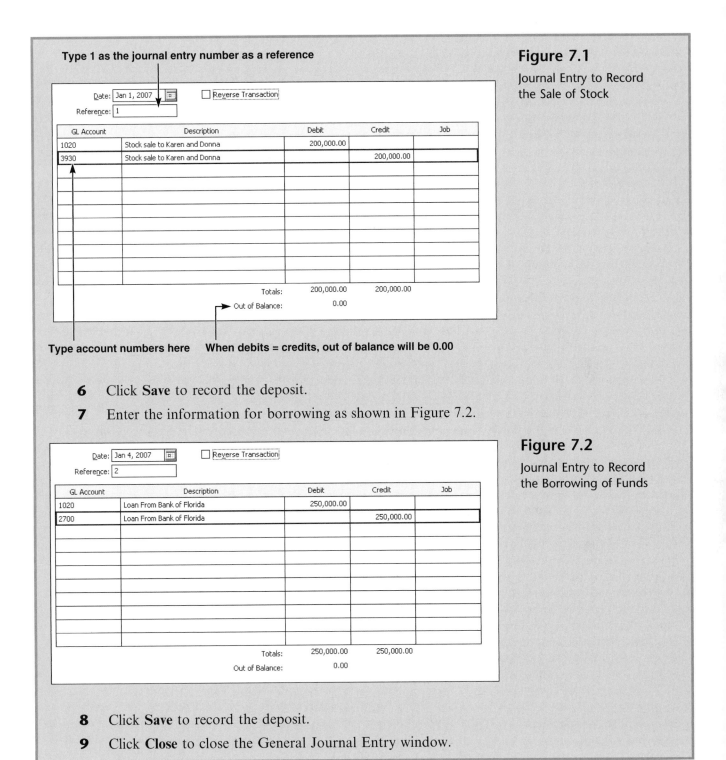

Figure 7.1

Journal Entry to Record
the Sale of Stock

Type 1 as the journal entry number as a reference

Type account numbers here   When debits = credits, out of balance will be 0.00

6   Click **Save** to record the deposit.

7   Enter the information for borrowing as shown in Figure 7.2.

Figure 7.2

Journal Entry to Record
the Borrowing of Funds

8   Click **Save** to record the deposit.

9   Click **Close** to close the General Journal Entry window.

"Do we always record transactions with journal entries like I did in college?" you ask.

"Actually, no," Karen answers, "usually we use source documents like receipts but those transactions affect revenues or accounts receivable. Peachtree's receipts process is reserved for prepayments, cash sales of products or services, or payments on account. We'll get to those types of transactions shortly."

You have now recorded two different cash-oriented financing activities: the sale of stock to investors and the borrowing of funds on a long-term basis. Now it's time to look at recording cash-oriented investing activities.

Recording Cash-Oriented Investing Activities

After recording the cash received from investors and creditors, the company decided to temporarily invest those funds into a money-market account with its bank. By transferring those funds from its checking to a money market account, the company expected to generate some interest revenue until the funds were needed. To accomplish this transfer, Karen wrote check number 1001 on January 8 from the company's checking account with Bank of Florida and deposited the check into the new money market account with ETrade.

"Do we have a general ledger account for this?" you ask.

"No, but we can create one while we record this transaction," Karen answers.

To create a new general ledger account, add a new vendor, and record the purchase of money market funds:

1 Open the **Banking** center from the Navigation bar.

2 Click the **Write Checks** button and then select **New Check** from the pop-up menu.

3 Select **Checking Account** from the drop-down list of accounts and then click **OK**.

4 Click the magnifying glass icon in the **Vendor ID** text box and then click **New** to go to the **Maintain Vendors** window.

5 Type **11100** in the Vendor ID text box and then press [**Tab**].

6 Type **ETrade** in the Name text box.

7 Click the **Purchase Default** tab.

8 Click the magnifying glass icon in the **Expense Account** text box and then click **New**.

9 Type **1030** in the Account ID text box and then press [**Tab**].

10 Type **Short-Term Investments** in the Description text box.

11 Select **Cash** as the Account Type. Your Maintain Chart of Accounts window should look like Figure 7.3.

Figure 7.3

Creating a New Account

Click Save to save your new account

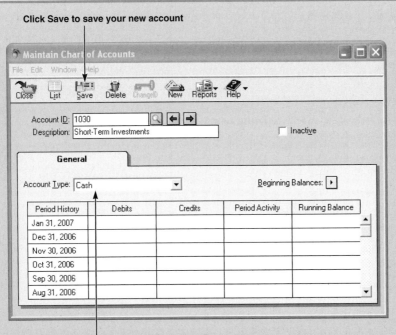

Be sure to select the proper account type when creating a new account. The default account type is Cash and students often forget to change this when creating new accounts!

12 Click **Save** and then click **Close**.

13 Type **1030** in the Expense Account text box. Your Maintain Vendors window should look like Figure 7.4.

Figure 7.4

Creating a New Vendor

Click Save to save this new vendor

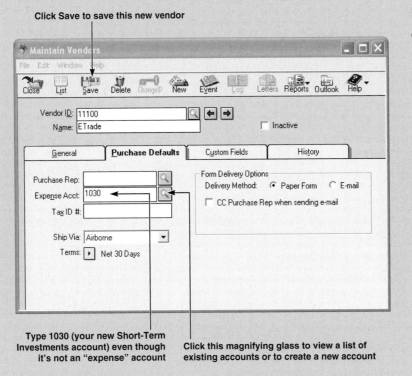

Type 1030 (your new Short-Term Investments account) even though it's not an "expense" account

Click this magnifying glass to view a list of existing accounts or to create a new account

14 Click **Save** and then click **Close**.

15 Type **11100** in the Vendor ID box.

16 Type **1001** as the check number.

17 Type **01/08/07** as the date.

18 Type **300000** as the check amount.

19 Be sure that **1020** is selected as the Cash Account.

20 Type **1030** (it actually should already be there) in the Expense Account text box.

> **Trouble?** The Expenses Account title is somewhat misleading because you can type or select any account to appear here, including assets.

21 Your Write Checks window should look like Figure 7.5.

Figure 7.5

Creating a New Check

Click this magnifying glass to view a list of existing vendors or to create a new vendor

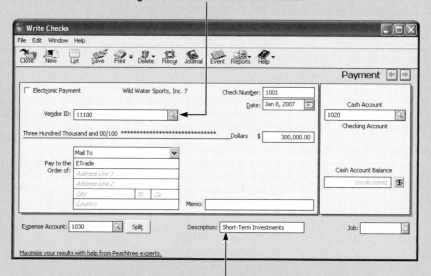

Once you type an account in the Expense Acct text box, that account's description appears here

22 Click **Save** to record this transaction. Do not close this window.

Wild Water also had other cash-oriented investment activity in January. On January 10, it purchased new office furniture for the sales, marketing, and service staff from the local Staples store and new equipment for the service bays from AJ Marine Equipment.

"How should we classify the purchase of furniture and fixtures since the only fixed asset account we have is Property and Equipment?" you ask.

"Since we won't have much invested in fixed assets, we'll just lump everything together into the existing account," Karen responds. "Peachtree now has a tracking system we could use to monitor the location of our various fixed assets, but since we won't have that many individual assets, we won't worry about tracking them at this point."

To record the purchase of furniture and equipment:

1   Type **1002** as the check number (if it is not already there).

Trouble? If you previously closed the Write Checks window, open it again by clicking the **Write Checks** icon from the Banking center.

2   Type **01/10/07** as the date of purchase in the Write Checks window.

3   Click the magnifying glass icon in the **Vendor ID** text box and then click **New**.

4   Type **11200** in the Vendor ID text box and then press [**Tab**].

5   Type **Staples** in the Name text box.

6   Click the **Purchase Default** tab.

7   Type **1500** in the Expense Account text box.

8   Click **Save** and then click **Close**.

9   Type **11200** into the Vendor ID text box.

10   Type **70000** as the check amount. Your new check should look like Figure 7.6.

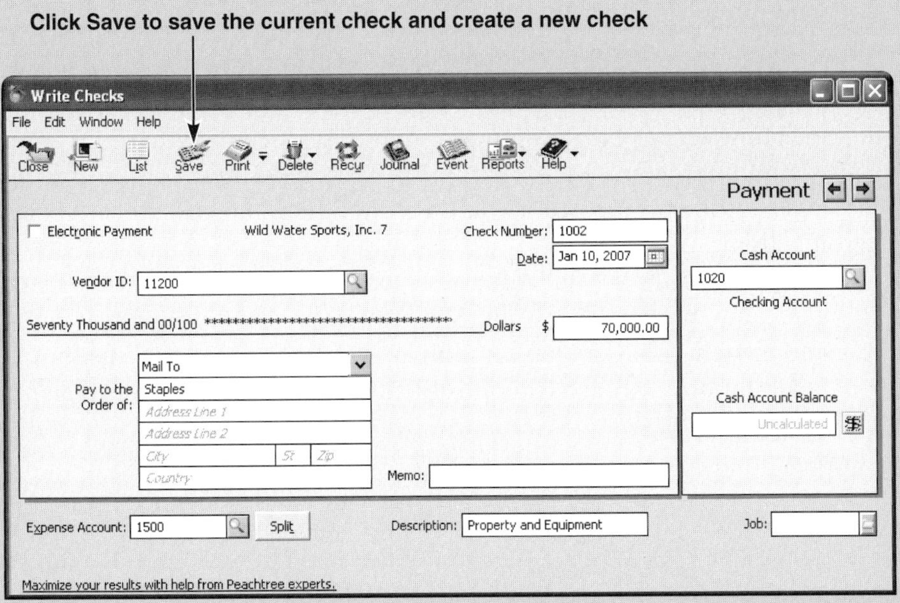

Click Save to save the current check and create a new check

Figure 7.6

Check to Purchase New Furniture

11   Click **Save** and then click **New** to enter another purchase.

12 Type **1003** as the check number (again it should already be there).

13 Type **01/10/07** as the date of purchase in the Write Checks window.

14 Click the magnifying glass icon in the **Vendor ID** text box and then click **New**.

15 Type **11300** in the Vendor ID text box and then press [**Tab**].

16 Type **AJ Marine Equipment** in the Name text box.

17 Click the **Purchase Default** tab.

18 Type **1500** in the Expense Account text box.

19 Click **Save** and then click **Close**.

20 Type **11300** in the Vendor ID text box.

21 Type **100000** as the check amount.

22 Click **Save** and then click **Close**.

"When is depreciation recorded on fixed assets?" you ask.

"Not until the end of the accounting period, before we create financial statements," Karen responds. "But we have lots to do before that."

Recording Cash-Oriented Operating Activities

"There are many cash-oriented operating activities," Karen comments. "These kinds of activities include receiving and recording orders from customers, invoicing those orders when products or services are delivered, and collecting cash from customers. They also include ordering products from vendors, receiving those products and recording bills, paying for those bills or other expenses as they become due, and of course recording payroll activities."

Karen explains that Wild Water uses both sales and purchase orders to help manage its business activities. She remarks that, typically, neither sales orders nor purchase orders have an impact on financial statements, but they do play an important role as a control feature in Peachtree. So she plans on using them.

"For example," she says, "in January, we had two customers order boats. One was a special order, and one was for a boat we didn't have in stock. We sold Florida Sports Camp a customized item 206 Malibu WakeSetter XTI for $70,000 plus tax. They gave us their address as 78 Hwy 150, Orlando, FL 31310. We also sold Performance Rentals (a new customer whose address is 15 Hwy 22, Orlando, FL 32807), a Tige 22v (a new item with Item ID = 301 and cost of $63,000) for $78,750 plus tax. Both of these boats were sold on a cash-only basis so both customers' credit terms need to reflect that fact. We recorded sales orders 101 and 102 for those sales, respectively." Karen reminds you that sales orders are internal documents and do not constitute as sales for accounting purposes. Karen decides first to show you the sales orders recorded when the customers placed their order, then she'll show you how the two deposits on sales were accounted for, and then she'll show you the purchase orders generated to order boats from the vendors.

To update a customer's information, create a new customer, and create a sales order:

1 Open the **Customers & Sales** center from the Navigation bar.

2 Click **Customers** and then select **View and Edit Customers**.

3 Double-click Customer ID **50005**.

4 Update this existing customer's record by typing the address **78 Hwy 150, Orlando, FL 31310**.

5 Click the **Terms and Credit** tab.

6 Uncheck the **Use Standard Terms and Credit** check box and change the terms and credit information as shown in Figure 7.7.

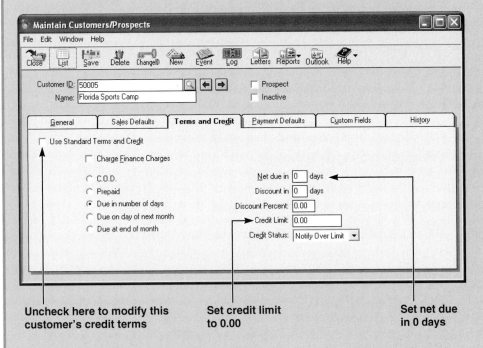

Figure 7.7

Updating Terms and Credit

Uncheck here to modify this customer's credit terms

Set credit limit to 0.00

Set net due in 0 days

7 Click **Save** and then click **Close**.

8 Click **New** to add a new customer.

9 Type **50006** in the Customer ID text box and then press [**Tab**].

10 Type **Performance Rentals** in the Name text box.

11 Type **15 Hwy 22, Orlando, FL 32807** as the customers' address. Your new customer window should look like Figure 7.8.

Figure 7.8

Add a New Customer

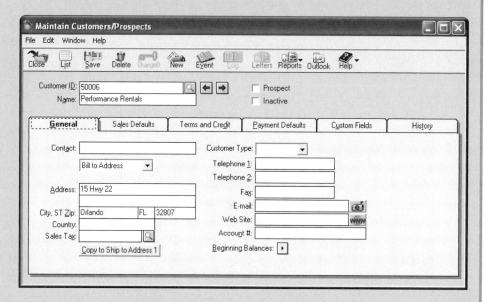

12 Click the **Terms and Credit** tab.

13 Uncheck the **Use Standard Terms and Credit** check box and change the terms and credit information as you did for Florida Sports Camp above.

14 Click **Save** and then click **Close** to add this new customer.

15 Close the Customer List.

16 Click **Sales Orders** and then select **New Sales Order**.

17 Select Customer ID **50005**.

18 Type **1/10/07** as the Date.

19 Type **1/30/07** as the Ship By date.

20 Type **101** as the SO No. (Sales Order Number)

21 Select **Cust. Pickup** in the Ship Via text box.

22 Type **1** in the Quantity text box.

23 Type **206** in the Item text box.

24 Select **01** in the Sales Tax Code text box. Your new sales order should look like Figure 7.9.

Type Item ID here

Type sales order number in this text box

Figure 7.9

Sales Order 101

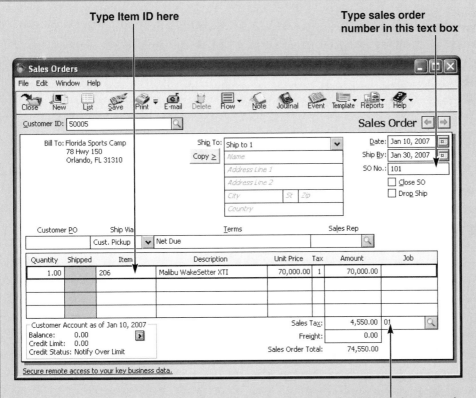

Be sure to set sales tax code to 01 as shown here

25 Click **Save**. This sales order is saved, and a new blank sales order is revealed.

26 Select Customer ID **50006**.

27 Type **1/11/07** as the Date.

28 Type **1/30/07** as the Ship By date.

29 Type **102** as the SO No. (Sales Order Number)

30 Select **Cust. Pickup** in the Ship Via text box.

31 Type **1** in the Quantity text box.

32 Click the magnifying glass icon in the **Item** text box and then click **New**.

33 Type **301** as the Item ID.

34 Type **Tige 22v** as the Description.

35 Select **Stock item** as the Item Class.

36 Type **Tige 22v** as the General Description. (Note that the text appears red indicating a misspelled word.)

37 Press the **F7** key or select **Check spelling** from the Edit menu and then select **Add** to add this word to the global dictionary.

38 Press the **F7** key again or select **Check spelling** from the Edit menu and then select **Add** to add this word to the global dictionary as well.

Trouble? Adding these words to the global dictionary works fine if you're using Peachtree at home or at work since that dictionary will be available for you all the time. However, if you are working in a lab environment on different computers or those computers are reset nightly to their original settings, chances are the next time you access this or other documents where these words appear they will once again be red. This is because the dictionary is global to Peachtree, not to your individual file. Thus, you can either ignore the misspelling or re-add the word to the dictionary.

39 Type **78750** as Price Level 1.

40 Type **63000** as the Last Unit Cost.

41 Select **Average** as the Cost Method.

42 Leave **4000** as the GL Sales Acct.

43 Leave **1200** as the GL Inventory Acct.

44 Leave **5000** as the GL Cost of Sales Acct.

45 Leave **1** as the Item Tax Type.

46 Select **10200** as the Preferred Vendor ID. Your Maintain Inventory Items window should look like Figure 7.10.

Figure 7.10

Adding a New Inventory Item

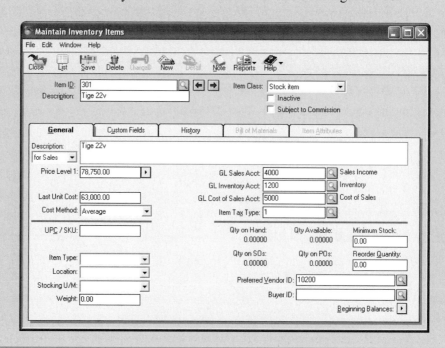

47 Click **Save** and then click **Close**.

48 Type **301** in the item box again if it doesn't automatically appear.

49 Select **01** in the Sales Tax Code text box.

50 Click **Save** and then click **Close**.

In both transactions, the customer was required to pay a 25% deposit upon order ($17,500.00 and $19,687.50, respectively).

"How do you account for the amounts received?" you ask.

"We treat them just like payments received from customers, but since there is no invoice to allocate them to, we just leave them as credit balances in customers' accounts," Karen answers. "Accounting would normally require you to treat this as unearned revenue and record them as liabilities; however, we only make adjustments for credit balances in accounts if, prior to preparing financial statements, we still have remaining credits in customer accounts."

Remember, in both cases, customers remitted cash to Wild Water, but a sale could not be recorded because the products had not been delivered and thus the earnings process was not complete.

To record the receipt of deposits on future sales:

1 Open the **Customers & Sales** center from the Navigation bar.

2 Click **Receive Money** and then select **Receive Money from Customer**.

3 Select **Checking Account** and then click **OK**.

4 Click on the magnifying glass icon across from the **Customer ID** box. From the drop-down menu, select **50005 Florida Sports Camp** as the customer from which the first cash payment was received.

5 Type **8755** in the Reference text box as the customer's check number.

6 Type **SR0001** in the Receipt Number text box.

7 Type the date **1/11/07**.

8 Select **Check** as the payment method.

9 Check the **Prepayment** check box (above the **Job** column near the bottom of the screen) since this is not a cash sale or payment on account.

10 Type **Deposit on boat order** in the Description text box.

11 Type **17500** in the Amount text box. Your Receipts window should look like Figure 7.11.

Figure 7.11

Receipt of Deposit from Florida Sports Camp

Leave this box blank as we'll deposit this amount later

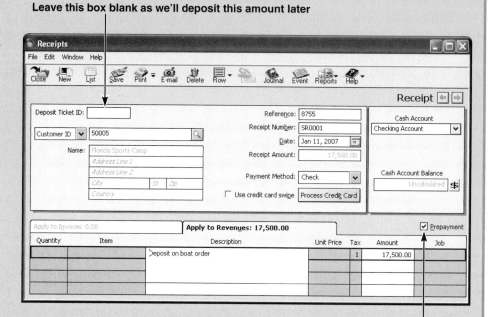

Place a check here to indicate this is a customer prepayment

12 Click **Save** to record the receipt and get ready for another. Click the magnifying glass icon in the **Customer ID** text box.

13 Select **50006 Performance Rentals** as the customer from which the second deposit was received.

14 Type **987452** in the Reference text box as the credit card receipt number.

15 Type **SR0002** in the Receipt Number text box.

16 Type the date as **1/11/07**.

17 Select **MasterCard** as the payment method.

18 Check the **Prepayment** check box since this is not a cash sale or payment on account.

19 Type **Deposit on boat order** in the Description text box.

20 Type **19687.50** in the Amount text box.

21 Click **Save** and then click **Close**.

"We then had to order those boats from the manufacturers using purchase orders 4001 and 4002. Let me show you how purchase orders are used in Peachtree."

"Are all purchase orders related to customers?" you ask.

"Not necessarily," Karen responds. "Sometimes we order for inventory to have in our showroom, but in these two we were ordering boats for specific customers."

To create a purchase order:

1 Open the **Vendors & Purchases** center from the Navigation bar.

2 Click **Purchase Orders** and select **New Purchase Order**.

3 Select **10000** from the Vendor ID drop-down list.

4 Type **1/11/07** as the date.

5 Type **4001** as the purchase order number.

6 Type **1** as the quantity.

7 Type **206** as the item (Malibu WakeSetter XTI).

8 Select **Best Way** in the Ship Via text box. Your purchase order should now look like Figure 7.12.

Click here to save this purchase order

Figure 7.12

Purchase Order 4001

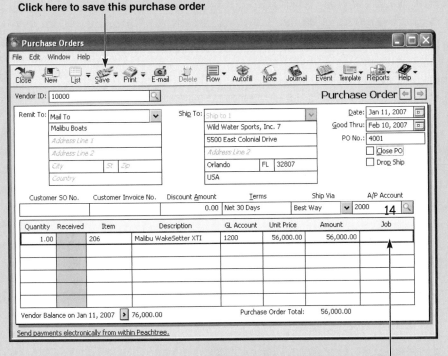

Even though this purchase order is related to a specific customer order, Peachtree will not allow stock items to be assigned to jobs

9 Click **Save** to save this purchase order and open a new one.

10 Select **10200 Tige Boats** from the Vendor ID drop-down list.

11 Type **1/11/07** as the date (if it's not already there).

12 Type **4002** as the purchase order number.

13 Type **1** as the quantity.

14 Type **301** as the item.

15 Select **Best Way** in the Ship Via text box. Your purchase order should look like Figure 7.13.

Figure 7.13

Purchase Order 4002

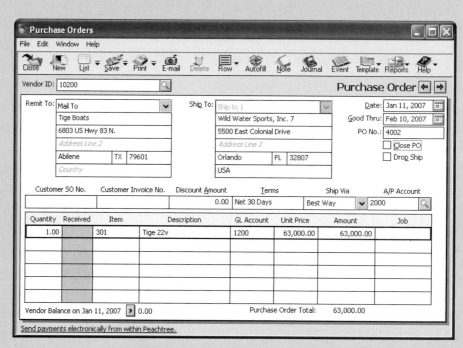

16 Click **Save** and then click **Close** to add this new purchase order.

Karen has shown you how to create purchase orders and now would like to show you how the customers' deposits should be accounted for.

"Typically we collect cash from sales on account, such as sales made to customers where we gave them credit terms like net 30," Karen comments. "If you recall when we set up our accounting system on January 1, 2007, we had some customers who owed us money from previous sales. The balances owed were reflected in accounts receivable."

"Do you record those cash collections like we just recorded the previous cash receipts?" you ask.

"Yes, plus we had some cash sales during January which I'll show you as well," Karen answers. "We had one cash boat sale and one cash boat service during the month, both from new customers."

To record cash collected on account:

1   Click **Receive Money** from the Customers & Sales center and then select **Receive Money from Customer**.

2   Select **50002 Buena Vista Water Sports** from the Customer ID drop-down list.

3   Type **65454** in the Reference text box as the customer's check number.

4   Type **SR0003** in the Receipts text box.

5   Type **1/15/07** as the date received.

6   Select **Check** as the payment method.

7   Place a check in the **Pay** check box next to the 30,000.00 amount due shown in the Apply to Invoices tab. Your screen should look like Figure 7.14.

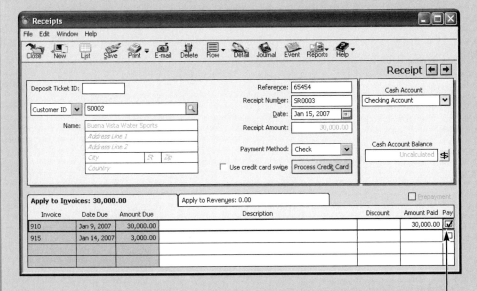

Figure 7.14

Receipt of Cash on Account

Place a check in this box to indicate what this customer is paying for

8   Click **Save** but don't close this window.

To record cash sales to a new customer:

1 Click the magnifying glass icon in the **Customer ID** text box and then click **New**.

2 Type **50007** in the Customer ID text box and then press [**Tab**].

3 Type **Seth Backman** in the Name text box.

4 Type **140 Fir Ave., Miami, FL 33109** as the customers' address.

5 Click **Save** and then click **Close**.

6 Select **50007** from the Customer ID text box.

7 Type **161** in the Reference text box as the customer's check number.

8 Type **SR0004** as the Receipt Number.

9 Type **1/16/07** as the date of sale.

10 Select **Check** as the Payment Method.

11 Type **1** as the Quantity sold.

12 Select **202 Malibu Sportster LX** from the drop-down list of items.

13 Type **01** as the Sales Tax Code. Your screen should look like Figure 7.15.

Figure 7.15

Recording a Cash Sale

Type 202 as the item sold for cash

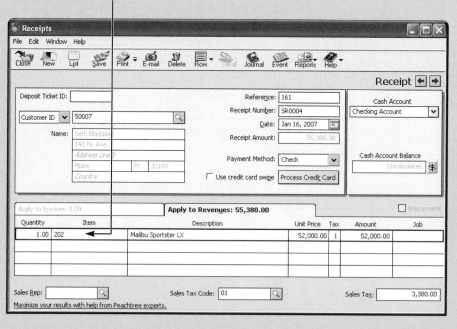

14 Click **Save** and then click **Close**.

"Have all of these cash receipt transactions been recorded in our checking account?" you ask.

"Peachtree treats all cash receipts (payments on account, advance payments, etc.) as undeposited amounts unless we place a deposit ticket number in the receipts window. This is because bank deposits are often made at a different time than cash is actually received," Karen answers. "We've made those deposits now, so let me show you how we record them in Peachtree."

To record cash deposits made to banks:

1 Click the **Bank Deposits** in the Customers & Sales center and then click **New Bank Deposit**.

2 Click in the **Deposit** check box on the rows with the two 1/11/07 receipts.

3 Type **1/12/07** as the date of deposit.

4 Type **1** in the Deposit Ticket ID text box.

5 Be sure **1020** is the Account ID to which you are depositing these funds. Your window should look like Figure 7.16.

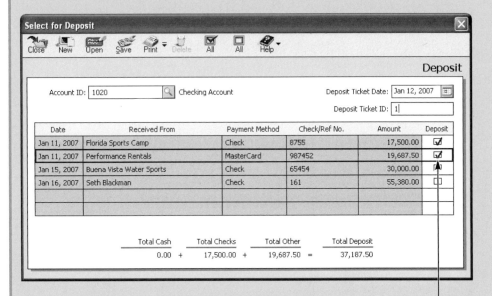

Figure 7.16

Selecting Receipts for Deposit

Place checks in these boxes to indicate which receipts are to be deposited

6 Click **Save**.

7 Click in the **Deposit** check box on the rows with the 1/15/07 and 1/16/07 receipts.

8 Type **1/16/07** as the date of deposit.

9 Type **2** in the Deposit Ticket ID text box.

10 Click **Save** and then click **Close**.

You have now accounted for the payments received from customers and the bank deposits which reflect amounts deposited to the checking account. Karen explains that the next item on your list is to record the inventory received from Purchase Order 1001 and the related payment to the vendor.

"When inventory received is related to a purchase order, it's important to do more than just record the check that paid for the inventory," Karen points out. "We also have to close out the purchase order and properly record the receipt of inventory. In this case, we received the two boats ordered under Purchase Orders 4001 and 4002. Both of these were cash-only purchases in that the vendor did not extend us credit and thus payment was due on receipt. Therefore, we have to receive inventory first creating an asset (inventory) and a liability (accounts payable). Then we'll have to write a check to pay the liability."

To record the receipt of inventory:

1 Open the Inventory & Services center.

2 Click **Receive Inventory** and then select **Receive Inventory** from the pop-up menu.

3 Select **10000** from the Vendor ID drop-down list.

4 Type **1/29/07** as the date.

5 Type **MB20397** as Malibu's Invoice No.

6 Select **4001** from the Apply to Purchase Order No. drop-down list.

7 Type **1** in the Received text box. Your window should look like Figure 7.17.

Figure 7.17

Recording the Receipt of Inventory and Bill

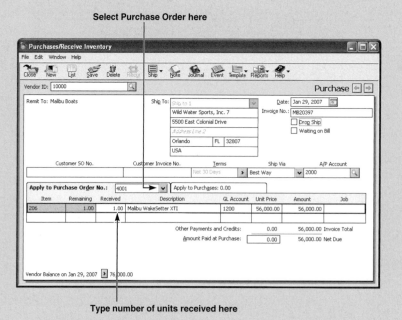

Select Purchase Order here

Type number of units received here

8 Click **Save** to record receipt of this inventory.

9 Select **10200** from the Vendor ID drop-down list.

10 Type **1/30/07** as the date.

11 Type **T2309443** as Tige's Invoice No.

12 Select **4002** from the Apply to Purchase Order No. drop-down list.

13 Type **1** in the Received text box. Your window should look like Figure 7.18.

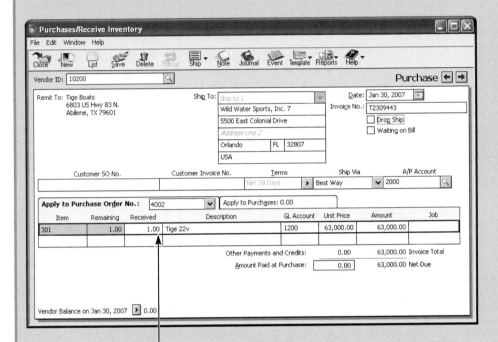

Figure 7.18

Recording the Receipt of Additional Inventory and Bill

Type number of units received here

14 Click **Save** to record receipt of this inventory and then click **Close**.

To record the payment of inventory:

1 Open the **Vendors & Purchases** center, click **Pay Bills**, and then select **Pay Bill**.

2 Select **10000** as the Vendor ID.

3 Type **1004** as the check number if it is not already present.

4 Type **1/29/07** as the check date.

5 Click in the **Pay** check box on the row containing the 56,000.00 amount. *Note:* The date due indicates that this invoice isn't due until 2/28 and that an earlier invoice was actually due 1/14. Malibu shipped the company this product on a pay on receipt basis even though the Peachtree system showed Wild Water Sports as having 30 days credit. Karen makes a note to follow up with Malibu on the credit terms. See Figure 7.19.

Figure 7.19

Payment of Malibu Bill

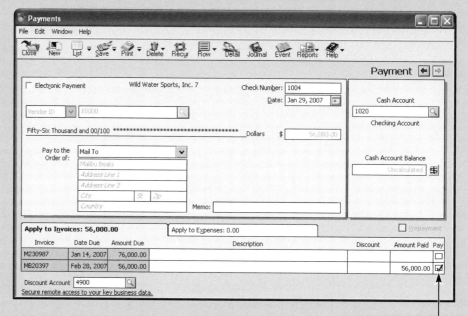

Clicking in this Pay checkbox places the 56,000.00 amount in both the Amount Paid text box and the payment amounts sections of the check

6 Click **Save**.

7 Select **10200** as the Vendor ID.

8 Type **1005** as the check number if it is not already present.

9 Type **1/30/07** as the check date.

10 Click in the **Pay** check box on the row containing the 63,000.00 amount. See Figure 7.20.

11 Click **Save** and then click **Close**.

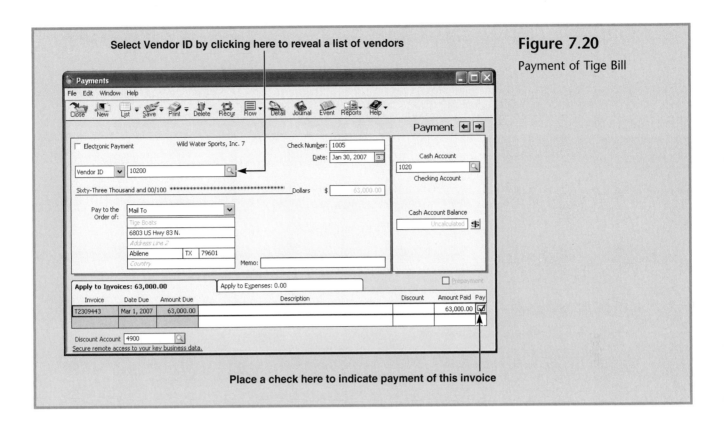

Figure 7.20

Payment of Tige Bill

Karen explains that, as a result of paying these vendors for boats received under purchase orders, cash has decreased and inventory has increased. Both customers, for whom these boats were ordered, were contacted, and they picked up their boats on January 30.

"I'll show you how we record the sales of these boats via the invoice process," Karen says. "Remember that both of these customers remitted their deposits when we placed the order, and thus we only need to collect the remaining 75% balance owed."

"How do we account for the deposits already received?" you ask.

"Recall that, when we received these deposits earlier in January, we credited each of these customer's accounts receivable balances," she answers. "Because of that, we need to use the invoicing process to record the sales first, apply the existing credits, and then record the receipt of the balance due on the sale. Florida Sports Camp remitted $57,050 as the balance due on its purchase, while Performance Rentals remitted $64,181.25."

To record sales, the application of advanced deposits received, and the receipt of payment for the balance due:

1 Open the **Customer & Sales** center, click **Sales Invoices**, and then select **New Sales Invoice**.

2 Select **50005 Florida Sports Camp** from the Customer ID drop-down list.

3 Type **1/30/07** as the invoice date and **10001** as the Invoice No.

4 Select **101** in the Apply to Sales Order No. text box. (This links this invoice with the previously recorded sales order for this customer.)

5 Type **1** in the Shipped text box.

6 Click the button next to the words **Amount Paid at Sale**.

7 Type **4532** in the Reference text box (this is Florida Sports Camp's check number).

8 Type **57050** in the Receipt Amount text box.

9 Select **Check** as the Payment Method. Your Receive Payment window should look like Figure 7.21.

Figure 7.21

Time of Sale Receipt

Leave this blank as you'll deposit this to the bank later

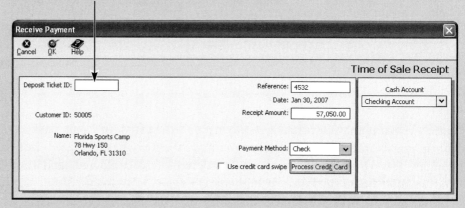

10 Click **OK**.

11 Click **Save** to save this invoice and then click the Invoice left arrow button (in the upper right corner of the invoice screen) to return to the partially paid invoice as shown in Figure 7.22.

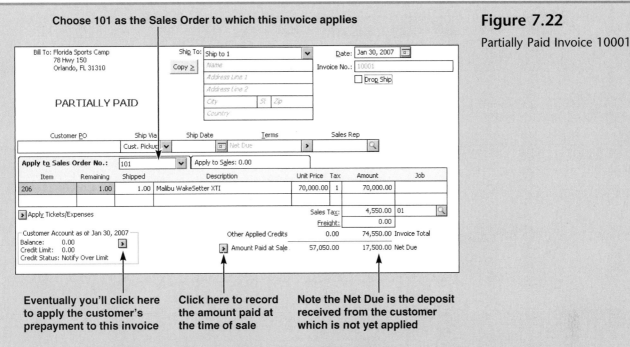

Figure 7.22

Partially Paid Invoice 10001

12 Note that the invoice indicates a net amount due of $17,500.00 but that the balance reflected in the lower left-hand corner of the invoice indicates a balance of 0.00. Click the arrow button located next to the 0.00 amount to reveal the Customer Ledger shown in Figure 7.23.

Wild Water Sports, Inc. 7
Customer Ledgers
For the Period From Jan 1, 2007 to Jan 30, 2007
Filter Criteria includes: 1) IDs from 50005 to 50005. Report order is by ID. Report is printed in Detail Format.

Customer ID Customer	Date	Trans No	Type	Debit Amt	Credit Amt	Balance
50005	1/11/07	8755	CRJ		17,500.00	-17,500.00
Florida Sports Camp	1/30/07	10001	SJ	74,550.00		57,050.00
	1/30/07	4532	CRJ		57,050.00	0.00
Report Total				74,550.00	74,550.00	0.00

Figure 7.23

Florida Sports Camp Customer Ledger

Double-click on this row to view the original cash receipt accounted for as a prepayment

13 Double-click the row containing the **17,500.00** amount.

14 Uncheck the **Prepayment** check box.

15 Click the **Apply to Invoices** tab.

16 Check the **Pay** check box to apply this previously recorded prepayment to invoice 10001 just recorded as shown in Figure 7.24.

Figure 7.24

Applying a Prepayment

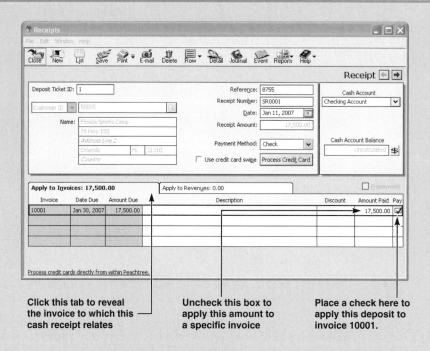

Click this tab to reveal the invoice to which this cash receipt relates

Uncheck this box to apply this amount to a specific invoice

Place a check here to apply this deposit to invoice 10001.

17 Click **Save** to save your changes and then click **Close** to close the Receipts window.

18 Click **Close** to close the Customer Ledger window, and close the Sales/Inventory window.

19 Click **Sales Invoices** from the Customers & Sales from the Navigation bar and then select **View and Edit Sales Invoices**.

20 Double-click Invoice No. **10001** to reveal the paid in full invoice with a Net Due of 0.00 as shown in Figure 7.25.

Figure 7.25

Paid in Full Invoice

This invoice is now shown as paid in full once we applied the prepayment

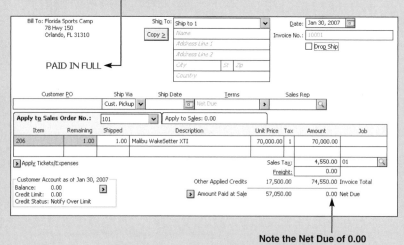

Note the Net Due of 0.00

21 Click **Close** to close invoice 10001 and click **Close** to close the Sales Invoice List.

22 Click **Sales Invoices** and then select **New Sales Invoice**.

23 Select **50006** from the Customer ID drop-down list.

24 Type **1/30/07** as the invoice date and **10002** as the Invoice No.

25 Select **102** in the Apply to Sales Order No. text box.

26 Type **1** in the Shipped text box.

27 Click the button next to the words **Amount Paid at Sale**.

28 Type **10885** in the Reference text box (this is Florida Sports Camp's check number).

29 Type **64181.25** in the Receipt Amount text box.

30 Select **Check** as the Payment Method.

31 Click **OK**.

32 Click **Save** to save this invoice and then click the Invoice left arrow button to return to the partially paid invoice.

33 Click the arrow button located next to the 0.00 amount in the lower left box.

34 Double-click the row containing the **19,687.50** amount.

35 Uncheck the **Prepayment** check box.

36 Click the **Apply to Invoices** tab.

37 Check the **Pay** check box to apply this previously recorded prepayment to invoice 10002 just recorded.

38 Click **Save** to save your changes and then click **Close** to close the Receipts window.

39 Click **Close** to close the Customer Ledger window.

40 Click **Close** to close the Sales/Invoicing window.

Karen comments that in the examples shown, the prepayment could be applied to an invoice in total. In other words, there was no left over prepayment. If, however, a prepayment was for an amount larger than the invoice to which it is being applied, the same steps shown are taken but in addition a new prepayment must be recorded for the difference. Let's take for example the Florida Sports Camp sale. If the prepayment had been $20,000.00 instead of $19,687.50 the difference ($312.50) would have recorded as another prepayment and the $19,687.50 would have been applied to the sales invoice. The result would have been a credit balance of $312.50 and the sales invoice would have been recorded as paid in full.

Now that the invoices are recorded, sales and accounts receivable have been increased, cost of goods sold has been increased, and inventory has been decreased. Wild Water has also recorded the receipt of full payment from the customers, but they haven't recorded the related deposit to their bank account.

To record the deposit of funds from boat sales:

1 Click **Bank Deposits** from the Banking center and then select **New Bank Deposit**.

2 Type **1/30/07** as the Deposit Ticket Date.

3 Type **3** as the Deposit Ticket ID.

4 Click in both check boxes under the Deposit title to record a total deposit of 121,231.25.

5 Click **Save** and then click **Close**.

"Next," Karen comments, "I'd like to show you how Wild Water will pay for monthly expenses and bills. Currently, most of our vendors want us to pay on receipt of their bills, so we've been recording expenses only when we pay the bills. In a couple of months, we will be in a position to ask for credit terms from most of our vendors. In the meantime, we write checks at the end of the month to pay for expenses."

One of the payments was for insurance for the year, which will be treated as prepaid insurance and adjusted prior to preparing financial statements. A second payment represents inventory parts received (oil, air filters, and oil filters used in servicing boats). Still another represents an amount due to Malibu Boats, which was established as a liability when the company was first set up. This payment requires the use of Peachtree's bill payment process. The balance of Wild Water's payments this month relates to expenses already incurred.

"Let's first look at how we pay for expenses and then how we pay for inventory parts received," Karen suggests.

To record checks written for expenses:

1 Click **Write Checks** in the Banking center and then select **New Check**.

2 Type **1006** as the check number if it is not already there.

3 Type **1/31/07** as the check date.

4 Click the magnifying glass in the Vendor ID text box and then click **New** to create a new vendor.

5 Type **11400** as the new Vendor ID.

6 Type **Manchester Insurance** in the Name text box.

7 Type the vendor's address as **234 Wilshire Blvd., Los Angeles, CA 91335**.

8 Click the **Purchase Defaults** tab.

9 Select **1400 Prepaid Expenses** in the Expense Account text box.

10 Click the arrow button next to Terms in the lower left-hand corner of the window.

11 Uncheck Standard Terms, type **0** in the **Net due in** text box and **0** in the **Credit limit** box, and then click **OK**.

12 Click **Save** and then click **Close**.

13 Select **11400** as the Vendor ID.

14 Type **22000** as the check amount. Your Write Checks window should look like Figure 7.26.

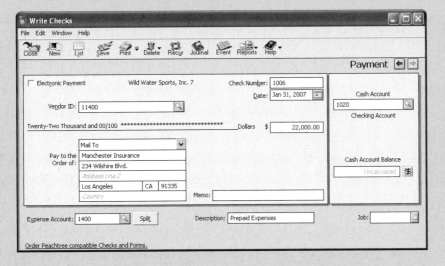

Figure 7.26

Check 1006 to Manchester Insurance

15 Click **Save**.

16 Type **1007** as the check number if it is not already there.

17 Type **1/31/07** as the check date if it is not already there.

18 Click the magnifying glass in the Vendor ID text box and then click **New** to create a new vendor.

19 Type **11600** as the new Vendor ID.

20 Type **Central Florida Gas & Electric** in the Name text box.

21 Click the **Purchase Defaults** tab.

22 Select **6400 Utilities Expenses** in the Expense Account text box.

23 Click the arrow button next to Terms in the lower left-hand corner of the window.

24 Uncheck Standard Terms, type **0** in the **Net due in** text box and 0 in the **Credit limit** box, and then click **OK**.

25 Click **Save** and then click **Close**.

26 Select **11600** as the Vendor ID.

27 Type **1/31/07** as the check date if it is not already there.

28 Type **890** as the amount.

29 Click **Save**.

30 Click the magnifying glass in the Vendor ID text box and then click **New** to create a new vendor.

31 Type **11700** as the new Vendor ID.

32 Type **Verizon** in the Name text box.

33 Click the **Purchase Defaults** tab.

34 Select **6500 Telephone Expenses** in the Expense Account text box.

35 Click the arrow button next to Terms in the lower left-hand corner of the window.

36 Uncheck Standard Terms, type **0** in the **Net due in** text box and **0** in the **Credit limit** box, and then click **OK**.

37 Click **Save** and then click **Close**.

38 Select **11700** as the Vendor ID.

39 Type **1008** as the check number if it is not already there.

40 Type **1/31/07** as the check date if it is not already there.

41 Type **1700** as the amount.

42 Click **Save** and then click **Close**.

To record inventory parts received and paid for:

1 Open the **Inventory & Services** center, click **Receive Inventory**, and then select **Receive Inventory**.

2 Click the magnifying glass in the Vendor ID text box and then click **New** to create a new vendor.

3 Type **11500** as the new Vendor ID.

4 Type **Chevron/Mobil** in the Name text box.

5 Type the vendor's address as **2389 Peachtree Blvd., Atlanta, GA 30311**.

6 Click the **Purchase Defaults** tab.

7 Select **1230 Inventory Parts** in the Expense Account text box.

8 Click the arrow button next to Terms in the lower left-hand corner of the window.

9 Uncheck Standard Terms, type **0** in the **Net due in** text box and **0** in the **Credit limit** box, and then click **OK**.

10 Click **Save** and then click **Close**.

11 Select **11500** as the Vendor ID.

12 Type **1/31/07** as the Date.

13 Type **EM239879978** as the Invoice No.

14 Type **25** as the Quantity on the first row of the Apply to Purchases tab.

15 Select **904 Air Filter** from the Item drop-down list.

16 Type **150** as the Quantity on the second row.

17 Select **901 Engine Oil** from the Item drop-down list.

18 Type **25** as the Quantity on the third row.

19 Select **902 Oil Filter** from the Item drop-down list. Your screen should look like Figure 7.27.

Trouble? If there are not enough rows on your inventory receipt, simply enlarge the Purchases/Receipts Inventory window and more rows will appear.

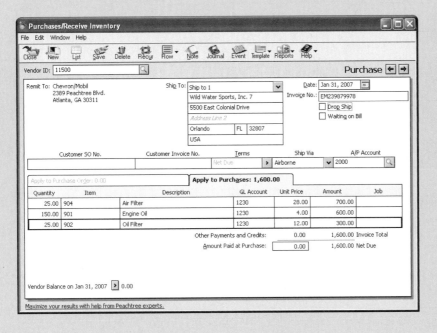

Figure 7.27

Receiving Inventory Parts

20 Click **Save** and then click **Close**.

"Let's now look at how we pay for bills already established in accounts payable," Karen suggests.

To record checks written to pay bills:

1 Click **Pay Bills** in the Vendors & Purchases center and then select **Pay Bills**.

2 Select **11500** from the Vendor ID text box.

3 Type **1009** in the Check Number text box.

4 Type **1/31/07** as the Date.

5 Click the **Apply to Invoices** tab.

6 Check the **Pay** box in the row containing invoice EM239879978.

7 Click **Save**.

8 Select **10000** from the Vendor ID text box.

9 Type **1010** in the Check Number text box.

10 Type **1/31/07** as the Date.

11 Click the Apply to Invoices tab.

12 Check the Pay box in the row containing invoice M230987 as shown in Figure 7.28.

Figure 7.28

Payment of Bills

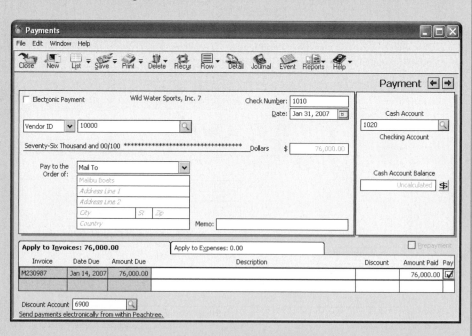

13 Click **Save** and then click **Close**.

Now it's time to calculate payroll. Karen explains that entering information about payroll is a little tricky since Wild Water has decided not to use Peachtree's payroll service. To participate at any level would have required a monthly or annual fee, and, since Wild Water Sports has so few employees, the company has decided to manually compute payroll.

"Is that why we previously set up Wild Water to calculate payroll manually?" you ask.

"Exactly," Karen answers. "That was a part of the Peachtree setup process. Now we are going to enter payroll information for the month of January."

"Wouldn't it be faster to use the payroll service?" you ask.

"Well, yes," Karen responds, "but, as you'll see, entering payroll withholding and tax information manually isn't that difficult."

"Peachtree has a nice time sheet capability which is how we'll track Ryder's and Pat's time," Karen explains. "It also has a job cost tracking feature so that, when either Ryder or Pat works on a specific boat, their time can be automatically charged to a customer and a specific job for that customer. Time sheets are typically used when a company is trying to keep track of hours worked on specific jobs. They are not required. Many companies who don't track job costs will only enter the hours for each employee right before processing the payroll. However, in this company's situation, time sheets are very helpful. Before we can enter the employees' time, we must make sure that a customer/job entry is set up. Later we'll do this during the month as each job is started, but for now we'll enter them after the fact. Two jobs were started in the last couple days of January—one for Florida Sports Camp and one for Freebirds. Let me show you how to create those jobs entries, both of which are for customers we've already created in Peachtree."

To create new jobs for existing customers:

1 Open the **Customers & Sales** center, click **Jobs,** and then select **New Job** from the pop-up menu.

2 Type **3001** in the Job ID text box.

3 Click the magnifying glass in the For Customer text box and then click **New**.

4 Type **50008** as the Customer ID and **Alisa Hay** as the Customer Name.

5 Enter this customer's address as **2999 Dover Blvd. Daytona Beach, FL 32114**.

6 Click the **Terms and Credit** tab and change this customer's terms to net due in **0** days with a **0.00** credit limit.

7 Click **Save** and then click **Close**.

8 Select **50008** from the list of customers provided in the For Customer text box. Your Maintain Jobs window should look like Figure 7.29.

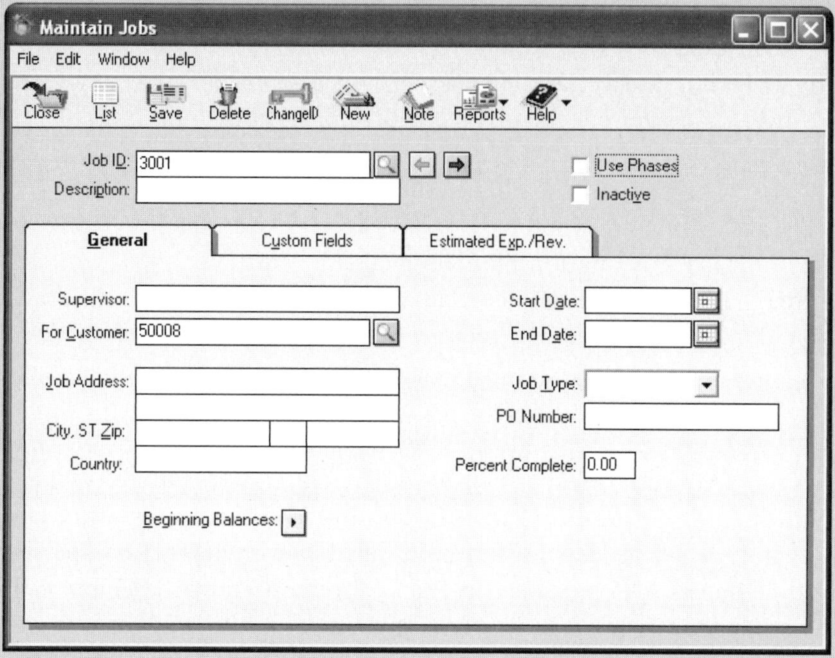

Figure 7.29

Adding a New Job

9 Click **Save** to save this new job.

10 Click **New** to add a new job.

11 Add a new Job ID **3002**, with no description for customer **50005** and **Save**; then add a new Job ID **3003** with no description for customer **50004** and **Save**.

12 Be sure to save both jobs after creating them and then close the Maintain Jobs window.

With the new jobs added, Karen explains that you can now enter the hours worked into Peachtree's time sheets which are organized by week.

To complete weekly time sheets for January:

1 Open the **Employees & Payroll** center, click **Time and Expense Tickets**, and then select **New Time Ticket**.

2 Click the **Weekly Tab**.

3 Select **003** from the drop-down list of employees by clicking the magnifying glass.

4 Type **1/1/07** in the Week Including text box.

5 Click in the Activity Item column, click the magnifying glass, and then click **New** to add a new activity. (*Note:* All time sheet entries for employees require an activity item.)

6 Create a new activity by typing **801** as the Item ID, select **Activity item** as the Item Class, and type **Office Work** in the Description text box.

7 Click **Save** and then click **Close** to close the Maintain Inventory Items window.

8 Select **801** as the Activity Item.

9 Choose **Administrative** from the Cust/Job/Administrative column as shown in Figure 7.30.

Select Administrative from this list of alternatives **Click here to view a drop-down list of employees**

Figure 7.30

Entering Time Ticket Information

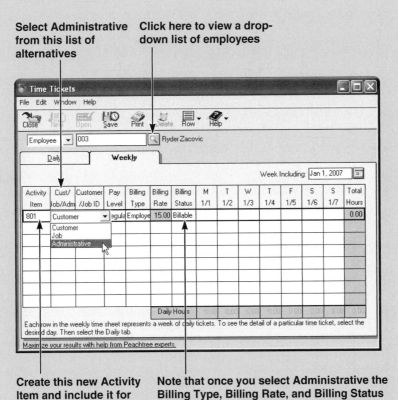

Create this new Activity Item and include it for this row's activity **Note that once you select Administrative the Billing Type, Billing Rate, and Billing Status column information for this row will change**

10 Type **6** as the hours worked on T 1/4 and then press [**Tab**] to move to the next date.

11 Type **4** as the hours worked on F 1/5 and then press [**Tab**]. The Weekly tab should look like Figure 7.31.

Figure 7.31

Entering Hours into the Time Ticket Window for Ryder Zacovic (ID 003)

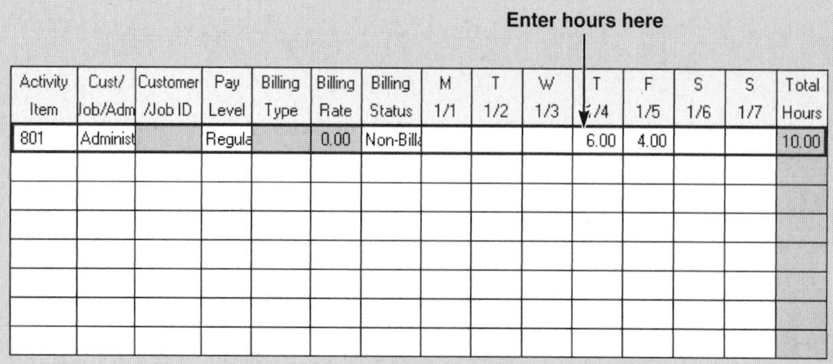

Enter hours here

Activity Item	Cust/ Job/Adm	Customer /Job ID	Pay Level	Billing Type	Billing Rate	Billing Status	M 1/1	T 1/2	W 1/3	T 1/4	F 1/5	S 1/6	S 1/7	Total Hours
801	Administ		Regula		0.00	Non-Billa				6.00	4.00			10.00

12 Click **Save** to save this weekly time sheet. (Entering time tickets on a weekly time sheet also automatically creates daily time tickets.)

13 Click **Close** to close this weekly time sheet.

14 Click **Time and Expense Tickets**, and then select **New Time Ticket**. (The Time Ticket window should open with the Weekly tab open.)

15 Select Employee ID **004**. (Be sure the Week Including text box still states Jan 1, 2007.)

16 Select **801** as the Activity Item.

17 Choose **Administrative** from the Cust/Job/Administrative column.

18 Type **4** as the hours worked on T 1/4 and then press [**Tab**] to move to the next date.

19 Type **6** as the hours worked on F 1/5 and then press [**Tab**]. The Weekly tab should look like Figure 7.32.

Figure 7.32

Entering Hours into the Time Ticket Window for Pat Ng (ID 004)

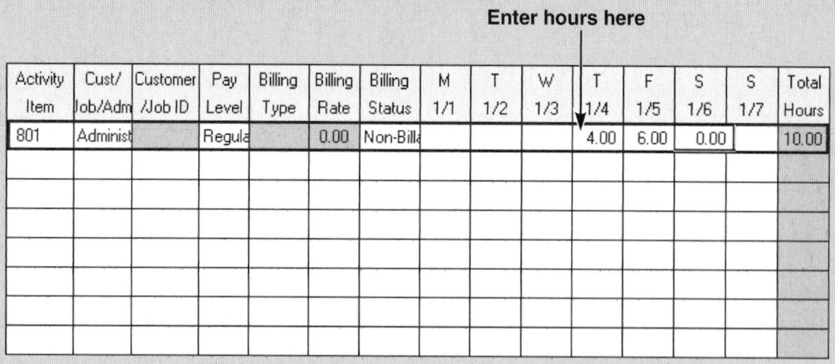

Enter hours here

Activity Item	Cust/ Job/Adm	Customer /Job ID	Pay Level	Billing Type	Billing Rate	Billing Status	M 1/1	T 1/2	W 1/3	T 1/4	F 1/5	S 1/6	S 1/7	Total Hours
801	Administ		Regula		0.00	Non-Billa				4.00	6.00	0.00		10.00

20 Click **Save**. The hours you have just input should match up with the table below.

Employee/Date	Ryder Zacovic (ID 003)	Job - Activity Item	Pat Ng (ID 004)
Week of 1/1			
1/4	6 hrs.	n/a - 801	4 hrs.
1/5	4 hrs.	n/a - 801	6 hrs.

21 Use the following table to enter hours for Ryder and Pat administrative/office work for the week of 1/8 (follow the same steps as described above).

Employee/Date	Ryder Zacovic (ID 003)	Job - Activity Item	Pat Ng (ID 004)
Week of 1/8			
1/8	8 hrs.	n/a - 801	2 hrs.
1/10	6 hrs.	n/a - 801	4 hrs.
1/12	4 hrs.	n/a - 801	6 hrs.

22 Use the following table to enter hours for Ryder and Pat for the week of 1/22 (follow the same steps as described above). Enter only the office work hours provided by the table as we'll enter the last entry in the next step.

Employee/ Date	Ryder Zacovic (ID 003)	Job - Activity Item	Pat Ng (ID 004)
Week of 1/22			
1/24	8 hrs.	n/a - 801	8 hrs.
1/25	8 hrs.	n/a - 801	8 hrs.
1/26	7 hrs.	n/a - 801	8 hrs.
	1 hrs.	3001 - 101	n/a

23 For the last row in the table above, select Activity Item **101**, **Job**, **3001**, **Regular**, **Activity rate**, and **Billable** and then type **1** in column F 1/26 as shown in Figure 7.33. This represents Ryder's work on Job 3001 which can now be billed to the customer.

Note the office work hours entered as before

Activity Item	Cust/ Job/Adm	Customer /Job ID	Pay Level	Billing Type	Billing Rate	Billing Status	M 1/22	T 1/23	W 1/24	T 1/25	F 1/26	S 1/27	S 1/28	Total Hours
801	Administ		Regula		0.00	Non-Billa			8.00	8.00	7.00			23.00
101	Job	3001	Regula	Activity	125.00	Billable					1.00			1.00

Job hours require a different activity item, a specific job ID, designation of a billing type (Activity rate in this case) and a billing status = Billable

Figure 7.33

Weekly Time Sheet for Ryder Zacovic for the Week Including 1/22/07

24 Use the following table to enter hours for Ryder and Pat for the week of 1/29 (follow the same steps as described above).

Employee/Date	Ryder Zacovic (ID 003)	Job - Activity Item	Pat Ng (ID 004)
Week of 1/29			
1/29	–	3002 – 102	6 hrs.
1/29	–	3002 – 105	1 hrs.
1/29	–	n/a – 801	1 hrs.
1/30	3 hrs.	3003 – 103	—
1/30	4 hrs.	3003 – 106	—
1/30	1 hrs.	n/a – 801	—

25 The resulting weekly time sheets should look like Figure 7.34 and Figure 7.35.

Figure 7.34

Pat Ng's Time Sheet for the Week Including 1/29

Activity Item	Cust/ Job/Adm	Customer /Job ID	Pay Level	Billing Type	Billing Rate	Billing Status	M 1/29	T 1/30	W 1/31	T 2/1	F 2/2	S 2/3	S 2/4	Total Hours
102	Job	3002	Regula	Activity	250.00	Billable	6.00							6.00
105	Job	3002	Regula	Activity	75.00	Billable	1.00							1.00
801	Administ		Regula		0.00	Non-Billa	1.00							1.00

Note different rows for different activity items even though this time sheet only covers one day

Figure 7.35

Ryder Zacovic's Time Sheet for the Week Including 1/29

Activity Item	Cust/ Job/Adm	Customer /Job ID	Pay Level	Billing Type	Billing Rate	Billing Status	M 1/29	T 1/30	W 1/31	T 2/1	F 2/2	S 2/3	S 2/4	Total Hours
103	Job	3003	Regula	Activity	175.00	Billable		3.00						3.00
106	Job	3003	Regula	Activity	80.00	Billable		4.00						4.00
801	Administ		Regula		0.00	Non-Billa		1.00						1.00

26 Click **Close** to close the Weekly Time Sheet window.

"That takes care of January's hourly time sheets, but now we have to manually process payroll for those time sheets and for our two salaried employees," Karen explains. "Processing payroll for salaried employees simply requires us to enter the end of period date, in this case a month end of 1/31, and specify the taxes to be withheld and the employer's tax expenses. The same is basically true for our hourly employees at Wild Water Sports since both of our hourly employees' payroll is based on time ticket hours."

To process payroll for January:

1 From the Employees & Payroll center, click **Pay Employees** and then select **Enter Payroll For One Employee**.

2 If a warning message appears, click in the check box labeled **Do not display this message again** and then click **OK**.

3 Choose **Checking Account** as the cash account used for this transaction and then click **OK**.

4 Type **1011** as the Check Number.

5 Type **1/31/07** in the Date text box.

6 Type **1/31/07** in the Pay Period Ends text box.

7 Select Employee ID **001**.

8 Enter information for Donna Chandler's paycheck from Figure 7.36. Be sure to put employee tax amounts as negative numbers and company amounts as positive numbers.

The salary amount comes from our original employee setup

Make sure your net check equals this amount

Figure 7.36

Donna Chandler's Paycheck for the Pay Period Ending 1/31/07

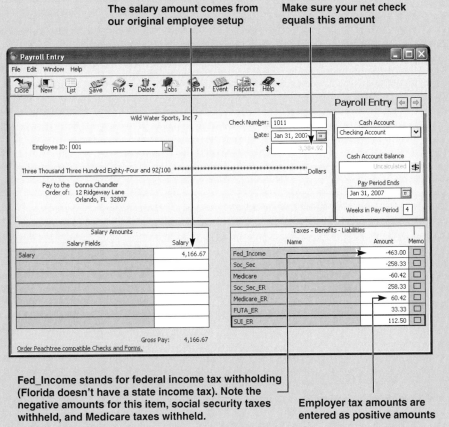

Fed_Income stands for federal income tax withholding (Florida doesn't have a state income tax). Note the negative amounts for this item, social security taxes withheld, and Medicare taxes withheld.

Employer tax amounts are entered as positive amounts

9 Click **Save**.

10 Select Employee ID **003**.

11 Type **1012** as the Check Number.

12 Since you have already entered Ryder's hours via time sheets, the 60 hours should show up in the lower left-hand corner of your check.

> *Trouble?* If no hours are showing, you may not have the correct pay period selected. Be sure your Pay Period Ends text box shows Jan 31, 2007. The text (Employee uses Time Ticket hours) should also appear under the Employee ID. If it doesn't, go back to the setup for this employee and make sure their setup specifies that this employee uses time ticket hours.

13 Enter information for Ryder Zacovic's paycheck from Figure 7.37. Once again, be sure to put employee tax amounts as negative numbers and company amounts as positive numbers.

Figure 7.37

Ryder Zacovic's paycheck for the Pay Period Ending 1/31/07

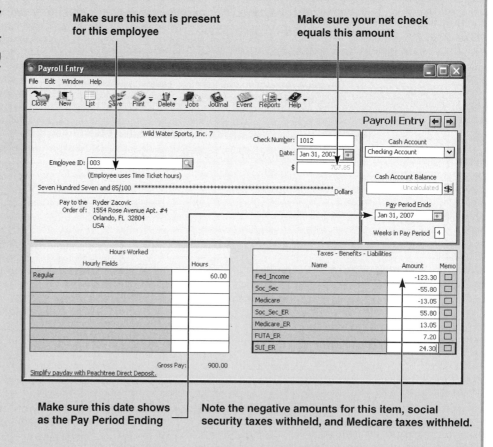

Make sure this text is present for this employee

Make sure your net check equals this amount

Make sure this date shows as the Pay Period Ending

Note the negative amounts for this item, social security taxes withheld, and Medicare taxes withheld.

14 Click **Save**.

15 Continue the payroll process based on the following payroll information.

Employee/Item	Karen 002	Pat 004
Check Number	1013	1014
Salary/Hours worked	4,166.67	54
Fed_Income	−710.00	−133.16
Soc_Sec	−258.33	−60.26
Medicare	−60.42	−14.09
Soc_Sec_ER	258.33	60.26
Medicare_ER	60.42	14.09
FUTA_ER	33.33	7.78
SUI_ER	112.50	26.24
Net check amount	3,137.92	764.49

16 Click **Close** to close the Payroll Entry window.

"How did you determine the withholding amounts and the other tax items?" you ask.

"Withholding amounts came from the payroll tax withholding tables I downloaded from the Internal Revenue Services' Web site at http://www.irs.gov," says Karen. "The others were provided by our local CPA, as follows: Social Security is 6.2% of earnings, Medicare is 1.45% of earnings, and federal unemployment is 0.8% of earnings up to $7,000, while state unemployment is 2.7% of earnings up to $7,000." (See Appendix A—"Payroll Taxes.")

Karen further explains that, since the hourly employees' time was recorded on time sheets, she did not have to enter hours on each employee's paycheck. If, however, the company didn't use time sheets, it would enter hours worked by hourly employees in each Payroll Entry window.

"What about the customer jobs we charged for Ryder's and Pat's time?" you ask. "Don't we have to bill the customers for the time charged?"

"Yes," Karen answers. "You are quite perceptive. As it turns out, these jobs were completed and the boats were picked up by the customers. If they were not complete, we would wait to bill them until they were complete. Let me show you the process for generating an invoice based on time recorded via the payroll system."

To bill customers for time recorded via the payroll system:

1 Open the **Customers & Sales** center, click **Sales Invoices**, and then select **New Sales Invoice**.

2 Select Customer ID **50008**.

3 Type **1/30/07** as the date.

4 Type **10003** as the Invoice No.

5 Click the arrow button next to **Apply Tickets/Expenses**.

6 Place a check in the **Use** column and select the option button to **Use Item Description for Invoicing** as shown in Figure 7.38.

Figure 7.38

Applying Payroll Costs Incurred on a Job

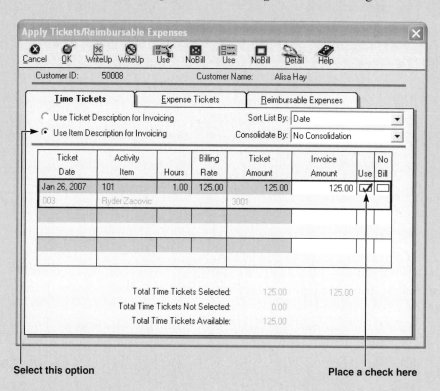

Select this option

Place a check here

7 Click **OK**.

8 Add 5 quarts of engine oil and 1 oil filter to the invoice, specify job **3001** for both, and specify sales tax code **01**. Your invoice should look like Figure 7.39.

Figure 7.39

Invoice 10003

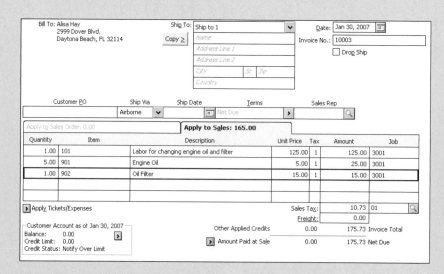

9 Click the arrow button next to the text **Amount Paid at Sale**.

10 Type **4** as the Deposit Ticket ID since this amount was then directly deposited into the company's checking account.

11 Type **9845** in the Reference text box of the Receive Payment window.

12 Type **175.73** as the Receipt Amount and then click **OK**.

13 Your new invoice should now indicate a 0.00 Net Due.

14 Click **Save** and then click **Close**.

15 Click **50004** from the Customers list in the Customers & Sales center to edit Freebirds data.

16 Type **1000 Boomer St. Tallahassee FL 32303** as its address, click **Save**, and then click **Close**.

17 Click **Sales Invoices** and select **New Sales Invoice** from the Customers & Sales center.

18 Select Customer ID **50004**.

19 Type **1/31/07** as the date.

20 Type **10004** as the Invoice No.

21 Click the arrow button next to **Apply Tickets/Expenses**.

22 Place a check in the **Use** column for both rows presented and select the option button to **Use Item Description for Invoicing** as shown in Figure 7.40.

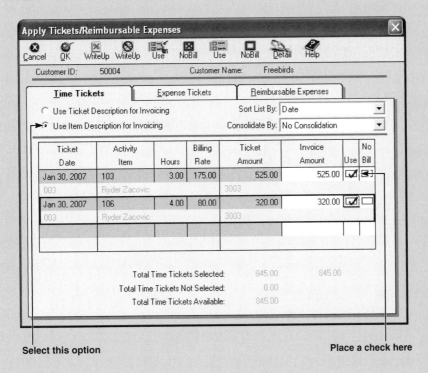

Figure 7.40

Applying Payroll Costs Incurred on a Job

23 Click **OK**.

24 Select **01** as the sales tax code.

25 Click the arrow button next to the text **Amount Paid at Sale**.

26 Type **9412332** in the Reference text box of the Receive Payment window.

27 Type **899.93** as the Receipt Amount and then click **OK**.

28 Your new invoice should now indicate a 0.00 Net Due as shown in Figure 7.41.

Figure 7.41

Invoice 10004

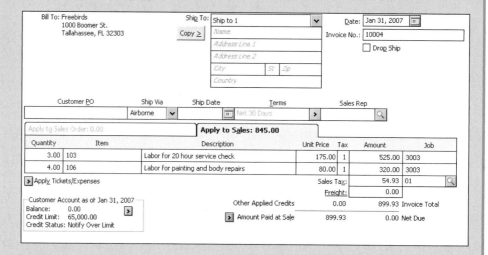

29 Click **Save**.

30 Select Customer ID **50005**.

31 Type **1/31/07** as the date.

32 Type **10005** as the Invoice No.

33 Click the arrow button next to **Apply Tickets/Expenses**.

34 Place a check in the Use column for both rows presented, select the option button to Use Item Description for Invoicing, and then click **OK**.

35 Select **01** as the sales tax code.

36 Click the arrow button next to the text **Amount Paid at Sale**.

37 Type **1254** in the Reference text box of the Receive Payment window.

38 Type **1677.38** as the Receipt Amount and then click **OK**.

39 Your new invoice should now indicate a 0.00 Net Due as shown in Figure 7.42.

Figure 7.42

Invoice 10005

Bill To: Florida Sports Camp		
78 Hwy 150		
Orlando, FL 31310		

Ship To: Ship to 1

Copy ≥

Name
Address Line 1
Address Line 2
City   St   Zip
Country

Date: Jan 31, 2007
Invoice No.: 10005
☐ Drop Ship

Customer PO	Ship Via	Ship Date	Terms	Sales Rep
	Airborne		Net Due	

Apply to Sales Order : 0.00   **Apply to Sales: 1,575.00**

Quantity	Item	Description	Unit Price	Tax	Amount	Job
6.00	102	Labor for engine tune up	250.00	1	1,500.00	3002
1.00	105	Labor for cleaning boats	75.00	1	75.00	3002

Apply Tickets/Expenses

Sales Tax:	102.38	01
Freight:	0.00	

Customer Account as of Jan 31, 2007
Balance: 0.00
Credit Limit: 0.00
Credit Status: Notify Over Limit

Other Applied Credits   0.00   1,677.38 Invoice Total
Amount Paid at Sale   1,677.38   0.00 Net Due

40 Click **Save** and then click **Close** in the Sales/Invoicing window.

"Did we deposit funds collected from those last two transactions?" you ask. "No," Karen answers. "We won't deposit them until the next month."

You've now recorded many operating activities, including cash sales, purchase orders, writing checks, and processing payroll, and you'd like to know how the business did for the month.

Evaluate a Firm's Performance and Financial Position

The best way to evaluate a firm's performance and financial position at this point is to generate an income statement and a balance sheet as of January 31, 2007. Karen suggests that you apply what you have learned from past experiences with Peachtree to create and print a standard income statement and a standard balance sheet for January.

To prepare a standard income statement and a balance sheet for January:

1 Set the System Date to **1/31/07**.

2 Open the Company center and then click **View All Financial Statements** from the list of Recently Used Financial Statements.

3 Double-click <**Standard**> **Income Stmnt** from the Select a Report window.

4 Uncheck the Print Page Numbers and Show Zero Amounts check boxes.

5 Click **OK** to view the income statement for January as shown in Figure 7.43.

Figure 7.43

Income Statement for January 2007

Wild Water Sports, Inc. 7
Income Statement
For the One Month Ending January 31, 2007

Revenues	Current Month			Year to Date	
Sales Income	$ 200,750.00	98.73	$	200,750.00	98.73
Service Income	2,545.00	1.25		2,545.00	1.25
Parts Income	40.00	0.02		40.00	0.02
Total Revenues	203,335.00	100.00		203,335.00	100.00
Cost of Sales					
Cost of Sales	160,632.00	79.00		160,632.00	79.00
Total Cost of Sales	160,632.00	79.00		160,632.00	79.00
Gross Profit	42,703.00	21.00		42,703.00	21.00
Expenses					
Wages Expense	10,205.34	5.02		10,205.34	5.02
Payroll Tax Expense	1,137.88	0.56		1,137.88	0.56
Utilities Expense	890.00	0.44		890.00	0.44
Telephone Expense	1,700.00	0.84		1,700.00	0.84
Total Expenses	13,933.22	6.85		13,933.22	6.85
Net Income	$ 28,769.78	14.15	$	28,769.78	14.15

6 Click **Print** from the button bar and then **OK** to print this statement.

7 Click **Close**.

8 Double-click < **Standard** > **Balance Sheet** from the Select a Report window.

9 Make sure the Print Page Numbers and Show Zero Amounts check boxes are unchecked.

10 Click **OK** to view the balance sheet for January as shown in Figures 7.44 and 7.45.

```
                    Wild Water Sports, Inc. 7
                         Balance Sheet
                       January 31, 2007
                            ASSETS

Current Assets
  Checking Account                    $        22,366.61
  Short-Term Investments                      300,000.00
  Accounts Receivable                          66,300.00
  Inventory                                   330,400.00
  Inventory Parts                               1,568.00
  Prepaid Expenses                             22,000.00
                                      _____

  Total Current Assets                                      742,634.61

Property and Equipment
  Property and Equipment                      245,000.00
  Accum. Depreciation-Prop&Eqt                 (7,500.00)
                                      _____

  Total Property and Equipment                              237,500.00

Other Assets
                                      _____

  Total Other Assets                                              0.00

  Total Assets                        $                     980,134.61
                                                          ============
```

Figure 7.44

Asset Section of the Balance Sheet as of January 31, 2007

```
                    Wild Water Sports, Inc. 7
                         Balance Sheet
                       January 31, 2007
                  LIABILITIES AND CAPITAL

Current Liabilities
  Accounts Payable                    $         1,000.00
  Sales Tax Payable                            13,216.79
  Federal Payroll Taxes Payable                 2,990.86
  FUTA Payable                                     81.64
  State Payroll Taxes Payable                     275.54
                                      _____

  Total Current Liabilities                                  17,564.83

Long-Term Liabilities
  Long Term Debt-Noncurrent                    633,800.00
                                      _____

  Total Long-Term Liabilities                               633,800.00

  Total Liabilities                                         651,364.83

Capital
  Common Stock                                 300,000.00
  Net Income                                    28,769.78
                                      _____

  Total Capital                                             328,769.78

  Total Liabilities & Capital         $                     980,134.61
                                                          ============
```

Figure 7.45

Liabilities and Capital Section of the Balance Sheet as of January 31, 2007

11 Click **Print** from the button bar and then **OK** to print this statement.

12 Click **Close**.

"Is there a way for us to see what transactions made up these balances?" you ask.

"Yes," Karen responds. "We'll print a Find Transactions report which will show us every transaction recorded in chronological order. It will include the type of transaction, the date it was recorded, a number reference (like check number, invoice number, etc.), the name of the entity (vendor name, customer name, employee name, etc.), the balance sheet account affected (checking, accounts receivable, undeposited funds, etc.), other accounts affected (inventory, revenue, expenses, etc.), and the amount. Let me show you how to create this report."

To prepare a transaction list by date report for January:

1 Click **Company Reports** from the Select a Report window.

2 Double-click **Find Transactions Report**.

3 If your system date is still set at 1/31/07, the report you get will only show you transactions recorded on 1/31/07. To change the report to reflect all transactions recorded in January 07, click the **Options** button on the report button bar.

4 Change the From date to **1/1/07** and then click **OK**.

5 Click **Print** from the report button bar and then click **OK** to print. The report shown in Figure 7.46 should appear.

Trouble? On occasion you might accidentally enter the wrong date for a transaction (for example, accepting the default date which might be before January 2007 or after January 2007). This might occur if you forgot to set the system date to some date in January 2007. If you're pretty sure you entered a transaction but don't see it on your transactions list, dates are likely your problem. To verify this, try entering 1/1/06 as the From date and 12/31/09 as the To date. If your missing transaction appears, double-click it to correct the date, and you'll be good to go!

6 Click **Close** and then click **Yes** to save it.

7 Type **Find Transactions Report 1/07** as the new name of the report and then click **Save**.

8 Close the Select a Report window.

Figure 7.46 Find Transactions Report

Wild Water Sports, Inc. 7
Find Transactions Report
For the Period From Jan 1, 2007 to Jan 31, 2007

Filter Criteria includes: 1) All Transaction Types. Report order is by Date.

Date	Type	Reference	ID	Name	Amount
1/1/07	General Journal Entry	1			200,000.00
1/4/07	General Journal Entry	2			250,000.00
1/4/07	Time Ticket	000001	003	Ryder Zacovic	
1/4/07	Time Ticket	000003	004	Pat Ng	
1/5/07	Time Ticket	000002	003	Ryder Zacovic	
1/5/07	Time Ticket	000004	004	Pat Ng	
1/8/07	Payment	1001	11100	ETrade	300,000.00
1/8/07	Time Ticket	000005	003	Ryder Zacovic	
1/8/07	Time Ticket	000008	004	Pat Ng	
1/10/07	Payment	1002	11200	Staples	70,000.00
1/10/07	Payment	1003	11300	AJ Marine Equipment	100,000.00
1/10/07	Sales Order	101	50005	Florida Sports Camp	74,550.00
1/10/07	Time Ticket	000006	003	Ryder Zacovic	
1/10/07	Time Ticket	000009	004	Pat Ng	
1/11/07	Purchase Order	4001	10000	Malibu Boats	56,000.00
1/11/07	Purchase Order	4002	10200	Tige Boats	63,000.00
1/11/07	Receipt	8755	50005	Florida Sports Camp	17,500.00
1/11/07	Receipt	987452	50006	Performance Rentals	19,687.50
1/11/07	Sales Order	102	50006	Performance Rentals	83,868.75
1/12/07	Time Ticket	000007	003	Ryder Zacovic	
1/12/07	Time Ticket	000010	004	Pat Ng	
1/15/07	Receipt	65454	50002	Buena Vista Water Sports	30,000.00
1/16/07	Receipt	161	50007	Seth Blackman	55,380.00
1/24/07	Time Ticket	000011	003	Ryder Zacovic	
1/24/07	Time Ticket	000015	004	Pat Ng	
1/25/07	Time Ticket	000012	003	Ryder Zacovic	
1/25/07	Time Ticket	000016	004	Pat Ng	
1/26/07	Time Ticket	000013	003	Ryder Zacovic	
1/26/07	Time Ticket	000014	003	Ryder Zacovic	125.00
1/26/07	Time Ticket	000017	004	Pat Ng	
1/29/07	Payment	1004	10000	Malibu Boats	56,000.00
1/29/07	Purchase	MB20397	10000	Malibu Boats	56,000.00

Figure 7.46 Cont'd

8/8/06 at 13:14:20.48

Wild Water Sports, Inc. 7
Find Transactions Report
For the Period From Jan 1, 2007 to Jan 31, 2007

Filter Criteria includes: 1) All Transaction Types. Report order is by Date.

Date	Type	Reference	ID	Name	Amount
1/29/07	Time Ticket	000018	004	Pat Ng	1,500.00
1/29/07	Time Ticket	000019	004	Pat Ng	75.00
1/29/07	Time Ticket	000020	004	Pat Ng	
1/30/07	Payment	1005	10200	Tige Boats	63,000.00
1/30/07	Purchase	T2309443	10200	Tige Boats	63,000.00
1/30/07	Receipt	10885	50006	Performance Rentals	64,181.25
1/30/07	Receipt	4532	50005	Florida Sports Camp	57,050.00
1/30/07	Receipt	9845	50008	Alisa Hay	175.73
1/30/07	Sale/Invoice	10001	50005	Florida Sports Camp	74,550.00
1/30/07	Sale/Invoice	10002	50006	Performance Rentals	83,868.75
1/30/07	Sale/Invoice	10003	50008	Alisa Hay	175.73
1/30/07	Time Ticket	000021	003	Ryder Zacovic	525.00
1/30/07	Time Ticket	000022	003	Ryder Zacovic	320.00
1/30/07	Time Ticket	000023	003	Ryder Zacovic	
1/31/07	Payment	1006	11400	Manchester Insurance	22,000.00
1/31/07	Payment	1007	11600	Central Florida Gas & Electric	890.00
1/31/07	Payment	1008	11700	Verizon	1,700.00
1/31/07	Payment	1009	11500	Chevron/Mobil	1,600.00
1/31/07	Payment	1010	10000	Malibu Boats	76,000.00
1/31/07	Payroll Entry	1011	001	Donna Chandler	3,384.92
1/31/07	Payroll Entry	1012	003	Ryder Zacovic	707.85
1/31/07	Payroll Entry	1013	002	Karen Wilson	3,137.92
1/31/07	Payroll Entry	1014	004	Pat Ng	764.49
1/31/07	Purchase	EM23987997	11500	Chevron/Mobil	1,600.00
1/31/07	Receipt	1254	50005	Florida Sports Camp	1,677.38
1/31/07	Receipt	9412332	50004	Freebirds	899.93
1/31/07	Sale/Invoice	10004	50004	Freebirds	899.93
1/31/07	Sale/Invoice	10005	50005	Florida Sports Camp	1,677.38

Report Total: 1,957,472.5

Number of Transactions: 60

"Not bad for our first month," Karen comments. "But we need to pay off some of the debt acquired with the company acquisition. Plus, we can't forget that some costs such as interest and depreciation expenses have not been accrued or paid, so this information is not complete."

End Note

The two of you decide to quit for the day because you've accomplished quite a lot. You've recorded the firm's financing, investing, and operating activities for the month of January, which included processing purchase orders, receiving inventory, paying for inventory and other bills, recognizing cash sales, and writing checks, including some for payroll. Next up are February transactions and a few noncash activities.

Chapter 7 Questions

1 Compare and contrast operating, investing, and financing activities.

2 Describe some of the financing activities you recorded for Wild Water in January.

3 Describe some of the investing activities you recorded for Wild Water in January.

4 Describe some of the operating activities you recorded for Wild Water in January.

5 How should you account for advanced deposits received on customer orders?

6 Do sales orders increase revenue? If not, why not?

7 How are cash sales of products on hand recorded?

8 What steps are involved when a company receives inventory ordered from a vendor that requires immediate payment?

9 When is it appropriate to use time sheets for payroll?

10 What is involved in the processing of payroll for Wild Water Sports?

Chapter 7 Assignments

merchandising

Job Costing

1 *Adding More Information to Wild Water Sports*

Restore the file **Wild Water Sports, Inc 7A** found on the text CD or downloaded from the text Web site and then add the following transactions in chronological order. Be sure to set the system date to **2/1/07** and the accounting period to **Period 2 — 02/01/07 — 02/28/07**.

Date	Transaction
2/1/07	Received five sets of tune-up parts (Item 903) from Delco (new vendor with ID = 11800 with terms pay on receipt of product) on its invoice 9874564. Wrote Check No. 1015 for $1,000 as payment for those parts.
2/1/07	Accepted a new job (3004) to tune up a boat owned by Orlando Water Sports.
2/1/07	Paid $24,000 to Coe Marketing (new vendor with ID = 11850) for new advertising campaign, which will last one year, with Check No. 1016. (*Hint:* All prepaid balances are recorded to the prepaid expense account.)
2/1/07	Deposited funds received 1/31 of $2,577.31 into the checking account using Deposit Ticket 5.
2/2/07	Created Purchase Order No. 4003 to MB Sports (ID 10100) to order an MB B52 V23 Team Edition (a new item ID = 401) on behalf of our customer, Performance Rentals. Cost: $60,000, Sales Price: $75,000. Credit terms due on receipt, Ship Via Best Way.

2/2/07	Collected $18,750 as an advance payment from Performance Rentals (its Check No. 2001) which was equal to the 25% down payment required on all boat orders. (Use Receipt Number SR0005.)
2/2/07	Recorded Sales Order 103 from Performance Rentals for 1 item 401 for customer pickup by 2/28 including sales tax.
2/2/07	Pat Ng worked four hours on Job No. 3004 tuning up a boat owned by Orlando Water Sports using billing type Activity Rate. (*Hint:* Record on a time ticket now!)
2/3/07	Recorded journal entry 3 for receipt of $100,000 from a new investor, Sam Ski, in exchange for common stock representing a 25% interest in the company.
2/3/07	Recorded invoice 10006 to Orlando Water Sports for Job No. 3004 based on work performed by Pat Ng and one set of tune-up parts (item 903). $1,331.25 was collected at the time of sale with Check No. 9774.
2/5/07	Deposited the advance payment received from Performance Rentals and the check received from Orlando Water Sports using Deposit Ticket ID 6.
2/5/07	Received Check No. 390 for $3,000 as payment on account from Buena Vista Water Sports using Receipt Number SR0006.
2/5/07	Recorded journal entry 4 for receipt of a $50,000 check, No. 188774, from CitiBank (new Vendor ID = 11050) as the proceeds from a three-year 6% loan negotiated by Sam Ski. The company plans to use these funds in the future to pay down some older, more expensive debt. (Record this debt to account 2700.)
2/6/07	Wrote Check No. 1017 in the amount of $75,000 to ETrade as a short-term investment.
2/6/07	Deposited $3,000 check received on 2/5 using Deposit Ticket 7.
2/6/07	Created Purchase Order No. 4004 to Malibu Boats to order a Malibu Sunscape LSV (ID – 203) and a Malibu Vride (ID – 204) on behalf of a new customer, Fantasy Sports (ID = 50009), located at 345 Sunset Rd., Orlando, FL 31312. (Specify sales tax code 01 for the new customer and Cust. Pickup as the Ship Via option.)
2/6/07	Recorded Sales Order 104 to Fantasy Sports for customer pickup by 3/31/07 for 1 item 203 and 1 item 204 both of which were ordered from Malibu on Purchase Order No. 4004.
2/6/07	Collected $28,250 as an advance payment from Fantasy Sports (its Check No. 1005), which was equal to the 25% down payment required on all boat orders using Receipt Number SR0007.
2/8/07	Received Check No. 1988 for $43,000 as payment on account from Orlando Water Sports using Receipt Number SR0008.
2/8/07	Sold a Malibu WakeSetter VLX (Item ID = 205) from inventory to Walking on Water for $57,000 plus tax of $3,705 and recorded the sale with Receipt Number SR0009. Received the customer's Check No. 232 as payment in full. Updated the customer's address as 874 Nightingale Dr., Kissimmee, FL 34743.
2/8/07	Accepted a new job (ID = 3005) to paint a boat owned by Alisa Hay.
2/9/07	Made a deposit of $131,955 from checks received on 2/6 and 2/8 using Deposit Ticket 8.
2/9/07	Ryder Zacovic worked five hours on Job No. 3005 painting a boat owned by Alisa Hay. (Be sure to use the Activity rate as the Billing Type.)
2/10/07	Recorded invoice 10007 to Alisa Hay under Job No. 3005 based on work performed by Ryder Zacovic. Check No. 741 collected $426. (If a notice of going over the credit limit appears, you can ignore it since this is a cash sale.)
2/12/07	Deposited $426 from Alisa Hay using Deposit Ticket 9.
2/15/07	Wrote Check No. 1018 to Sunset Auto (New Vendor ID 11550) for $45,000 to purchase a truck for the business. (Record as Property and Equipment.)
2/19/07	Recorded receipt of the MB B52 V23 Team Edition ordered on behalf of Performance Rentals on Purchase Order No. 4003. Wrote Check No. 1019 to MB Sports for $60,000 as payment for this purchase based on its invoice 230987.

2/20/07   Created invoice 10009 to Performance Rentals for sale of MB B51 V23 based on Sales Order 103. Record receipt of payment made at the time of sale from Performance Rentals of $61,125 with its Check No. 23098. Applied the deposit received when this boat was ordered. (If a notice of going over the credit limit appears, you can ignore it since this is a cash sale.)

2/21/07   Deposited Performance Rentals' check received 2/20 using Deposit Ticket 10.

2/26/07   Wrote Check No. 1020 to pay MasterCard bill of $1,000. (*Hint:* Use the Pay Bills function to record this transaction just like in the text.)

2/26/07   Wrote Check No. 1021 to Central Florida Gas & Electric for $930 for utilities expense.

2/26/07   Wrote Check No. 1022 to Verizon for $1,820 for telephone expense.

2/26/07   Wrote Check No. 1023 to Brian Szulczewski (New Vendor ID = 11825) for $2,700 for advertising expense.

2/26/07   Wrote Check No. 1024 to Staples for $4,500 for other office expenses.

2/28/07   Record time sheet information provided in Table 7.1 below *Note:* Some of these hours are related to jobs for which time had already been recorded and should already be on your time sheet. Those hours are designated in the following table with an *. All other hours not designated by an * are for administrative office work activities.

2/28/07   Process payroll per the information provided in Table 7.2, starting with Check No. 1025.

Table 7.1
Time Sheet Information

Date	Ryder 003	Date	Pat 004
2/1	8 hrs.	2/2	4 hrs.*
2/6	5 hrs.	2/5	8 hrs.
2/8	5 hrs.	2/7	8 hrs.
2/9	5 hrs.*	2/12	8 hrs.
2/13	8 hrs.	2/14	8 hrs.
2/15	8 hrs.	2/19	8 hrs.
2/20	8 hrs.	2/21	8 hrs.
2/22	8 hrs.	2/26	8 hrs.
2/28	8 hrs.	2/27	8 hrs.
Total	63 hrs.		68 hrs.

Table 7.2
Payroll Information for Wild Water Sports

Employee/Item	Donna 001	Karen 002	Pat 004	Ryder 003
Check Number	1025	1026	1027	1028
Earnings/Hours	4,166.67	4,166.67	68	63
Federal Withholding	−463.00	−710.00	−167.69	−129.47
Social Security Employee	−258.33	−258.33	−75.89	−58.59
Medicare Employee	−60.42	−60.42	−17.75	−13.70
Social Security Company	258.33	258.33	75.89	58.59
Medicare Company	60.42	60.42	17.75	13.70
Federal Unemployment	33.33	33.33	9.79	7.56
State Unemployment	112.50	112.50	33.05	25.52
Check Amount	3,384.92	3,137.92	962.67	743.24

Print the following with no page numbers and no zero amounts and with the accounting period set to Period 2:

a. Standard income statement.

b. Standard balance sheet.

c. Find transactions report for the period February 1 through February 28, 2007.

2 *Adding More Information to Central Coast Cellular*

merchandising

Restore the backup you made for Central Coast Cellular in Chapter 6 into a new company folder. (Do not restore this backup into an existing folder.) Change the company name to include Ch 7 at the end so that the new company name is **Central Coast Cellular Ch 7**. (See the Preface to this book for more detailed instructions on how to do this.) Change the system date to **1/1/09** and the accounting period to **Period 1 – 1/1/09 – 1/31/09**. Add the following business events:

Date	Transaction
1/2/09	Mr. Van Morrison deposited $200,000 of his personal funds into the company checking account and received 25,000 shares of common stock.
1/2/09	The company signed a lease with Central Coast Leasing (Vendor ID CCL, 2830 McMillan Ave #7, San Luis Obispo, CA 93401, 805-544-2875) to rent retail space at $3,000 a month for five years. Payment is due on the 13th of the month. The default expense account for this vendor is account 6300.
1/6/09	The company temporarily invested $75,000 by writing Check No. 3001 to Schwab Investments (Vendor ID SI, 1194 Pacific Street, San Luis Obispo, CA 93401, 805-788-0502). *Hint:* You will need to create a new other current assets account type named Short-Term Investments, Account ID = 1300. This will be the default expense account for this vendor.
1/7/09	The company borrowed and then deposited $125,000 from Wells Fargo Bank (Vendor ID WF, 665 Marsh St., San Luis Obispo, CA 93401, 805-541-0143) due in five years with annual interest of 8% and payments made monthly. The default expense account for this vendor is account 2700.
1/8/09	The company purchased office furniture by writing Check No. 3002 for $20,000 to Russco (Vendor ID R, 3046 S. Higuera St. #A, San Luis Obispo, CA 93401, 805-547-8440). The default expense account for this vendor is account 1500.
1/9/09	Using Purchase Order No. 101, the company ordered 40 ELX588 and 60 ET19LX phones from Ericsson. Using Purchase Order No. 102, the company ordered 25 N3285, 50 N8290, and 15 N8890 phones from Nokia.
1/9/09	The company purchased supplies from Russco for $3,000 using Check No. 3003. These supplies are expected to last over the next year. You'll need to add an other current assets type of account 1410 called Supplies.
1/13/09	The company wrote Check No. 3004 to Central Coast Leasing for $6,000 ($3,000 for January's rent, and $3,000 as a prepaid expense).
1/14/09	The company received and deposited an advance payment of $10,000 from the City of San Luis Obispo (a customer) as part of a consulting contract to be started in February using Deposit Ticket 001 to deposit its Check No. 2034978.
1/15/09	The company received a shipment of phones from Ericsson on Purchase Order No. 101. Items were received and a bill recorded due in 30 days. All items ordered were received. Ericsson's invoice A3908 was included with the shipment.

1/16/09   The company created sales receipt 501 to record 50 hours of consulting services and the sale of 25 Ericsson LX588 phones to Sterling Hotels Corporation. A check was received and deposited for $7,425 using Deposit Ticket 002.

1/16/09   On January 16, 2009, the company paid semimonthly payroll using the regular checking account starting with Check No. 3005 for the period January 4 to January 16, 2003. Megan Paulson worked 80 hours during the period. (*Hint:* Be sure Megan was set up with a Pay Method = Hourly - Hours per Pay Period.) Payroll tax information is shown in Table 7.3.

	Tax or Withholding/Employee	Rodriguez	Bruner	Paulson
Table 7.3	Check Number	3005	3006	3007
Payroll Information for	Gross Pay	$2,000.00	$1,500.00	$960.00
Central Coast Cellular	Federal Withholding	−300.00	−225.00	−144.00
	Social Security Employee	−124.00	−93.00	−59.52
	Medicare Employee	−29.00	−21.75	−13.92
	State Withholding	−100.00	−75.00	−48.00
	SDI	−10.00	−7.50	−4.80
	Social Security Company	124.00	93.00	59.52
	Medicare Company	29.00	21.75	13.92
	FUTA	6.40	4.80	3.07
	SUTA-4.8	24.00	18.00	11.52
	California Employee Training Tax	2.00	1.50	0.96
	Check Amount	1,437.00	1,077.75	689.76

This is a continuous assignment in that the next chapter will use the work you've accomplished here as the basis for recording additional business events. After you've printed the following reports, create a backup of this file and store it on some type of external medium (flash drive, Internet site, CD, disk, etc.). The backup file should be named **Central Coast Cellular Ch 7** for easy identification later. You'll be restoring this file in the next chapter. Print the following with no page numbers and no zero amounts:

a. Standard income statement for the one month ending January 31, 2009.

b. Standard balance sheet as of January 31, 2009.

c. Find transactions report for the period January 1 through January 16, 2009.

Chapter 7 Case Problem 1
ALOHA PROPERTY MANAGEMENT

Restore the backup you made for Aloha in Chapter 6 into a new company folder. (Do not restore this backup into an existing folder.) (See the Preface to this book for more detailed instructions on how to do this.) Change the company name to include Ch 7 at the end so that the new company name is

Aloha Property Management Ch 7. Change the system date to **1/1/08** and the accounting period to **Period 1 — 1/1/08 — 1/31/08**. Add the following business events:

Date	Transaction
1/3/08	Adventure Travel purchased common stock from Aloha in exchange for $50,000 cash which was deposited to the company's regular checking account.
1/4/08	Received payment on account from General Motors (GM) in the amount of $75,000 on its Check No. 6874. Use Deposit Ticket 001.
1/7/08	Wrote Check No. 984 for $40,000 to World Investments (WI) as a short-term investment. (*Hint:* Create a new other current asset type account called Short-Term Investments—Account Number 10700.)
1/8/08	Wrote Check No. 985 for $24,000 to GEICO Insurance (GEICO) as payment for a one-year insurance policy with coverage provided from January 1, 2008, through December 31, 2008, and recorded this transaction as Prepaid Expenses—Account Number 14000.
1/9/08	Collected two checks from a new customer, Pixar Studios (PX). The two checks, a $14,000 check (Check No. 2348907) and a $10,000 check (Check No. 2348908), were for two different deposits on future rentals. Record these as two different receipts. No receipt numbers are used.
1/9/08	Deposited the checks received from Pixar into the Bank of Hawaii using Deposit Ticket 002.
1/11/08	Recorded Sales Receipt No. 5115 for rent of Villa Unit #1 for one week. Collected MasterCard payment in full of $3,120 from a new customer, Coast Union Bank (CU). (*Hint:* Select MasterCard as the Payment Method.)
1/11/08	Recorded invoice 7508 for rental of Moana Unit #4 for one week to Sara Rice. Recorded receipt of balance owed of $6,480 with Check No. 654.
1/11/08	Recorded Sales Receipt No. 5116 for rent of Villa Unit #2 for one week. Collected MasterCard payment in full of $4,680 from a new customer, Berkshire Hathaway (BH).
1/12/08	Deposited checks and MasterCard payments of $14,280 to the regular checking accounting using Deposit Ticket 003.
1/14/08	Wrote Check No. 986 for $23,000 to Furniture King (FK) as payment for new furniture. Recorded this to account 15000.
1/15/08	Wrote Check No. 987 for $4,500 as payment on account to Reilly Custodial. (*Hint:* Use Vendors/Pay Bills.)
1/18/08	Recorded Sales Receipt No. 5117 for rent of Moana Unit #3 and Villa Unit #3 for one week each. Collected American Express (AMEX) payment in full of $8,528 from a new customer, Bridgette Hacker (BRH).
1/18/08	Recorded Sales Receipt No. 5118 for rent of Moana Unit #4 for one week. Collected Check No. 909 as payment in full of $12,480 from a new customer, Lockheed Martin (LM).
1/18/08	Recorded invoice 7509 for rental of Villa Unit #1 and #2 for one week to Boeing, terms net 30.
1/21/08	Deposited $21,008 of undeposited funds to the regular checking account with Deposit Ticket 004.
1/23/08	Paid Reilly Custodial $3,000 on Check No. 988 for maintenance expenses. (Use account 70000.)
1/24/08	Collected a $5,125 deposit from a new customer, Exxon Mobil (EM) (its Check No. 30035). No receipt numbers are used.
1/25/08	Recorded invoice 7510 for rental of Villa Unit #4 for one week to Brice Montoya. Recorded receipt of balance owed of $3,240 with Check No. 1874.

1/28/08	Deposited $8,365 of undeposited funds to regular checking account with Deposit Ticket 005.
1/30/08	Wrote Check No. 989 for $12,000 to Pacific Electric (PE) to account 78000 Utilities Expenses.
1/30/08	Wrote Check No. 990 for $3,700 to AT&T (ATT) to account 76000 Telephone Expenses.
1/30/08	Wrote Check No. 991 for $15,000 to Sunset Media (SM) to account 60100 Advertising Expenses.
1/31/08	Process payroll per the information provided in Table 7.4. Use Regular Checking account.

Table 7.4 Earnings Information for Aloha Property Management	**Pay/Tax/Withholding**	**Aki**	**Castillo**
	Check Number	992	993
	Hours	n/a	150
	Rate	$75,000	$20.00
	Gross Pay	6,250.00	3,000.00
	Federal Withholding	−856.25	−411.00
	Social Security Employee	−387.50	−186.00
	Medicare Employee	−90.63	−43.50
	State Withholding	−442.33	−195.33
	SDI (State Disability Ins.)	−1.25	−0.60
	Social Security Employer	387.50	186.00
	Medicare Company	90.63	43.50
	Federal Unemployment	50.00	24.00
	SUI (State Unemployment)	187.50	90.00
	HI E&T	0.63	0.30
	Check Amount	4,472.04	2,163.57

Requirements

This is a continuous case in that the next chapter will use the work you've accomplished here as the basis for recording additional business events. After you've printed the following reports create a backup of this file and store it on some type of external medium (flash drive, Internet site, CD, disk, etc.). The backup file should be named **Aloha Property Management Ch 7** for easy identification later. You'll be restoring this file in the next chapter. Print the following with no page numbers and no zero amounts:

    a. Standard balance sheet

    b. Standard income statement

    c. Statement of cash flows

    d. Transaction list by date

Chapter 7 Case Problem 2
OCEAN VIEW FLOWERS

merchandising

Restore the backup you made for Ocean View Flowers in Chapter 6 into a new company folder. (Do not restore this backup into an existing folder.)

(See the Preface to this book for more detailed instructions on how to do this.) Change the company name to include Ch 7 at the end so that the new company name is **Ocean View Flowers Ch 7**. Change the system date to **1/1/08** and the accounting period to **Period 1 − 1/1/08 − 1/31/08**. Add the following business events:

Date	Transaction
1/4/08	The company sold common stock to Scott Wilson (add as a vendor with ID = SW), an investor, for $100,000 cash. The company deposited the check into the regular checking account. (Remember to use a general journal entry for this type of transaction.)
1/7/08	The company borrowed $50,000 from Santa Barbara Bank & Trust (add as a new vendor with ID = SBBT). The long-term note payable is due in three years with interest due annually at 10%. The company deposited the check into the regular checking account. (Remember to use a general journal entry for this type of transaction.)
1/8/08	The company temporarily invested $25,000 in a certificate of deposit due in three months, which will earn 7% per annum. Check No. 101, drawn on the regular checking account, was made payable to Prudent Investments (PI), 100 Main Street, San Francisco, CA 95154.
1/11/08	The company purchased furniture from Stateside Office Supplies (SOS), 324 G St., Lompoc, CA 93436, for $20,000 with Check No. 102.
1/14/08	The company purchased computer equipment from Gateway Computers (GC), 100 Cowabunga Blvd., Sioux City, IA 23442, for $15,000 with Check No. 103.
1/14/08	The company created Purchase Order No. 01 to order the following new items from Brophy Bros. Farms, which specializes in daylilies. It ordered 1,000 Almond Puff Daylilies (AP) at a cost of $12, 2,000 Calistoga Sun Daylilies (CS) at a cost of $8, and 500 Caribbean Pink Sands Daylilies (CPS) at a cost of $13. All daylilies are sold at a 100% markup (2 times cost) and are recorded to GL Sales account 40000. (Rename this account to Daylilies Sales.) Cost of goods sold are recorded to GL Cost of Goods Sold account 50000. (Rename this account to Cost of Goods Sold − Flowers.) (Also, be sure to use Average Cost for these inventory items. Remember if you use a different costing method by accident, you'll need to delete this item and then recreate it!)
1/15/08	The company paid payroll. All employees worked the entire period. Kelly Gusland worked 60 hours and Margie Conner 75 hours. Checks were written using the regular checking account. Payroll taxes and withholding for employees during the period 1/1/08 through 1/15/08 are shown in Table 7.5. (Be sure you have correctly established the hourly rate in the employee's file located in the Pay Info tab across from the G/L account.)
1/18/08	The company received its order in full from Brophy Bros. Farms (Purchase Order No. 01) receiving its invoice BB34908.
1/21/08	The company paid Stateside Office Supplies for purchase of supplies expected to last over the next six months using Check No. 109 for $1,500. Record this into a new other current assets type account 14300 called Supplies.
1/22/08	The company recorded its first cash sale (Sales Receipt No. 1000) to Valley Florists in which it sold 100 Almond Puffs, 100 Calistoga Suns, and 100 Caribbean Pink Sands. The $6,600 Check No. 0809 was deposited directly to the regular checking account using Deposit Ticket 5001. (Note that there is no sales tax for Ocean View because it is a wholesaler.)

1/25/08   The company recorded its second cash sale (Sales Receipt No. 1001) to Eastern Scents in which it sold 600 Almond Puffs and 300 Caribbean Pink Sands. The $22,200 VISA charge (20349802) was deposited directly to the regular checking account using Deposit Ticket 5002. (Note that there is no sales tax for Ocean View because it is a wholesaler.)

1/28/08   The company received an advance payment on account (Sales Receipt No. 1002) from FTD with Check No. 92384 in the amount of $5,000, which was deposited to the regular checking account using Deposit Ticket 5003.

1/29/08   Paid the Brophy Bros. bill with Check No. 110 in the amount of $34,500.

1/30/08   The company wrote Check No. 111 to Hawaiian Farms for $3,000 to pay rent expense, Check No. 112 to Edison, Inc. (E) for $500 to pay utilities expense, and Check No. 113 to General Telephone & Electric (GTE) for $400 to pay telephone expense (a new expense type account 77100). (Be sure to modify the expense account for Hawaiian Farms for this expenditure.)

1/31/08   The company paid payroll for the period ended January 31, 2008. All employees worked the entire period. Kelly Gusland worked 65 hours, and Margie Conner worked 70 hours. Payroll taxes and withholding for employees during the period 1/16/08 through 1/31/08 are shown in Table 7.6.

Table 7.5 Earnings Information for Ocean View Flowers 1/1/08 through 1/15/08	Employee/Tax or Withholding	Thomas	Gusland	Conner	McAninch	Comstock
	Check	104	105	106	107	108
	Hours/Salary	2,916.67	60	75	2,500.00	2,083.34
	Federal Income	−667.00	−118.00	−118.00	−402.00	−286.00
	Social Security	−180.83	−55.80	−55.80	−155.00	−129.17
	Medicare	−42.29	−13.05	−13.05	−36.25	−30.21
	State	−192.30	−19.32	−9.32	−153.55	−61.86
	SDI	−14.58	−4.50	−4.50	−12.50	−10.42
	Social Security Company	180.83	55.80	55.80	155.00	129.17
	Medicare Company	42.29	13.05	13.05	36.25	30.21
	FUTA	23.33	7.20	7.20	20.00	16.67
	SUI	1.46	0.45	0.45	1.25	1.04
	California Training Tax	2.92	0.90	0.90	2.50	2.08
	Check Amount	1,819.67	689.33	699.33	1,740.70	1,565.68

Table 7.6 Earnings Information for Ocean View Flowers 1/16/08 through 1/31/08	Employee/Tax or Withholding	Thomas	Gusland	Conner	McAninch	Comstock
	Check	114	115	116	117	118
	Hours/Salary	2,916.67	65	70	2,500.00	2,083.34
	Federal Income	−667.00	−130.00	−109.00	−402.00	−286.00
	Social Security	−180.83	−60.45	−52.08	−155.00	−129.17
	Medicare	−42.29	−14.14	−12.18	−36.25	−30.21
	State	−192.30	−23.63	−8.12	−153.55	−61.86
	SDI	−14.58	−4.88	−4.20	−12.50	−10.42
	Social Security Company	180.83	60.45	52.08	155.00	129.17
	Medicare Company	42.29	14.14	12.18	36.25	30.21
	FUTA	23.33	7.80	6.72	20.00	16.67
	SUI	1.46	0.49	0.42	1.25	1.04
	California Training Tax	2.92	0.98	0.84	2.50	2.08
	Check Amount	1,819.67	741.90	654.42	1,740.70	1,565.68

This is a continuous case in that the next chapter will use the work you've accomplished here as the basis for recording additional business events. After you've printed the following reports, create a backup of this file and store it on some type of external medium (flash drive, Internet site, CD, disk, etc.). The backup file should be named **Ocean View Flowers Ch 7** for easy identification later. You'll be restoring this file in the next chapter. Print the following with no page numbers and no zero amounts:

a. Standard balance sheet

b. Standard income statement

c. Statement of cash flows

d. Transaction list by date

Comprehensive Problems

Comprehensive Problem 1: SARAH DUNCAN, CPA

Sarah Duncan, CPA, is starting her new practice, as a corporation at One Constellation Road, Vandenberg Village, CA 93436. She'll start effective 9/1/09 and use a 12-month calendar year (January 1–December 31) for financial and tax purposes under the accrual accounting method on a real time basis. She'll be using Peachtree's manual payroll calculations feature to account for herself and her one employee, and her federal tax ID number, EIN, and California EDD number is 574-85-4125. (Be sure to set payroll to manual calculations and perform payroll setup before entering transactions below.) Sarah lives at 259 St. Andrews Way, Vandenberg Village, CA 93436. Her Social Security Number is 574-85-4125 and employee ID = SD. She's married and earns $72,000 per year and has an hourly billing rate of $150. Bob Humphrey, her other employee, lives at 453 Sirius, Vandenberg Village, CA 93436. His Social Security Number is 632-78-1245 and employee ID = BH. He's single and earns $20 per hour and has an hourly billing rate of $100. Her business, of course, is in the Accounting Services area as a certified public accountant and thus she uses the "Accounting Agency" chart of accounts. She does not collect sales tax for her services, nor does she use sales receipts because she invoices her clients for services provided and gives them 15-day credit terms and a standard $10,000 credit limit. She does accept credit card payments and tracks time spent on each client's services for billing purposes. She will have two payroll items: salary and hourly. All payroll costs (salary, wages, and employee and employer payroll taxes) are recorded to a new account called Payroll Expenses (Account ID 77100). In addition to normal payroll taxes, California charges employers a training tax which needs to be set up with the field name: CA_Train. All state taxes, employee and employer, accrue to G/L account 23600 (State payroll taxes payable), while all federal taxes, employee and employer, accrue to G/L account 23400 (Federal payroll taxes payable). She will perform accounting, tax, and consulting services. Sarah and her employee are paid monthly, but file weekly time sheets on Friday of each week. Clients are also invoiced on Fridays of each week once time sheets have been processed. Her vendors usually give her 30-day credit terms. Add the following transactions (*Note:* Be sure to enter these transactions in the proper date period.):

Date	Transaction
9/01/09	Opened a business checking account with a $50,000 deposit as her investment in the business in exchange for common stock.
9/01/09	Purchased a $15,000 copier (Equipment) from Xerox Corporation, completely financed with a note payable for three years with monthly payments of $463.16 due starting 10/1/09.
9/01/09	Signed an engagement letter to perform tax services for Valley Medical Group (ID = VMG), a new client located at 234 Third St., Lompoc, CA 93436.
9/04/09	Purchased furniture and fixtures from Sam Snead (ID = SS), a prior tenant in her rented office space, for $4,000 using Check No. 1001.
9/04/09	Sarah worked five hours each day on 9/2, 9/3, and 9/4 on the Valley Medical tax job and three hours more on each of those days that were not billable related to administrative work. Bob worked six hours each day on 9/3 and 9/4 on the Valley Medical tax job and two more hours on each of those days that were not billable related to staff training. (*Hint:* You'll need to create three activity items: Tax services (ID = TAX), Administrative (ID = AD), and Staff Training (ID = ST).)
9/04/09	Created invoice 5001 to Valley Medical based on time costs incurred using terms net 15.
9/07/09	Wrote Check No. 1002 for $15,000 to Dean Witter (ID = DW) to purchase an investment. Create a new other current assets type of account 14300 called Short-Term Investment.
9/07/09	Wrote Check No. 1003 to Wiser Realty (ID = WR) as payment for the first and last months' rent and security deposit for $9,000 (one-third for rent expense and two-thirds prepaid).
9/08/09	Signed an engagement letter to perform accounting services for Pactuco (ID = P), a new client located at 345 Central Ave., Lompoc, CA 93436.
9/09/09	Signed an engagement letter to perform consulting services for Celite Corporation (ID = C), a new client located at 20 Central Ave., Lompoc, CA 93436.
9/09/09	Received a payment in the amount of $5,000 from Celite Corporation (its Check No. 86546) as an advance on services to be rendered. Sarah anticipates completing services for this client by the end of the month. She then deposited the check into the regular checking account using Deposit Ticket 300.
9/11/09	Sarah worked five hours each day on 9/7, 9/8, and 9/9 on the Valley Medical job, and three more hours on each of those days which were not billable. She also worked eight hours on 9/10 on the Pactuco job performing accounting services and eight hours on 9/11 on the Celite job performing consulting services. Bob worked five hours each day on 9/7, 9/8, and 9/9 on the Valley Medical tax job and three more hours on each of those days which were not billable. He also worked eight hours on 9/10 on the Pactuco job performing accounting services and eight hours on 9/11 on the Celite job performing consulting services. Create two new activities: Accounting Services (ID = A) and Consulting Services (ID = C).
9/11/09	Created invoices. 5002, 5003, and 5004 to Valley Medical, Pactuco, and Celite based on time costs incurred using terms net 15. Apply credits available for Celite.
9/14/09	Signed an engagement letter to perform consulting services for Lompoc Hospital (ID = LH), a new client located at 233 D St., Lompoc, CA 93436.

9/15/09	Sold the short-term investments for $16,500 with the proceeds from the sale remaining in the short-term investment account. (Record the gain of $1,500 as other income and related increase in the short-term investment account via a journal entry.)
9/16/09	Received a payment of $7,200 from Valley Medical Group on its Check No. 2340987 as payment on account and deposited it to the regular checking account using Deposit Ticket 301.
9/18/09	Sarah worked four hours each day from 9/14 to 9/18 on the Pactuco job performing accounting services and two hours on 9/14 and 9/15 on the Celite job performing consulting services. She also worked five hours each on 9/17 and 9/18 on the Lompoc Hospital job performing consulting services. Bob worked eight hours 9/14 on the Valley Medical tax job, eight hours on 9/15 on the Pactuco job performing accounting services, and eight hours each day on 9/16 and 9/17 on the Celite job performing consulting services. On 9/18, he attended four hours of staff training at a local university.
9/18/09	Created invoices 5005, 5006, 5007, and 5008 to Valley Medical, Pactuco, Celite, and Lompoc Hospital based on time costs incurred using terms net 15. Apply credits available for Celite. (Remember: To apply a portion of a previously received deposit, you must create a new receipt for the remainder of the deposit not yet applied.)
9/25/09	Sarah worked six hours each day from 9/21 through 9/24 on the Pactuco accounting engagement and two hours each of those days as nonbillable hours doing administrative work. Bob worked six hours each day from 9/21 through 9/24 and seven hours on 9/25 on the Lompoc Hospital job performing consulting services.
9/25/09	Created invoices 5009 and 50010 to Pactuco and Lompoc Hospital based on time costs incurred using terms net 15.
9/29/09	Wrote Check No. 1004 to Pacific Gas & Electric (ID = PGE) for $400 in utilities expenses.
9/29/09	Wrote Check No. 1005 to Mark Jackson Insurance (ID = MJ) for $8,000 in liability insurance for the year 9/1/09 through 8/31/10. (Record as a prepaid expense!)
9/29/09	Wrote Check No. 1006 to Allan Hancock College (ID = AHC) for $300 in professional development expense for Bob's training.
9/29/09	Check No. 1007 was voided.
9/29/09	Received invoice 20938 from Verizon Wireless (ID = VW) in the amount of $525 for telephone expenses for September. Terms are net 30.
9/29/09	Received invoice 123897 from Staples (ID = S) in the amount of $1,500 for supplies (create a new other current assets account 14600). Terms are net 30.
9/30/09	Paid herself her $6,000 monthly salary and her assistant Bob Humphrey for 123 hours of work at $20 per hour, as shown in Table 7.7.

Requirements

Create a Peachtree file for Sarah Duncan, CPA. Modify the company name to include Ch 7 at the end so that the company name is **Sarah Duncan, CPA Ch 7**. Change the system date to **9/1/09**. Add vendors, inventory items, customers, and employees first and then record business transactions in chronological order (remember dates are in the month of September 2009). After you've printed the following reports (with no page numbers and no zero amounts), create a backup of this file and store it on some type of external medium (flash drive, Internet site, CD, disk, etc.). The backup file should be named **Sarah Duncan, CPA Ch 7** for easy identification later.

Pay/Tax/Withholding	Duncan	Humphrey
Hours	n/a	123
Rate	n/a	20.00
Check Number	1008	1009
Gross Pay	6,000.00	2,460.00
Federal Withholding	−770.50	−305.05
Social Security Employee	−372.00	−152.52
Medicare Employee	−87.00	−35.67
CA Withholding	−231.40	−77.98
CA Disability	−4.80	−1.97
Social Security Employer	372.00	152.52
Medicare Company	87.00	35.67
Federal Unemployment	48.00	19.68
CA Unemployment	204.00	83.64
CA Training Tax	6.00	2.46
Check Amount	4,534.30	1,886.81

Table 7.7

Earnings Information
for Sarah Duncan, CPA

a. Customer ledgers

b. Vendor ledgers

c. Employee list

d. Item list

e. Standard balance sheet

f. Standard income statement

g. Statement of cash flows

h. Find transactions report

merchandising

Comprehensive Problem 2: PACIFIC BREW INC.

Pacific Brew Inc. was incorporated January 1, 2008, upon the issuance of 50,000 shares of $1 par value common stock for $50,000 worth of net assets (orginally belonging to Michael Patrick as a sole proprietor). Thus, beginning assets, liabilities, and equity are:

Account	Description	Debits	Credits
1020	Checking Account	47,500	
1100	Accounts Receivable	250	
1200	Inventory	2,750	
2000	Accounts Payable		500
3930	Common Stock		50,000

The company is located at 500 West Ocean, Arcata, CA 95521. Michael Patrick, as president, oversees this beer distributor's operations (use the simplified chart of accounts for a distribution company). The company will use a calendar year using 12-month periods, has a federal employer ID number of 77-1357465, and plans to use Peachtree's inventory (average costing method), purchase orders, and manual payroll features on a real time basis using the accrual method of accounting. The company does not collect sales taxes. Customers are given a $10,000 credit limit and 30-day terms. Vendors typically give the company 30-day terms as well and a $30,000 credit limit.

In addition to distributing beer, Pacific Brew provides consulting services to customers on bar operations, menu plans, and beverage selection. These services are billed to customers at the rate of $85 per hour and are recorded in an income account called other income. (*Hint:* Create a new item ID = C, description = Consulting, class = Service.)

Pacific has two other employees, as shown below. Federal withholding, unemployment, Social Security, and Medicare are paid to the U.S. Treasury, while California withholding, unemployment, employee disability, and employee training tax (which needs to be set up with the field name: CA_Train) are paid to the EDD (Employment Development Department). Payroll is paid semimonthly with gross pay recorded to a new account 6090 (Salaries & Wages Expense). State taxes accrue to account 2350 (State Payroll Taxes Payable) and federal payroll taxes accrue to account 2330 (Federal Payroll Taxes Payable). All payroll taxes are calculated manually. Vendors, inventory items, customers, and employees are listed below.

Vendors

Name	Mad River	Lost Coast	JD Salinger (landlord)	Humboldt
Vendor ID	MR	LC	JD	H
Address	195 Taylor Way	123 West Third St.	101 Market St.	865 10th St.
City	Blue Lake	Eureka	San Francisco	Arcata
State	CA	CA	CA	CA
Zip	95525	95501	94102	95521
Phone	707-555-4151	707-555-4484	415-555-6141	707-555-2739
Beg Bal	$500 (MR2800)	$0	$0	$0

Inventory

Item ID	Description	Cost	Price	Beginning Quantity
302	Mad River Pale Ale	5.00	6.00	100
303	Mad River Stout	6.00	7.00	125
304	Mad River Amber Ale	4.00	5.00	100
305	Mad River Porter	5.50	6.50	200
402	Lost Coast Pale Ale	5.25	6.25	0
403	Lost Coast Stout	6.25	7.25	0
404	Lost Coast Amber Ale	4.25	5.25	0
502	Humboldt Pale Ale	5.50	6.50	0
506	Humboldt IPA	6.50	7.50	0
507	Humboldt Red Nectar	7.00	8.00	0

Customers

Name	Avalon Bistro	Hole in the Wall	Ocean Grove
ID	AB	HW	OG
Address	1080 3rd St	590 G St.	570 Ewing St.
City	Arcata	Arcata	Trinidad
State	CA	CA	CA
Zip	95521	95521	95570
Phone	707-555-0500	707-555-7407	707-555-5431
Beg Bal	$250	$0	$0

Name	River House	Michael's Brew House	Bon Jovi's
ID	RH	MB	BJ
Address	222 Weller St.	2198 Union St.	4257 Petaluma Hill
City	Petaluma	San Francisco	Santa Rosa
State	CA	CA	CA
Zip	95404	94123	95404
Phone	707-555-0123	415-555-9874	707-555-5634
Beg Bal	$0	$0	$0

Employees

Name	Michael Patrick	Shawn Lopez	Emilio Duarte
ID	MP	SL	ED
Address	333 Spring Rd.	234 University Dr.	23 Palm Dr. #23
City	Arcata	Arcata	Arcata
State	CA	CA	CA
Zip	95521	95521	95521
Phone	707-555-9847	707-555-1297	707-555-6655
SS#	655-85-1253	702-54-8746	012-58-4654
Earnings	Salary—$2083.33	Wages—$12/hour	Wages—$11/hour
Filing Status	Married	Single	Single

Chronological List of Business Transactions

Date	Transaction
12/31/07	Be sure you've recorded beginning balances as per above.
1/04/08	Using Purchase Order No. 1001, ordered 500 each of Item 302, 303, 304, and 305 for immediate delivery. Terms: due on receipt, from Mad River. (Change terms for this vendor.)
1/04/08	Using Purchase Order No. 1002, ordered 400 each of Item 502, 506, and 507 for immediate delivery. Terms: due on receipt, from Humboldt.
1/04/08	Using Purchase Order No. 1003, ordered 300 each of Item 402, 403, and 404 for immediate delivery on net 30-day terms, from Lost Coast.
1/07/08	Rented a warehouse from JD Salinger, landlord, for $2,500 per month by paying first and last month's rent with Check No. 101 for $5,000.
1/07/08	Purchased furniture and office equipment from JD Salinger for $8,000 with Check No. 102 (record to Property & Equipment Account 1500).
1/09/08	Borrowed $40,000 from Wells Fargo Bank (ID = WF) as a long-term note payable due in three years.

1/10/08   Invested $30,000 in a Wells Fargo Bank certificate of deposit for 60 days with Check No. 103. (Create a new cash type account, ID = 1050, description = Certificates of Deposit.)

1/10/08   Purchased several computer systems and printers (classified as Property & Equipment). Check No. 104 was written for $10,200 to West Coast Computer Supply (ID = WCCS) to purchase the systems.

1/11/08   Received all items ordered on Purchase Order No. 1001 to Mad River. The full amount ($10,250) was paid at purchase based on invoice MR2987, reference Check No. 105.

1/11/08   Provided 50 hours of consulting services on Sales Receipt 5001 to Michael's Brew House. A check in the amount of $4,250 was deposited into the checking account with Deposit Ticket A4001 that same day.

1/14/08   Received all items ordered on Purchase Order No. 1002 to Humboldt. The full amount ($7,600) was paid at purchase based on invoice H2098, reference Check No. 106.

1/14/08   Received and shipped an order (Sales Receipt 5002) to Bon Jovi's for 25 units of Item 305, 30 units of Item 506, and 50 units of Item 507. Check payment of $787.50 was deposited into the checking account that same day with Deposit Ticket A4002.

1/15/08   Provided 60 hours of consulting services (Sales Receipt 5003) to River House. Payment of $5,100 was deposited into the checking account that same day with Deposit Ticket A4003.

1/16/08   Received and shipped an order (Sales Receipt 5004) to Ocean Grove for 30 units of Item 304, 40 units of Item 302, and 50 units of Item 502. VISA credit card payment of $715 was deposited into the checking account that same day with Deposit Ticket A4004.

1/16/08   Received and shipped an order (Sales Receipt 5005) to Avalon Bistro for 40 units of Item 302, 50 units of Item 507, and 35 units of Item 506. Check payment of $902.50 was deposited into the checking account that same day with Deposit Ticket A4005.

1/16/08   Received and shipped an order (Sales Receipt 5006) to Michael's Brew House for 100 each of Items 302, 305, and 506. MasterCard payment of $2,000 was deposited into the checking account that same day with Deposit Ticket A4006.

1/16/08   Paid employees for the period ended 1/16/08. See tax information in Table 7.8.

Pay/Tax/Withholding	Duarte	Lopez	Patrick
Check	107	108	109
Hours Worked	80	75	n/a
Gross Pay	880.00	900.00	2,083.33
Federal Withholding	−120.56	−123.30	−285.42
Social Security Employee	−54.56	−55.80	−129.17
Medicare Employee	−12.76	−13.05	−30.21
CA—Withholding	−48.40	−49.50	−114.58
CA—Disability	−4.40	−4.50	−10.42
Social Security Company	54.56	55.80	129.17
Medicare Company	12.76	13.05	30.21
Federal Unemployment	7.04	7.20	16.67
CA—Unemployment Company	26.40	27.00	62.50
CA—Employment Training Tax	0.88	0.90	2.08
Check Amount	639.32	653.85	1,513.53

Table 7.8

Earnings Information for Pacific Brew Inc.

Requirements

Create a Peachtree file for Pacific Brew. Modify the company name to include Ch 7 at the end so that the company name is **Pacific Brew Ch 7**. Change the system date to **1/1/08**. Add vendors, inventory items, customers, and employees first and then record business transactions in chronological order (remember dates are in the month of January 2008). After you've printed the following reports (with no page numbers and no zero amounts), create a backup of this file and store it on some type of external medium (flash drive, Internet site, CD, disk, etc.). The backup file should be named **Pacific Brew Ch 7** for easy identification later. You'll be restoring this file in Chapter 11.

    a. Customer ledgers

    b. Vendor ledgers

    c. Employee list

    d. Item list

    e. Standard balance sheet

    f. Standard income statement

    g. Statement of cash flows

    h. Find transactions report

merchandising

Comprehensive Problem 3: SUNSET SPAS INC.

Sunset Spas Inc. was incorporated January 1, 2007, upon the issuance of 10,000 shares of $2 par value common stock for $100,000. Located at 300 West Street, Del Mar, CA 92014, Bryan Christopher, president, will oversee this spa retailer's operation (use the Retail Company Extensive Version chart of accounts). The company will follow accrual accounting, use real time posting, have 12 monthly accounting periods, and have a federal employer ID number of 77-9851247 and a California EDD number of 012-3435-8. It plans to use Peachtree's inventory, purchase orders, and payroll features. The following tables list the suppliers it purchases from, the items it intends to carry in inventory, and the customers it has lined up. The customers' billing and shipping addresses are the same. The company collects 7.75% sales tax (Sales Tax Code = TAX, description = CA Sales Tax) which is remitted to one tax authority (ID = SBE, description = Sales Tax) on all spa sales that are credited to account 23100 (Sales Tax Payable). Payments are made quarterly to the California State Board of Equalization (ID = CSBE). No sales tax is collected on installation services.

In addition to selling spas, Sunset Spas also provides consulting and installation services to customers. Consulting services are billed to customers at the rate of $80 per hour, while installation services are billed to customers at the rate of $75 per hour, and both are recorded in an income account 40200 called Sales: Services. Spa sales are recorded in an income account 40000 titled Sales: Merchandise. The company uses the average inventory cost method. All customers currently have credit terms of "due on receipt." Vendors typically require payment on delivery.

Sunset also employs two other people, as shown below. Federal withholding, federal unemployment (FUTA), Social Security, and Medicare are paid to the U.S. Treasury (ID − UST), while California withholding, state unemployment (SUTA), employee disability, and employee training tax (CA_Train) are paid to the Employment Development Department (ID = EDD). Payroll is paid semimonthly with employees paid a salary recorded to account 77000 and employees paid hourly wages recorded to account 77500. State taxes accrue to account 23600 (State Payroll Taxes Payable), and federal payroll taxes accrue to account 23400 (Federal Payroll Taxes Payable). All payroll taxes are calculated manually.

Vendors

Name	Sundance Spas	Cal Spas
ID	SS	CS
Address	14525 Monte Vista Ave.	1462 East Ninth Street
City	Chino	Pomona
State	CA	CA
Zip	91710	91766
Phone	909-614-0679	909-623-8781

Customers

Name	J's Landscaping	Marriott Hotels	Pam's Designs
ID	J	MH	PD
Address	12 Bones Way	97444 Miramar	5144 Union
City	San Diego	San Diego	San Diego
State	CA	CA	CA
Zip	92354	92145	92129
Phone	858-555-1348	858-555-7407	707-555-5748

Employees

Name	Bryan Christopher	Loriel Sanchez	Sharon Lee
ID	BC	LS	SL
Address	12 Mesa Way	2342 Court	323 Ridgefield Pl.
City	Del Mar	Del Mar	Del Mar
State	CA	CA	CA
Zip	92014	92014	92014
Phone	858-555-1264	858-555-3365	858-555-9874
SS#	556-95-4789	475-54-8746	125-58-8452
Earnings	Salary — $2,500	Wages — $13/hr	Wages — $12/hr
Filing Status	Married (one income)	Single (one income)	Single

Inventory Items

ID	Description	Vendor	Cost	Price
201	Maxus	Sundance	$5,000	$7,000
202	Optima	Sundance	$6,000	$8,000
203	Cameo	Sundance	$7,000	$9,000
301	Galaxy	Cal Spas	$4,500	$6,500
302	Ultimate	Cal Spas	$5,500	$7,500
303	Aqua	Cal Spas	$7,500	$9,500
C	Consulting			$80/hour
I	Installation			$75/hour

Chronological List of Business Transactions

Date	Transaction
1/03/07	Sold 10,000 shares of no-par common stock for $100,000 cash to various shareholders. Deposited these funds into the regular checking account.
1/04/07	Borrowed $200,000 from Hacienda Bank as a long-term note payable due in three years. The money was deposited into the company's regular checking account.
1/05/07	Using Purchase Order No. 5001, ordered 10 each of Items 201, 202, and 203 for immediate delivery. Terms: Net due, from Sundance Spas.
1/05/07	Using Purchase Order No. 5002, ordered five each of Items 301, 302, and 303 for immediate delivery. Terms: Net due, from Cal Spas.
1/08/07	Rented a retail store front from K Realty (ID = K), landlord, for $3,000 per month by paying first month's rent and a deposit with Check No. 101 for $6,000. This is a long-term lease for five years.
1/08/07	Purchased shelving, desks, and office equipment from Office Max (ID = OM) for $8,000 with Check No. 102. (Shelving and desks = $4,500, equipment = $3,500)
1/09/07	Invested $30,000 in a short-term investment with Poole Investments (ID = PI) with Check No. 103. Create a new other current assets account 14800 called Short-Term Investments.
1/10/07	Purchased several computer systems and printers (classified as equipment). Check No. 104 was written for $8,900 to Coast Computer Supply (ID = CCS) to purchase the systems.
1/11/07	Received all items ordered on Purchase No. Order 5001 from Sundance Spas. Received and paid invoice 98789 with Check No. 105 for $180,000.
1/11/07	Provided 10 hours of consulting to J's Landscape on Sales Receipt 7001. Consulting services are taxable. Payment of $862 was deposited into the bank that same day with Deposit Ticket 901. (*Hint:* Be sure consulting was already set up as a service item (ID = C) that is billed at $80 per hour, is taxable, and is recorded into an income account 40200 Sales: Services.)
1/12/07	Received all items ordered on Purchase Order No. 5002 from Cal Spas. Received and paid invoice A9892 with Check No. 106 for $87,500.
1/15/07	Received an order and delivered three Item 301, one Item 202, and one Item 303 to Pam's Design on Sales Receipt 7002. Payment of $39,867.50 was deposited into the checking account with Deposit Ticket 902.
1/15/07	Provided eight hours of consulting services on Sales Receipt 7003 to Marriott. Payment of $689.60 was deposited into the checking account that same day with Deposit Ticket 903.

1/16/07 Received an order and delivered three Item 201 and two Item 203 to J's Landscape on Sales Receipt 7004. Payment of $42,022.50 was deposited into the checking account that same day with Deposit Ticket 904.

1/16/07 Received a deposit from Marriott Hotels for future consulting services of $5,000, which was deposited into the checking account that same day with Deposit Ticket 905. Reference its Check No. 3098.

1/16/07 Paid employees. Sanchez worked 75 hours and Lee worked 83 hours during the period ended 1/16/07. See tax information in Table 7.9.

Pay/Tax/Withholding	Christopher	Sanchez	Lee	**Table 7.9**
Check	107	108	109	Earnings Information for
Hours	n/a	75	83	Sunset Spas
Rate	2,500.00	13.00	12.00	
Gross Pay	2,500.00	975.00	996.00	
Federal Withholding	−342.50	−133.58	−136.45	
Social Security Employee	−155.00	−60.45	−61.75	
Medicare Employee	−36.25	−14.14	−14.44	
CA—Withholding	−137.50	−53.63	−54.78	
CA—Disability	−12.50	−4.88	−4.98	
Social Security Employer	155.00	60.45	61.75	
Medicare Company	36.25	14.14	14.44	
Federal Unemployment	20.00	7.80	7.97	
CA—Unemployment	6.25	2.44	2.49	
CA—Employment Training Tax	2.50	0.98	1.00	
Check Amount	1,816.25	708.32	723.60	

Requirements

Create a Peachtree file for Sunset Spas. Modify the company name to include Ch 7 at the end so that the company name is **Sunset Spas Ch 7**. Change the system date to **1/1/07**. Add vendors, inventory items, customers, and employees first and then record business transactions in chronological order (remember dates are in the month of January 2007). After you've printed the following reports (with no page numbers and no zero amounts), create a backup of this file and store it on some type of external medium (flash drive, Internet site, CD, disk, etc.). The backup file should be named **Sunset Spas Ch 7** for easy identification later. You'll be restoring this file in Chapter 11.

   a. Customer ledgers

   b. Vendor ledgers

   c. Employee list

   d. Item list

e. Standard balance sheet

f. Standard income statement

g. Statement of cash flows

h. Find transactions report

Additional Business Activities

Learning Objectives

In this chapter, you will:

- Record additional business transactions classified as financing activities, such as repayment of loans.
- Record additional business transactions classified as investing activities, such as selling short-term investments for a gain or loss.
- Record additional business transactions classified as operating activities, such as purchasing and selling inventory on account.
- Record business transactions classified as noncash investing and financing activities, such as the purchase of equipment with long-term debt.

Case: **Wild Water Sports, Inc.**

You and Karen have finished entering business events which took place during the months of January and February and are ready to begin recording transactions for March. Karen explains that so far the transactions entered have involved cash-related financing activities such as owner contributions; cash-related investing activities such as equipment purchases; and cash-related operating activities such as creating purchase orders, receipt of customer payments, cash sales, making deposits, receiving inventory, payment of purchases, invoicing time and costs, payment of expenses, accounting for employees' time, and payment of payroll.

In March and April, the company had similar business events to record in addition to some new ones. During these months, the company entered into some additional cash-related financing activities such as the payment of loans, additional cash-related investing activities such as the sale of short-term investments, and additional cash-related operating activities such as the purchase and sale of inventory on account and the related payment and receipt of those transactions. Further, the company entered into some noncash investing and financing activities when it purchased some equipment with long-term debt.

Karen suggests that you work through these transactions for March, paying particular attention to those you haven't experienced yet.

Recording Additional Financing Activities

You recall that as of December 31, 2006, the company had a long-term liability of $383,800. Then in January, the company borrowed an additional $250,000 from Bank of Florida, which was due in five years and carried a 5% interest cost.

"When do we make payments on those loans?" you ask.

"Our agreement on the $250,000 loan with Bank of Florida called for monthly payments of $4,717.81 beginning February 4," Karen answers. "I was so busy with Peachtree and the business that I completely forgot! I wrote two checks yesterday to cover our first two payments, and the bank has been kind enough to waive the late payment fee."

The company also borrowed an additional $50,000 from Citibank on February 5. Payments on that loan are due annually. The loan payable of $383,800 has payments due July 1 of every year.

To record the checks written to make payment on the Bank of Florida loan:

1 Start the Peachtree program.

2 Restore the **Wild Water Sports, Inc 8** file from your Data Files CD or download it from the Internet. See "Data Files CD" in Chapter 1 if you need more information.

3 Set the system date to **3/1/07** and the accounting period to **Period 3**.

4 Click **Write Checks** from the Banking center and then select **New Check**. The Write Checks window appears with your current system date.

5 Type **1029** as the Check Number. The bank had provided a loan amortization schedule as shown in Figure 8.1.

6 Click the magnifying glass in the Vendor ID text box and then click **New**.

7 Type **11025** as the new Vendor ID, **Bank of Florida** as the name and 2700 – **Long-Term Debt-Noncurrent** as the purchase default expense account, click **Save**, and then click **Close**.

8 Select **11025** as the Vendor ID in the Write Checks window for your Check No. 1029.

Month	Payment	Interest	Principle	Balance
				$250,000.00
1	$4,717.81	$1,041.67	$3,676.14	$246,323.86
2	$4,717.81	$1,026.35	$3,691.46	$242,632.40
3	$4,717.81	$1,010.97	$3,706.84	$238,925.56
4	$4,717.81	$ 995.52	$3,722.29	$235,203.27
5	$4,717.81	$ 980.01	$3,737.79	$231,465.48
6	$4,717.81	$ 964.44	$3,753.37	$227,712.11
7	$4,717.81	$ 948.80	$3,769.01	$223,943.10
8	$4,717.81	$ 933.10	$3,784.71	$220,158.39
9	$4,717.81	$ 917.33	$3,800.48	$216,357.91
10	$4,717.81	$ 901.49	$3,816.32	$212,541.59
11	$4,717.81	$ 885.59	$3,832.22	$208,709.37
12	$4,717.81	$ 869.62	$3,848.19	$204,861.19

Figure 8.1

Loan Amortization Schedule

9 Type **4717.81** as the check amount.

10 Click the **Split** button in the lower left-hand corner of the check.

11 Type **2700** as the Account No. and then press [**Tab**] two times.

12 Type **3676.14** as the new amount for this row.

13 Press [**Tab**] two times again to move to the beginning of the next row and the Account No. column.

14 Click the magnifying glass in this text box and then click **New** to open the Maintain Chart of Accounts window.

15 Type **6725** as the new Account ID and type **Interest Expense** as the Description.

16 Select **Expenses** from the Account Type drop-down list.

17 Click **Save** and then click **Close** to close the Maintain Chart of Accounts window.

18 Press [**Tab**] two times. Your Split Transaction window should look like Figure 8.2.

Figure 8.2

Splitting Transactions
Between Accounts

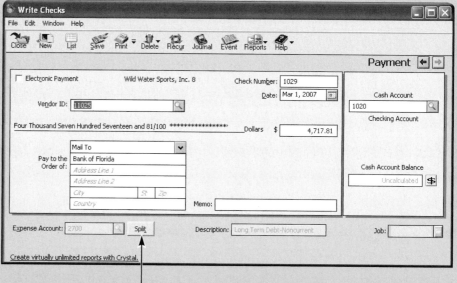

19 Click **OK** to close the Split Transaction window. Your check should look like Figure 8.3.

Figure 8.3

Check to Pay Installment
on Long-Term Debt

If your check affects multiple accounts you would click this
Split button to reveal the Split Transactions window

20 Click **Save** to record the check.

21 Using the amortization schedule above, enter information for Check No. 1030, on the same date, to record the second payment using interest expense and principle information provided. (*Note*: This transaction will have the same check amount but different interest expense and debt reduction.)

22 Click **Save** and then **Close** to record the check.

With the addition of a new owner, and the related funds received from their investment, the company decided to pay down the older, higher interest 10% debt with Bank of Orlando. It made a payment of $387,690.58, which accounted for interest at 10% for 37 days ($3,890.58), and paid the principle balance due of $383,800. Before the company made this payment, it decided to transfer $300,000 from its short-term investment account with ETrade to its Bank of Florida checking account. Karen suggests you try recording this transfer made with ETrade Check No. 101 and the loan payment that was made on 3/6 with Check No. 1031.

To record the electronic transfer of funds and record payment on a loan:

1 Click **Write Checks** from the Banking center and then select **New Check**. The Write Checks window appears with your current system date. Note that the default Cash Account is 1020 (Checking Account).

2 Click the magnifying glass in the Cash Account text box and select **1030 Short-Term Investments**.

3 Type **101** as the Check Number and **3/6/07** as the date.

4 Select **11025 – Bank of Florida** as the Vendor ID.

5 Type **300000** as the check amount.

6 Select **1020** as the Expense Account. (In reality, this is not an expense account but the account we want to record this transaction to.) Your check should look like Figure 8.4.

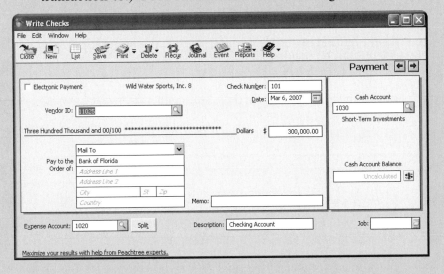

Figure 8.4

Check to Transfer Funds from Short-Term Investments to Checking

7 Click **Save**.

8 Click the magnifying glass in the Cash Account text box and select **1020 Checking Account**.

9 Type **1031** as the Check Number and **3/6/07** as the date.

10 Create a new vendor with ID 11030, Bank of Orlando, default Expense Acct 2700.

11 Select **11030 – Bank of Orlando** as the Vendor ID.

12 Type **387690.58** as the check amount.

13 Click the **Split** button in the lower left-hand corner of the check.

14 Type **2700** as the Account No. and then press [**Tab**] two times.

15 Type **383800** as the new amount for this row.

16 Press [**Tab**] two times again to move to the beginning of the next row and the Account No. column.

17 Type **6725** as the Account No. and then press [**Tab**] two times.

18 Type **3890.58** as the new amount for this row. Your Split Transaction window should look like Figure 8.5.

Figure 8.5

Split of Bank of Orlando Debt Repayment

Select Account No. here

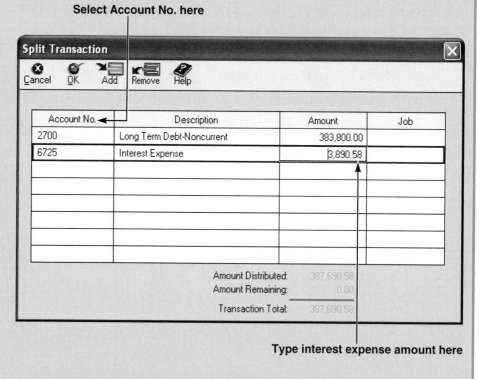

Type interest expense amount here

19 Click **OK** to close the Split Transaction window.

20 Click **Save** and then click **Close**.

You have now recorded payments of long-term debt. Now it's time to look at some additional investing activities.

Recording Additional Investing Activities

You may recall from your accounting courses that investing activities generally result in the acquisition of noncurrent assets from buying or selling investment securities or productive equipment. Wild Water Sports engaged in several investing activities that you and Karen need to record in March. The company made some additional short-term investments, and it sold previously purchased investment securities for a profit.

In February, Wild Water Sports made an investment with ETrade for $75,000. On March 7, it sold that investment for a profit of $3,000. All funds were retained with ETrade. In addition, it used $35,000 of those money market funds to purchase stock in Apple Computer, again as a short-term investment.

"These types of transactions are best recorded with a general journal entry," Karen says. "Although the $3,000 gain is a receipt of cash, Peachtree's receipts process is reserved for prepayments, cash sales of products or services, or payments on account."

"So is this just like the recording of loan or stock sale proceeds?" you ask.

"Exactly," Karen answers.

To record short-term investment activity:

1 Click **General Journal Entry** from the Company center.

2 Type **3/7/07** as the date and type **5** as the Reference.

3 Select **1030** as the first GL Account, type **Sale of investments for a gain** as the Description, and then type **3000** as the Debit amount.

4 Select **7100** as the second GL Account, leave **Sale of investments for a gain** in the Description, and then type **3000** as the Credit amount.

5 Click **Save** and then click **Close**.

6 Click **Account Register** from the Banking center.

7 Change the Cash Account to **1030 Short-Term Investments**.

8 Note that the transaction you just recorded is not shown. That transaction was recorded on 3/7/07, but your system date is 3/1/07. Thus, Peachtree doesn't show you any transactions after that date.

9 Close the Account Register window.

10 Change the system date to **3/31/07**.

11 Reopen the Account Register window and note how the 3/7/07 transaction is now shown as in Figure 8.6.

Figure 8.6

Account Register

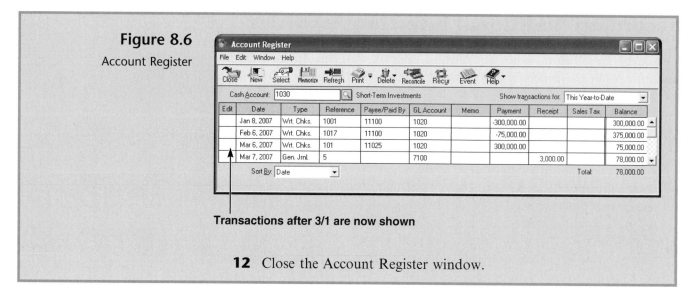

Transactions after 3/1 are now shown

12 Close the Account Register window.

"Why didn't we record the Apple Computer stock purchase in our records?" you ask.

"Well, remember that the funds used to purchase this stock were already in our short-term investment account," Karen answers. "Thus, this is just a reallocation of our short-term investment from a money market category to a stock category. We, as shareholders, consider both the money market funds and the stock investment to be short-term investments; thus, we don't differentiate them in the accounting records."

Recording Additional Operating Activities

Donna has been working hard establishing credit with the company's suppliers. Recently, she's convinced Malibu, MB Sports, and Tige to give Wild Water 15-day credit terms with a credit limit of $70,000. Several purchase orders have been created to acquire more inventory for the company's showroom and to purchase inventory ordered by some new customers.

"Now that we have some credit with our suppliers, we'll be able to offer credit to some of our better customers," Karen points out. Now that the company has secured a 15-day credit line with Malibu, MB, and Tige, vendor information in Peachtree needs to be updated. Karen demonstrates the process of modifying vendor information for terms.

To update vendor records for changes in terms:

1 Click the **Vendors** button in the Vendors & Purchases center and then click **View and Edit Vendors**.

2 Double-click **Malibu Boats** to open the Edit Vendor window.

3 Click the **Purchase Defaults** tab.

4 Click the **Terms** arrow.

5 Uncheck Use Standard Terms, type **15** in the Net due in text box, and then type **70000** as the credit limit. See Figure 8.7.

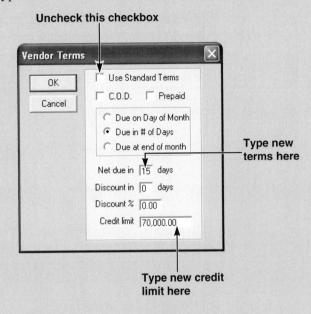

Figure 8.7
Adjusting Vendor Terms

6 Click **OK** to save this change in credit terms and then click **Save** to save this vendor's updated information.

7 Perform this same process for MB Sports and Tige.

8 Close all open windows.

Karen suggests that you now input the purchase orders created in March and the related bills received from suppliers.

To record purchase orders for the month of March:

1 Click the **Vendors** button in the Vendors & Purchases center and then click **View and Edit Vendors**.

2 Double-click **Malibu Boats** to open the Maintain Vendor window.

3 Type **1 Malibu Ct., Merced, CA 95340** as this vendor's address and then click **Save**.

4 Close the Maintain Vendors and Vendor List windows.

5 Click the **Purchase Order** from the Vendors & Purchases center and then select **New Purchase Order**.

6 Enter purchase order information as shown in Figure 8.8.

Figure 8.8

Malibu Purchase
Order No. 4005

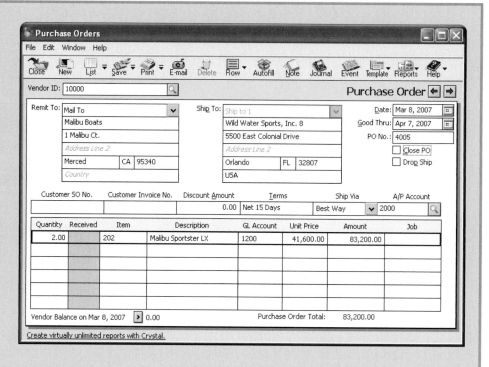

7   Click **Save**.

8   Create Purchase Order No. 4006 to Tige Boats on 3/12/07 ordering 1 Tige 22v (301) and 1 Tige 24v (a new item with ID 302, a cost of $70,000, and a sales price of $87,500 using the average cost method and cost of goods sold and income accounts as all other boats).

9   Create Purchase Order No. 4007 to MB Sports on 3/12/07 ordering 1 MB 220V (a new item with ID 402, a cost of $52,000, and a sales price of $65,000 using the same cost method and a cost of goods sold and income accounts as all other boats) for a new customer (ID 50010, Spirit Adventures, 500 Butterfly Lake Rd., Fort Lauderdale, FL 33308 using the standard terms and credit).

10   Close all windows.

Some of the boats ordered on the purchase orders entered above were received in the month of March. Since these were all ordered on account, Peachtree requires that you record the receipt of inventory at the same time you record the receipt of the bill invoicing the company for payment. In addition, boats ordered with Purchase Order No. 4004 issued in February were received in March.

To record receipt of inventory and bill:

1 Click **Receive Inventory** from the Inventory & Services center and then select **Receive Inventory**.

2 Select **10000** as the Vendor ID.

3 Select Purchase Order No. **4004** from the Apply to Purchase Order No. drop-down list.

4 Type **3/6/07** as the date.

5 Type **MB23987** as the Invoice No.

6 Type **1** in the Received column for both boats ordered.

7 Select **Best Way** from the Ship Via drop-down list and then click **Save.**

8 Select **10000** as the Vendor ID.

9 Select Purchase Order No. **4005** from the Apply to Purchase Order No. drop-down list.

10 Type **3/15/07** as the date.

11 Type **MB24002** as the Invoice No.

12 Type **2** in the Received column.

13 Select **Best Way** from the Ship Via drop-down list and then click **Save.**

14 Select **10200** as the Vendor ID.

15 Select Purchase Order No. **4006** from the Apply to Purchase Order No. drop-down list.

16 Type **3/28/07** as the date.

17 Type **T02398** as the Invoice No.

18 Type **1** in the Received column for both boats ordered.

19 Select **Best Way** from the Ship Via drop-down list, click **Save,** and then click **Close.**

Two service-related jobs (3006 and 3007) were started and completed in the month of March. Both were to customers who were invoiced for the work and given 15-day credit terms. Karen explains that in both of these cases, jobs need to be created, time recorded, and invoices generated. First off, she suggests that you update credit terms for two existing customers.

To update customer terms and address:

1 Click **Customers & Sales**, click **Customers**, and then select **View and Edit Customers**.

2 Double-click **Buena Vista Water Sports**.

3 Type **100 Disney Way, Orlando, FL, 31310** as the customer's address.

4 Click the **Terms and Credit** tab.

5 Change the Terms to Net due in 15 days, click **Save**, and then click **Close**.

6 Change the Terms to Net due in 15 days for Performance Rentals as well. Then change its credit limit to $10,000.

7 Click **Save** and then click **Close**.

8 Close the Customer List as well.

Next, you need to create the jobs (for tracking purposes) and assign jobs to customers.

To create new jobs:

1 Click **Jobs** and then select **New Job**.

2 Type **3006** as the Job ID and then type or select **50002** in the For Customer text box.

3 Click **Save**.

4 Create a second new job 3007 for customer 50006.

5 Close the Maintain Jobs window.

Karen explains that as employees work on various jobs, time must be entered and assigned to a job or customer, and an activity must always be specified.

To enter employee time on jobs:

1 Open the Employees & Payroll center, click **Time and Expense Tickets**, and then select **New Time Ticket**.

2 Select **003** Ryder Zacovic as the employee name.

3 Click the **Weekly** tab.

4 Type **3/12/07** in the Week Including text box and then press [**Tab**] two times.

5   Enter the information shown in Figure 8.9.

Select Employee 003

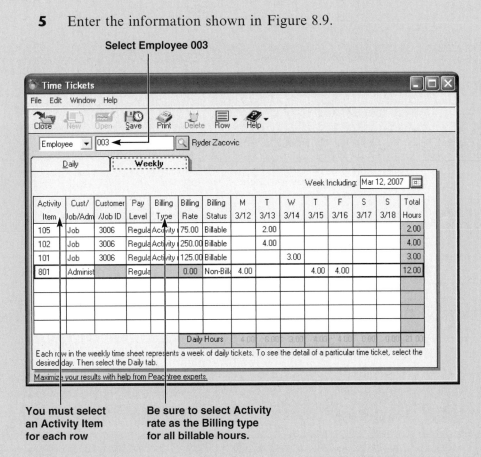

You must select
an Activity Item
for each row

Be sure to select Activity
rate as the Billing type
for all billable hours.

Figure 8.9

Ryder Zacovic Time Tickets
for the Week Including
3/12/07

6   Click **Save**.

7   Enter the information shown in Figure 8.10.

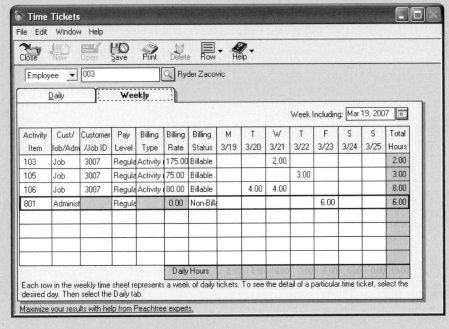

Figure 8.10

Ryder Zacovic Time Tickets
for the Week Including
3/19/07

8   Click **Save** and then **Close**.

"Now that the jobs are complete and time has been charged to a job, it's time to bill the customer for work performed and parts used," Karen explains.

"Do we use sales orders for service activities?" you ask.

"I guess we can," Karen responds. "But for now I just use sales orders to record customer orders for boats to be delivered in the future."

To invoice customers for job-related work:

1 Open the Customers & Sales center.

2 Click **Sales Invoices** and then select **New Sales Invoice**.

3 Select **50002** Buena Vista Water Sports from the Customer ID list.

4 Type **3/16/07** as the invoice date.

5 Type **10010** as the invoice number.

6 Click the **Apply Tickets/Expenses** button.

7 Check the **Use** check box for all items presented and then select the **Use Item Description for Invoicing** option button as shown in Figure 8.11.

Figure 8.11

Applying Tickets to an Invoice

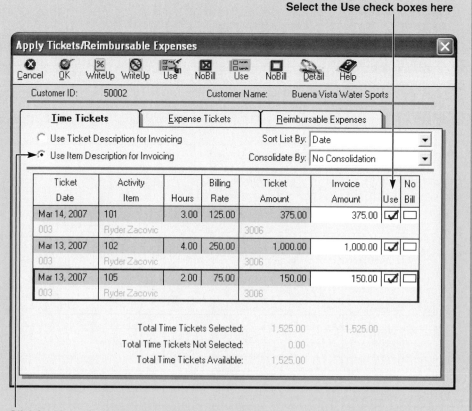

Select the Use check boxes here

Click in this option button

8 Click **OK** to close the window and apply information to the invoice.

9 Add the Ship Via information and tune-up parts, engine oil, air filter, and oil filter to the invoice as shown in Figure 8.12.

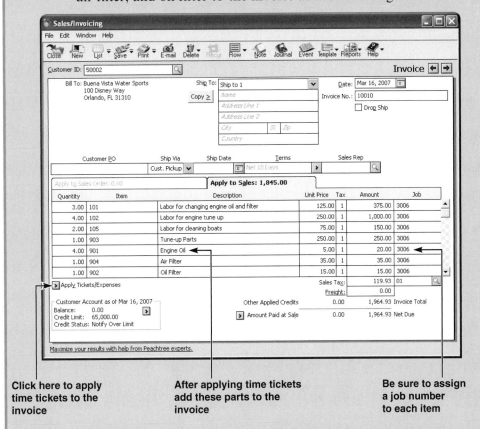

Figure 8.12

Invoice for Service and Parts

Click here to apply time tickets to the invoice

After applying time tickets add these parts to the invoice

Be sure to assign a job number to each item

Trouble? You may have to increase the window size to view all of the line items for this invoice.

10 Click **Save**.

11 Select **50006** Performance Rentals from the Customer ID list.

12 Type **3/23/07** as the invoice date.

13 Type **10008** as the invoice number.

14 Click the **Apply Tickets/Expenses** button.

15 Check the **Use** check box for all items presented and then select **Activity Item** from the Consolidate By list as shown in Figure 8.13.

16 Click **OK** to accept this time ticket application.

Figure 8.13

Apply Time Tickets

Select Activity Item as the Consolidate By option

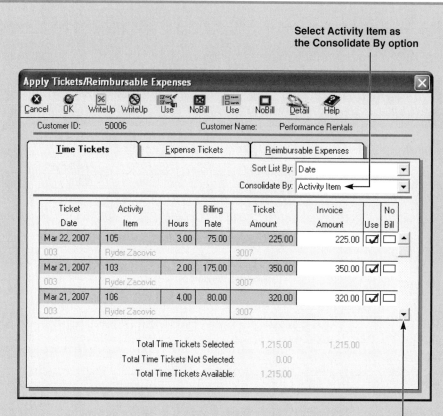

Be sure to select all four time tickets for this employee that applies to this job. Scroll down the window to see 1 additional time ticket not shown here.

17 Select **01** as the Sales Tax code and then select **Cust. Pickup** from the Ship Via list. Your invoice should look like Figure 8.14.

Figure 8.14

Performance Rentals Invoice 10008

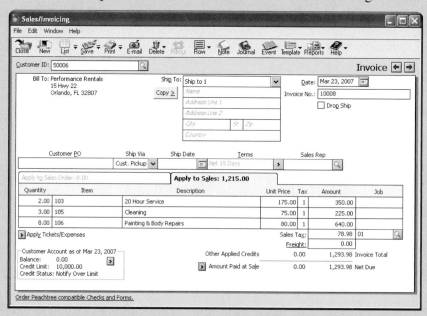

18 Click **Save** and then click **Close**.

There was one cash boat purchase during the month to a new customer, Sonia Garcia. She purchased a Malibu Vride off the showroom floor on March 12 for $51,120 using Check No. 8593 including sales tax.

To record a cash sale and deposit cash received:

1 Click **Receive Money** from the Customers & Sales center and then select **Receive Money from Customer**.

2 Type **11** as the Deposit Ticket ID since this amount was deposited at the same time as the product was sold.

3 Create a new customer: 50011 Sonia Garcia with cash terms: i.e., no credit (check the C.O.D box and put a 0 in the credit limit box).

4 Select **50011** as the Customer ID for this cash receipt.

5 Type **8593** in the Reference text box as the customer's check number.

6 Type **SR0010** in the Receipts text box.

7 Type **3/12/07** as the date received.

8 Select **Check** as the payment method.

9 Click on the **Apply to Revenues** tab.

10 Type **1** as the Quantity sold.

11 Select **204 Malibu Vride** from the drop-down list of items.

12 Type **01** as the Sales Tax code. Your screen should look like Figure 8.15.

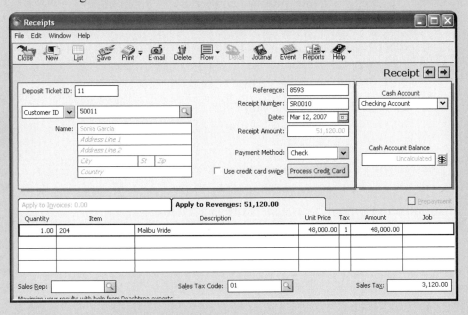

Figure 8.15

Cash Sale to Sonia Garcia

13 Click **Save** and then click **Close**.

Three invoices were generated in the month of March for boat sales. One, to Fantasy Sports (Sales Order 104), was invoiced with invoice 10011 and represented an order received during the month for which Fantasy had already paid a deposit. Upon Fantasy's request, Donna approved net 30 credit terms on the balance owed and the temporary increase in credit. The other two were sales from the showroom floor: on account on invoices 10012 and 10013, respectively.

To record invoices from the sale of boats on account and apply deposits received:

1 Click **Sales Invoices** from the Customers & Sales center and then click **New Sales Invoice**.

2 Select **50009** Fantasy Sports from the Customer ID list.

3 Type **3/7/07** as the invoice date.

4 Type **10011** as the invoice number.

5 Select **104** from the Apply to Sales Order No. list.

6 Type **1** in the Shipped column from both items 203 and 204.

7 Click **Save** to save this invoice. Click **Yes** to allow the sale to be recorded even though it exceeds the customer's credit limit. (*Note*: This is a temporary increase as future sales will still be limited to the standard $65,000 credit limit.)

8 Click the **back arrow** in the Sales/Invoicing window until you see the invoice 10011 you just created.

9 Click on the **arrow** button next to the Customer Account section in the lower left corner of the invoice.

10 Click the Options button in the button bar, change the range of dates for the Customer Ledger which appears to **1/1/07 to 3/31/07**, and then click **OK**.

11 Double-click the transaction reported on **2/6/07** to bring up the receipt you recorded in February where Fantasy Sports paid their $28,250 deposit.

12 Uncheck the **Prepayment** check box.

13 Click the **Apply to Invoices** tab and then type **28250** in the Amount Paid column as shown in Figure 8.16.

14 Click **Save** and then click **Yes** when asked if it is ok to record a transaction in a different period. Then click **Close**.

15 Click **Close** again to close the customer ledger.

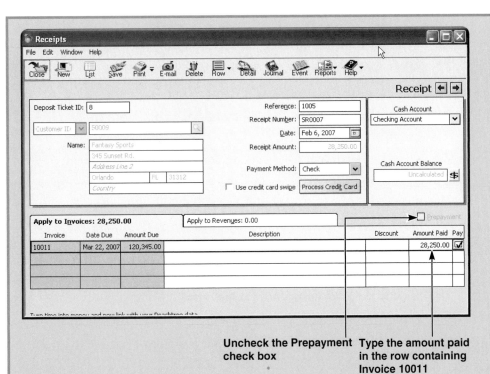

Figure 8.16

Applying a Deposit
to an Invoice

**Uncheck the Prepayment
check box**

**Type the amount paid
in the row containing
Invoice 10011**

16 Click the **back arrow** in the Sales/Invoicing window again
until you see the invoice 10011 you just adjusted. It should
look like Figure 8.17.

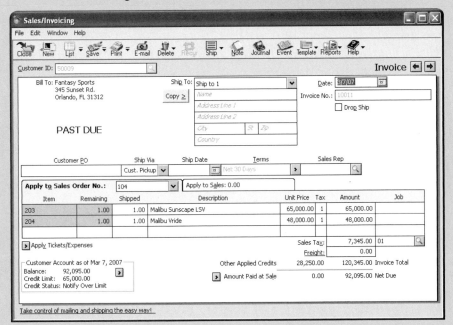

Figure 8.17

Modified Invoice after
Applying Deposit

17 Click **New**.

18 Select **50004** Freebirds from the Customer ID list.

19 Type **3/23/07** as the invoice date.

20 Type **10012** as the invoice number.

21 Select **Cust. Pickup** from the Ship Via list.

22 Type **2** in the Quantity column and select **203** as the Item.

23 Select **01** as the Sales Tax code and then click **Save** to save this invoice.

24 Click **Yes** to accept the over the credit limit notification.

25 Change the terms for customer 50005 Florida Sports Camp to the standard terms of net **30** and **$65,000** credit limit.

26 Select **50005** Florida Sports Camp from the Customer ID list.

27 Type **3/29/07** as the invoice date.

28 Type **10013** as the invoice number.

29 Select **Cust. Pickup** from the Ship Via list.

30 Type **1** in the Quantity column and select **301** as the Item.

31 Select **01** as the Sales Tax code and then click **Save** to save this invoice.

32 Click **Yes** to accept the over the credit limit notification.

33 Click **Close**.

"How do we know when to accept an over the credit limit situation?" you ask.

"Each case is different," Karen answers. "Once we get some history of good payment from a customer, we will permanently change their credit limit. In the meantime, the Peachtree system will remind us when we exceed the credit limits we established for each individual customer."

At the end of the month, Wild Water Sports received a check from Performance Rentals for $10,000 as a deposit toward the purchase of a boat on its showroom floor.

To record receipt of deposit from Performance Rentals:

1 Open the Customer & Sales center, click **Receive Money**, and then select **Receive Money From Customer**.

2 Type **12** as the Deposit Ticket ID.

3 Type **8774** as the check number received in the Reference text box.

4 Select **50006** Performance Rentals from the Customer ID list.

5 Type **SR0011** in the Receipt Number text box.

6 Type **3/31/07** as the date.

7 Check the **Prepayment** check box.

8 Type **10000** as the amount. Your receipt should look like Figure 8.18.

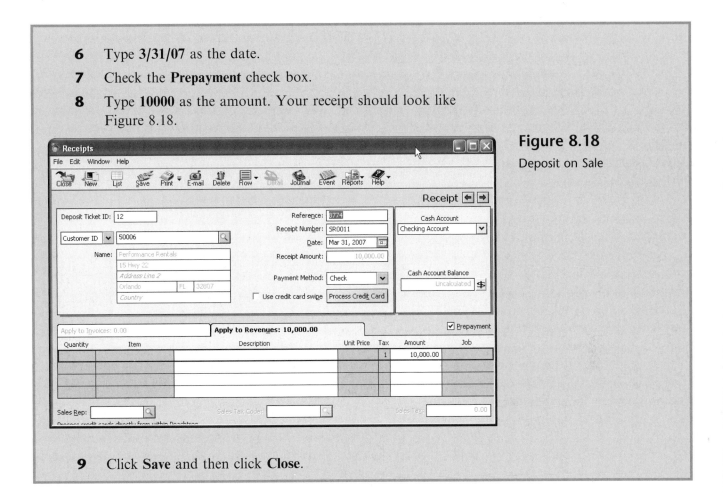

Figure 8.18

Deposit on Sale

9 Click **Save** and then click **Close**.

"When do we get around to paying the bills and collecting cash from these invoices?" you ask.

"It's important to pay bills on a timely basis to keep your suppliers happy and keep our good credit," Karen answers. "First off, we can view what bills are outstanding and when they are due and then choose which to pay and when."

To choose which bills to pay and pay bills:

1 Set the system date to **3/31/07**.

2 Click **Analysis** from the menu and then select **Payment Manager**.

3 Click the **Bracket** button from the button bar.

4 Select **Total** from the Days Past Due drop-down list. See Figure 8.19.

Figure 8.19

Payment Manager

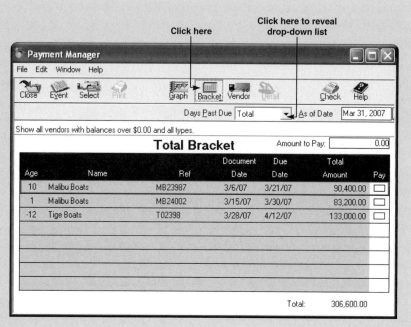

5 Note the oldest bill you have is to Malibu Boats for $90,400. You decide to pay this bill only. Close the Payment Manager window.

6 Open the Vendors & Purchases center, click **Pay Bills**, and then select **Pay Bill**.

7 Type **1032** as the check number.

8 Type **3/21/07** as the payment date.

9 Select Vendor ID **10000** Malibu Boats.

10 Place a check in the **Pay** column on the row containing the $90,400 amount. Your screen should look like Figure 8.20.

Figure 8.20

Payment to Malibu Boats

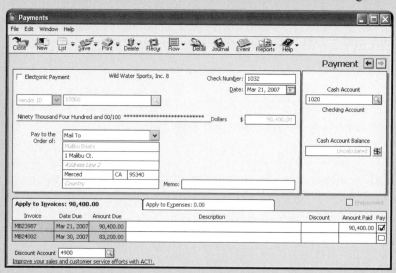

11 Click **Save** and then click **Close**.

Karen explains that by using the Payment Manager, you could have selected more bills to be paid and actually printed and recorded the checks right there. However, you are currently hand writing checks so you used the Payment Manager just to see what bills were due, hand wrote the check, and then use the Pay Bills feature to record the check written.

"We also collected two payments from customers on account in March," Karen says. "Orlando Water Sports paid us $5,300.00 on 3/21, and Buena Vista paid us $1,964.93 on 3/29."

To record cash collections on account and related deposit:

1 Open the Customers & Sales center, click **Receive Money**, and then select **Receive Money from Customer**.

2 Select **50001** Orlando Water Sports as the Customer ID.

3 Type **9152** as the Reference and **SR0012** as the Receipt Number.

4 Type **3/21/07** as the Date received.

5 Select **Check** as the Payment Method.

6 Place a check in the **Pay** column of the row containing invoice 906 for $5,300. Your screen should look like Figure 8.21.

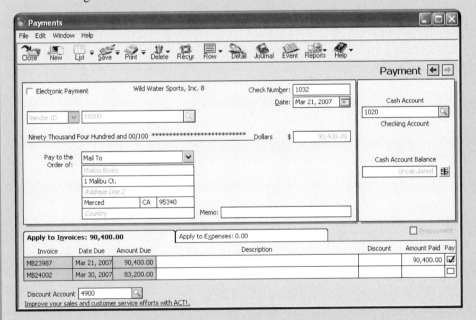

Figure 8.21

Receipt from Orlando Water Sports

7 Click **Save**.

8 Select **50002** Buena Vista Water Sports as the Customer ID.

9 Type **741** as the Reference and **SR0013** as the Receipt Number.

10 Type **3/29/07** as the Date received.

11 Select **Check** as the Payment Method.

12 Place a check in the **Pay** column of the row containing invoice 10010 for $1,964.93.

13 Click **Save** and then click **Close**.

14 Click **Bank Deposits** from the Customers & Sales center and then select **New Bank Deposit**.

15 Select the two deposits shown in the Select for Deposit window.

16 Type **3/29/07** as the deposit date.

17 Type **13** as the Deposit Ticket ID.

18 Click **Save** and then click **Close** to record the deposit and close the window.

"In addition to paying bills from vendors for merchandise purchased, the company also has to pay its sales tax and payroll tax obligations," Karen reminds you. "Before we can do that and pay the rest of our end of the month bills and payroll, we'll need to transfer some funds from our short-term investment account at ETrade to our checking account."

Karen offers to make the electronic transfer of $40,000 from ETrade to Bank of Florida, and you agree to record the accounting effect of that transfer and record checks to pay the sales tax and payroll tax obligations.

To record the transfer funds:

1 From the Company center, click **General Journal Entry**.

2 Create the journal entry shown in Figure 8.22.

Figure 8.22

Journal Entry to Transfer Funds from ETrade

Date: Mar 29, 2007   ☐ Reverse Transaction
Reference: 6

GL Account	Description	Debit	Credit	Job
1020	To record the transfer of funds from ETrade	40,000.00		
1030	To record the transfer of funds from ETrade		40,000.00	

Totals: 40,000.00   40,000.00
Out of Balance: 0.00

3 Click **Save** and then click **Close**.

"How do we know how much to pay in sales and payroll taxes?" you ask.

"Peachtree doesn't have a quick way to determine that," Karen answers, "but we plan on paying the sales and payroll tax obligations with monthly deposits based on reports available in Peachtree. In March, we will pay amounts owing for the two months ended in February, but in April we will pay amounts owing from March, etc. For sales taxes, we'll use the Taxable/Exempt Sales report to identify the amount of sales taxes collected and owed. For payroll taxes, we'll use the Payroll Register report to identify the amount of taxes withheld from employees and the amount of taxes we owe as an employer.

To pay sales tax and payroll tax obligations owed as of 2/28/07:

1 Click **Reports** and then click **Accounts Receivable**.

2 Scroll down the list of reports and double-click **Taxable/ Exempt Sales**.

3 Click the **Options** button, type **1/1/07** as the From date, type **2/28/07** as the To date, and then click **OK**. See Figure 8.23.

Figure 8.23

Sales Tax Liability

Wild Water Sports, Inc. 8
Taxable/Exempt Sales
For the Period From Jan 1, 2007 to Feb 28, 2007
Filter Criteria includes: Report is printed in Summary Format.

Authority ID	Authority Description	Tax Rate	Taxable Sale	Tax Amount	Exempt Sales	Total Sales
Florida	State of Florida	6.50000	336,985.00	21,904.04		336,985.00
Florida	Total State of Florida		336,985.00	21,904.04		336,985.00

4 Click **Print** and then click **OK** to print the report. Note the liability amount of $21,904.04 as we'll write that check in a minute.

5 Click **Close** to close the report.

6 From the Select a Report window (which should still be open), click **Payroll** and then double-click **Payroll Register**.

7 Click the **Options** button, type **1/1/07** as the From date, type **2/28/07** as the To date, and then click **OK**.

8 Scroll to the bottom of the report to see the Summary Total as shown in Figure 8.24.

9 Click **Print** and then click **OK** to print the report. Note the liability amounts as we'll also write that check in a minute.

10 Click **Close** to close the report.

11 Close the Select a Report window as well.

Figure 8.24

Payroll Register 1/1/07
to 2/28/07

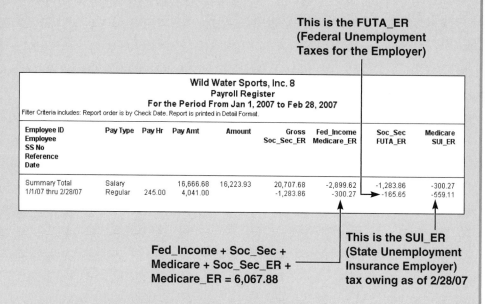

This is the FUTA_ER (Federal Unemployment Taxes for the Employer)

Wild Water Sports, Inc. 8
Payroll Register
For the Period From Jan 1, 2007 to Feb 28, 2007
Filter Criteria includes: Report order is by Check Date. Report is printed in Detail Format.

Employee ID Employee SS No Reference Date	Pay Type	Pay Hr	Pay Amt	Amount	Gross Soc_Sec_ER	Fed_Income Medicare_ER	Soc_Sec FUTA_ER	Medicare SUI_ER
Summary Total 1/1/07 thru 2/28/07	Salary Regular	245.00	16,666.68 4,041.00	16,223.93	20,707.68 -1,283.86	-2,899.62 -300.27	-1,283.86 -165.65	-300.27 -559.11

Fed_Income + Soc_Sec + Medicare + Soc_Sec_ER + Medicare_ER = 6,067.88

This is the SUI_ER (State Unemployment Insurance Employer) tax owing as of 2/28/07

12 From the Banking center, click **Write Checks** and then select **New Check**.

13 Type **1033** as the Check Number.

14 Type **3/29/07** as the Date.

15 Type **12000** as the Vendor ID.

16 Type **21904.04** as the amount.

17 Type **2310** Sales Tax Payable (it should already be there) as the Expense Account.

18 Click **Save**.

19 Type **1034** as the Check Number (it should already be there).

20 Type **3/29/07** as the Date.

21 Type **12000** as the Vendor ID.

22 Type **559.11** as the amount. (*Note*: This amount came from the Payroll Register in Figure 8.24.)

23 Type **2350** State Payroll Taxes Payable as the Expense Account.

24 Click **Save**.

25 Type **1035** as the Check Number (it should already be there).

26 Type **3/29/07** as the Date.

27 Add U.S. Treasury as a new vendor with Vendor ID = 12100 and default expense Acct. = 2330 Federal Payroll Taxes Payable.

28 Type **12100** as the Vendor ID.

29 Type **6233.53** as the amount.

30 Click the **Split** button to split the distribution of this check amount into two accounts. Type the accounts and amounts as shown in Figure 8.25. Note the amounts come from Figure 8.24.

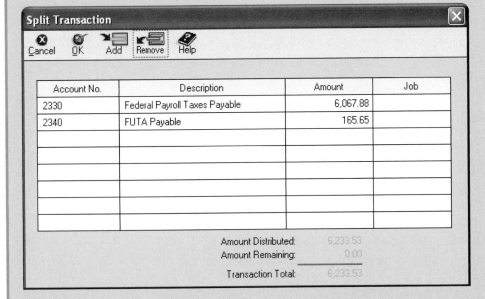

Figure 8.25

Split Transaction Detail

31 Click **OK**, click **Save**, and then click **Close** to close the Write Checks window.

"How can we be sure the correct amounts were paid?" you ask.

"Well, we can verify ending balances by looking in the general ledger," Karen answers. "Let's take a look."

To verify sales tax and payroll tax amounts have been recorded:

1 Click **Reports** and then click **General Ledger**.

2 Double-click **General Ledger** from the list of reports available.

3 Click the **Options** button and then select **Range** from the Time Frame drop-down list.

4 Select **Period 1** in the From drop-down list and **Period 3** in the To drop-down list.

5 Click **OK**.

6 Scroll down to account 2310 Sales Tax Payable as shown in Figure 8.26.

Figure 8.26

Account 2310 from the
General Ledger

Ending balance for February

				Wild Water Sports, Inc. 8			
				General Ledger			
				For the Period From Jan 1, 2007 to Mar 31, 2007			
Filter Criteria includes: Report order is by ID. Report is printed with Truncated Transaction Descriptions and in Detail Format.							
Account ID **Account Description**	**Date**	**Reference**	**Jrnl**	**Trans Description**	**Debit Amt**	**Credit Amt**	**Balance**
2310	1/1/07			Beginning Balance			
Sales Tax Payable	1/16/07	161	CRJ	Seth Blackman - St		3,380.00	
	1/30/07	10001	SJ	Florida Sports Ca		4,550.00	
	1/30/07	10002	SJ	Performance Rent		5,118.75	
	1/30/07	10003	SJ	Alisa Hay - State of		10.73	
	1/31/07	10004	SJ	Freebirds - State of		54.93	
	1/31/07	10005	SJ	Florida Sports Ca		102.38	
				Current Period Ch		13,216.79	-13,216.79
	2/1/07			Beginning Balance			-13,216.79
	2/3/07	10006	SJ	Orlando Water Spo		81.25	
	2/8/07	232	CRJ	Walking on Water -		3,705.00	
	2/10/07	10007	SJ	Alisa Hay - State of		26.00	
	2/20/07	10009	SJ	Performance Rent		4,875.00	
				Current Period Ch		8,687.25	-8,687.25
	3/1/07			Beginning Balance			-21,904.04
	3/7/07	10011	SJ	Fantasy Sports - St		7,345.00	
	3/12/07	8593	CRJ	Sonia Garcia - Stat		3,120.00	
	3/16/07	10010	SJ	Buena Vista Water		119.93	
	3/23/07	10008	SJ	Performance Rent		78.98	
	3/23/07	10012	SJ	Freebirds - State of		8,450.00	
	3/23/07	10013	SJ	Florida Sports Ca		5,118.75	
	3/29/07	1033	CDJ	Florida Departmen	21,904.04		
				Current Period Ch	21,904.04	24,232.66	-2,328.62
	3/31/07			**Ending Balance**			**-24,232.66**

Payment made in March

7 Note that the ending balance on 2/28/07 equals the payment made in March.

8 Scroll down to account 2330 Federal Payroll Taxes and note the 0 current balance as shown in Figure 8.27.

Figure 8.27

Account 2330 from the
General Ledger

				Wild Water Sports, Inc. 8			
				General Ledger			
				For the Period From Jan 1, 2007 to Mar 31, 2007			
Filter Criteria includes: Report order is by ID. Report is printed with Truncated Transaction Descriptions and in Detail Format.							
Account ID **Account Description**	**Date**	**Reference**	**Jrnl**	**Trans Description**	**Debit Amt**	**Credit Amt**	**Balance**
	3/1/07			Beginning Balance			-6,067.88
	3/29/07	1035	CDJ	US Treasury - Fed	6,067.88		
				Current Period Ch	6,067.88		
	3/31/07			**Ending Balance**			6,067.88

Note the 0 ending balance as the payment (check 1035) equaled the beginning balance.

9 Scroll down to account 2350 State Payroll Taxes Payable also noting the 0 current balance.

10 Click **Close** to close the General Ledger report.

11 Close the Select a Report window as well.

"All that is left for March is for us to record checks written for expenses and to record payroll," Karen states. "Our expenses are about the same each month, so you shouldn't see too much variation in what you did the last two months. We didn't have much in the way of service this month, and so Pat didn't work and Ryder just worked the hours we recorded earlier."

To record end of the month expenses:

1 Click **Write Checks** from the Banking center and then select **New Check**.

2 Type **1036** as the Check Number.

3 Type **3/30/07** as the Date.

4 Select **11600** Central Florida Gas & Electric as the Vendor ID.

5 Type **1050** as the amount.

6 Note that account **6400** — Utilities should already be selected from the Account drop-down list. If it is not, select it now.

7 Click **Save**.

8 Type **1037** as the Check Number if it is not already there.

9 Type **3/30/07** as the Check Date if it is not already there.

10 Select **11700** Verizon as the Vendor ID.

11 Type **1500** as the amount.

12 Note that account **6500** — Telephone should already be selected from the Account drop-down list. If it is not, select it now.

13 Click **Save** and then click **Close**.

To record end of the month payroll:

1 Click **Pay Employees** from the Employees & Payroll center and then select **Enter Payroll for One Employee**.

2 Type **1038** as the Check Number.

3 Type **3/30/07** as the Check Date and **3/31/07** as the Pay Period Ends date.

4 Enter payroll information as specified below. (*Note:* Pat Ng did not work this period.)

Employee/Item	Donna 001	Karen 002	Ryder 003
Check Number	1038	1039	1040
Earnings	4,166.67	4,166.67	600.00
Federal Withholding	−463.00	−710.00	−82.20
Social Security Employee	−258.33	−258.33	−37.20
Medicare Employee	−60.42	−60.42	−8.70
Social Security Company	258.33	258.33	37.20
Medicare Company	60.42	60.42	8.70
Federal Unemployment	33.33	33.33	4.80
FL Unemployment Company	112.50	112.50	16.20
Check Amount	3,384.92	3,137.92	471.90

5 When complete, close the Payroll Entry window.

Recording Noncash Investing and Financing Activities

Although noncash investing and financing activities do not affect the cash position of a company, they do have an impact on a firm's financial position. One example of such an activity was Wild Water Sport's purchase of computer equipment in March that was completely financed with long-term debt (a $5,000 note payable to Staples with no interest and no payment due until 10/1/08). Karen explains the nature of this transaction to you and demonstrates how it should be recorded.

To record the purchase of equipment with long-term debt:

1 From the Company center, click **General Journal Entry**.

2 Create the journal entry shown in Figure 8.28.

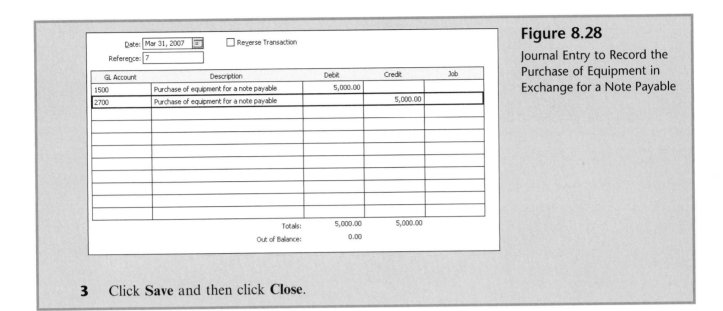

Figure 8.28

Journal Entry to Record the Purchase of Equipment in Exchange for a Note Payable

3   Click **Save** and then click **Close**.

Evaluate a Firm's Performance and Financial Position

Once again, the best way to evaluate a firm's performance and financial position at this point is to generate an income statement and balance sheet. Karen suggests you do this for the entire three months ended March 31, 2007 (the first quarter of 2007), and prepare a find transactions report like you did last month.

To prepare a standard income statement and a balance sheet for January:

1   Set the system date to **3/31/07**.

2   Open the Company center and then click **View All Financial Statements** from the list of Recently Used Financial Statements.

3   Double-click **<Standard> Income Stmnt** from the Select a Report window.

4   Uncheck the Print Page Numbers and Show Zero Amounts check boxes.

5   Click **OK** to view the income statement for March as shown in Figure 8.29.

Figure 8.29

Income Statement for March 2007

	Wild Water Sports, Inc. 8			
	Income Statement			
	For the Three Months Ending March 31, 2007			
	Current Month		Year to Date	
Revenues				
Sales Income	$ 369,750.00	99.18	$ 702,500.00	98.97
Service Income	2,740.00	0.73	6,685.00	0.94
Parts Income	320.00	0.09	610.00	0.09
Total Revenues	372,810.00	100.00	709,795.00	100.00
Cost of Sales				
Cost of Sales	296,056.00	79.41	562,488.00	79.25
Total Cost of Sales	296,056.00	79.41	562,488.00	79.25
Gross Profit	76,754.00	20.59	147,307.00	20.75
Expenses				
Wages Expense	8,933.34	2.40	29,641.02	4.18
Payroll Tax Expense	996.06	0.27	3,304.95	0.47
Utilities Expense	1,050.00	0.28	2,870.00	0.40
Telephone Expense	1,500.00	0.40	5,020.00	0.71
Other Office Expense	0.00	0.00	4,500.00	0.63
Advertising Expense	0.00	0.00	2,700.00	0.38
Interest Expense	5,958.60	1.60	5,958.60	0.84
Gain/Loss-Sale of Assets Exp	(3,000.00)	(0.80)	(3,000.00)	(0.42)
Total Expenses	15,438.00	4.14	50,994.57	7.18
Net Income	$ 61,316.00	16.45	$ 96,312.43	13.57

6 Click **Print** from the button bar and then **OK** to print this statement.

7 Click **Close**.

8 Double-click **< Standard > Balance Sheet** from the Select a Report window.

9 Make sure the Print Page Numbers and Show Zero Amounts check boxes are unchecked.

10 Click **OK** to view the balance sheet for March as shown in Figures 8.30 and 8.31.

Wild Water Sports, Inc. 8
Balance Sheet
March 31, 2007

ASSETS

Current Assets		
Checking Account	$ 47,392.42	
Short-Term Investments	38,000.00	
Accounts Receivable	320,707.73	
Inventory	295,600.00	
Inventory Parts	2,112.00	
Prepaid Expenses	46,000.00	
Total Current Assets		749,812.15
Property and Equipment		
Property and Equipment	295,000.00	
Accum. Depreciation-Prop&Eqt	(7,500.00)	
Total Property and Equipment		287,500.00
Other Assets		
Total Other Assets		0.00
Total Assets	$	1,037,312.15

Figure 8.30

Assets Section of the Balance Sheet as of March 31, 2007

Wild Water Sports, Inc. 8
Balance Sheet
March 31, 2007

LIABILITIES AND CAPITAL

Current Liabilities		
Accounts Payable	$ 216,200.00	
Sales Tax Payable	24,232.66	
Federal Payroll Taxes Payable	2,622.00	
FUTA Payable	71.46	
State Payroll Taxes Payable	241.20	
Total Current Liabilities		243,367.32
Long-Term Liabilities		
Long Term Debt-Noncurrent	297,632.40	
Total Long-Term Liabilities		297,632.40
Total Liabilities		540,999.72
Capital		
Common Stock	400,000.00	
Net Income	96,312.43	
Total Capital		496,312.43
Total Liabilities & Capital	$	1,037,312.15

Figure 8.31

Liabilities and Capital Section of the Balance Sheet as of March 31, 2007

11 Click **Print** from the button bar and then **OK** to print this statement.

12 Click **Close**.

To prepare a find transactions report for March:

1 Click **Company Reports** from the Select a Report window.

2 Double-click **Find Transactions Report**.

3 If your system date is still set at **3/31/07**, the report you get will only show you transactions recorded on 3/31/07. To change the report to reflect all transactions recorded in March 07, click the **Options** button on the report button bar.

4 Change the From date to **3/1/07** and then click **OK**.

5 Click **Print** from the report button bar and then click **OK** to print. The report shown in Figure 8.32 should appear.

6 Click **Save**.

7 Type **Find Transactions Report 3/07** as the new name of the report and then click **Save**.

8 Click **Close** to close the report and then close the Select a Report window.

Figure 8.32 Find Transaction Report

8/19/06 at 11:41:04.59

Wild Water Sports, Inc. 8
Find Transactions Report
For the Period From Mar 1, 2007 to Mar 31, 2007

Filter Criteria includes: 1) All Transaction Types. Report order is by Date.

Date	Type	Reference	ID	Name	Amount
3/1/07	Payment	1029	11025	Bank of Florida	4,717.81
3/1/07	Payment	1030	11025	Bank of Florida	4,717.81
3/6/07	Payment	101	11025	Bank of Florida	300,000.00
3/6/07	Payment	1031	11030	Bank of Orlando	387,690.58
3/6/07	Purchase	MB23987	10000	Malibu Boats	90,400.00
3/7/07	General Journal Entry	5			3,000.00
3/7/07	Sale/Invoice	10011	50009	Fantasy Sports	120,345.00
3/8/07	Purchase Order	4005	10000	Malibu Boats	83,200.00
3/12/07	Purchase Order	4006	10200	Tige Boats	133,000.00
3/12/07	Purchase Order	4007	10100	MB Sports	50,000.00
3/12/07	Receipt	8593	50011	Sonia Garcia	51,120.00
3/12/07	Time Ticket	000042	003	Ryder Zacovic	
3/13/07	Time Ticket	000043	003	Ryder Zacovic	150.00
3/13/07	Time Ticket	000044	003	Ryder Zacovic	1,000.00
3/14/07	Time Ticket	000045	003	Ryder Zacovic	375.00
3/15/07	Purchase	MB24002	10000	Malibu Boats	83,200.00
3/15/07	Time Ticket	000046	003	Ryder Zacovic	
3/16/07	Sale/Invoice	10010	50002	Buena Vista Water Sports	1,964.93
3/16/07	Time Ticket	000047	003	Ryder Zacovic	
3/20/07	Time Ticket	000048	003	Ryder Zacovic	320.00
3/21/07	Payment	1032	10000	Malibu Boats	90,400.00
3/21/07	Receipt	9152	50001	Orlando Water Sports	5,300.00
3/21/07	Time Ticket	000049	003	Ryder Zacovic	350.00
3/21/07	Time Ticket	000050	003	Ryder Zacovic	320.00
3/22/07	Time Ticket	000051	003	Ryder Zacovic	225.00
3/23/07	Sale/Invoice	10008	50006	Performance Rentals	1,293.98
3/23/07	Sale/Invoice	10012	50004	Freebirds	138,450.00
3/23/07	Sale/Invoice	10013	50005	Florida Sports Camp	83,868.75
3/23/07	Time Ticket	000052	003	Ryder Zacovic	
3/28/07	Purchase	T02398	10200	Tige Boats	133,000.00
3/29/07	General Journal Entry	6			40,000.00
3/29/07	Payment	1033	12000	Florida Department of Revenue	21,904.04

Figure 8.32 Cont'd

Wild Water Sports, Inc. 8
Find Transactions Report
For the Period From Mar 1, 2007 to Mar 31, 2007

Filter Criteria includes: 1) All Transaction Types. Report order is by Date.

Date	Type	Reference	ID	Name	Amount
3/29/07	Payment	1034	12000	Florida Department of Revenue	559.11
3/29/07	Payment	1035	12100	US Treasury	6,233.53
3/29/07	Receipt	741	50002	Buena Vista Water Sports	1,964.93
3/30/07	Payment	1036	11600	Central Florida Gas & Electric	1,050.00
3/30/07	Payment	1037	11700	Verizon	1,500.00
3/30/07	Payroll Entry	1038	001	Donna Chandler	3,384.92
3/30/07	Payroll Entry	1039	002	Karen Wilson	3,137.92
3/30/07	Payroll Entry	1040	003	Ryder Zacovic	471.90
3/31/07	General Journal Entry	7			5,000.00
3/31/07	Receipt	8774	50006	Performance Rentals	10,000.00
				Report Total:	**1,863,615.2**
				Number of Transactions:	**42**

"Not bad for our first three months," Karen comments. "But we still need to accrue some revenues and expenses, adjust some prepaid assets and unearned revenue, and record depreciation."

End Note

You've now helped Karen understand even more of Peachtree's features, including how to record the repayment of loans, sale of investments, receipt of inventory items and related bills, credit sales, and the receipt of payments on account.

Chapter 8 Questions

1 What information, contained in a loan amortization schedule, is part of the payment information recorded in Peachtree?

2 How does a firm account for transfer of funds from one bank to another bank in Peachtree?

3 How do you update vendor records for changes in terms?

4 Consider this statement: "Peachtree records revenue when an invoice is generated even though cash has not been received." Is this practice acceptable? Why or why not?

5 How do you record the receipt of inventory and the related bill in Peachtree?

6 How is time accumulated on jobs?

7 How did Wild Water know how much time to bill customers for service rendered?

8 How does Peachtree prevent you from recording a sale to a customer in excess of their credit limit?

9 What information does the Payment Manager provide?

10 What are noncash investing and financing activities, and how are they recorded in Peachtree?

Chapter 8 Assignments

1 *Adding More Information to Wild Water Sports*

Restore the file **Wild Water Sports, Inc 8A** found on the text CD or download it from the text Web site, and then add the following transactions in chronological order. Be sure to set the system date to **4/1/07** and the accounting period to **Period 4 − 04/01/07 − 04/30/07**.

merchandising

Date	Transaction
4/2/07	Wrote Check No. 1041 for $4,717.81 as payment 3 on loan to Bank of Florida. See loan amortization schedule in Figure 8.1 for interest and principle breakdown.
4/3/07	Received $92,095 as payment on account from Fantasy Sports on its Check No. 234 for Wild Water's sales receipt SR0014.
4/4/07	Deposited payment received from Fantasy Sports on Deposit Ticket 14.
4/4/07	Paid Malibu Boats bill by writing Check No. 1042 for $83,200.
4/5/07	Created Purchase Order No. 4008 to Tige to purchase one Tige 22v and one Tige 24v for showroom floor inventory to be shipped via Best Way.

4/6/07	Received 1 MB 220V and bill (invoice MB23049) on Purchase Order No. 4007 from MB Sports.
4/9/07	Received $1,293.98 as payment on account from Performance Rentals on its Check No. 987 for Wild Water's sales receipt SR0015.
4/9/07	Accepted a new job (3008) to service a boat owned by Seth Blackman.
4/9/07	Pat Ng worked four hours on each day, April 9, 11, 12, and 13, doing office work. He worked two hours performing an engine service and three hours cleaning on Job No. 3008 on April 10 which were billed at the activity rate.
4/10/07	Recorded the sale of Apple Computer stock, originally purchased for $25,000 for a loss of $2,000 with journal entry 8. (Just record the loss as the proceeds remained in the short-term investments account.)
4/11/07	Deposited payment received from Performance Rentals using Deposit Ticket 15.
4/11/07	Created invoice 10014 to Spirit Adventures to record sale of an MB 220v terms net 30 for $69,225 including tax.
4/11/07	Created invoice 10015 to Seth Backman for service under Job No. 3008 and five quarts of oil, one air filter, and one oil filter, terms net 30 for $585.75 including tax.
4/11/07	Created Purchase Order No. 4009 to MB Sports to purchase one MB 220v and one MB B52 V23 for showroom floor inventory shipped Best Way.
4/12/07	Received $83,868.75 as payment on account from Florida Sports Camp on its Check No. 8741.
4/12/07	Deposited payment received from Florida Sports Camp using Deposit Ticket 16.
4/12/07	Recorded the transfer of $20,000 from short-term investments to checking with journal entry 9.
4/13/07	Paid Tige Boats bill by writing Check No. 1043 for $133,000.
4/16/07	Accepted a new job (3009) to paint a boat owned by Fantasy Sports.
4/16/07	Ryder Zacovic worked six hours on each day, April 17 thru April 20, which were nonbillable office work. He worked eight hours painting and repairing on Job No. 3009 on April 16 which are billed at the activity rate.
4/17/07	Created invoice 10016 to High Flying Fun (a new customer with ID = 50012) to record sale of one Tige 24v and one Malibu WakeSetter XTI terms net 15 and a credit limit of $200,000 for customer pickup for a total of $167,737.50 including tax.
4/18/07	Created sales receipt SR0017 to Orlando Water Sports to record the sale of one Malibu Sunsetter LXi in exchange for its Check No. 10005.
4/18/07	Deposited payment received from Orlando Water Sports using Deposit Ticket 17.
4/20/07	Created invoice 10017 to Fantasy Sports for service under Job No. 3009.
4/23/07	Created Purchase Order No. 4010 to Malibu Boats to purchase one Malibu Sportster LX for Freebirds, one Malibu Sunscape LSV for Buena Vista Water Sports, one Malibu WakeSetter VLX, and one Malibu Vride for showroom floor inventory.
4/24/07	Received all items ordered on Purchase Order No. 4009 from MB Sports. Also received its invoice MB234987.
4/24/07	Received all items ordered and bill on Purchase Order No. 4008 from Tige Boats. Also received its invoice T023948.
4/25/07	Created invoice 10018 to Half Moon Sports (a new customer with ID 50013) to record sale of one MB 220v terms net 15 and a credit limit of $75,000.
4/26/07	Purchased another computer, printer, and other electronic equipment from Staples for $12,000, again completely financed with a note payable with no interest and no payment due until 11/1/08. Record this transaction using journal entry 10.

4/27/07	Created and printed a payroll register for the month of March. Paid payroll tax liabilities accrued as of 3/31/07 of $2,934.66 using Check No. 1044 to the Florida Dept. of Revenue and Check No. 1045 to the U.S. Treasury.
4/27/07	Paid sales tax liability as of 3/31/07 of $24,232.66 to the Florida Dept. of Revenue using Check No. 1046.
4/27/07	Wrote Check No. 1047 to Central Florida Gas & Electric for $1,250 for utilities expense.
4/27/07	Wrote Check No. 1048 to Verizon for $1,800 for telephone expense.
4/27/07	Wrote Check No. 1049 to Brian Szulczewski for $3,000 for advertising expense. Pat Ng performed four hours of office work each a day (Monday–Friday) for the weeks of 4/2, 4/16, and 4/23 in addition to the hours already recorded for the week of 4/9. Ryder Zacovic performed four hours of office work each a day (Monday–Friday) for the weeks of 4/2, 4/9, and 4/23 in addition to the hours already recorded for the week of 4/16.
4/30/07	Received $681.60 as payment on account from Fantasy Sports on its Check No. 1874 using Wild Water's sales receipt SR0018.
4/30/07	Received $585.75 as payment on account from Seth Blackman on his Check No. 1547 using Wild Water's sales receipt SR0019.
4/30/07	Received $13,000 as a deposit from Freebirds on its Check No. 2514 towards the purchase of a Malibu Sportster LX ordered 4/23. *Note:* Do not apply this amount to its existing balance. Use Wild Water's sales receipt SR0020.
4/30/07	Received $16,250 as a deposit from Buena Vista Water Sports on its Check No. 8742 towards the purchase of a Malibu Sunscape LSV ordered 4/23. Use Wild Water's sales receipt SR0021.
4/30/07	Deposited $30,517.35 of checks received 4/30 into checking account using Deposit Ticket 18.
4/30/07	Process payroll per the information provided below in Table 8.1 starting with Check No. 1050. (Be sure to change the pay period date.)

Employee/Item/07	Donna 001/07	Karen 002	Ryder 003	Pat 004
Check Number	1050	1051	1052	1053
Earnings	4,166.67	4,166.67	1,380.00	1,458.00
Federal Withholding	−463.00	−710.00	−189.06	−199.75
Social Security Employee	−258.33	−258.33	−85.56	−90.40
Medicare Employee	−60.42	−60.42	−20.01	−21.14
Social Security Company	258.33	258.33	85.56	90.40
Medicare Company	60.42	60.42	20.01	21.14
Federal Unemployment	0	0	11.04	11.66
State Unemployment	0	0	37.26	39.37
Check Amount	3,384.92	3,137.92	1,085.37	1,146.71

Table 8.1

Payroll Information for Wild Water Sports

Print the following with no page numbers and no zero amounts and with the accounting period set to **Period 4**:

a. Standard income statement

b. Standard balance sheet

c. Find transactions report for the period April 1 through April 30, 2007

2   *Adding More Information: Central Coast Cellular*

Restore the backup you made for Central Coast Cellular in Chapter 7 into a new company folder. (Do not restore this backup into an existing folder.) Change the company name to include Ch 8 at the end so that the new company name is **Central Coast Cellular Ch 8**. Change the system date to **1/1/09** and the accounting period to **Period 1 – 1/1/09 – 1/31/09**. Add the following business events:

Date	Transaction
1/20/09	The company received a shipment of phones from Nokia on Purchase Order No. 102. Items were received and invoice 209387 was recorded due in 30 days.
1/21/09	The company invoiced the City of San Luis Obispo, using invoice 10001 for 20 Nokia 8290 phones, 15 Nokia 8890 phones, 30 hours of consulting time, and 35 commissions earned on cell phone contracts (cell phone contracts are a new service item ID = COM, name = Commissions, valued at $50 per contract, and recorded to a new income account titled Commissions, ID = 4050).
1/22/09	The company purchased equipment in the amount of $95,000 cash from Kyle Equipment, Inc. (a new vendor with ID = KYLE) using Check No. 3008. *Hint:* This is equipment, a long-lived asset, and thus you need to record this purchase as an asset to account 1500.
1/24/09	The company paid the Ericsson bill of $6,500 with Check No. 3009.
1/31/09	The company paid the semimonthly payroll starting with Check No. 3010 for the period of January 16 to January 31, 2003. Megan Paulson worked 85 hours during the period. Payroll tax information is shown in Table 8.2.

Table 8.2 Payroll Information for Central Coast Cellular	**Tax or Withholding/Employee**	**Rodriguez**	**Bruner**	**Paulson**
	Check Number	3010	3011	3012
	Gross Pay/Hours	$2,000.00	$1,500.00	85
	Federal Withholding	−300.00	−225.00	−153.00
	Social Security Employee	−124.00	−93.00	−63.24
	Medicare Employee	−29.00	−21.75	−14.79
	CA—Withholding	−100.00	−75.00	−51.00
	CA—Disability Employee	−10.00	−7.50	−5.10
	Social Security Company	124.00	93.00	63.24
	Medicare Company	29.00	21.75	14.79
	Federal Unemployment	6.40	4.80	3.26
	CA—Unemployment (SUI)	24.00	18.00	12.24
	California Employee Training Tax	2.00	1.50	1.02
	Check amount	1,437.00	1,077.75	732.87

This is a continuous assignment in that the next chapter will use the work you've accomplished here as the basis for recording additional business events. After you've printed the following reports, create a backup of this file and store it on some type of external medium (flash drive, Internet site, CD, disk, etc.). The backup file should be named **Central Coast Cellular Ch 8** for easy identification later.

You'll be restoring this file in the next chapter. Print the following with no page numbers and no zero amounts:

a. Standard income statement for the one month ending January 31, 2009

b. Standard balance sheet as of January 31, 2009

c. Find transactions report for the period January 20 through January 31, 2009

Chapter 8 Case Problem 1
ALOHA PROPERTY MANAGEMENT

Restore the backup you made for Aloha in Chapter 7 into a new company folder. (Do not restore this backup into an existing folder.) Change the company name to include Ch 8 at the end so that the new company name is **Aloha Property Management Ch 8**. Change the system date to **2/1/08**. Add the following business events:

service

Date	Transaction
2/1/08	Wrote Check No. 994 for $31,000 to GMAC Mortgage (ID = GMAC) as an installment payment on a 7% loan payable. (Interest Expense, $22,604; Notes Payable Noncurrent, $8,396.)
2/1/08	Recorded invoice 7511 for rental of Moana Units #1, #3, #4, and Villa Units #1 and #4 for one week to Pixar (ID = PX). Applied $14,000 of the advance payment to this invoice, noted terms due on receipt, and recorded receipt of balance owed of $14,080. (When you apply credits, type 14000 in the column Amt. To Use and then click **Done**.) Deposited Pixar Check No. 38771 for $14,080 into regular checking account using Deposit Ticket 005.
2/4/08	Received payment on account from Apple Computer of $25,000 on its Check No. 987426. Deposited check into regular checking account using Deposit Ticket 007.
2/4/08	Received a bill from Reilly Custodial for maintenance expenses of $3,500 with terms of net 15 on their invoice AB1725.
2/5/08	Collected a $15,000 deposit (on Check No. Z100333) from new customer American Airlines (AA) using Deposit Ticket 008.
2/7/08	Received a bill from Blue Sky Pools (its invoice 3600) for maintenance expenses of $1,800. (Blue Sky may have changed Aloha's credit terms to net 15.)
2/8/08	Recorded invoice 7512 for rental of Moana Unit #4 and Villa Units #1 and #4 for one week to Pixar. Applied $10,000 of Pixar's advance payment to this invoice, noted terms due on receipt, and recorded receipt of balance owed of $11,840.
2/8/08	Deposited Pixar check for $11,840 into checking account.
2/8/08	Recorded sales receipt 5119 for rent of Moana Units #1, #2, and #3 for one week each. Collected American Express payment in full of $8,840 from new customer Accenture (ACC).
2/8/08	Deposited Accenture's American Express credit card payment of $8,840 into the checking account.
2/11/08	Received a bill from Pacific Electric for utilities expenses of $2,600 with terms of net 15 on their invoice Q33789.

2/15/08   Recorded invoice 7513 for rental of Moana Unit #3 and Villa Unit #4 for one week to Exxon. Applied Exxon's advance payment to this invoice, noted terms due on receipt, and recorded receipt of balance owed of $5,275 from Exxon's Check No. 943098.

2/15/08   Deposited Exxon's check for $5,275 into checking account.

2/18/08   Received a bill from Service Connection (SC) (a new vendor) for repairs expense of $5,200. Terms are net 15.

2/20/08   Received a bill from Sunset Media for advertising of $1,450 on their invoice 4392. Terms are net 30.

2/22/08   Recorded invoice 7514 for rental of all units for one week to Boeing terms net 30. Invoice total $39,728.

2/25/08   Collected a $3,250 deposit on their check 83546 from new customer Los Angeles (UCLA).

2/26/08   Collected a $7,500 deposit on their check 75624 from new customer Berkely (UCB).

2/26/08   Deposited both checks into checking account.

2/27/08   Paid all bills due on or before 2/28/08 for a total of $9,700 using Check Nos. 995–997. Note that even though there are four bills which require payment, two are to the same vendor (Blue Sky Pools) and thus only three checks are required.

2/28/08   Paid sales tax due as of 1/31/08 of $2,128 with Check No. 998.

2/28/08   Paid payroll tax liabilities due as of 1/31/08. $2,756.51 in federal taxes are paid to the U.S. Treasury. $640.44 in total state taxes are all paid to the State of Hawaii Department of Taxation using ID 874525. (*Note:* The company has a dispute with the state unemployment system and has been directed not to remit the $277.50 owed as of 1/31/08.) Use Check Nos. 999 and 1000. *Hint:* Remember to use the payroll register to determine these amounts. Add up all federal amounts and then all state amounts less the state unemployment amount owing as of 1/31/08.

2/29/08   Process payroll per the information provided in Table 8.3 starting with Check No. 1001.

	Pay/Tax/Withholding	Aki	Castillo
Table 8.3	Hours	n/a	160
Payroll Information for Aloha Property Management	Rate	75,000	20.00
	Gross Pay	6,250.00	3,200.00
	Federal Withholding	−856.25	−438.40
	Social Security Employee	−387.50	−198.40
	Medicare Employee	−90.63	−46.40
	HI Withholding	−442.33	−210.53
	HI Disability	−1.25	−0.64
	Social Security Employer	387.50	198.40
	Medicare Company	90.63	46.40
	Federal Unemployment	50.00	25.60
	HI Unemployment	187.50	96.00
	HI E& T	0.63	0.32
	Check amount	4,472.04	2,305.63

Requirements

This is a continuous case in that the next chapter will use the work you've accomplished here as the basis for recording additional business events. After you've printed the following reports, create a backup of this file and store it on some type of external medium (flash drive, Internet site, CD, disk, etc.). The backup file should be named **Aloha Property Management Ch 8** for easy identification later. You'll be restoring this file in the next chapter. Print the following with no page numbers and no zero amounts:

a. Standard balance sheet

b. Standard income statement

c. Statement of cash flows

d. Find transactions report for the period 2/1/08 to 2/29/08

Chapter 8 Case Problem 2
OCEAN VIEW FLOWERS

merchandising

Restore the backup you made for Ocean View Flowers in Chapter 7 into a new company folder. (Do not restore this backup into an existing folder.) Change the company name to include Ch 8 at the end so that the new company name is **Ocean View Flowers Ch 8**. Change the system date to **2/1/08** and the accounting period to **Period 2 – 2/1/08 – 2/28/08**. Add the following business events:

Date	Transaction
2/1/08	The company repaid a portion of the long-term debt it borrowed from Santa Barbara Bank & Trust with regular checking account Check No. 119 in the amount of $1,000. (All of this payment was principal, and none was interest.)
2/4/08	The company prepaid a one-year liability insurance policy to State Farm Insurance (new vendor with ID = SFI with Union Bank Check No. 120 in the amount of $2,500. (The transaction was properly recorded to Prepaid Expenses.)
2/5/08	The company created Purchase Order No. 2 to Vordale Farms for the items shown in Table 8.4 below to be purchased on terms net 30. All Anthuriums are to be recorded in account 40100 – Anthuriums Sales, an income account type, which you will have to create. (Use average cost.)
2/8/08	The company cashed in $5,000 of its $25,000 certificate of deposit early and received $5,200, which was deposited into the regular checking account. The $200 difference represents interest revenue and should be recorded with journal entry 3. (Be sure to change the company's interest income account title to **Interest Revenue** before entering this transaction.)
2/12/08	The company received the bills shown in Table 8.5. (Accept any terms changes and add any new vendors necessary.)

2/15/08	The company paid payroll. All employees worked the entire period. Kelly Gusland worked 62 hours. Margie Conner worked 72 hours. Checks were written using the regular checking account starting with Check No. 121. Payroll taxes and withholding for employees are shown in Table 8.6.
2/18/08	The company received items and entered the bill (invoice VF323 from Purchase Order No. 2 to Vordale Farms on terms net 30).
2/22/08	The company created invoices to customers as shown in Table 8.7.
2/25/08	The company paid the GTE and Edison bills using Union Bank Check Nos. 126 and 127.
2/26/08	The company received Check No. AD32908 for $9,000 as payment on account from Latin Ladies. The check was deposited using Deposit Ticket 1.
2/26/08	The company purchased a warehouse and land for $300,000 ($30,000 of the purchase price is attributable to the land). A cash payment using Check No. 128 for $30,000 was made to Hawaiian Farms to pay for the land. The warehouse was purchased for $270,000 by signing a long-term note payable to Bank of California who then remitted the $270,000 to Hawaiian Farms. Use journal entry 4 to record the warehouse purchase.
2/26/08	The company paid payroll for the period ended February 29, 2008. All employees worked the entire period. Kelly Gusland worked 50 hours. Margie Conner worked 45 hours. Checks were written using the regular checking account starting with Check No. 129. (Do not print these checks.) Payroll taxes and withholding for employees are shown in Table 8.8.

Table 8.4

Purchase Order No. 2 Information

Anthuriums	Quantity Ordered	Cost	Sales Price
Bright Red (ID = BRA)	700	20.00	35.00
Peach (ID = PA)	800	22.00	40.00
White (ID = WA)	600	27.00	50.00

Table 8.5

Bills Received

Vendor	Invoice #	Amount	Terms	Expense
GTE (GTE)	654654	250	Net 30	Telephone expense
Edison (E)	79411	300	Net 30	Utilities expense
FlowerMart (FM)	914222	60	Net 30	Supplies expense

Tax or Withholding/ Employee	Thomas	Gusland	Conner	McAninch	Comstock
Check Number	121	122	123	124	125
Salary/Hours	2,916.67	62	72	2,500.00	2,083.34
Federal Withholding	−667.00	−123.00	−113.00	−402.00	−286.00
Social Security Employee	−180.83	−57.66	−53.57	−155.00	−129.17
Medicare Employee	−42.30	−13.48	−12.53	−36.25	−30.20
CA—Withholding	−192.30	−20.93	−8.60	−153.55	−61.86
CA—Disability Employee	−14.58	−4.65	−4.32	−12.50	−10.42
Social Security Company	180.83	57.66	53.57	155.00	129.17
Medicare Company	42.30	13.48	12.53	36.25	30.20
Federal Unemployment	9.33	7.44	6.91	16.00	16.67
CA—Unemployment (SUI)	0.58	0.46	0.43	1.00	1.05
California Employee Training Tax	1.17	0.93	0.86	2.00	2.08
Check Amount	1,819.66	710.28	671.98	1,740.70	1,565.69

Table 8.6

Payroll Taxes and Withholding for Employees from February 1, 2008, through February 15, 2008

Customer	Invoice #	Item Sold	Quantity	Terms	Invoice
Latin Ladies	10001	Calistoga Sun Daylilies	400	Net 30	9,000
		Caribbean Pink Sands	100		
California Beauties	10002	White Anthuriums	500	Net 30	25,000
FTD	10003	Bright Red Anthuriums	300	Net 30	10,500

Table 8.7

Customer Invoices

Tax or Withholding/ Employee	Thomas	Gusland	Conner	McAninch	Comstock
Check Number	129	130	131	132	133
Salary/Hours	2,916.67	50	45	2,500.00	2,083.34
Federal Withholding	−667.00	−96.00	−64.00	−402.00	−286.00
Social Security Employee	−180.83	−46.50	−33.48	−155.00	−129.17
Medicare Employee	−42.30	−10.88	−7.83	−36.25	−30.20
CA—Withholding	−192.30	−13.32	0.00	−153.55	−61.86
CA—Disability Employee	−14.58	−3.75	−2.70	−12.50	−10.42
Social Security Company	180.83	46.50	33.48	155.00	129.17
Medicare Company	42.30	10.88	7.83	36.25	30.20
Federal Unemployment	0.00	6.00	4.32	0.00	6.00
CA—Unemployment (SUI)	0.00	0.38	0.27	0.00	0.37
California Employee Training Tax	0.00	0.75	0.54	0.00	0.75
Check Amount	1,819.66	579.55	431.99	1,740.70	1,565.69

Table 8.8

Payroll Taxes and Withholding for Employees from February 16, 2008, through February 29, 2008

Requirements

This is a continuous case in that the next chapter will use the work you've accomplished here as the basis for recording additional business events. After you've printed the following reports, create a backup of this file and store it on some type of external medium (flash drive, Internet site, CD, disk, etc.). The backup file should be named **Ocean View Flowers Ch 8** for easy identification later. You'll be restoring this file in the next chapter. Print the following with no page numbers and no zero amounts:

a.   Standard balance sheet

b.   Standard income statement

c.   Statement of cash flows

d.   Find transactions report for the period 2/1/08 to 2/29/08

Adjusting Entries and Bank Reconciliations

9

Learning Objectives

In this chapter, you will:

- Accrue expenses incurred but not yet recorded.
- Accrue revenues earned but not yet recorded.
- Record expenses incurred but previously deferred.
- Adjust for unearned revenue.
- Prepare a bank reconciliation and record related adjustments.
- Evaluate a firm's performance and financial position.

Case: **Wild Water Sports, Inc.**

Karen has recorded the majority of Wild Water's financing, investing, and operating activities for January through April 2007. To help her prepare financial statements for the first quarter, she asks you to prepare any necessary adjusting entries for the period January 1 through March 31, 2007.

"Some people have trouble with adjusting entries," you remark, "but I'm not one of them. I was always helping my classmates understand these types of journal entries. Why don't I give them a try?"

"Okay with me," Karen responds. "Traditional journal entries are available in Peachtree as you've already seen." Karen explains that in Peachtree the most common adjusting entries—accruing expenses, accruing revenue, recording asset expirations, and recording liability reductions—can be made by using the General Journal Entry item in the Company center.

Accruing Expenses

Wild Water Sports had a long-term liability of $383,800 when Karen and Donna made their initial investment. That loan was paid off along with accrued interest on March 6, 2007. The remaining balance in the loan payable account represents three different loans. The first, a $250,000, five-year, 5% loan from the Bank of Florida, was made on January 4, 2007. The second was a $50,000, three-year, 6% loan from Citibank that was made on February 5, 2007. The third was just recently acquired when the company purchased a computer from Staples for $5,000. In March, the company made two payments on the Bank of Florida loan.

According to the loan amortization schedule (see Figure 8.1), a payment of $4,717.81 is due to be made at the beginning of April on the $250,000 loan of which $1,010.97 represents interest owed. (*Note:* This payment was made in Ch. 8, on April 2, using Check No. 1041.) As of March 31, 2007, that interest should be included in interest expense for March. Payments are due annually on the $50,000 loan. Thus, as of March 31, 2007, the company owes $750 of interest calculated as **Principle × Rate × Time** (**PRT** = $50,000 × 6% × 3/12). The Staples loan bears no interest.

"Peachtree does not automatically assign journal entry numbers for reference," Karen points out. "The journal numbers we'll assign for March 31 adjustments may follow journal entries used for April business events. What's important is the date specified in the journal."

"Okay," you respond. "I'll take the information provided and create the adjustment necessary for interest expense as of March 31."

To accrue interest expense:

1 Start the Peachtree program.

2 Restore the **Wild Water Sports, Inc 9** file from your Data Files CD or download it from the Internet. See "Data Files CD" in Chapter 1 if you need more information.

3 Set the system date to **3/31/07** and the accounting period to **Period 3**.

4 From the Company center, click **General Journal Entry**.

5 The journal entry date should already indicate Mar 31, 2007.

6 Type **11** as the reference.

7 Select **6725** – Interest Expense as the first account.

8 Type **To accrue interest expense on long-term debt** in the Description text box.

9 Type **1010.97** as the amount in the Debit column. This will increase interest expense (an expense account).

10 Click the magnifying glass in the second row in the GL Account column and then click **New** to create a new account. Create a new account by typing ID = **2200**, Description = **Accrued Interest Payable**, and Account Type = **Other Current Liabilities**, click **Save**, and then click **Close**.

11 Select **2200** – Accrued Interest Payable as the second account and then press **[Tab]**.

12 Type **To accrue interest expense on long-term debt** in the Description text box for this row.

13 Type **1010.97** as the amount in the Credit column. This will increase Accrued Interest Payable. The resulting journal entry should look like Figure 9.1.

GL Account	Description	Debit	Credit	Job
6725	To accrue interest expense on long-term debt	1,010.97		
2200	To accrue interest expense on long-term debt		1,010.97	
	Totals:	1,010.97	1,010.97	
	Out of Balance:	0.00		

Date: Mar 31, 2007   ☐ Reverse Transaction
Reference: 11

Figure 9.1

Accruing Interest Expense

14 Click **Save**.

15 Accept **12** as the Reference.

16 Select **6725** – Interest Expense as the first account.

17 Type **To accrue interest expense on long-term debt** in the Description text box.

18 Type **750** as the amount in the Debit column.

19 Select **2200** – Accrued Interest Payable as the second account and then press **[Tab]**.

20 Accept **To accrue interest expense on long-term debt** in the Description text box for this row.

21 Type **750** as the amount in the Credit column.

22 Click **Save** and then click **Close**.

Karen explains that this process properly reflects interest expenses in the correct accounting period (first quarter of 2007) and establishes the liability as of March 31, 2007. However, in April, when the company pays the next installment on the $250,000 loan, Karen will have to remember that the interest has already been accrued.

"Either that, or we can reverse the adjustment as of April 1 and then just record the next payment as we've done in the past with a portion of the payment going to interest expense and a portion going to reduce the loan principle," you suggest.

"I like that idea," Karen answers. "Do we do the same for the $50,000 loan?"

"No," you respond. "The $50,000 loan is on an annual payment plan, and if we reversed the journal entry as of April 1, we'd have to reestablish it as of March 31 and accrue more interest for the second quarter. I suggest we reverse the first accrual only."

Karen explains that reversing a journal entry can be accomplished in one of two ways. One alternative is to actually create the reversing journal entry in the next period: in this case on April 1. A second and more common alternative is to use the automatic reversal process provided in Peachtree. This process is generated when you click the **Reverse Transaction** check box available on every journal entry.

"This is confusing," you say.

"I know," Karen answers. "Let me walk you through this. First off, I'll go back and edit the journal entry we just recorded to accrue interest via journal entry 11 for $1,010.97. All I have to do is place a check in the **Reverse Transaction** check box, and a journal entry, the exact opposite of journal entry 11, will appear on the first of the month following our original entry. Since the original entry was 3/31/07, the reversing journal entry will appear 4/1/07 and use the same reference number: 11."

To reverse an accrual entry:

1 From the Company center, click **General Journal Entry**.

2 Click the **arrows** to go back through recorded journal entries until you find journal entry 11.

3 Click in the **Reverse Transaction** check box as shown in Figure 9.2.

Figure 9.2

Reversing Entry

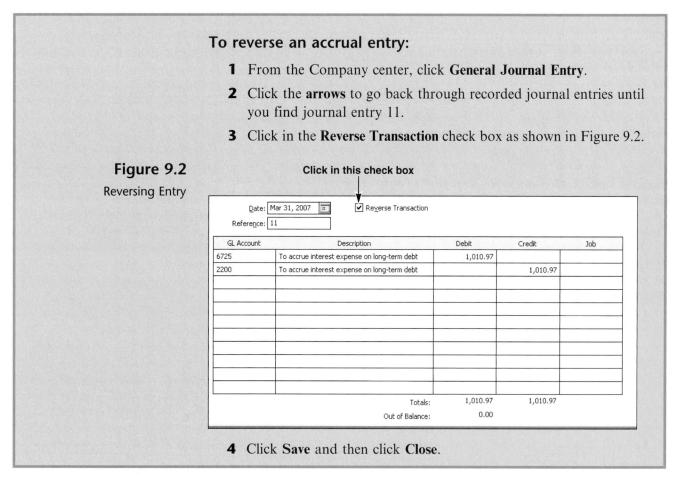

"After this entry was recorded on April 1, the accrued interest payable balance was 0 and interest expense for April has a credit balance of $1,010.97. Now," you explain, "when we record the next payment on this loan, we can use the amortization schedule to record the interest paid and reduction of principle. The payment will reduce cash and increase interest expense by $1,010.97 creating a balance of 0 in interest expense for April. If we need to provide GAAP-based financial statements in April, we'll need to accrue interest owed at April 30. Let me show you what the general ledger accounts look like after these entries."

To view the effects of the interest accrual and related reversal:

1   From the Company center, click **View** next to General Ledger from the listing of Company Reports located in the upper right-hand corner of your window.

2   Click the **Options** button and change the To: date of the report to **Period 4** so that the report will reflect transactions affecting general ledger accounts for both Periods 3 and 4 and then click **OK**.

3   Scroll down the General Ledger report to account 2200. See Figure 9.3.

This is the original entry increasing the liability

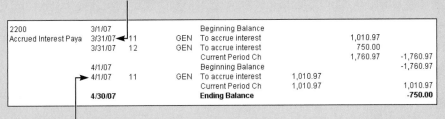

This is the automatic reversing entry decreasing the liability

Figure 9.3

Account 2200 for Periods 3 and 4

4   Now scroll down the General Ledger report to account 6725. See Figure 9.4.

This is the original entry increasing the expense

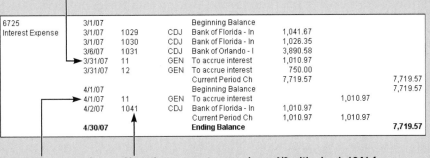

This is the automatic reversing entry decreasing the expense

Note the payment we made on 4/2 with check 1041 for interest owed as of 3/31. The net effect of the reversal and payment is 0 for April.

Figure 9.4

Account 6725 for Periods 3 and 4

5   See the callouts above and then close this report.

Accruing Revenue

Karen tells you that she can also use journal entries to record revenue earned on investments. She points out that during the quarter the company had some short-term investments with ETrade that earned money market interest if they were not invested in stock. The interest is paid quarterly. Since no interest was paid during the quarter, no interest revenue has been recorded. After checking with ETrade's investment advisor, Karen learns that $1,890.41 of interest revenue was earned but unpaid as of March 31, 2007. She decides to accept Peachtree's description of interest revenue as interest income.

> **To accrue interest revenue:**
>
> **1** From the Company center, click **General Journal Entry**.
> **2** The journal entry date should already indicate Mar 31, 2007.
> **3** Type **13** as the reference.
> **4** Select **1030** — Short-Term Investments as the first account.
> **5** Type **To accrue interest revenue on short-term investments** in the Description text box.
> **6** Type **1890.41** as the amount in the Debit column.
> **7** Select **4100** — Interest Income as the second account.
> **8** Type **1890.41** as the amount in the Credit column.
> **9** Click **Save**.

"I thought we were going to record more interest revenue," you say. "Why did we choose to record this as interest income?"

"Peachtree doesn't follow the accounting convention of recording interest revenue," Karen points out. "Peachtree was originally created as a tool for businesses preparing tax returns, and the Internal Revenue Service (IRS) uses the income reference for interest instead of revenue. Rather than changing the account title, we'll just use interest income."

"Another issue we have to address is whether any products were delivered to customers but not recorded as sales at the end of the month," Karen comments. "For example, our records show that we delivered a boat to Spirit Adventures on March 31, but we didn't invoice them until April 2. Thus, as of March 31, 2007, we need to accrue that additional revenue, sales tax, and cost of goods sold."

"Don't you also have to reduce inventory since our records show that boat in inventory March 31?" you ask.

"Exactly," Karen answers, "plus, since this transaction is recorded as an invoice in April, we'll need to reverse this accrual entry on April 1."

To adjust for sales occurring in March but not invoiced until April:

1 Accept **3/31/07** as the journal entry date.

2 Place a check in the **Reverse Transaction** check box.

3 Accept **14** as the Reference.

4 Select **1100 – Accounts Receivable** as the first account.

5 Type **To accrue revenue and costs on sales** in the Description text box.

6 Type **69225** as the amount in the Debit column. Press [**Tab**] three times.

7 Select **4000 – Sales Income** as the second account. Press [**Tab**] two times.

8 Type **65000** as the amount in the Credit column. Press [**Tab**] two times.

9 Select **2310 – Sales Tax Payable** as the third account.

10 Type **4225** as the amount in the Credit column. Press [**Tab**] two times.

11 Select **5000 – Cost of Goods Sold** as the fourth account.

12 Type **52000** as the amount in the Debit column. Press [**Tab**] three times.

13 Select **1200 – Inventory** as the fifth account.

14 Type **52000** as the amount in the Credit column.
Your journal entry should look like Figure 9.5.

Date: Mar 31, 2007   ☑ Reverse Transaction
Reference: 14

GL Account	Description	Debit	Credit	Job
1100	To accrue revenue and costs on sales	69,225.00		
4000	To accrue revenue and costs on sales		65,000.00	
2310	To accrue revenue and costs on sales		4,225.00	
5000	To accrue revenue and costs on sales	52,000.00		
1200	To accrue revenue and costs on sales		52,000.00	
	Totals:	121,225.00	121,225.00	
	Out of Balance:	0.00		

Figure 9.5

Accruing Sales Revenue

15 Click **Save** and then click **Close**.

"Where did you get the cost of good sold and inventory asset information?" you ask.

"I got it from our list of items which provides the sales price, income account, and cost," Karen answers. "When we accrue the sales revenue, we must also accrue the related cost of good sold."

"How about the sales tax payable?" you ask. "Why didn't we just use our normal sales tax payable account?"

"I didn't use the normal sales tax payable account because that account is tied to the payment of sales tax and this accrual is for our records only. When the invoice is recorded in April, the normal sales tax account will be increased."

Karen explains that this is another case where it is best to reverse this accrual the first of the next month so that when the actual invoice is recorded in April, it will be offset by the previous accrual.

"This accrual accounting process is a lot of work!" you comment.

"Yes," Karen agrees. "But at least we get a picture of our performance and financial position based on when events occur, not just when we get around to recording them."

Recording Expenses Incurred but Previously Deferred

The adjustments that you and Karen just recorded accounted for previously unrecorded transactions. Now Karen wants to show you how to record adjustments that affect previously recorded business activity, such as the prepayment of expenses and the purchase of fixed assets.

On February 1, 2007, Wild Water Sports paid $24,000 to Coe Marketing for a one-year advertising campaign. Since this payment represented an expenditure that benefited more than the one accounting period, it was correctly recorded to prepaid expenses, an asset account.

On March 31, 2007, two months of the time period covered by the ad campaign had expired. Thus, two-twelfths of the cost ($4,000) should be recorded as advertising expense and the prepaid advertising account reduced accordingly. Each month thereafter, one-twelfth of the cost ($2,000) should be recorded as advertising expense and the prepaid expense account reduced accordingly.

To adjust prepaid expenses for advertising consumed:

1 From the Company center, click **General Journal Entry**.

2 Accept 3/31/07 as the journal entry date.

3 Type **15** as the Reference.

4 Select **6600** — Advertising Expense as the first account.

5   Type **To adjust prepaid expenses for advertising consumed** in the Description text box.

6   Type **4000** as the amount in the Debit column.

7   Select **1400** – Prepaid Expenses as the second account.

8   Type **4000** as the amount in the Credit column.

9   Click **Save**.

On January 31, 2007, Wild Water Sports paid $22,000 to Manchester Insurance for a one-year liability insurance policy covering it for the calendar year 2007. Once again, since this payment represented an expenditure that benefited more than one accounting period, it was correctly recorded to prepaid expenses, an asset account.

On March 31, 2007, three months of the time period covered by the insurance policy had expired. Thus, three-twelfths of the cost ($5,500) should be recorded as insurance expense and the prepaid expense account reduced accordingly. Each month thereafter, one-twelfth of the cost ($1,833.33) should be recorded as insurance expense and the prepaid insurance account reduced accordingly.

To adjust prepaid expenses:

1   Accept 3/31/07 as the journal entry date.

2   Accept **16** as the Reference.

3   Select **6950** – Insurance Expense as the first account.

4   Type **To adjust prepaid expenses for insurance consumed** in the Description text box.

5   Type **5500** as the amount in the Debit column.

6   Select **1400** – Prepaid Expenses as the second account.

7   Type **5500** as the amount in the Credit column.

8   Click **Save**.

A similar adjustment called *depreciation* is needed to allocate the cost of previously recorded depreciable plant and equipment assets. Wild Water Sports has one account for all property, plant, and equipment. Depreciation on said plant and equipment is usually accumulated in a separate contra-asset account on the balance sheet for control purposes.

While Peachtree does have a separate module available to track individual assets and calculate depreciation, Karen has chosen not to use this feature. Instead, she maintains a separate spreadsheet to track when assets were purchased, how much depreciation should be recorded, and when assets are sold. Her analysis indicates that $10,333 of depreciation should be recorded as of March 31, 2007, to reflect depreciation for the first quarter of 2007. Of that balance, $5,583 is related to equipment, $2,500 is related to furniture & fixtures, and $2,250 is related to truck.

To record depreciation expense:

1 Accept **3/31/07** as the journal entry date.
2 Accept **17** as the Reference.
3 Select **7050** – Depreciation Expense as the first account.
4 Type **To depreciate assets** in the Description text box.
5 Type **10333** as the amount in the Debit column.
6 Select **1900** – Accumulated Depreciation as the second account.
7 Type **10333** as the amount in the Credit column.
8 Click **Save** and then click **Close**.

You find the above procedures very straightforward but are curious about the financial statement impact of these adjusting entries so far. You wonder if Peachtree provides a way to view financial statements so you can see what effect these adjustments have had. Karen tells you that Peachtree does have such a feature—you can view financial statements at any time without having to post entries. She suggests that you look at the balance sheet as of March 31, 2007, to see the effect of these adjustments on the balance sheet.

To examine the balance sheet as of March 31, 2007:

1 Click **Reports**, click **Financial Statements**, and then double-click **< Standard > Balance Sheet**.
2 Make sure the Print Page Numbers and Show Zero Amounts check boxes are unchecked and then click **OK**.
3 View the assets section of the balance sheet as shown in Figure 9.6.
4 Close all windows.

Figure 9.6

Balance Sheet After
Adjusting Entries So Far

Wild Water Sports, Inc. 9
Balance Sheet
March 31, 2007

ASSETS

Current Assets		
Checking Account	$ 47,392.42	
Short-Term Investments	39,890.41	
Accounts Receivable	389,932.73	
Inventory	243,600.00	
Inventory Parts	2,112.00	
Prepaid Expenses	36,500.00	
Total Current Assets		759,427.56
Property and Equipment		
Property and Equipment	295,000.00	
Accum. Depreciation-Prop&Eqt	(17,833.00)	
Total Property and Equipment		277,167.00
Other Assets		
Total Other Assets		0.00
Total Assets	$	1,036,594.56

Karen notes that the ending balance in prepaid expenses ($36,500) is made up of two items: prepaid advertising ($20,000) and prepaid insurance ($16,500). The prepaid advertising as of March 31, 2007 makes sense since 10 months of the ad campaign are left (10 months × $2,000 per month = $20,000). She also notes that the balance in prepaid insurance as of March 31, 2007 also makes sense since 9 months of insurance coverage are left (9 months × $1,833.33 per month = $16,500). She also notes the new balances in the accumulated depreciation accounts.

Having tackled prepaid asset and depreciable asset adjustments, you and Karen are now ready to move on to the last adjustment category—adjusting unearned revenue.

Adjusting for Unearned Revenue

On March 31, 2007, Wild Water Sports received $10,000 from its customer Performance Rentals as a deposit on a boat in stock. On this date, Performance Rentals had an existing balance outstanding, but you and Karen chose to account for this as a separate transaction and not apply this payment to the amount due. As described in Chapter 8, Karen recorded this transaction by increasing the checking account and decreasing Performance Rental's Accounts Receivable. Karen has decided to reclassify it as unearned revenue, a liability, on March 31, 2007. Here's why: Cash has been received, but the boat has not been delivered. Thus, on March 31, you need to reclassify the $10,000 to an unearned revenue account (a liability). When the company actually sells the boat to Performance Rentals in a future period, Wild Water will create an invoice, decrease the liability, and increase sales revenue.

The effect of this adjusting journal entry is to increase accounts receivable and increase unearned revenue (in our case an account called Customer Deposits), reflecting the fact that Wild Water still has a balance owed by Performance Rentals of $1,293.98 and owes Performance Rentals $10,000 if it doesn't deliver the boat on which Performance placed the deposit. Karen chooses to automatically reverse this entry in the next accounting period, which will reallocate this $10,000 as a credit to Accounts Receivable and remove it from customer deposits. However, she warns you that reversing this entry assumes that in the next accounting period a sale will take place and this $10,000 credit will be offset against an increase in accounts receivable from the sale. If this doesn't occur in April, you will need to reclassify the $10,000 as unearned revenue (customer deposit) again.

To reclassify the $10,000 as unearned revenue (customer deposit) at 3/31/07:

1 From the Company center, click **General Journal Entry**.
2 Accept **3/31/07** as the journal entry date.
3 Type **18** as the Reference.
4 Check the **Reverse Transaction** box.
5 Select **1100 – Accounts Receivable** as the first account.
6 Type **To reclassify amounts to unearned revenue** in the Description text box.
7 Type **10000** as the amount in the Debit column.
8 Select **2400 – Customer Deposits** as the second account.
9 Type **10000** as the amount in the Credit column.
10 Click **Save**.

"I always like to print out a copy of my adjustments to make sure everything was recorded correctly," Karen comments. "Peachtree has a journal feature that we can use to print just those transactions occurring on March 31 and April 1 so we can see the effects of our adjustments."

To print the journal for March 31 and April 1:

1 Click **Reports** from the Peachtree menu, click **General Ledger**, and then double-click **General Journal**.

2 Click the **Options** button.

3 Uncheck the Include Accounts with Zero Amounts check box.

4 Uncheck the Truncate Transactions Descriptions check box.

5 Type **3/31/07** in the From text box.

6 Type **4/1/07** in the To text box.

7 Click **OK**.

8 Click the **Design** button and resize the Reference, Trans Description, and any other columns you'd like so that your report fits on one page.

9 Click the **Preview** button, click **Print**, and then click **OK** to print the general journal. Your printout should look like Figure 9.7.

Figure 9.7

General Journal Entries from 3/31 and 4/1

Wild Water Sports, Inc. 9
General Journal
For the Period From Mar 31, 2007 to Apr 1, 2007
Page: 1

Filter Criteria includes: Report order is by Date. Report is printed in Detail Format.

Date	Account ID	Reference	Trans Description	Debit Amt	Credit Amt
3/31/07	6725	11	To accrue interest expense on long-term debt	1,010.97	
	2200		To accrue interest expense on long-term debt		1,010.97
3/31/07	6725	12	To accrue interest expense on long-term debt	750.00	
	2200		To accrue interest expense on long-term debt		750.00
3/31/07	1030	13	To accrue interest revenue on short-term investments	1,890.41	
	4100		To accrue interest revenue on short-term investments		1,890.41
3/31/07	1100	14	To accrue revenue and costs on sales	69,225.00	
	4000		To accrue revenue and costs on sales		65,000.00
	2310		To accrue revenue and costs on sales		4,225.00
	5000		To accrue revenue and costs on sales	52,000.00	
	1200		To accrue revenue and costs on sales		52,000.00
3/31/07	6600	15	To adjust prepaid expenses for advertising consumed	4,000.00	
	1400		To adjust prepaid expenses for advertising consumed		4,000.00
3/31/07	6950	16	To adjust prepaid expenses for insurance consumed	5,500.00	
	1400		To adjust prepaid expenses for insurance consumed		5,500.00
3/31/07	7050	17	To depreciate assets	10,333.00	
	1900		To depreciate assets		10,333.00
3/31/07	1100	18	To reclassify amounts to unearned revenue	10,000.00	
	2400		To reclassify amounts to unearned revenue		10,000.00
3/31/07	1500	7	Purchase of equipment for a note payable	5,000.00	
	2700		Purchase of equipment for a note payable		5,000.00
4/1/07	6725	11	To accrue interest expense on long-term debt		1,010.97
	2200		To accrue interest expense on long-term debt	1,010.97	
4/1/07	1100	14	To accrue revenue and costs on sales		69,225.00
	4000		To accrue revenue and costs on sales	65,000.00	
	2310		To accrue revenue and costs on sales	4,225.00	
	5000		To accrue revenue and costs on sales		52,000.00
	1200		To accrue revenue and costs on sales	52,000.00	
4/1/07	1100	18	To reclassify amounts to unearned revenue		10,000.00
	2400		To reclassify amounts to unearned revenue	10,000.00	
		Total		291,945.35	291,945.35

10 Click **Close** to close the Journal window.

11 Click **No** when asked if you want to save this report as modified.

12 Close the Select a Report window.

Karen explains that most of these journals represent the adjustments you just made and seem to be in order. She points out that each transaction has a transaction number, a type, a date, a journal number (if applicable), names, accounts, debits, and credits.

Preparing a Bank Reconciliation and Recording Related Adjustments

Every month, Bank of Florida sends Wild Water Sports a bank account statement that lists all deposits received by the bank and all checks and payments that have cleared the bank as of the date of the statement. You and Karen examine the bank statements for the months of January, February, and March, which indicate an ending balance of $37,172.23 as of March 31, 2007. Normally, you would reconcile your statement each month, but you've been a little busy these last couple of months. You now turn your attention toward reconciling that balance with the balance reported by Peachtree. You note that Peachtree indicates an ending checking account balance of $37,392.42 at that same date. You believe that most of the difference between these two amounts is probably attributable to "outstanding checks" that Wild Water Sports has written but that the bank hasn't yet paid, deposits it has recorded that have not been received by the bank, bank service charges, and interest income.

A review of all three statements shows that all checks recorded by Wild Water Sports have been paid by the bank except payroll checks written on March 30, 2007, totaling $6,994.74. All deposits recorded by the company have been received by the bank except one dated March 29, 2007, for $7,264.93. Bank charges per the bank statement total $75, which has not yet been recorded by the company. Interest income credited to the company's bank account in the amount of $125 also has not yet been recorded by the company.

To reconcile the bank statement as of 3/31/07:

1 From the Banking center, click **Reconcile Accounts**.

2 Select **1020** as the Account to Reconcile.

3 Type **3/31/07** as the Statement Date.

4 Select **All** from the Show drop-down list.

5 Type **37172.23** as the Statement Ending Balance (box at bottom right of screen).

6 Type **125** as the Interest Income, **3/31/07** as the Date, and **4100** as the Account.

7 Type **75** as the Service Charges, **3/31/07** as the Date, and **6850** as the Account.

8 Place a check mark next to all of the checks, payments, and service charges except Check Nos. 1038, 1039, and 1040. (These are the payroll checks issued 3/30/07 which have not yet cleared the bank.)

9 Place a check mark next to all of the Deposits, Interest, and Other Credits except the deposit #13 of $7,264.93 dated 3/29/07 and the $10,000.00 deposit #12 dated 3/31/07.

10 Click in the **Date** column title to sort these transactions in descending date order (earliest to latest).

11 Scroll to the top of the listing. Your screen should look like Figure 9.8.

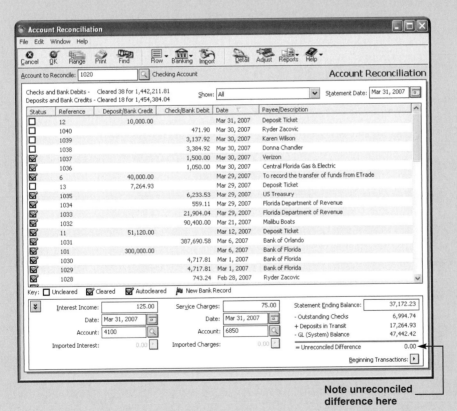

Figure 9.8

Account Reconciliation

Note unreconciled difference here

12 Note the unreconciled difference of 0.00 in the lower right corner of the window.

13 Click **OK** to complete the reconciliation.

14 Click **Reports, Account Reconciliation** and then double-click **Account Reconciliation** from the Select a Report window. Your window should look like Figure 9.9.

Figure 9.9

Account Reconciliation Report for Account 1020 as of March 31, 2007

Wild Water Sports, Inc. 9
Account Reconciliation
As of Mar 31, 2007
1020 - Checking Account
Bank Statement Date: March 31, 2007
Filter Criteria includes: Report is printed in Detail Format.

Beginning GL Balance				164,775.11
Add: Cash Receipts				68,384.93
Jess: Cash Disbursement				(225,767.62)
Add (Less) Other				40,050.00
Ending GL Balance				47,442.42
Ending Bank Balance				37,172.23
Add back deposits in transit				
	Mar 31, 2007	12	10,000.00	
	Mar 29, 2007	13	7,264.93	
Total deposits in transit				17,264.93
(Less) outstanding checks				
	Mar 30, 2007	1038	(3,384.92)	
	Mar 30, 2007	1039	(3,137.92)	
	Mar 30, 2007	1040	(471.90)	
Total outstanding checks				(6,994.74)
Add (Less) Other				
Total other				
Unreconciled difference				0.00
Ending GL Balance				47,442.42

15 Click **Print** and then click **OK** to print this reconciliation.

16 Close all open windows.

The only adjustments created in this bank reconciliation were the recognition of bank service fees and interest income. Peachtree automatically records these in the checking account. Once reconciled, Peachtree also inserts a check mark next to each transaction that has cleared the bank in the check register.

Evaluate a Firm's Performance and Financial Position

Once again, the best way to evaluate a firm's performance and financial position at this point is to generate an income statement and balance sheet. Karen suggests you do this for the entire three months ended March 31, 2007 (the first quarter of 2007), and prepare a find transactions report like you did last month.

To prepare a standard income statement and a balance sheet for January:

1 Set the system date to **3/31/07**.

2 Open the Company center and then click **View All Financial Statements** from the list of Recently Used Financial Statements.

3 Double-click **< Standard > Income Stmnt** from the Select a Report window.

4 Uncheck the Print Page Numbers and Show Zero Amounts check boxes.

5 Click **OK** to view the income statement for March as shown in Figure 9.10.

Figure 9.10

Income Statement for March 2007 after Adjusting Entries and Bank Reconciliation

Wild Water Sports, Inc. 9
Income Statement
For the Three Months Ending March 31, 2007

	Current Month			Year to Date	
Revenues					
Sales Income	$ 434,750.00	98.85	$	767,500.00	98.80
Service Income	2,740.00	0.62		6,685.00	0.86
Parts Income	320.00	0.07		610.00	0.08
Interest Income	2,015.41	0.46		2,015.41	0.26
Total Revenues	439,825.41	100.00		776,810.41	100.00
Cost of Sales					
Cost of Sales	348,056.00	79.14		614,488.00	79.10
Total Cost of Sales	348,056.00	79.14		614,488.00	79.10
Gross Profit	91,769.41	20.86		162,322.41	20.90
Expenses					
Wages Expense	8,933.34	2.03		29,641.02	3.82
Payroll Tax Expense	996.06	0.23		3,304.95	0.43
Utilities Expense	1,050.00	0.24		2,870.00	0.37
Telephone Expence	1,500.00	0.34		5,020.00	0.65
Other Office Expense	0.00	0.00		4,500.00	0.58
Advertising Expense	4,000.00	0.91		6,700.00	0.86
Interest Expense	7,719.57	1.76		7,719.57	0.99
Service Charge Expense	75.00	0.02		75.00	0.01
Insurance Expense	5,500.00	1.25		5,500.00	0.71
Depreciation Expense	10,333.00	2.35		10,333.00	1.33
Gain/Loss-Sale of Assets Exp	(3,000.00)	(0.68)		(3,000.00)	(0.39)
Total Expenses	37,106.97	8.44		72,663.54	9.35
Net Income	$ 54,662.44	12.43	$	89,658.87	11.54

6 Click **Print** from the button bar and then **OK** to print this statement.

7 Click **Close**.

8 Double-click **< Standard >** **Balance Sheet** from the Select a Report window.

9 Make sure the **Print Page Numbers** and **Show Zero Amounts** check boxes are unchecked.

10 Click **OK** to view the balance sheet for March as shown in Figures 9.11 and 9.12.

Figure 9.11

Assets Section of the Balance Sheet as of March 31, 2007, after Adjusting Entries and Bank Reconciliation

Wild Water Sports, Inc. 9
Balance Sheet
March 31, 2007

ASSETS

Current Assets		
Checking Account	$ 47,442.42	
Short-Term Investments	39,890.41	
Accounts Receivable	399,932.73	
Inventory	243,600.00	
Inventory Parts	2,112.00	
Prepaid Expenses	36,500.00	
Total Current Assets		769,477.56
Property and Equipment		
Property and Equipment	295,000.00	
Accum. Depreciation - Prop&Eqt	(17,833.00)	
Total Property and Equipment		277,167.00
Other Assets		
Total Other Assets		0.00
Total Assets		$ 1,046,644.56

11 Click **Print** from the button bar and then **OK** to print this statement.

12 Close all windows.

Wild Water Sports, Inc. 9
Balance Sheet
March 31, 2007

LIABILITIES AND CAPITAL

Current Liabilities		
Accounts Payable	$ 216,200.00	
Accrued Interest Payable	1,760.97	
Sales Tax Payable	28,457.66	
Federal Payroll Taxes Payable	2,622.00	
FUTA Payable	71.46	
State Payroll Taxes Payable	241.20	
Customer Deposits	10,000.00	
Total Current Liabilities		259,353.29
Long-Term Liabilities		
Long Term Debt-Noncurrent	297,632.40	
Total Long-Term Liabilities		297,632.40
Total Liabilities		556,985.69
Capital		
Common Stock	400,000.00	
Net Income	89,658.87	
Total Capital		489,658.87
Total Liabilities & Capital	$	1,046,644.56

Figure 9.12

Liabilities and Capital Section of the Balance Sheet as of March 31, 2007, after Adjusting Entries and Bank Reconciliation

To prepare a find transactions report for March:

1 Click **Company Reports** from the Select a Report window.

2 Double-click **Find Transactions Report 3/07**.

Trouble? If this report isn't shown, you probably forgot to save it as requested. If so, change the report to reflect all transactions recorded in March 07 by clicking the **Options** button on the report button bar. Change the From date to **3/1/07** and then click **OK**.

3 Click **Print** from the report button bar and then click **OK** to print. The report shown in Figure 9.13 should appear.

Figure 9.13 Find Transactions Report

Wild Water Sports, Inc. 9
Find Transactions Report
For the Period From Mar 1, 2007 to Mar 31, 2007

Page: 1

Filter Criteria includes: 1) All Transaction Types. Report order is by Date.

Date	Type	Reference	ID	Name	Amount
3/1/07	Payment	1029	11025	Bank of Florida	4,717.81
3/1/07	Payment	1030	11025	Bank of Florida	4,717.81
3/6/07	Payment	101	11025	Bank of Florida	300,000.00
3/6/07	Payment	1031	11030	Bank of Orlando	387,690.58
3/6/07	Purchase	MB23987	10000	Malibu Boats	90,400.00
3/7/07	General Journal Entry	5			3,000.00
3/7/07	Sale/Invoice	10011	50009	Fantasy Sports	120,345.00
3/8/07	Purchase Order	4005	10000	Malibu Boats	83,200.00
3/12/07	Purchase Order	4006	10200	Tige Boats	133,000.00
3/12/07	Purchase Order	4007	10100	MB Sports	52,000.00
3/12/07	Receipt	8593	50011	Sonia Garcia	51,120.00
3/12/07	Time Ticket	000042	003	Ryder Zacovic	
3/13/07	Time Ticket	000043	003	Ryder Zacovic	150.00
3/13/07	Time Ticket	000044	003	Ryder Zacovic	1,000.00
3/14/07	Time Ticket	000045	003	Ryder Zacovic	375.00
3/15/07	Purchase	MB24002	10000	Malibu Boats	83,200.00
3/15/07	Time Ticket	000046	003	Ryder Zacovic	
3/16/07	Sale/Invoice	10010	50002	Buena Vista Water Sports	1,964.93
3/16/07	Time Ticket	000047	003	Ryder Zacovic	
3/20/07	Time Ticket	000048	003	Ryder Zacovic	320.00
3/21/07	Payment	1032	10000	Malibu Boats	90,400.00
3/21/07	Receipt	9152	50001	Orlando Water Sports	5,300.00
3/21/07	Time Ticket	000049	003	Ryder Zacovic	350.00
3/21/07	Time Ticket	000050	003	Ryder Zacovic	320.00
3/22/07	Time Ticket	000051	003	Ryder Zacovic	225.00
3/23/07	Sale/Invoice	10008	50006	Performance Rentals	1,293.98
3/23/07	Sale/Invoice	10012	50004	Freebirds138,450.00	
3/23/07	Sale/Invoice	10013	50005	Florida Sports Camp	83,868.75
3/23/07	Time Ticket	000052	003	Ryder Zacovic	
3/28/07	Purchase	T02398	10200	Tige Boats133,000.00	
3/29/07	General Journal Entry	6			40,000.00
3/29/07	Payment	1033	12000	Florida Department of Revenue	21,904.04

Figure 9.13 Cont'd

Page: 2

Wild Water Sports, Inc. 9
Find Transactions Report
For the Period From Mar 1, 2007 to Mar 31, 2007

Filter Criteria includes: 1) All Transaction Types. Report order is by Date.

Date	Type	Reference	ID	Name	Amount
3/29/07	Payment	1034	12000	Florida Department of Revenue	559.11
3/29/07	Payment	1035	12100	US Treasury	6,233.53
3/29/07	Receipt	741	50002	Buena Vista Water Sports	1,964.93
3/30/07	Payment	1036	11600	Central Florida Gas & Electric	1,050.00
3/30/07	Payment	1037	11700	Verizon	1,500.00
3/30/07	Payroll Entry	1038	001	Donna Chandler	3,384.92
3/30/07	Payroll Entry	1039	002	Karen Wilson	3,137.92
3/30/07	Payroll Entry	1040	003	Ryder Zacovic	471.90
3/31/07	General Journal Entry	03/31/07			125.00
3/31/07	General Journal Entry	03/31/07			75.00
3/31/07	General Journal Entry	11			1,010.97
3/31/07	General Journal Entry	12			750.00
3/31/07	General Journal Entry	13			1,890.41
3/31/07	General Journal Entry1	41			21,225.00
3/31/07	General Journal Entry	15			4,000.00
3/31/07	General Journal Entry	16			5,500.00
3/31/07	General Journal Entry	17			10,333.00
3/31/07	General Journal Entry	18			10,000.00
3/31/07	General Journal Entry	7			5,000.00
3/31/07	Receipt	8774	50006	Performance Rentals	10,000.00
				Report Total:	**2,020,524.5**
				Number of Transactions:	**52**

4 Click **Close** to close the report and then close the Select a Report window.

End Note

You've now helped Karen record various adjustments including accrued expenses, accrued revenues, expiration of prepaid and depreciable assets, creation of unearned revenue, and one which reflected the completion of bank reconciliation.

practice

Chapter 9 Questions

1 What is the typical formula used to calculate interest?

2 Give an example of accrued revenue other than the examples given in this chapter. Explain how this example of accrued revenue would be adjusted using journal entries.

3 Give an example of an accrued expense other than the example given in this chapter. Explain how this example of accrued expense would be adjusted using journal entries.

4 Give an example of asset expiration other than the example given in this chapter. Explain how this example would be adjusted using journal entries.

5 Give an example of unearned revenue, and explain the process for period-end adjustments involving unearned revenue.

6 Explain how to access general journal entries.

7 What center would you use to start bank reconciliations?

8 What account is typically used to record service charges?

9 When you've finished reconciling a bank account, what should be the difference between the ending balance and the cleared balance?

10 What information is included in the account reconciliation report?

Chapter 9 Assignments

1 *Adding More Information to Wild Water Sports*

Restore the file **Wild Water Sports, Inc 9A** found on the text CD or download it from the text Web site, and then add the following transactions in chronological order. Be sure to set the system date to **4/30/07** and the accounting period to **Period 4 — 04/01/07 — 04/30/07**.

Date	Adjustment
5/1	Invoice 10019 was recorded on this date for the sale of a Malibu Sportster LX to Alisa Hay for $52,000 plus tax. (Even though this isn't an adjusting entry, record it in Peachtree to illustrate how the accrual and reversal work.)
4/30	Accrue interest expense of $995.52 on the $250,000 loan as per the amortization schedule in Figure 8.1. Use journal entry 19. Don't forget to reverse the entry.
4/30	Accrue interest expense of $250 on the $50,000 loan. No reversal required. Use journal entry 20.

4/30	Accrue interest income of $100 on short-term investments. Use journal entry 21.
4/30	Records show that the company delivered a Malibu Sportster LX to Alisa Hay on April 30 but the company didn't invoice her until May 1. The boat was sold for $52,000 and cost $41,600. Sales tax in the amount of $3,380 was collected on 5/1 from the sale. Create journal entry 22 to adjust for this event. Be sure to indicate this transaction should be reversed in the next accounting period.
4/30	Adjust prepaid expenses (for advertising and insurance) for April similar to what you did for March in the chapter. Use journal entry 23.
4/30	Record depreciation expense of $3,870 for the month of April: for Equipment, for Furniture, and for the Truck. Use journal entry 24.
4/30	Reclassify the deposit received from Buena Vista Water Sports on 4/30/07 of $16,250 to Customer Deposits (unearned revenue). *Note:* The $10,000 Performance Rentals deposit remains. Thus, you'll need to reclassify that as well. Use journal entry 25 and remember to reverse this journal next period.
4/30	The Bank of Florida bank statement as of 4/30 has an ending balance of $54,475.02. All checks cleared the bank account except Check Nos. 1050 to 1053. All deposits cleared the bank account except the $30,517.35 deposit made 4/30. The bank statement shows interest income of $35 and bank charges of $25.

Print the following with no page numbers and no zero amounts and with the accounting period set to **Period 4**:

a.   Standard income statement for April 2007

b.   Standard balance sheet for April 30, 2007

c.   Account reconciliation report for the checking account as of April 30, 2007

d.   General journal from April 30 to May 1, 2007 (fit on one page)

2   *Adding More Information to Central Coast Cellular*

Restore the backup you made for Central Coast Cellular in Chapter 8 into a new company folder. (Do not restore this backup into an existing folder.) Change the company name to include Ch 9 at the end so that the new company name is **Central Coast Cellular Ch 9.** Change the system date to **1/31/09** and the accounting period to **Period 1 – 1/1/09 – 1/31/09**. Add the following adjusting journal entries and perform the bank reconciliation (*Note:* The company has chosen not to provide journal entry reference numbers.):

Date	Adjustment
1/31	Record depreciation expense of $1,000 for equipment and $500 for office furniture.
1/31	Accrue interest expense of $950. (Create a new interest expense account with ID = 6925 and a new accrued interest payable account with ID = 2050.) Set this entry up to automatically reverse the next accounting period.
1/31	Reclassify the credit balance of $10,000 in the City of San Luis Obispo account to unearned revenue (Customer Deposits).

1/31   The bank statement dated January 31, 2003, indicated a bank balance of $133,640.49, with all checks clearing except Check Nos. 3010, 3011, and 3012. All deposits cleared. A bank service charge of $80 was reported. Reconcile the bank statement.

This is a continuous assignment in that the next chapter will use the work you've accomplished here as the basis for recording additional business events. After you've printed the following reports, create a backup of this file and store it on some type of external medium (flash drive, Internet site, CD, disk, etc.). The backup file should be named **Central Coast Cellular Ch 9** for easy identification later. You'll be restoring this file in the next chapter. Print the following with no page numbers and no zero amounts:

a. Standard income statement for January 2009

b. Standard balance sheet for January 31, 2009

c. Account reconciliation report for the checking account as of January 31, 2009

d. General journal from January 30 to February 1, 2009 (fit on one page)

Chapter 9 Case Problem 1
ALOHA PROPERTY MANAGEMENT

service

Restore the backup you made for Aloha in Chapter 8 into a new company folder. (Do not restore this backup into an existing folder.) Change the company name to include Ch 9 at the end so that the new company name is **Aloha Property Management Ch 9**. Change the system date to **2/29/08** and the accounting period to Period 2 – 2/1/08 – 2/29/08. Add the following adjustments and bank reconciliation (*Note:* The company has chosen not to provide journal entry reference numbers.):

Date	Adjustment
2/29	Accrue interest expense of $22,555 on the $3,875,000 loan to account 23000 Accrued Expenses. Reverse this entry.
2/29	Accrue interest income of $210 on short-term investments.
2/29	Adjust prepaid insurance for January and February 2008 to insurance expense. *Hint:* Go to the original entry (recorded in Chapter 7) to determine the amount of the adjustment.
2/29	Record depreciation expense of $34,612 for the months of January and February 2008: $13,334 for the Moana building, $20,000 for the Villa building, and $1,278 for the Furniture.
2/29	Reclassify the deposits received from American Airlines, UCLA, and UCB on 2/5/08, 2/25/08, and 2/26/08, respectively, to unearned revenue (a new current liability account (Customer Deposits) numbered 24400). *Hint:* Create a Receipts List to view the receipts received in February.

2/29　　Complete the bank reconciliation. The Bank of Hawaii bank statement as of 2/29 has an ending balance of $115,292.39 for the regular checking account. All checks cleared the bank account except Check Nos. 998 through 1003. All deposits cleared the bank account except the $10,750 deposit made 2/26. The bank statement shows interest income of $175 and bank charges of $35.

This is a continuous case in that the next chapter will use the work you've accomplished here as the basis for recording additional business events. After you've printed the following reports, create a backup of this file and store it on some type of external medium (flash drive, Internet site, CD, disk, etc.). The backup file should be named **Aloha Property Management Ch 9** for easy identification later. You'll be restoring this file in the next chapter. Print the following with no page numbers and no zero amounts:

a. Standard income statement for February 2008

b. Standard balance sheet for February 29, 2008

c. Account reconciliation report for the checking account as of February 29, 2008

d. General journal from February 29 through March 1, 2008 (fit on one page)

Chapter 9 Case Problem 2
OCEAN VIEW FLOWERS

merchandising

Restore the backup you made for Ocean View Flowers in Chapter 8 into a new company folder. (Do not restore this backup into an existing folder.) Change the company name to include Ch 9 at the end so that the new company name is **Ocean View Flowers Ch 9**. Add the following adjustments and bank reconciliation:

Date	Adjustment
1/31	Change the system date to **1/31/08** and the accounting period to **Period 1 – 1/1/08 – 1/31/08**. The January bank statement reported an ending balance for the regular checking account of $76,340.29, bank service charges of $45, and interest revenue of $100 as of January 31, 2008. Deposits for $100,000, $50,000, $6,600, and $22,200 were received by the bank. Check Nos. 101–110 were paid by the bank. Reconcile the bank statement.
2/29	Change the system date to **2/29/08** and the accounting period to **Period 2 – 2/1/08 – 2/29/08**. Accrue loan interest expense of $3,190 on the $319,000 loan for two months interest to an account called Accrued Expenses (an existing current liability account ID = 23000). Use journal entry 5. Reverse this transaction next period.
2/29	Accrue interest revenue of $800 on a certificate of deposit with journal entry 6. (Record this to a new account called Accrued Interest Receivable, and other current asset, with ID = 11100.) Reverse this transaction next period.
2/29	Prepaid insurance of $100 expired for each month: January and February 2008. Use journal entry 7.

2/29	Record depreciation expense of $3,100: $2,000 for the building, $600 for the computer equipment, and $500 for the office equipment. Use journal entry 8.
2/29	Reclassify the deposit received from FTD on 1/28/08 to unearned revenue (a new current liability account called Customer Deposits ID = 24300). Use journal entry 9 and reverse this transaction next period. *Hint:* Create a Receipts List to view the receipts received in January.
2/29	A review of the shipping records indicates that a shipment that occurred on 2/28 was not invoiced until 3/3. Invoice 10004, recorded in the next accounting period, billed California Beauties $16,000 for 800 Calistoga Sun Daylilies, $7,200 for 300 Almond Puff Daylilies, and $20,000 for 500 Peach Anthuriums (cost: $22,600). Use journal entry 10 and reverse this transaction next period.
2/29	The February bank statement reported an ending balance of $65,579.61, bank service charges of $55, and interest revenue of $75 as of February 29, 2008. Deposits for $5,000 and $5,200 were received by the bank. Check Nos. 111–127 were paid by the bank.

This is a continuous case in that the next chapter will use the work you've accomplished here as the basis for recording additional business events. After you've printed the following reports, create a backup of this file and store it on some type of external medium (flash drive, Internet site, CD, disk, etc.). The backup file should be named **Ocean View Flowers Ch 9** for easy identification later. You'll be restoring this file in the next chapter. Print the following with no page numbers and no zero amounts:

a. Standard income statement for February 2008

b. Standard balance sheet for February 29, 2008

c. Account reconciliation report for the checking account as of January 31, 2008 (You will have to set the accounting period to **Period 1** to print this reconciliation.)

d. Account reconciliation report for the checking account as of February 29, 2008 (You will have to set the accounting period back to **Period 2** to print this reconciliation.)

e. General journal from February 29 through March 1, 2008 (fit on one page)

Budgeting

Learning Objectives

In this chapter, you will:

- Create budgets for revenues.
- Create budgets for expenses.
- Create a budgeted income statement.
- Create a budget vs. actual income statement.
- Create a budget for assets, liabilities, and equities.
- Create a budgeted balance sheet.
- Create a budget vs. actual balance sheet.

Case: **Wild Water Sports, Inc.**

Today Donna asks you and Karen to prepare financial statements for the first quarter of the year. She reminds you that you have already recorded all of the transactions for January through April, so you're ready to prepare the statements as of the end of the first quarter, March 31.

"But just preparing the statements is half the job," Karen points out. "We have to be able to interpret these statements. How will we know if the company is doing well?"

Donna is quick to respond, "At the beginning of the year, I used a spreadsheet program to establish budgets for the year. I can compare the actual results shown in the statements you prepare with these budgets."

"Doesn't Peachtree have a budgeting feature?" you ask.

"You're right!" exclaims Donna. "I didn't use that feature, but now that you mention it, I should have. Would the two of you mind entering my budget estimates into Peachtree as well?"

"Not at all," you respond.

After Donna leaves, Karen explains to you that Peachtree allows you to set up a budget for an account or for a customer within an account. To do this, you enter budget amounts for the income statement accounts or balance sheet accounts you wish to track.

"Are you able to track actual versus budgeted amounts?" you ask.

"Yes," Karen replies. "I'll show you how to use Peachtree's budget reports to examine the budget by itself, as well as how to compare Wild Water Sport's actual results to its budgeted amounts."

You have another question. "Can we create different budgets based on different assumptions in Peachtree?"

"No," Karen answers. "Peachtree allows you to have a different budget for different fiscal years, but you may have only one budget per fiscal year."

Karen explains that Peachtree allows you to set up budgets for specific accounts within financial statements or for all specific financial statements. While it is easier to budget for specific accounts, it might be more useful to prepare a budgeted income statement or budgeted balance sheet.

To begin, Karen suggests that you print Donna's spreadsheet budget and then the two of you can establish the monthly budget for revenues.

Budgeting Revenues

Peachtree provides a Maintain Budgets window to enter budget information. In this window, you specify fiscal year, account, and the corresponding amounts for each month. As you fill in this information, you are setting up a budget for a single account, such as a balance sheet or an income statement account.

You also ask about Peachtree's use of the term *income* instead of *revenues* for products and services. Karen reminds you that although *revenues* is the traditional accounting term for these items, Peachtree has chosen to classify them as "income" in the Type section of the chart of accounts.

Donna's budget predicts revenue of $200,000 in January 2007, with an increase of $50,000 each month throughout the year. Service and ports revenue are expected to remain constant, at $3,000 and $500 per month, respectively, throughout the year.

To create a budget for specific revenues:

1 Start the Peachtree program.

2 Restore the **Wild Water Sports, Inc 10** file from your Data Files CD or download it from the Internet. See "Data Files CD" in Chapter 1 if you need more information.

3 Set the system date to **3/31/07** and the accounting period to **Period 3**.

4 From the Company center, click **Budgets**.

5 Click the **Edit** menu and then click **Quick Action Buttons** to remove the check from this item and disable Quick Action Buttons. (These can be more of an obstacle than an aid.)

6 Select **Income Statement Accounts** from the Type drop-down list.

7 Select **01/01/2007 – 12/31/07** from the View Fiscal Year drop-down list. A partial view of the resulting Maintain Budgets window is shown in Figure 10.1.

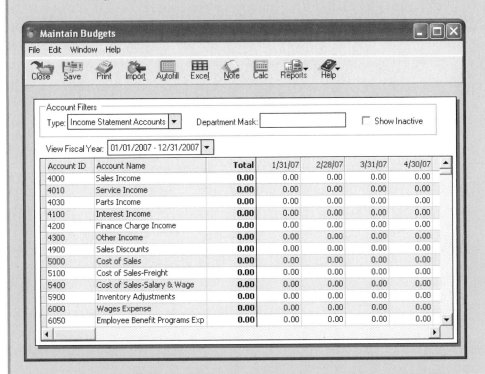

Figure 10.1

Partial View of the Maintain Budgets

8 Click in the cell at the intersection of the 1/31/07 column and the 4000 – Sales Income row. Type **200000**.

9 Continue entering budget amounts for revenues until your window looks like Figure 10.2.

Click here for example and then drag the mouse left or right to increase or decrease the column width

Figure 10.2

Revenue Budget

Account ID	Account Name	Total	1/31/07	2/28/07	3/31/07	4/30/07
4000	Sales Income	1,100,000.00	200,000.00	250,000.00	300,000.00	350,000.00
4010	Service Income	12,000.00	3,000.00	3,000.00	3,000.00	3,000.00
4030	Parts Income	2,000.00	500.00	500.00	500.00	500.00

Trouble? You may have to adjust column widths to view amounts. Click on the line dividing a column title as shown in the above figure and then drag the mouse left or right to increase or decrease the column width.

Now you're ready to set up budget amounts for expenses.

Budgeting Expenses

The budget for Wild Water Sports cost of goods sold depends on product sales. Donna estimated that product cost should amount to approximately 80% of sales since the company marks up the cost of boats 25% above their cost. Thus, as budgeted sales increase, so should budgeted cost of sales. Karen recalls that in January you set up the budget to include sales of $200,000. Thus, expected cost of sales should be 80% of the total January sales of $200,000, or $160,000. Each month thereafter, Donna expects sales to increase by $50,000. Accordingly, the related costs of good sold should increase monthly by 80% of $50,000, or $40,000.

Karen expects wages expense, the largest budgeted expense item for Wild Water Sports, to remain constant at $12,000 per month throughout the year. Depreciation expenses are expected to be $3,500 per month, insurance expenses $2,000 per month, printing and reproduction office expenses $1,000 per month, marketing and advertising expense $2,500 per month, interest expense $2,800 per month, telephone expenses $2,100 per month, and utilities $900 per month.

To create a budget for specific expenses:

1 Click in the cell at the intersection of the 1 column and the 5000 — Cost of Sales row. Type **160000** ($200,000 × 80%).

2 Type **200000**, **240000**, and **280000** as the Cost of Sales for February, March, and April, respectively.

3 Enter budgeted expenses for January as follows:

Account ID	Amount
6000	12,000
6400	900
6500	2,100
6550	1,000
6600	2,500
6725	2,800
6950	2,000
7050	3,500

4 Click and drag to select all budget amounts for January between Wages Expense and Depreciation Expense.

5 Right-click the selected cells and select **Copy** from the shortcut menu as shown in Figure 10.3.

Account ID	Account Name	Total	1/31/07	2/28/07	3/31/07	4/30/07
5000	Cost of Sales	880,000.00	160,000.00	200,000.00	240,000.00	280,000.00
5100	Cost of Sales-Freight	0.00	0.00	0.00	0.00	0.00
5400	Cost of Sales-Salary & Wage	0.00	0.00	0.00	0.00	0.00
5900	Inventory Adjustments	0.00	0.00	0.00	0.00	0.00
6000	Wages Expense	12,000.00	12,000.00	0.00	0.00	0.00
6050	Employee Benefit Programs Exp	0.00	0.00	0.00	0.00	0.00
6100	Payroll Tax Expense	0.00	0.00	0.00	0.00	0.00
6150	Bad Debt Expense	0.00	0.			
6200	Income Tax Expense	0.00	0.			
6250	Other Taxes Expense	0.00	0.			
6300	Rent or Lease Expense	0.00	0.			
6350	Maintenance & Repairs Expense	0.00	0.			
6400	Utilities Expense	900.00	900.			
6450	Office Supplies Expense	0.00	0.			
6500	Telephone Expense	2,100.00	2,100.			
6550	Other Office Expense	1,000.00	1,000.			
6600	Advertising Expense	2,500.00	2,500.			
6650	Commissions and Fees Expense	0.00	0.			
6700	Franchise Fees Expense	0.00	0.00	0.00	0.00	0.00
6725	Interest Expense	2,800.00	2,800.00	0.00	0.00	0.00
6750	Equipment Rental Expense	0.00	0.00	0.00	0.00	0.00
6800	Freight Expense	0.00	0.00	0.00	0.00	0.00
6850	Service Charge Expense	0.00	0.00	0.00	0.00	0.00
6900	Purchase Disc-Expense Items	0.00	0.00	0.00	0.00	0.00
6950	Insurance Expense	2,000.00	2,000.00	0.00	0.00	0.00
7000	Over and Short Expense	0.00	0.00	0.00	0.00	0.00
7050	Depreciation Expense	3,500.00	3,500.00	0.00	0.00	0.00
7100	Gain/Loss - Sale of Assets Exp	0.00	0.00	0.00	0.00	0.00

Shortcut menu: Select ▶ | Cut Ctrl+X | Copy Ctrl+C | Paste Ctrl+V | Clear Del | Adjust | Round to the Nearest ▶ | Quick Action Buttons | What's This?

Figure 10.3
Copying Budget Cells

6 Click and drag to select all budget amounts for February between Wages Expense and Depreciation Expense.

7 Right-click the selected cells and select **Paste** from the shortcut menu.

8 Repeat these steps for March and April since budgeted expenses for these items are identical for all four months being budgeted. Your completed expense budget should look like Figure 10.4.

9 Click **Save** to save all these budgeted amounts.

Now that all of the detail income and expense amounts have been created for the budget, you can create a budgeted income statement.

Figure 10.4

Budgeted Expenses

Account ID	Account Name	Total	1/31/07	2/28/07	3/31/07	4/30/07
5000	Cost of Sales	880,000.00	160,000.00	200,000.00	240,000.00	280,000.00
5100	Cost of Sales-Freight	0.00	0.00	0.00	0.00	0.00
5400	Cost of Sales-Salary & Wage	0.00	0.00	0.00	0.00	0.00
5900	Inventory Adjustments	0.00	0.00	0.00	0.00	0.00
6000	Wages Expense	48,000.00	12,000.00	12,000.00	12,000.00	12,000.00
6050	Employee Benefit Programs Exp	0.00	0.00	0.00	0.00	0.00
6100	Payroll Tax Expense	0.00	0.00	0.00	0.00	0.00
6150	Bad Debt Expense	0.00	0.00	0.00	0.00	0.00
6200	Income Tax Expense	0.00	0.00	0.00	0.00	0.00
6250	Other Taxes Expense	0.00	0.00	0.00	0.00	0.00
6300	Rent or Lease Expense	0.00	0.00	0.00	0.00	0.00
6350	Maintenance & Repairs Expense	0.00	0.00	0.00	0.00	0.00
6400	Utilities Expense	3,600.00	900.00	900.00	900.00	900.00
6450	Office Supplies Expense	0.00	0.00	0.00	0.00	0.00
6500	Telephone Expense	8,400.00	2,100.00	2,100.00	2,100.00	2,100.00
6550	Other Office Expense	4,000.00	1,000.00	1,000.00	1,000.00	1,000.00
6600	Advertising Expense	10,000.00	2,500.00	2,500.00	2,500.00	2,500.00
6650	Commissions and Fees Expense	0.00	0.00	0.00	0.00	0.00
6700	Franchise Fees Expense	0.00	0.00	0.00	0.00	0.00
6725	Interest Expense	11,200.00	2,800.00	2,800.00	2,800.00	2,800.00
6750	Equipment Rental Expense	0.00	0.00	0.00	0.00	0.00
6800	Freight Expense	0.00	0.00	0.00	0.00	0.00
6850	Service Charge Expense	0.00	0.00	0.00	0.00	0.00
6900	Purchase Disc-Expense Items	0.00	0.00	0.00	0.00	0.00
6950	Insurance Expense	8,000.00	2,000.00	2,000.00	2,000.00	2,000.00
7000	Over and Short Expense	0.00	0.00	0.00	0.00	0.00
7050	Depreciation Expense	14,000.00	3,500.00	3,500.00	3,500.00	3,500.00
7100	Gain/Loss - Sale of Assets Exp	0.00	0.00	0.00	0.00	0.00

Budgeted Income Statement

Now that Karen has entered budgetary information for several specific income statement accounts, she is curious to see a complete budget. Thus, she will create and print a budgeted income statement for the first quarter of 2007.

To create and print a budgeted income statement:

1 Click **Reports** from the button toolbar and then select **Budget**.

2 Click **Options** from the button toolbar.

3 Select **Per End (3/31/07)** from the To: drop-down list.

4 Uncheck the Include Accounts with Zero Amounts check box and then click **OK**. The resulting Budget is then displayed as shown in Figure 10.5.

	Wild Water Sports, Inc. 10 Budget For the Period From Jan 1, 2007 to Mar 31, 2007 Filter Criteria includes: 1) Types: Income Statement Accounts; 2) Active Accounts.				
Account ID	**Account Description**	**1/31/07**	**2/28/07**	**3/31/07**	**YTD Total**
4000	Sales Income	200,000.00	250,000.000	300,000.00	750,000.00
4010	Service Income	3,000.00	3,000.00	3,000.00	9,000.00
4030	Parts Income	500.00	500.00	500.00	1,500.00
5000	Cost of Sales	160,000.00	200,000.00	240,000.00	600,000.00
6000	Wages Expense	12,000.00	12,000.00	12,000.00	36,000.00
6400	Utilities Expense	900.00	900.00	900.00	2,700.00
6500	Telephone Expense	2,100.00	2,100.00	2,100.00	6,300.00
6550	Other Office Expense	1,000.00	1,000.00	1,000.00	3,000.00
6600	Advertising Expense	2,500.00	2,500.00	2,500.00	7,500.00
6725	Interest Expense	2,800.00	2,800.00	2,800.00	8,400.00
6950	Insurance Expense	2,000.00	2,000.00	2,000.00	6,000.00
7050	Depreciation Expense	3,500.00	3,500.00	3,500.00	10,500.00
	Revenue	203,500.00	253,500.00	303,500.00	760,500.00
	-Cost of Sales	−160,000.00	−200,000.00	−240,000.00	−600,000.00
	Gross Profit	43,500.00	53,500.00	63,500.00	160,500.00
	-Expenses	−26,800.00	−26,800.00	−26,800.00	−80,400.00
	Net Income	16,700.00	26,700.00	36,700.00	80,100.00

Figure 10.5

Budgeted Income Statement

5 Click **Print** and then click **OK** to print this budgeted income statement.

6 Click **Close** to close the budgeted income statement.

7 Close the Maintain Budgets window.

Karen explains that the above report just describes the current budget but does not compare that budget with actual results from the quarter ended March 31, 2007. She suggests that you create a budget versus actual report for the quarter ended March 31, 2007, showing only quarterly amounts.

"Why not monthly?" you ask.

"Remember we only made our adjusting entries at the end of March," Karen reminds you. "We didn't make adjusting entries at the end of January and February. As a result, our budget versus actual analysis on a monthly basis would reveal all sorts of discrepancies. Take insurance, for example. We budgeted insurance expense of $2,000 per month for January, February, and March. Our actual insurance expense will only be recorded in March when we made an adjusting entry for prepaid insurance. Thus, we'll be under budget in January and February and over budget in March just because of when we recorded our adjustments."

"Then why don't we make adjusting entries every month?" you ask.

"Good question," Karen answers. "We could, but it would take lots of time. Instead, we'll just produce financial statements every quarter, since that's when the bank wants to see how we're doing."

To create and print a budget versus actual report for the first quarter of 2007:

1 Click **Reports**, select **Financial Statements**, and then double-click **< Standard > Income/Budget**.

2 Uncheck the Print Page Numbers and Show Zero Amounts check boxes and then click **OK**. The resulting Income Statement Compared with Budget is then displayed as shown in Figure 10.6.

Figure 10.6

Budgeted Income Statement

Wild Water Sports, Inc. 10
Income Statement
Compared with Budget
For the Three Months Ending March 31, 2007

	Current Month Actual	Current Month Budget	Current Month Variance	Year to Date Actual	Year to Date Budget	Year to Date Variance
Revenues						
Sales Income	$ 434,750.00 $	300,000.00	134,750.00 $	767,500.00 $	750,000.00	17,500.00
Service Income	2,740.00	3,000.00	(260.00)	6,685.00	9,000.00	(2,315.00)
Parts Income	320.00	500.00	(180.00)	610.00	1,500.00	(890.00)
Interest Income	2,015.41	0.00	2,015.41	2,015.41	0.00	2,015.41
Total Revenues	439,825.41	303,500.00	136,325.41	776,810.41	760,500.00	16,310.41
Cost of Sales						
Cost of Sales	348,056.00	240,000.00	108,056.00	614,488.00	600,000.00	14,488.00
Total Cost of Sales	348,056.00	240,000.00	108,056.00	614,488.00	600,000.00	14,488.00
Gross Profit	91,769.41	63,500.00	28,269.41	162,322.41	160,500.00	1,822.41
Expenses						
Wages Expense	8,933.41	12,000.00	(3,066.66)	29,641.02	36,000.00	(6,358.98)
Payroll Tax Expense	996.06	0.00	996.06	3,304.95	0.00	3,304.95
Utilities Expense	1,050.00	900.00	150.00	2,870.00	2,700.00	170.00
Telephone Expense	1,500.00	2,100.00	(600.00)	5,020.00	6,300.00	(1,280.00)
Other Office Expense	0.00	1,000.00	(1,000.00)	4,500.00	3,000.00	1,500.00
Advertising Expense	4,000.00	2,500.00	1,500.00	6,700.00	7,500.00	(800.00)
Interest Expense	7,719.57	2,800.00	4,919.57	7,719.57	8,400.00	(680.43)
Service Charge Expense	75.00	0.00	75.00	75.00	0.00	75.00
Insurance Expense	5,500.00	2,000.00	3,500.00	5,500.00	6,000.00	(500.00)
Depreciation Expense	10,333.00	3,500.00	6,833.00	10,333.00	10,500.00	(167.00)
Gain/Loss-Sale of Assets Exp	(3,000.00)	0.00	(3,000.00)	(3,000.00)	0.00	(3,000.00)
Total Expenses	37,106.97	26,800.00	10,306.97	72,663.54	80,400.00	(7,736.46)
Net Income	$ 54,662.44 $	36,700.00	17,962.44 $	89,658.87 $	80,100.00	9,558.87

3 Click **Print** and then click **OK** to print this report.

4 Click **Close** to close the report.

Karen points out that, based on the budget vs. actual report, the company is doing pretty good. She'll ask Donna about budgeting for bank service charges and other income since neither was included in the budget. She also wants to investigate the actual office expenses, which, according to the report, were 50% over budget.

Budgeting Assets, Liabilities, and Equities

Karen explains to you that creating specific budgets for assets, liabilities, and stockholders' equity accounts is not a simple task. First, you cannot complete this task until the budget for revenues and expenses has been established. This is due to the relationship that exists between net income and retained earnings. Budgeted retained earnings are dependent on net income/net loss. That is, budgeted retained earnings must be increased by monthly net income and decreased by monthly net losses, if any.

Second, budgets for accounts receivable are dependent on sales, while budgets for inventory and accounts payable are dependent on cost of sales and projected sales. Budgeted accumulated depreciation accounts are increased by monthly depreciation expenses. Fortunately for you and Karen, Donna has already created this budget in her spreadsheet program.

Donna's budget for assets had forecasts for the cash financing activities of issuing more stock, offering credit terms to customers, buying more inventory for the showroom, temporarily investing some cash, and then eventually paying down some debt. She also planned to increase accounts payable by getting suppliers to offer credit terms as well.

Before you get started on the current period budget, you need to create budgeted beginning balances as of the start of the year (1/1/07), which, of course, should be the same balances you ended up with the previous year (12/31/06).

To create beginning balances as of 1/1/07:

1 With the Maintain Budgets window open, select **Balance Sheet Accounts** from the Type drop-down list.

2 Select **01/01/2006 – 12/31/2006** from the View Fiscal Year drop-down list.

3 Click in the cell at the intersection of the 12/31/06 column and the 1020 – Checking Account row. Type **25000**. Remember, even those these amounts represent ending balances, they also represent changes from the previous balances, which were all $0.

4 Continue by entering, in the 12/31/06 column, the following amounts (from the beginning balances established when you first created the Wild Water Sports file) for each account as specified:

Account ID	Amount
1020	25,000
1100	96,300
1200	372,000
1500	75,000
1900	7,500
2000	77,000
2700	383,800
3930	100,000

5 Click **Save**.

You have now established budgeted beginning balances for the current fiscal year. Karen suggests that you complete the current year budget changes one step at a time—first entering the budget for assets, then the budget for liabilities, and then for stockholders' equity. You agree with her suggestion and remind her that the budgeted amounts for these accounts are the changes expected for the period, not the ending balance expected for each quarter. For now, you'll just be creating budgeted changes for assets at the end of March 2007.

To create a budget for assets:

1 With the Maintain Budgets window open, select **Balance Sheet Accounts** from the Type drop-down list.

2 Select **01/01/2007 – 12/31/2007** from the View Fiscal Year drop-down list.

3 Click in the cell at the intersection of the 3/31/07 column and the 1020 – Checking Account row. Type **9250**.

4 Continue by entering the following amounts for each account as specified:

Account ID	Amount
1020	9,250
1030	50,000
1100	303,700
1200	−172,000
1230	2,000
1400	36,500
1500	220,000
1900	10,250

5 Your window should look like Figure 10.7.

Figure 10.7

Budgeted Change in Assets

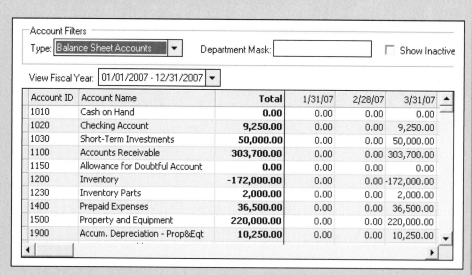

Account ID	Account Name	Total	1/31/07	2/28/07	3/31/07
1010	Cash on Hand	0.00	0.00	0.00	0.00
1020	Checking Account	9,250.00	0.00	0.00	9,250.00
1030	Short-Term Investments	50,000.00	0.00	0.00	50,000.00
1100	Accounts Receivable	303,700.00	0.00	0.00	303,700.00
1150	Allowance for Doubtful Account	0.00	0.00	0.00	0.00
1200	Inventory	-172,000.00	0.00	0.00	-172,000.00
1230	Inventory Parts	2,000.00	0.00	0.00	2,000.00
1400	Prepaid Expenses	36,500.00	0.00	0.00	36,500.00
1500	Property and Equipment	220,000.00	0.00	0.00	220,000.00
1900	Accum. Depreciation - Prop&Eqt	10,250.00	0.00	0.00	10,250.00

The liabilities and stockholders' equity items are less numerous and include accounts payable, loans payable, common stock, and retained earnings, to name a few. Loans payable was relatively easy to predict, as the owners of Wild Water Sports planned initially to borrow funds when they first opened up and then to pay down some of that debt when they took on another investor and sold some inventory. Common stock was also easy since Donna and Karen knew what they were going to invest and had already planned on a fourth investor. Retained earnings were linked to Donna's estimate for net income, and since they started the year with no retained earnings, ending retained earnings as of March 31 had to equal their budgeted net income since they hadn't planned to distribute any earnings via dividends. Once again, these budgeted amounts are predicted changes in account balances, not ending balances.

To create a budget for liabilities and stockholders' equity:

1 Scroll down the Maintain Budgets window until Accounts Payable is the top account shown.

2 Click in the cell at the intersection of the 3/31/07 column and the 2000 — Accounts Payable row. Type **123000**.

3 Continue by entering the following amounts for each account as specified:

Account ID	Amount
2000	123,000
2200	1,500
2310	15,400
2330	2,650
2340	100
2350	250
2700	−83,800
3930	300,000

4 Your window should look like Figure 10.8.

5 Click **Save**.

Now that all of the detail asset, liability, and stockholders' equity amounts have been created for the budget, you can create a budgeted balance sheet.

Figure 10.8

Budgeted Liabilities and Stockholders' Equity

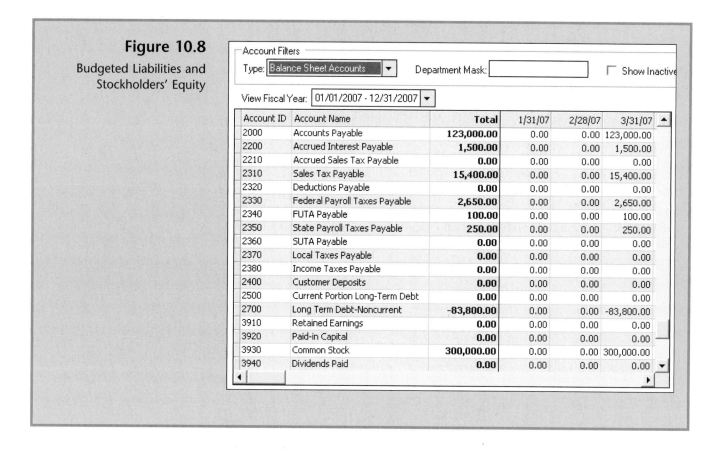

Budgeted Balance Sheet

Now that Karen has entered budgetary information for several specific balance sheet accounts, she is curious to see a complete budget. Thus, she will create and print a budgeted balance sheet for the quarter ended March 31, 2007.

To create and print a budgeted balance sheet:

1 Click **Reports** from the button toolbar and then select **Budget**.

2 Click **Options** from the button toolbar.

3 Select **Per Start (3/1/07)** from the From: drop-down list.

4 Select **Per End (3/31/07)** from the To: drop-down list.

5 Uncheck the Include Accounts with Zero Amounts check box.

6 Click **OK**.

7 Click **Design** and resize the columns so that the full account description shows.

8 Click **Preview**. The resulting budget is then displayed as shown in Figure 10.9.

Figure 10.9

Budgeted Balance Sheet

Wild Water Sports, Inc. 10A
Budget
For the Period From Mar 1, 2007 to Mar 31, 2007
Filter Criteria includes: 1) Types: Balance Sheet Accounts; 2) Active Accounts.

Account ID	Account Description	3/31/07	YTD Total
1020	Checking Account	9,250.00	9,250.00
1030	Sort-Term Investments	50,000.00	50,000.00
1100	Accounts Receivable	303,700.00	303,700.00
1200	Inventory	−172,000.00	−172,000.00
1230	Inventory Parts	2,000.00	2,000.00
1400	Prepaid Expenses	36,500.00	36,500.00
1500	Property and Equipment	220,000.00	220,000.00
1900	Accum. Depreciation-Prop&Eqt	10,250.00	10,250.00
2000	Accounts Payable	123,000.00	123,000.00
2200	Accrued Interest Payable	1,500.00	1,500.00
2310	Sales Tax Payable	15,400.00	15,400.00
2330	Federal Payroll Taxes Payable	2,650.00	2,650.00
2340	FUTA Payable	100.00	100.00
2350	State Payroll Taxes Payable	250.00	250.00
2700	Long Term Debt-Noncurrent	−83,800.00	−83,800.00
3930	Common Stock	300,000.00	300,000.00
	Assets	439,200.00	439,200.00
	Liabilities	59,100.00	59,100.00
	Equity	300,000.00	300,000.00

9 Click **Print** and then click **OK** to print this budget.

10 Click **Close** to close the report window.

"That doesn't look right," you say. "Assets don't equal liabilities plus equities!"

"You're correct," Karen responds. "I found that disconcerting as well. Since we had no beginning retained earnings, our ending retained earnings should be our current period income less dividends, which were zero. However, this budget also is linked to our budget for income which estimated net income of $80,100. Thus, ending retained earnings will be beginning retained earnings ($0) plus net income ($80,100) for a total of $80,100. When ending retained earnings is added to common stock, the change in total equity will equal $380,100. Now the balance sheet equation works: Change in Assets ($439,200) = Change in Liabilities ($59,100) + Change in Equity ($380,100).

Karen explains that once again the above report just describes the current budget but does not compare that budget with actual results from the quarter ended March 31, 2007. She suggests that you create a budget versus actual report for the balance sheet just like you did for the income statement as of the quarter ended March 31, 2007.

While getting ready to create this report, you discover that Peachtree doesn't have a predefined budget versus actual report for the balance sheet. However, Karen says she can quickly modify the existing standard balance sheet to add budget, variance, and % variance columns.

To create and print a balance sheet budget versus actual report as of the first quarter of 2007:

1   Click the **Reports** menu, select **Financial Statements**, and then double-click < **Standard** > **Balance Sheet**.

2   Uncheck the Print Page Numbers and Show Zero Amounts check boxes and then click **OK**.

3   Click **Save**.

4   Type **Balance Sheet/Budget** in the Name text box and then click **Save**.

5   Click **Design** and then double-click on the text **Balance Sheet**.

6   Type **Budget Versus Actual** in front of the words **Balance Sheet in the Text to Print** text box and then click **OK**.

7   Double-click the Text — Body row which contains the text **ASSETS**, select **Left of Column** from the Alignment drop-down list, and then click **OK**.

8   Double-click the **Text — Body** row which contains the text **LIABILITIES AND CAPITAL**, select **Left of Column** from the Alignment drop-down list, and then click **OK**.

9   Double-click on the text **Net Balance Current Period** shown as the second column title.

10 Click in the first row where column 1 is described. Type **30** in the Width text box.

11 Click in the second row where column 2 is described. Type **20** in the Width text box.

12 Click **Alignment Options**, select the **Data and Totals aligned in the column** option button, and then click **OK**.

13 Click in the 3rd row of the Column Description text box and check the Print check box. Select **Balance** from the Contents drop-down list. Type **20** in the Width text box and place a check in the Format/$ check box.

14 Select **Center of Column** from the Align Title drop-down list.

15 Select **Budget** from the Qualifier drop-down list. Your window should look like Figure 10.10.

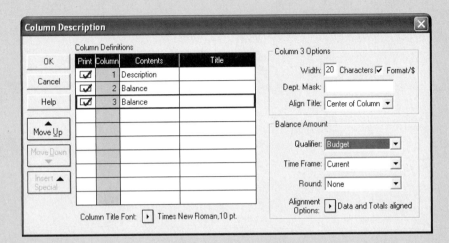

Figure 10.10
Modifying the Column Description

16 Click in the 4ᵗʰ row of the Column Description text box and check the Print check box. Select **Formula** from the Contents drop-down list. Type **20** in the Width text box.

17 Type **Actual** as the Title of Column 2, type **Budget** as the Title of Column 3, and then type **Variance** as the Title of Column 4.

18 Select **Center of Column** from the Align Title drop-down list.

19 Input the Formula Activity as shown in Figure 10.11.

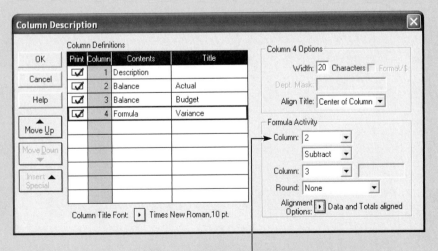

Figure 10.11
Creating a Variance Formula

Enter formula activity shown here. This formula will subtract budget figures in column 3 from actual figures in column 2 and display the result which will give us the variance between actual and budget

20 Click **OK**.

21 Click **Preview** and then click **OK**. The assets section of your report should look like Figure 10.12, and the liabilities and capital section of your report should look like Figure 10.13.

Figure 10.12

Assets Section of the Budget Versus Actual Balance Sheet

Wild Water Sports, Inc. 10
Budget Versus Actual Balance Sheet
March 31, 2007

		Actual		Budget	Variance
ASSETS					
Current Assets					
Checking Account	$	47,442.42	$	34,250.00	13,192.42
Short-Term Investments		39,890.41		50,000.00	(10,109.59)
Accounts Receivable		399,932.73		400,000.00	(67.27)
Inventory		243,600.00		200,000.00	43,600.00
Inventory Parts		2,112.00		2,000.00	112.00
Prepaid Expenses		36,500.00		36,500.00	0.00
Total Current Assets		769,477.56		722,750.00	46,727.56
Property and Equipment					
Property and Equipment		295,000.00		295,000.00	0.00
Accum. Depreciation-Prop&Eqt		(17,833.00)		(17,750.00)	(83.00)
Total Property and Equipment		277,167.00		277,250.00	(83.00)
Other Assets					
Total Other Assets		0.00		0.00	0.00
Total Assets	$	1,046,644.56	$	1,000,000.00	46,644.56

Figure 10.13

Liabilities and Capital Section of the Budget Versus Actual Balance Sheet

Wild Water Sports, Inc.10
Budget Versus Actual Balance Sheet
March 31, 2007

		Actual		Budget	Variance
LIABILITIES AND CAPITAL					
Current Liabilities					
Accounts Payable	$	216,200.00	$	200,000.00	16,200.00
Accrued Interest Payable		1,760.97		1,500.00	260.97
Sales Tax Payable		28,457.66		15,400.00	13,057.66
Federal Payroll Taxes Payable		2,622.00		2,650.00	(28.00)
FUTA Payable		71.46		100.00	(28.54)
State Payroll Taxes Payable		241.20		250.00	(8.80)
Customer Deposits		10,000.00		0.00	10,000.00
Total Current Liabilities		259,353.29		219,900.00	39,453.29
Long-Term Liabilities					
Long Term Debt-Noncurrent		297,632.40		300,000.00	(2,367.60)
Total Long-Term Liabilities		297,632.40		300,000.00	(2,367.60)
Total Liabilities		556,985.69		519,900.00	37,085.69
Capital					
Common Stock		400,000.00		400,000.00	0.00
Net Income		89,658.87		80,100.00	9,558.87
Total Capital		489,658.87		480,100.00	9,558.87
Total Liabilities & Capital	$	1,046,644.56	$	1,000,000.00	46,644.56

22 Click **Print** and then **OK** to print this report.

Karen points out that, based on the budget vs. actual report, the company is right on target. She'll ask Donna about budgeting for the customer deposit account since it was included in the budget. She does want to investigate the inventory asset account, which was $43,600 over budget, and sales tax payable, which was $13,057.66 over budget.

End Note

You and Karen have now entered all budgetary information for the first quarter of 2007. Donna can make changes to the budget at any time if additional information becomes available, and Peachtree will automatically update any related budget report.

Chapter 10 Questions

1 Explain how the budgeting process is accomplished in Peachtree.

2 Can multiple budgets be created in Peachtree? Explain.

3 In Peachtree, do the terms **revenues** and **income** mean the same thing?

4 How do you set up the budget for just income accounts?

5 Explain the typical relationship between cost of goods sold and sales in the budgeting process.

6 Compare the process of budgeting revenues and expenses with the process of budgeting assets, liabilities, and owners' equity and explain how this information is included in the Peachtree budgeting process.

7 Explain the typical relationship between accumulated depreciation and depreciation expense in the budgeting process and how this information is included in the Peachtree budgeting process.

8 Can you copy and paste in Peachtree budgets?

9 Does Peachtree have a built-in budget vs. actual income statement and balance sheet?

10 Explain the typical relationship between retained earnings and net income/loss in the budgeting process and how this information is included in the Peachtree budgeting process.

Chapter 10 Assignments

1 *Adding More Information to Wild Water Sports*

Restore the file **Wild Water Sports, Inc 10A** found on the text CD or download it from the text Web site. Be sure to set the system date to **4/30/07** and the accounting period to **Period 4 – 04/01/07 – 04/30/07** and then <u>modify</u> the existing budget as follows: Merchandise revenues for April are expected to be 10% higher than what is budgeted in March. Cost of goods sold for April is still estimated at 80% of sales. Wages expenses for April are expected to be $15,000. Changes in assets, liabilities, and equities are as follows:

Account ID	Amount
1020	25,750
1030	−20,000
1100	100,000
1200	90,000
1400	−4,250
1500	12,000
1900	3,500
2000	145,200
2200	500
2310	14,600

Print the following with no page numbers and no zero amounts and with the accounting period set to **Period 4**:

a. Budgeted income statement for the four months ended in April (*Hint:* Range is from 1/1/07 to 4/30/07.)

b. Budgeted versus actual income statement for April

c. Budgeted balance sheet for April

d. Budgeted versus actual balance sheet for April

2 *Adding More Information to Central Coast Cellular*

merchandising

Restore the backup you made for Central Coast Cellular in Chapter 9 into a new company folder. (Do not restore this backup into an existing folder.) Change the company name to include Ch 10 at the end so that the new company name is **Central Coast Cellular Ch 10**. Change the system date to **1/1/09** and the accounting period to **Period 1 − 1/1/09 − 1/31/09**. Add the following budget information:

Commissions of $2,000 are expected each month for the first quarter. Sales income of $18,000 is expected in January, increasing to $23,800 in February and to $29,680 in March. Cost of goods sold is estimated at $5,000, $7,500, and $10,000 for January, February, and March, respectively. Bank service charges and depreciation of $80 and $1,500, respectively, are expected each month. Loan interest expense and rent of $1,000 and $3,000, respectively, are expected each month. Wages expenses of $10,000 are expected in January, increasing by $2,000 each month thereafter. Telephone expenses of $500 are expected in January, increasing $100 each month thereafter. Utilities expenses of $300 are expected in January, increasing 5% each month thereafter.

Changes in assets, liabilities, and equities during January are as follows:

Account ID	Amount
1020	130,000
1100	14,000
1200	18,000
1300	68,500
1400	3,000
1410	3,000
1500	115,000
1900	1,500
2000	24,380
2050	1,000
2310	2,000
2330	3,000
2350	1,000
2700	120,000
3930	200,000

This is a continuous assignment in that the next chapter will use the work you've accomplished here as the basis for recording additional business events. After you've printed the following reports, create a backup of this file and store it on some type of external medium (flash drive, Internet site, CD, disk, etc.). The backup file should be named **Central Coast Cellular Ch 10** for easy identification later. You'll be restoring this file in the next chapter. Print the following with no page numbers and no zero amounts:

a. Budgeted income statement for the quarter (1/1/09–3/31/09)

b. Budgeted versus actual income statement for January

c. Budgeted balance sheet for January

d. Budgeted versus actual balance sheet for January

Chapter 10 Case Problem 1
ALOHA PROPERTY MANAGEMENT

service

Restore the backup you made for Aloha in Chapter 9 into a new company folder. (Do not restore this backup into an existing folder.) Change the company name to include Ch 10 at the end so that the new company name is **Aloha Property Management Ch 10**. Use that file to enter the following budget information for January and February. Be sure to change the system date to 1/1/08 and the Accounting Period to Period 1.

Rental income is expected to be $60,000 in January and $100,000 in February. Advertising is expected to be $12,500 in January (for an initial advertising campaign) and then $1,500 per month thereafter. Depreciation should be about $17,000 per month. Other expenses per month include insurance $2,000, interest $23,000, maintenance $4,650, repairs $2,500, telephone $4,000, wages $10,000, and utilities $3,000.

Beginning balances as of 1/1/08 were as follows:

Account ID	Amount
10200	15,000
11000	101,000
15500	5,000,000
17500	1,200,000
20000	6,300
27000	3,875,000
39003	10,000
39005	24,700

Changes in assets, liabilities, and equities during January and February are as follows:

Account ID	January	February
10200	53,000	49,000
10700	40,000	10,000
11000	−88,000	45,000
14000	20,000	5,000
15000	19,000	0
17000	0	1,000
17500	0	33,000
20000	3,650	750
23000	0	25,000
23100	5,000	4,000
23400	2,800	3,000
23600	1,200	1,300
24400	0	24,000
27000	0	−15,400
39003	50,000	0

This is a continuous case in that the next chapter will use the work you've accomplished here as the basis for recording additional business events. After you've printed the following reports, create a backup of this file and store it on some type of external medium (flash drive, Internet site, CD, disk, etc.). The backup file should be named **Aloha Property Management Ch 10** for easy identification later. You'll be restoring this file in the next chapter. Print the following with no page numbers and no zero amounts:

a. Budgeted income statement for the two months ended in February like that created in the chapter and illustrated in Figure 10.5

b. Budgeted versus actual income statement for the two months ended in February like that created in the chapter and illustrated in Figure 10.6

c. Budgeted balance sheet for January and February like that created in the chapter and illustrated in Figure 10.9

d. Budgeted versus actual balance sheet for February like that created in the chapter and illustrated in Figures 10.12 and 10.13

Chapter 10 Case Problem 2
OCEAN VIEW FLOWERS

merchandising

Restore the backup you made for Ocean View Flowers in Chapter 9 into a new company folder. (Do not restore this backup into an existing folder.) Change the company name to include Ch 10 at the end so that the new company name is **Ocean View Flowers Ch 10**. Enter the following budget information:

Account	January	February
Sales Daylilies	30,000	30,000
Sales Anthuriums	5,000	50,000
Interest Revenue	500	1,000
Cost of Sales - flowers	16,000	42,000
Depreciation	1,500	1,500
Insurance	100	100
Interest Expense	1,600	1,600
Legal Fees	500	500
Rent	1,400	1,400
Telephone	400	400
Wages Expense	20,000	20,000
Utilities	300	300

Changes in assets, liabilities, and equities during January and February are as follows:

Account ID	January	February
10200	70,000	−34,000
10700	25,000	−5,000
11000	0	80,000
12000	20,000	0
14300	2,000	0
15000	20,000	
15100	15,000	
15500	0	270,000
16900	0	30,000
17000	0	500
17100	0	500
17500	0	2,000
20000	1,300	47,800
23400	6,000	6,000
23600	1,000	1,000
27000	50,000	270,000
39003	100,000	0

This is a continuous case in that the next chapter will use the work you've accomplished here as the basis for recording additional business events. After you've printed the following reports, create a backup of this file and store it on some type of external medium (flash drive, Internet site, CD, disk, etc.). The backup file should be named **Ocean View Flowers Ch 10** for easy identification later. You'll be restoring this file in the next chapter. Print the following with no page numbers and no zero amounts:

a. Budgeted income statement for February

b. Budgeted versus actual income statement for February

c. Budgeted balance sheet for January and February

d. Budgeted versus actual balance sheet for February

Reporting Business Activities

Case: **Wild Water Sports, Inc.**

Now that you have entered the budget information for Wild Water Sport's first year and have entered in the first four months of operating, investing, and financing transactions as well as adjustments, you are ready to prepare financial statements to send to the bank for Wild Water Sport's first three months. Donna has asked you and Karen to prepare these statements and to provide any additional information that will help her better understand Wild Water's financial performance. You and Karen decide that you'll create a set of financial statements which includes the income statement, statement of retained earnings, balance sheet, and statement of cash flows.

In addition, you agree to provide Donna some related supporting schedules that are already built into Peachtree such as an inventory profitability report, a report of items sold to customers, and a report of items purchased from vendors. These will give Donna a better idea of the company's profitability and operating activities and support the numbers reported on the company's income statement.

"What about support for the numbers on the balance sheet?" you ask.

"We'll also create some detailed reports using Peachtree's analysis tools such as the Collections Manager, Payment Manager, and Financial Manager." Karen answers.

Karen suggests you help her create an aging of accounts receivable which will support the accounts receivable balance on the balance sheet, an inventory valuation report which will support the inventory balance on the balance sheet, and an aging of accounts payable which will support the accounts payable balance on the balance sheet. In addition, she suggests that printing key ratios and key balances found in the Financial Manager will help with an analysis of the company's financial position.

"Sounds like Peachtree saves hours of work," you remark. "Let's get started."

Creating a Set of Financial Statements

Karen decides to create one customized income statement for the three-month period ended March 31 without examining each month separately, because adjustments were made only as of March 31.

Karen explains that Peachtree enables you to create reports for any period you desire. It also lets you create separate columns for a time segment—such as a day, a week, four weeks, a month, a quarter, and so on—within each period. At the end of the fiscal year, Karen will create an income statement report for the year with separate columns for each quarter.

Karen decides to modify the < Standard > Income/Earnings report available in Peachtree to include just a year-to-date column and % of total revenues column.

"Do we have to go through this customization effort every time?" Karen asks.

"No," you reply. "Peachtree has a save feature that can 'save' or retain the customization—what columns we want, what period, what layout, and so on. That way, the next time we want a similar report, it will be available from a report list."

Restoring Peachtree Backup Files from Your CD

To create and save a customized income and retained earnings statement:

1 Start the Peachtree program.

2 Restore the **Wild Water Sports, Inc 11** file from your Data Files CD or download it from the Internet. See "Data Files CD" in Chapter 1 if you need more information.

3 Set the system date to **3/31/07** and the accounting period to **Period 3**.

4 Click **Reports**, click **Financial Statements**, and then click < **Standard** > **Income/Earnings**.

5 Uncheck the Print Page Numbers and Show Zero Amounts check boxes and then click **OK**.

6 Click the **Design** button.

7 Double-click the **Net Activity Current** column description.

8 Uncheck the Print check boxes for rows 2 and 3.

9 Remove the title from row 4.

10 Type **% of Total Revenues** as the title for row 5.

11 Change the width of column 3 for row 5 to **25**. The Column Description window should now look like Figure 11.1.

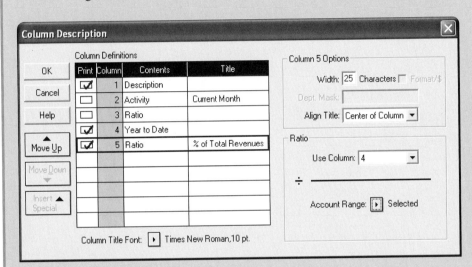

Figure 11.1

Modified Column Description

12 Click **OK**.

13 Double-click **Net Balance Current** column description.

14 Uncheck the Print check boxes for rows 2 and 3.

15 Change the width of column 3 for row 5 to **25** and then click **OK**.

16 Double-click **Net Activity Current** column description.

17 Uncheck the Print check boxes for rows 2 and 3.

18 Change the width of column 3 for row 5 to **25** and then click **OK**.

19 Click **Preview** and then click **OK**. Your modified income and retained earnings statement should look like Figure 11.2.

Figure 11.2

Modified Income
and Retained
Earnings Statement

Wild Water Sports, Inc. 11
Statement of Income and Retained Earnings
For the Three Months Ending March 31, 2007

		% of Total Revenues
Revenues		
Sales Income	767,500.00	98.80
Service Income	6,685.00	0.86
Parts Income	610.00	0.08
Interest Income	2,015.41	0.26
Total Revenues	776,810.41	100.00
Cost of Sales		
Cost of Sales	614,488.00	79.10
Total Cost of Sales	614,488.00	79.10
Gross Profit	162,322.41	20.90
Expenses		
Wages Expense	29,641.02	3.82
Payroll Tax Expense	3,304.95	0.43
Utilities Expense	2,870.00	0.37
Telephone Expense	5,020.00	0.65
Other Office Expense	4,500.00	0.58
Advertising Expense	6,700.00	0.86
Interest Expense	7,719.57	0.99
Service Charge Expense	75.00	0.01
Insurance Expense	5,500.00	0.71
Depreciation Expense	10,333.00	1.33
Gain/Loss-Sale of Assets Exp	(3,000.00)	(0.39)
Total Expenses	72,663.54	9.35
Net Income	89,658.87	11.54
Beginning Retained Earnings	0.00	
Adjustments To Date	0.00	
Ending Retained Earnings	89,658.87	

20 Click **Save**, type **Income/Earnings** as the new name of this statement, and then click **Save**.

21 Click **Print** and then click **OK**.

22 Click **Close**.

Karen suggests that you take note of the % of Total Revenues column. She explains how this column reports each item's percentage of total revenue. Cost of goods sold at 79.10% and wages expenses at 3.82% are the company's largest costs as a percentage of total revenue. Notice also that Wild Water's profit margin ratio (net income divided by total revenue) is 11.54%. You suggest a cup of coffee before you come back to customize a balance sheet.

You return to your office to create the balance sheet Donna needs as of 3/31/07. Karen explains to you that Peachtree can prepare balance sheets for any accounting period you specify. Since Donna needs balance results as of 3/31/07, the two of you start by preparing a standard balance sheet. You decide to customize the balance sheet to include a percentage column.

To create and save a customized balance sheet:

1 Click **< Standard > Balance Sheet** from the Select a Report window.

2 Uncheck the Print Page Numbers and Show Zero Amounts check boxes and then click **OK**.

3 Click the **Design** button.

4 Double-click the **Net Balance Current Period** column description.

5 Change the column width of column 2 to **15**.

6 Set Alignment Options of column 2 to **Data and Totals aligned**.

7 Add a 3rd row with **Ratio** as the Contents description and **%** as the Title.

8 Set the column width of column 3 to **8**.

9 Select **Center of Column** from the Align Title drop-down list for the new row.

10 Select **2** as the Use Column.

11 Click the arrow next to Account Range.

12 Select **1010** as the From Account Range, select **1900** as the To Account Range and then click **OK**. (This in effect selects all asset accounts.)

13 Click **OK** to close the Column Description window.

14 Set the Assets and Liabilities and Capital text body rows to a **Left of Column** Alignment.

15 Click **Preview** and then click **OK**. Your new balance sheet should look like Figures 11.3 and 11.4.

Figure 11.3

Modified Balance
Sheet—Assets Section

Wild Water Sports, Inc. 11
Balance Sheet
March 31, 2007

		%
ASSETS		
Current Assets		
Ckecking Account	$ 47,442.42	4.53
Short-Term Investments	39,890.41	3.81
Accounts Receivable	399,932.73	38.21
Inventory	243,600.00	23.27
Inventory Parts	2,112.00	0.20
Prepaid Expenses	36,500.00	3.49
Total Current Assets	769,477.56	73.52
Property and Equipment		
Property and Equipment	295,000.00	28.19
Accum. Depreciation-Prop&Eqt	(17,833.00)	(1.70)
Total Property and Equipment	277,167.00	26.48
Other Assets		
Total Other Assets	0.00	0.00
Total Assets	$ 1,046,644.56	100.00

16 Click **Print** and then click **OK**.

17 Click **Save**. Type **Balance Sheet** as the name of this new financial statement and then click **Save**.

18 Click **Close**.

Figure 11.4

Modified Balance Sheet—Liabilities and Capital Section

```
                    Wild Water Sports, Inc. 11
                         Balance Sheet
                        March 31, 2007
                                                              %

LIABILITIES AND CAPITAL

Current Liabilities
   Accounts Payable                 $      216,200.00      20.66
   Accrued Interest Payable                  1,760.97       0.17
   Sales Tax Payable                        28,457.66       2.72
   Federal Payroll Taxes Payable             2,622.00       0.25
   FUTA Payable                                 71.46       0.01
   State Payroll Taxes Payable                 241.20       0.02
   Customer Deposits                        10,000.00       0.96

   Total Current Liabilities               259,353.29      24.78

Long-Term Liabilities
   Long Term Debt-Noncurrent               297,632.40      28.44

   Total Long-Term Liabilities             297,632.40      28.44

   Total Liabilities                       556,985.69      53.22

Capital
   Common Stock                            400,000.00      38.22
   Net Income                               89,658.87       8.57

   Total Capital                           489,658.87      46.78

   Total Liabilities & Capital      $    1,046,644.56     100.00
```

Donna notices that Peachtree includes a line item called "Net Income" in the Capital section. Standard accounting practice does not allow inclusion of such an income statement category in a balance sheet. Usually, this net income is included in the retained earnings account.

Karen comments that at first she thought the percentage column was the same as the one shown in the income statement: the percentage each item is to the total revenue (what Peachtree calls "income"). But now she sees that this column shows the percentage of total assets. For example, the checking account is 4.53% of Wild Water Sport's total assets, and accounts receivable is 38.21% of total assets. She comments that it looks like a large portion of those assets came from accounts payable (20.66%) and loans payable (28.44%), and most of the balance is from capital (46.78%).

The last financial statement required is a statement of cash flows for the quarter. Karen explains that she'll have to modify this statement as well since all she wants is cash flows for the quarter, not for the month and the quarter, which is what the standard cash flow report provides.

To create and save a modified statement of cash flows:

1   Click < **Standard** > **Cash Flows** from the Select a Report window.

2   Uncheck the Print Page Numbers and Show Zero Amounts check boxes and then click **OK**.

3   Click the **Design** button.

4   Double-click the **Net Activity Current** column description.

5   Uncheck the Print check box from row 2.

6   Delete the title from row 3 and then click **OK**.

7   Do the same for all other sections of the statement of cash flows.

8   Click **Preview** and then click **OK**. Your statement of cash flows should look like Figure 11.5.

9   Click **Print** and then click **OK**.

10   Click **Save**. Type **Cash Flow** as the name of this new financial statement and then click **Save**.

11   Click **Close**.

Figure 11.5

Modified Statement of Cash Flows

Wild Water Sports, Inc. 11
Statement of Cash Flow
For the three Months Ended March 31, 2007

Cash Flows from operating activities		
Net Income	$	89,658.87
Adjustments to reconcile net		
income to net cash provided		
by operating activities		
Accum. Depreciation - Prop&Eqt		10,333.00
Accounts Receivable		(303,632.73)
Inventory		128,400.00
Inventory Parts		(2,112.00)
Prepaid Expenses		(36,500.00)
Accounts Payable		139,200.00
Accrued Interest Payable		1,760.97
Sales Tax Payable		28,457.66
Federal Payroll Taxes Payable		2,622.00
FUTA Payable		71.46
State Payroll Taxes Payable		241.20
Customer Deposits		10,000.00
Total Adjustments		(21,158.44)
Net Cash provided by Operations		68,500.43
Cash Flows from investing activities		
Used For		
Property and Equipment		(220,000.00)
Net cash used in investing		(220,000.00)
Cash Flows from financing activities		
Proceeds From		
Long Term Debt-Noncurrent		305,000.00
Common Stock		300,000.00
Used For		
Long Term Debt-Noncurrent		(391,167.60)
Net cash used in financing		213,832.40
Net increase <decrease> in cash	$	62,332.83
Summary		
Cash Balance at End of Period	$	87,332.83
Cash Balance at Beg of Period		(25,000.00)
Net Increase <Decrease> in Cash	$	62,332.83

In addition to the basic set of financial statements, Karen now plans to create some supporting schedules and graphs.

Creating Additional Reports for Analysis of Sales and Purchases

"This is very helpful information," Donna comments as she quickly skims the customized income and retained earnings statement, balance sheet, statement of cash flows, and budget versus actual reports you previously created. "I can see Wild Water's financial position, and how we stand in relation to where I thought we'd be. Can I see a bit more detail?" she asks. "I'm afraid I might miss something when I look at just the financial statements."

Both you and Karen agree that some additional detail would be helpful. In particular, Donna is anxious to know more about product sales and related costs. It is clear that one standard report which might be helpful is Peachtree's inventory profitability report. This report identifies each item sold during the period, how many were sold, what they cost, what gross profit was earned, the percentage of gross profit to sales, and the percentage of total sales provided by each item.

To create an inventory profitability report:

1 Click **Reports**, click Inventory, and then double-click **Inventory Profitability Report** from the Select a Report window.

2 Click the **Design** button and then click the **Options** button.

3 Uncheck the Include Items with no activity check box.

4 Select **Period 1, (1/1/07)** in the From drop-down list.

5 Click the **Fields** tab.

6 Uncheck the Show check box in row 1 next to Item ID and then click **OK**.

7 Click **Preview**. Your report should look like Figure 11.6.

8 Click **Print** and then click **OK**.

9 Click **Save**. Type **1st Qtr Inv. Profitability** as the name of this new report and then click **Save**.

10 Close both the newly saved report and the Select a Report windows.

<table>
<tr><td colspan="7">Wild Water Sports, Inc. 11
Inventory Profitability Report
For the Period From Jan 1, 2007 to Mar 31, 2007
Filter Criteria includes: 1) Stock/Assembly. Report order is by ID. Report is printed with Truncated Long Descriptions.</td></tr>
<tr><td>Item Description</td><td>Units Sold</td><td>Sales($)</td><td>Cost($)</td><td>Gross Profit($)</td><td>Gross Profit(%)</td><td>% of Total</td></tr>
<tr><td>Malibu Sportster LX</td><td>1.00</td><td>52,000.00</td><td>41,600.00</td><td>10,400.00</td><td>20.00</td><td>7.40</td></tr>
<tr><td>Malibu Sunscape LSV</td><td>3.00</td><td>195,000.00</td><td>156,000.00</td><td>39,000.00</td><td>20.00</td><td>27.73</td></tr>
<tr><td>Malibu Vride</td><td>2.00</td><td>96,000.00</td><td>76,800.00</td><td>19,200.00</td><td>20.00</td><td>13.65</td></tr>
<tr><td>Malibu WakeSetter VLX</td><td>1.00</td><td>57,000.00</td><td>45,600.00</td><td>11,400.00</td><td>20.00</td><td>8.11</td></tr>
<tr><td>Malibu WakeSetter XTI</td><td>1.00</td><td>70,000.00</td><td>56,000.00</td><td>14,000.00</td><td>20.00</td><td>9.96</td></tr>
<tr><td>Tige 22v</td><td>2.00</td><td>157,500.00</td><td>126,000.00</td><td>31,500.00</td><td>20.00</td><td>22.40</td></tr>
<tr><td>Tige 24v</td><td></td><td></td><td></td><td></td><td></td><td></td></tr>
<tr><td>MB B52 V23 Team Edition</td><td>1.00</td><td>75,000.00</td><td>60,000.00</td><td>15,000.00</td><td>20.00</td><td>10.67</td></tr>
<tr><td>Engine Oil</td><td>9.00</td><td>45.00</td><td>36.00</td><td>9.00</td><td>20.00</td><td>0.01</td></tr>
<tr><td>Oil Filter</td><td>2.00</td><td>30.00</td><td>24.00</td><td>6.00</td><td>20.00</td><td></td></tr>
<tr><td>Tune-up Parts</td><td>2.00</td><td>500.00</td><td>400.00</td><td>100.00</td><td>20.00</td><td>0.07</td></tr>
<tr><td>Air Filter</td><td>1.00</td><td>35.00</td><td>28.00</td><td>7.00</td><td>20.00</td><td></td></tr>
<tr><td></td><td>25.00</td><td>703,110.00</td><td>562,488.00</td><td>140,622.00</td><td></td><td>100.00</td></tr>
</table>

Figure 11.6

Inventory Profitability Report for the Quarter Ended 3/31/07

"Shouldn't the total sales shown on this report equal the revenues reported from the sales of boats and parts on the income statement?" you ask. "When I add the two revenue accounts (sales income of $767,500 and parts income of $610) from the income statement, I get $768,110. However, the inventory profitability report only shows $703,110, a $65,000 difference."

"That difference is the accrual adjusting entry (#14) we made at the end of March," Karen says. "Many of the detailed reports generated by Peachtree are based on typical source documents like invoices and exclude adjusting entries like the adjusting entry I just referred to." Karen creates the following reconciliation to explain the difference:

Sales as reported on the income statement	$768,110.00
Adjusting entry #14	65,000.00
Sales as reported on the inventory profitability report	$703,110.00

Another report Karen thinks might be interesting is the items sold to customers report for the quarter. This report identifies how many items were sold to each customer, the dollar amount of those sales, the cost of those sales, the gross profit on those sales, and the gross profit percentage.

To create an items sold to customers report:

1 Click **Reports**, click **Accounts Receivable**, and then double-click **Items Sold to Customers** from the Select a Report window.

2 Click the **Design** button and then click the **Options** button.

3 Type **1/1/07** in the From drop-down list.

4 Place a check in the **Print Report in Summary Format** check box.

5 Click the **Fields** tab.

6 Uncheck the Show check box in row 1 next to Customer ID and in row 3 next to the Item ID and then click **OK**.

7 Click **Preview**. Your report should look like Figure 11.7.

Figure 11.7

Items Sold to Customers
for the Quarter

Wild Water Sports, Inc. 11					
Items Sold to Customers					
For the Period From Jan 1, 2007 to Mar 31, 2007					
Filter Criteria includes: Report order is by Customer ID, Item ID. Report is printed in Summary Format.					
Name	Qty	Amount	Cost of Sales	Gross Profit	Gross Margin
Orlando Water Sports	5.00	1,250.00	200.00	1,050.00	84.00
Buena Vista Water Sports	16.00	1,845.00	256.00	1,589.00	86.12
Walking on Water	1.00	57,000.00	45,600.00	11,400.00	20.00
Freebirds	9.00	130,845.00	104,000.00	26,845.00	20.52
Florida Sports Camp	9.00	150.325.00	119,000.00	31,325.00	20.84
Performance Rentals	15.00	154,965.00	123,000.00	31,965.00	20.63
Seth Blackman	1.00	52,000.00	41,600.00	10,400.00	20.00
Alisa Hay	12.00	565.00	32.00	533.00	94.34
Fantasy Sports	2.00	113,000.00	90,400.00	22,600.00	20.00
Sonia Garcia	1.00	48,000.00	38,400.00	9,600.00	20.00
Report Totals	71.00	709,795.00	562,488.00	147,307.00	20.75

8 Click **Print** and then click **OK**.

9 Click **Save**. Type **1st Qtr Items Sold** as the name of this new report and then click **Save**.

10 Close both the newly saved report and the Select a Report windows.

Once again, you have to reconcile this report to revenues reported on the income statement. This report includes revenues from the sales of boats and parts as well as revenues from services provided. The total revenue report from these items on the income statement for the quarter was $774,795 (sales income of $767,500 + parts income $610 + service income $6,685). Once again, the difference between the total revenue shown on the items sold to customers report of $709,795 and the total revenue reported on the income statement of $774,795 is the $65,000 accrual discussed above. Karen creates the following reconciliation:

Sales as reported on the income statement	$774,795.00
Adjusting entry #14	65,000.00
Sales as reported on the inventory profitability report	$709,795.00

A third report Karen thinks might be interesting is the items purchased from vendors report for the quarter.

To create an items purchased from vendors report:

1 Click **Reports**, click **Accounts Payable**, and then double-click **Items Purchased from Vendors** from the Select a Report window.

2 Click the **Design** button and then click the **Options** button.

3 Type **1/1/07** in the From drop-down list.

4 Select **10000** in the From drop-down list for Vendor ID and **10200** in the To drop-down list for Vendor ID to restrict the list of vendors to only those whose vendor ID is between 10000 and 10200. This will give you a list of just those vendors from whom the company purchases inventory.

5 Click the **Fields** tab.

6 Uncheck the Show check box in row 1 next to Vendor ID and in row 7 next to the Item ID and then click **OK**.

7 Click **Preview**. Your report should look like Figure 11.8.

Figure 11.8

Items Purchased from Vendors for the Quarter

Wild Water Sports, Inc. 11
Items Purchased from Vendors
For the Period From Jan 1, 2007 to Mar 31, 2007
Filter Criteria includes: 1) Vendor IDs from 10000 to 10200. Report order is by Vendor ID, Item ID. Report is printed in Detail Format.

Name	Item Description	Qty	Amount
Malibu Boats	Malibu Sportster LX	2.00	83,200.00
	Malibu Sunscape LSV	1.00	52,000.00
	Malibu Vride	1.00	38,400.00
	Malibu WakeSetter XTI	1.00	56,000.00
		5.00	229,600.00
MB Sports	MB B52 V23 Team Edition	1.00	60,000.00
		1.00	60,000.00
Tige Boats	Tige 22v	2.00	126,000.00
	Tige 24v	1.00	70,000.00
		3.00	196,000.00
Report Totals		9.00	485,600.00

8 Click **Print** and then click **OK**.

9 Click **Save**. Type **1st Qtr Items Purchased** as the name of this new report and then click **Save**.

10 Click **Close** and close Select a Report.

When you show Donna these reports, she comments that they will be very helpful. But she wants to see even more information derived from the financial statements—specifically, she wants to see detailed reports on accounts receivable, accounts payable, and inventory.

Creating Additional Reports for Managing Accounts Receivable, Accounts Payable, Inventory, and Your Business

With Peachtree, you can generate many supporting reports for the financial statements—what accountants consider traditional support in the form of schedules. Karen reads through Peachtree Help and discovers several reports that Peachtree generates that will help Donna—the collection aging report, payment aging report, financial manager reports, and an inventory valuation report. The collection aging report stratifies the amounts owed by customers by the number of days outstanding. The older the balance, the more likely it won't be collected. The payment aging report stratifies the amounts owed by the company to its vendors by the number of days outstanding. The financial manager report provides key financial ratios and balances. The inventory valuation report identifies the items remaining in inventory as of a particular date. It specifies the quantity on hand, the items value (cost), and the percentage of inventory value by item.

To create the collection aging and payment aging reports:

1 Click **Analysis** and then click **Collection Manager**.

2 Select the **Numeric** Display option button to see the collection aging report in Figure 11.9.

3 Click **Print** to print this report and then click **Close** to close this window.

4 Click **Analysis** and then click **Payment Manager**.

Click here for
numeric version
of report

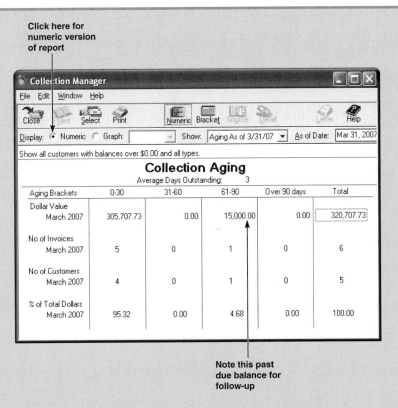

Figure 11.9

Collection Aging Report

Note this past
due balance for
follow-up

5 Select the **Numeric** Display option button to see the payment aging report in Figure 11.10.

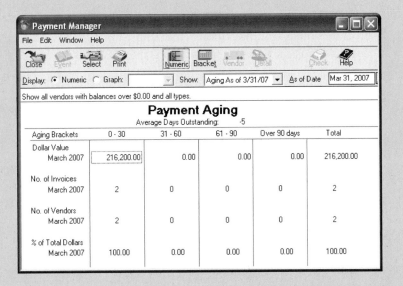

Figure 11.10

Payment Aging Report

6 Click **Print** to print this report and then click **Close** to close this window.

Karen reminds you to reconcile these two reports to accounts receivable and accounts payable amounts as reported on the balance sheet. The balance sheet reported accounts receivable of $399,932.73, while the collection aging report stated total accounts receivable of $320,707.73. The difference is partially attributed to the accrual of revenue and related amounts to be collected for sales tax. The remaining difference is attributed to a journal entry created to reclassify $10,000 received as a deposit on account to unearned revenue. Karen creates the following reconciliation:

Accounts receivable as reported on the balance sheet	$399,932.73
Adjusting entry #18 to reclassify unearned revenue	10,000.00
Adjusting entry #14	69,225.00
Accounts receivable as reported on the collection aging report	$320,707.73

When you compare the above payable aging report and the Accounts Payable balance per the financial statement you note that both amounts agree.

"This won't always be the case," Karen explains. "If we had made an adjusting entry to accrue some expenses, the balance in the payable aging report would have been different than the balance in Accounts Payable as reported on the balance sheet, and thus we would have had to create a reconciliation to explain the difference."

Karen notes the past due balances from a customer and will follow up tomorrow. She notes the Accounts Payable balance is current as of 3/31/07. She explains that the last analysis report she wants to create will provide typical financial management information like profitability ratios and liquidity ratios like the current ratio.

To create the financial manager reports:

1 Click **Analysis** and then click **Financial Manager**.

2 Select the **Business Summary** Display option button to see the ratios report in Figure 11.11.

3 Click **Print** to print this report.

4 Select the **Key Balances** Display option button to see the report in Figure 11.12.

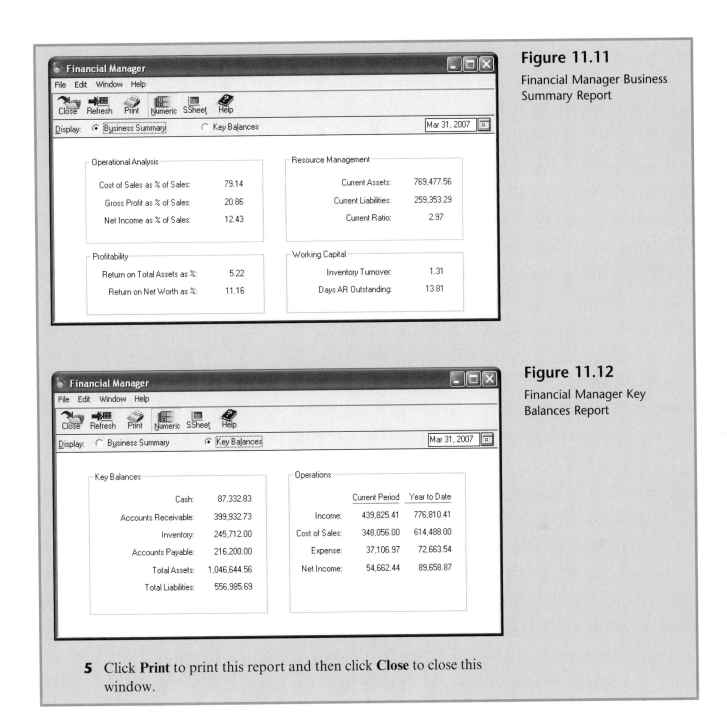

Figure 11.11

Financial Manager Business Summary Report

Figure 11.12

Financial Manager Key Balances Report

5 Click **Print** to print this report and then click **Close** to close this window.

Karen believes that both the business summary and key balances reports will help Donna negotiate with the bank and give her quick access to ratios and balances. She needs one more report to help her identify the detail behind the balance sheet inventory amount.

To create the financial manager reports:

1 Click **Reports**, click **Inventory**, and then click **Inventory Valuation Report**.

2 Click **Options** and then uncheck the Truncate Long Description and Include Items with no quantity on hand.

3 Click the **Fields** tab and uncheck the Show check box for the first two rows: Item ID and Item Class and for the fourth row: Stocking U/M.

4 Click **OK** and then click **Design**. Resize the Item Description column to include all text.

5 Click **Preview** to view the inventory valuation report shown in Figure 11.13.

Figure 11.13

Inventory Valuation Report

Wild Water Sports, Inc. 11
Inventory Valuation Report
As of Mar 31, 2007
Filter Criteria includes: 1) Stock/Assembly. Report order is by ID.

Item Description	Cost Method	Qty on Hand	Item Value	Avg Cost	% of Inv Value
Malibu Sunsetter LXI	Average	1.00	48,000.00	48000.00	16.12
Malibu Sportster LX	Average	2.00	83,200.00	41600.00	27.95
Malibu Vride	Average	1.00	38,400.00	38400.00	12.90
Malibu WakeSetter XTI	Average	1.00	56,000.00	56000.00	18.81
Tige 24v	Average	1.00	70,000.00	70000.00	23.51
Engine Oil	Average	141.00	564.00	4.00	0.19
Oil Filter	Average	23.00	276.00	12.00	0.00
Tune-up Parts	Average	3.00	600.00	200.00	0.20
Air Filter	Average	24.00	672.00	28.00	0.23
			297,712.00		100.00

6 Click **Print** and then click **OK** to print this report.

7 Click **Close** and then click **No** when asked if you want to save changes.

8 **Close** Select a Report.

Karen notes that once again the balance in this report doesn't equal the amount reported as inventory on the general ledger of $245,712 (in the inventory and inventory parts accounts). The difference between the two is the $52,000 accrual on March 31, 2007, where inventory was reduced and cost of goods sold was charged for $52,000. Karen creates the following reconciliation:

Inventory and inventory parts as reported on the balance sheet	$245,712.00
Adjusting entry #14	52,000.00
Inventory as reported on the inventory valuation report	$297,712.00

To help understand all of these reconciliations, Karen prepared the following summary reconciliation for all accounts:

	A/R	Inventory	A/P	Sales (Items Sold to Cust.)	Sales (Inv. Profit)
As reported on the financial statement	399,932.73	245,712.00	216,200.00	774,795.00	768,110.00
Adjusting entry	(10,000.00)	-	-	-	-
Adjusting entry	(69,225.00)	52,000.00	-	(65,000.00)	(65,000.00)
As reported on the supporting schedule	320,707.73	297,712.00	216,200.00	709,795.00	703,110.00

Exporting Reports to Excel

Karen explains that in Peachtree you can export any reports you create to Microsoft's Excel spreadsheet program.

"Why export to Microsoft Excel when Peachtree gives us so many report options?" you ask.

Karen explains that, occasionally, she may need to change a report's appearance or contents in ways that are not available within Peachtree. Since the changes you make in Excel do not affect your Peachtree data, you are free to customize a report as needed or even change report data to run "what if" scenarios.

Karen reads through Peachtree Help and discovers that exporting a report to Excel is as simple as clicking a new button on the report's button bar. She suggests that the two of you experiment with this feature by exporting a standard income statement.

To export the standard income statement to Excel:

1 Click **Reports**, click **Financial Statements**, and then double-click **< Standard > Income Stmnt.**

2 Uncheck the Print Page Numbers and the Show Zero Amounts check boxes and then click **OK**.

3 Click **Excel**.

4 Select the **Create a new Microsoft Excel workbook** option button under File option.

5 Check the **Use freeze panes** check box under Excel options.

6 Select the **Raw data layout** option button under Report layout option.

7 Select the **Send header to Page Setup in Excel** option button.

8 Click **OK**.

9 In Excel, click **File**, click Page Setup, select the **Portrait** orientation, and then click **OK** to see the Excel report created in Figure 11.14.

Figure 11.14

Excel Format Income Statement

	A	B	C	D	E
1		Current Month		Year to Date	
2	Revenues				
3	Sales Income	$ 434,750.00	98.85	$ 767,500.00	98.80
4	Service Income	2,740.00	0.62	6,685.00	0.86
5	Parts Income	320.00	0.07	610.00	0.08
6	Interest Income	2,015.41	0.46	2,015.41	0.26
7					
8	Total Revenues	439,825.41	100.00	776,810.41	100.00
9					
10					
11	Cost of Sales				
12	Cost of Sales	348,056.00	79.14	614,488.00	79.10
13					
14	Total Cost of Sales	348,056.00	79.14	614,488.00	79.10
15					
16	Gross Profit	91,769.41	20.86	162,322.41	20.90
17					
18	Expenses				
19	Wages Expense	8,933.34	2.03	29,641.02	3.82
20	Payroll Tax Expense	996.06	0.23	3,304.95	0.43
21	Utilities Expense	1,050.00	0.24	2,870.00	0.37
22	Telephone Expense	1,500.00	0.34	5,020.00	0.65
23	Other Office Expense	0.00	0.00	4,500.00	0.58
24	Advertising Expense	4,000.00	0.91	6,700.00	0.86
25	Interest Expense	7,719.57	1.76	7,719.57	0.99
26	Service Charge Expense	75.00	0.02	75.00	0.01
27	Insurance Expense	5,500.00	1.25	5,500.00	0.71
28	Depreciation Expense	10,333.00	2.35	10,333.00	1.33
29	Gain/Loss - Sale of Assets Exp	(3,000.00)	(0.68)	(3,000.00)	(0.39)
30					
31	Total Expenses	37,106.97	8.44	72,663.54	9.35
32					
33	Net Income	$ 54,662.44	12.43	$ 89,658.87	11.54

Trouble? To export reports to Excel, you must have Microsoft Excel 97 or a higher version installed on your computer.

10 Select cell **C3** in the report just exported. Note that the export process has created not only a spreadsheet with values, but also one with formulas.

11 Click **File** in Excel and then click **Print Preview**.

12 Click **Setup** and then click the **Sheet** tab in the Page Setup window. Place a check mark in the Gridlines and Row and column headings check boxes. (This will enable the printing of gridlines and row and column headings.)

13 Click the **Page** tab, click the **Fit to**: option button to scale printing to one page wide and one page tall, and then click **OK**.

14 Click **Print** in the Excel Print Preview window and then click **OK** in the Print window to print the Excel document you just created. Your spreadsheet should look like Figure 11.15.

Figure 11.15

Printed Excel Document

Wild Water Sports, Inc. 11
Income Statement
For the Three Months Ending March 31, 2007

	A	B	C	D	E
1		Current Month		Year to Date	
2	Revenues				
3	Sales Income	$ 434,750.00	98.85	$ 767,500.00	98.80
4	Service Income	2,740.00	0.62	6,685.00	0.86
5	Parts Income	320.00	0.07	610.00	0.08
6	Interest Income	2,015.41	0.46	2,015.41	0.26
7					
8	Total Revenues	439,825.41	100.00	776,810.41	100.00
9					
10					
11	Cost of Sales				
12	Cost of Sales	348,056.00	79.14	614,488.00	79.10
13					
14	Total Cost of Sales	348,056.00	79.14	614,488.00	79.10
15					
16	Gross Profit	91,769.41	20.86	162,322.41	20.90
17					
18	Expenses				
19	Wages Expense	8,933.34	2.03	29,641.02	3.82
20	Payroll Tax Expense	996.06	0.23	3,304.95	0.43
21	Utilities Expense	1,050.00	0.24	2,870.00	0.37
22	Telephone Expense	1,500.00	0.34	5,020.00	0.65
23	Other Office Expense	0.00	0.00	4,500.00	0.58
24	Advertising Expense	4,000.00	0.91	6,700.00	0.86
25	Interest Expense	7,719.57	1.76	7,719.57	0.99
26	Service Charge Expense	75.00	0.02	75.00	0.01
27	Insurance Expense	5,500.00	1.25	5,500.00	0.71
28	Depreciation Expense	10,333.00	2.35	10,333.00	1.33
29	Gain/Loss - Sale of Assets Exp	(3,000.00)	(0.68)	(3,000.00)	(0.39)
30					
31	Total Expenses	37,106.97	8.44	72,663.54	9.35
32					
33	Net Income	$ 54,662.44	12.43	$ 89,658.87	11.54
34					

15 Click **File** in Excel and then **Exit** to quit the Excel program.

16 Click **No** to not save the spreadsheet since it will no longer be used.

17 Close all windows in Peachtree.

End Note

You've completed the reports for Donna and decide to deliver them to her office. After quickly skimming each report, she compliments you and Karen on your fine work and you turn to walk back to your office.

As you walk back to your office, you comment, "That was a pretty good review of the accounting basics and now I've learned to use a computerized accounting system. Life is good!"

Chapter 11 Questions

1 Identify the three supporting schedules that support the operating activities of a company reported on the income statement, as illustrated in this chapter.

2 Identify the four supporting schedules that support the balance sheet, as illustrated in this chapter.

3 How is the profit margin ratio calculated?

4 What are the steps necessary to create a % of Total Assets column to the balance sheet?

5 Once created, what does the % of Total Assets column mean?

6 What information does the inventory profitability report provide?

7 What information does the items sold to customers report provide?

8 What information does the collection aging report provide?

9 What information does the payment aging report provide?

10 What information does the inventory valuation report provide?

Chapter 11 Assignments

1 *Adding More Information to Wild Water Sports*

Restore the file **Wild Water Sports, Inc 11A** found on the text CD or download it from the text Web site. Be sure to set the system date to **4/30/07** and the accounting period to **Period 4 – 04/01/07 – 04/30/07** and then create, save, and print the following reports with no page numbers and without zero balance accounts (as you did in the chapter):

merchandising

a. Statement of income and retained earnings for the four months ending April 30, 2007, with a % of Total Revenues column

b. Balance sheet as of April 30, 2007, with a % column

c. Statement of cash flow for the four months ending April 30, 2007

d. Inventory profitability report for the four months ending April 30, 2007

e. Items sold to customers report for the four months ending April 30, 2007

f. Items purchased from vendors report for the four months ending April 30, 2007, from only those vendors who sell Wild Water inventory

g. Collection aging report as of April 30, 2007

h. Payment aging report as of April 30, 2007

i. Business summary report as of April 30, 2007

j. Key balances report as of April 30, 2007

k. Inventory valuation report as of April 30, 2007

l. Export the inventory profitability report created above to Excel and then print the Excel spreadsheet from Excel with row and column headers and gridlines in landscape orientation

m. Prepare a summary reconciliation to explain any differences between the supporting schedules and the financial statements you just created like the one created in the chapter

merchandising

2   *Adding More Information to Central Coast Cellular*

Restore the backup you made for Central Coast Cellular in Chapter 10 into a new company folder. (Do not restore this backup into an existing folder.) Change the company name to include Ch 11 at the end so that the new company name is **Central Coast Cellular Ch 11**. Change the system date to **1/31/09** and the accounting period to **Period 1 – 1/1/09 – 1/31/09** and then create, save, and print the following reports with no page numbers and without zero balance accounts (as you did in the chapter):

a. Statement of income and retained earnings for January 2009 with a % of Total Revenues column

b. Balance sheet as of January 31, 2009, with a % column

c. Statement of cash flow for January 2009

d. Inventory profitability report for January 2009

e. Items sold to customers report for January 2009

f. Items purchased from vendors report for January 2009 for all vendors

g. Collection aging report as of January 31, 2009

h. Payment aging report as of January 31, 2009

i. Business summary report as of January 31, 2009

j. Key balances report as of January 31, 2009

k. Inventory valuation report as of January 31, 2009

l. Export the inventory profitability report you created to Excel and then print the Excel spreadsheet from Excel with row and column headers and gridlines in landscape orientation

m. Reconciliation of financial statement amounts and supporting schedules

Chapter 11 Case Problem 1

ALOHA PROPERTY MANAGEMENT

service

Restore the backup you made for Aloha in Chapter 10 into a new company folder. (Do not restore this backup into an existing folder.) Change the company name to include Ch 11 at the end so that the new company name is **Aloha Property Management Ch 11**. Change the system date to **2/29/08** and the accounting period to **Period 2 − 2/1/08 − 2/29/08** and then create, save, and print the following reports with no page numbers and without zero balance accounts (like you did in the chapter). *Note:* Since this is a service company, no inventory profitability, inventory valuation, or items purchased from vendors reports are required:

a. Statement of income and retained earnings for the two months ending February 29, 2008, with a % of Total Revenues column

b. Balance sheet as of February 29, 2008, with a % column

c. Statement of cash flow for the two months ending February 29, 2008

d. Items sold to customers report for the two months ending February 29, 2008 (Uncheck the Show check boxes for both the Customer ID and Item ID fields. Then check the Item Description Show check box. With the item Description field selected, click the **Move UP** button until the Item Description field is right below the Name field.)

e. Collection aging report as of February 29, 2008

f. Payment aging report as of February 29, 2008

g. Business summary report as of February 29, 2008

h. Key balances report as of February 29, 2008

i. Export the statement of income and retained earnings report you created to Excel and then print the Excel spreadsheet from Excel with row and column headers and gridlines in portrait orientation. Use the Fit to 1 page width option.

merchandising

Chapter 11 Case Problem 2
OCEAN VIEW FLOWERS

Restore the backup you made for Ocean View Flowers in Chapter 10 into a new company folder. (Do not restore this backup into an existing folder.) Change the company name to include Ch 11 at the end so that the new company name is **Ocean View Flowers Ch 11**. Change the system date to **2/29/08** and the accounting period to **Period 2 – 2/1/08 – 2/29/08** and then create and print the following reports with no page numbers and without zero balance accounts (as you did in the chapter):

a. Statement of income and retained earnings for the two months ending February 29, 2008, with a % of Total Revenues column

b. Balance sheet as of February 29, 2008, with a % column

c. Statement of cash flow for the two months ending February 29, 2008

d. Inventory profitability report for the two months ending February 29, 2008

e. Items sold to customers report for the two months ending February 29, 2008

f. Items purchased from vendors report for the two months ending February 29, 2008

g. Collection aging report as of February 29, 2008

h. Payment aging report as of February 29, 2008

i. Business summary report as of February 29, 2008

j. Key balances report as of February 29, 2008

k. Inventory valuation report as of February 29, 2008

l. Export the inventory valuation report you created to Excel and then print the Excel spreadsheet from Excel with row and column headers and gridlines in landscape orientation

m. Prepare a summary reconciliation to explain any differences between the supporting schedules and the financial statements you just created like the one created in the chapter

Comprehensive Problems

Comprehensive Problem 1: SPORTS CITY

merchandising

Restore the file **Sports City** found on the text CD or download it from the text Web site. Be sure to set the system date to **1/31/07** and the accounting period to **Period 1 — 01/01/07 — 01/31/07**. The previous accountant had used a different computer accounting system. You chose to convert that work to Peachtree and the file you just restored is the result of that effort. You note the existing sales tax rate already present in the Peachtree file is 8%. Now you need to record the following additional business transactions in chronological order (remember, dates are in the month of January 2007).

Chronological List of Business Transactions

Date	Transaction
1/16	Purchased office supplies from vendor Office Max for $250 with Check No. 4.
1/16	Received terms net 10 days from Nike and Wilson Sporting Goods. Update vendor records accordingly.
1/17	Received items and entered a bill (invoice 23423) from Nike for a previously recorded Purchase Order No. 1 (terms: net 10).
1/18	Received items and entered a bill (invoice 984) from Wilson Sporting Goods for a previously recorded Purchase Order No. 2 (terms: net 10).
1/19	Hired a new employee, ID AF, Anne Franks, 112 East Fir #3, Lompoc, CA 93436, a single woman, Social Security number 233-89-4232. She will earn an hourly wage of $8.00, is paid semimonthly like all employees, and is subject to all payroll taxes including the training tax.
1/22	Received a $400 payment on account from Cabrillo High School (its Check No. 354), which is grouped with other undeposited funds. (Used sales receipt SR 001.)
1/23	Invoiced Buena Vista Elementary (a new customer with ID Buena Vista, 300 Aldeberan St., Vandenberg Village, CA 93436 and terms due in 5 days and a credit limit of $3,000) for 100 shirts and 5 footballs with invoice 3.
1/23	Received a $600 payment on account (its Check No. 0933, Sports City's sales receipt SR 002) from Lompoc High School, which is also grouped with other undeposited funds.
1/24	Borrowed $10,000 from Mid-State Bank with a short-term note payable. Use journal entry 1.
1/25	Wrote checks to pay all bills due by 1/31/07 using Check Nos. 5 — 9 for a total of $18,993.90. (This excludes the state sales taxes owed.)
1/29	Deposited by mail all previously received but undeposited payments, totaling $1,000, to Mid-State Bank with Deposit Ticket 0001.
1/31	Recorded depreciation of $2,000 on furniture & fixtures with journal entry 2.
1/31	Recorded the expiration of $3,000 in prepaid rent with journal entry 3.
1/31	Reclassified the advance payment made by Arroyo Grande High School to unearned revenue (a new other current liability account with ID 2300) with journal entry 4.
1/31	Paid all employees for the pay period 1/16 — 1/31. Ms. Franks worked 75 hours during this period. (See following tax information table.)

1/31   Reconciled the bank account. The ending bank balance per the statement is $5,333.52. The bank charged a $40 service charge. Check Nos. 10, 11, and 12 for the January 31 payroll do not appear on the statement, nor does the $1,000 deposited by mail on January 29.

	Sam Snead	Kelly Flowers	Anne Franks
Check Number	10	11	12
Gross Pay	1,458.33	1,250.00	600.00
Federal Withholding	−244.00	−147.00	−73.00
Social Security Employee	−90.41	−77.50	−37.20
Social Security Employer	90.41	77.50	37.20
Medicare Employee	−21.14	−18.12	−8.70
Medicare Employer	21.14	18.12	8.70
CA—Withholding	−57.39	−40.72	−7.66
CA—Disability Employee	−7.29	−6.25	−3.00
CA—Training Tax	1.46	1.25	0.60
Federal Unemployment	11.66	10.00	4.80
CA—Unemployment	0.73	0.62	0.30
Check Amount	1,038.10	960.41	470.44

Budget information for January through March 2007 is as follows (*Note:* You are to round budget data to the nearest whole dollar.):

Account	January 07	Following
Sales	$10,000	15% increase each month thereafter
Cost of Sales	$6,000	60% of sales
Depreciation	$2,000	Constant each month thereafter
Payroll	$6,500	$500 increase each month thereafter
Rent	$3,000	Constant each month thereafter
Telephone	$100	5% increase each month thereafter
Utilities	$200	5% increase each month thereafter

Create, save, and print the following reports with no page numbers and without zero balance accounts (as you did in this and previous chapters):

a. Account reconciliation report of Mid-State Bank checking account for January 2007

b. Budgeted income statement accounts for January through March 2007

c. Budgeted versus actual income statement for January 2007

d. Statement of income and retained earnings for January 2007 with a % of Total Revenues column

e. Balance sheet as of January 31, 2007, with a % column

f. Statement of cash flows for January 2007

g. Inventory profitability report for January 2007

h. Items sold to customers report for January 2007 (print in detail, not summary, format)

i. Items purchased from vendors report for January 2007 (print in detail, not summary, format)

j. Collection aging report as of January 31, 2007

k. Payment aging report as of January 31, 2007

l. Business summary report as of January 31, 2007

m. Key balances report as of January 31, 2007

n. Inventory valuation report as of January 31, 2007

o. Export the inventory profitability report you created to Excel and then print the Excel spreadsheet from Excel with row and column headers and gridlines in landscape orientation

p. Prepare a summary reconciliation to explain any differences between the supporting schedules and the financial statements you just created like the one created in the chapter

Comprehensive Problem 2: PACIFIC BREW INC.

merchandising

Restore the backup you made for Pacific Brew Inc. in Chapter 7 into a new company folder. (Do not restore this backup into an existing folder.) Change the company name to include Ch 11 at the end so that the new company name is **Pacific Brew Ch 11**. Change the system date to **1/1/08** and the accounting period to **Period 1 − 1/1/08 − 1/31/08**. Add the following business events:

Chronological List of Business Transactions

Date	Transaction
1/17	Received all items ordered on Purchase Order No. 1003 to Lost Coast (terms net 30) on its invoice LC9873.
1/17	Received invoice 2039480 from Staples (a new vendor) for $2,500 of office supplies purchased on account terms net 15. These supplies will be used over the next six months; thus, you will need to create an office supplies (ID 1300 other current asset) account.
1/17	Using Purchase Order No. 1004, ordered 1,000 of Item 402, 1,500 of Item 403, and 2,000 of Item 404 for Best Way delivery, terms: net 30 from Lost Coast.
1/18	Using Purchase Order No. 1005, ordered 750 each of Items 302, 303, 304, and 305 for Best Way delivery, terms: net 30 from Mad River.
1/18	The manager believes the company charges too little for its products and increases all product prices 50%. (Use Peachtree Help to find out how to change item sales prices by calculating new item prices for a range of items. Adjust Price Level 1 by multiplying the current price by 50% with no rounding. Be careful to only do this once! For example, the new price for Item 302 should be $9.00, and the new price for Item 402 should be $9.38.)

1/21	Changed terms for vendor Humboldt to the standard net 30 days. Then using Purchase Order No. 1006, ordered 500 each of Items 502, 506, and 507 for Best Way delivery, from Humboldt.
1/21	Received and shipped via Best Way an order to Bon Jovi's for 200 units of Item 302, 150 units of Item 303, and 100 units of Item 507. Invoice 7001 was generated to bill the customer on net 30 terms.
1/22	Received and shipped via Best Way an order to Ocean Grove for 100 units each of Items 302, 304, and 305. Invoice 7002 was generated to bill the customer on net 30 terms.
1/23	Received and shipped via Best Way an order to Avalon Bistro for 150 units each of Items 502, 506, and 507. Invoice 7003 was generated to bill the customer on net 30 terms.
1/24	Received all items ordered and entered a bill (invoice 098732) from Purchase Order No. 1004 to Lost Coast.
1/24	Received invoice 232 from Verizon (a new vendor ID = V) for telephone services for the month of January in the amount of $500, terms: net 10.
1/24	Received invoice 121223 from the City of Arcata (a new vendor ID = CA) for utility services for the month of January in the amount of $1,500, terms: net 10.
1/25	Received Check No. 9388 as payment on account from Bon Jovi's of $4,575 on invoice 7001, which will be deposited later in the week.
1/28	Received Check No. 1233334 as an advance on future orders from River House in the amount of $1,200, which will be deposited later.
1/29	Deposited $5,775 in checks received earlier to Wells Fargo using Deposit Ticket A4007.
1/30	Modified terms for Mad River to net 15 from net due. Received all items ordered and entered invoice 82798 from Purchase Order No. 1005 to Mad River.
1/30	Paid bills from Verizon, City of Arcata, and Staples for a total of $4,500, assigning Check Nos. 110, 111, and 112, respectively.
1/30	Received and shipped an order (SR 5007) to Hole in the Wall for 250 units each of Items 303, 305, and 404. Payment of $7,032.50 (with its Check No. 3232) was deposited and mailed to Wells Fargo Bank that same day using Deposit Ticket A4008.
1/30	Paid employees. Duarte worked 83 hours, and Lopez worked 79 hours during the period. See tax information in the table on the next page.
1/31	Recorded depreciation of $800 for the month with journal entry 2.
1/31	Recorded the use of office supplies of $400 with journal entry 3.
1/31	Reclassified the $1,200 payment from River House to customer deposits with journal entry 4.
1/31	Accrued interest income on the certificate of deposit short-term investment of $2,000 with journal entry 5.
1/31	Accrued interest expense on long-term note payable of $2,600 with journal entry 6. (*Hint:* You'll have to create a new interest expense account ID = 6875 and a new accrued interest payable account ID = 2390.)
1/31	Reconciled the Wells Fargo bank account. No bank service charges were noted on the bank statement. The ending bank balance was $28,673.30. All deposits were recorded by the bank except the $7,032.50 deposit recorded 1/30/08. All checks cleared the bank except those issued on 1/31/08 for payroll.

1/31   Budget income statement account information for January through March is
          as follows. Sales income of $35,000 is expected in January, increasing
          $5,000 each month thereafter. Cost of goods sold of $15,000 is expected in
          January, increasing $2,500 each month thereafter. Depreciation, interest, rent,
          and office supplies expenses are expected to remain constant at $1,000,
          $2,000, $2,500, and $500, respectively. Telephone expenses of $450 are
          budgeted for January and are expected to increase $50 each month thereafter.
          Wages expenses are budgeted at $8,500 for January and February and then
          $10,000 for March. Utilities expense is budgeted at $1,200 for January and
          is expected to increase by 5% each month thereafter. Interest income of
          $1,500 is expected each month.

1/31   Budget balance sheet account information for January is as follows.

Checking Account	$40,000
Certificates of Deposit	30,000
Accounts Receivable	10,000
Inventory	45,000
Office Supplies	2,000
PP& E	23,000
Accounts Payable	50,650
Federal Payroll Taxes Payable	3,000
State Payroll Taxes Payable	1,000
Notes Payable	40,000
Common Stock	50,000

No changes in balance sheet accounts are expected in February and March
except retained earnings, which, of course, will change by the amount of net
income budgeted above.

	Duarte	Lopez	Patrick
Check Number	113	114	115
Gross Pay	913.00	948.00	2,083.33
Federal Withholding	−125.08	−129.88	−285.42
Social Security Employee	−56.61	−58.78	−129.17
Medicare Employee	−13.24	−13.75	−30.21
CA—Withholding	−50.22	−52.14	−114.58
CA—Disability	−4.57	−4.74	−10.42
CA—Employment Training Tax	0.91	0.95	2.08
Social Security Employer	56.61	58.78	129.17
Medicare Company	13.24	13.75	30.21
Federal Unemployment	7.30	7.58	16.67
CA—Company Unemployment	27.39	28.44	62.50
Check Amount	663.28	688.71	1,513.53

Create and print the following reports with no page numbers and without
zero balance accounts (like you did in this and previous chapters):

a. Bank reconciliation report for January 2008

b. Budgeted income statement accounts for January through
    March 2008 with a YTD column

c. Budgeted versus actual income statement for the month of January 2008

d. Budgeted balance sheet accounts for January through March 2008 with a YTD column

e. Budgeted versus actual balance sheet for the month ended January 2008 with Budget, Variance, and % Variance columns

f. Statement of income and retained earnings for the month of January 2008 with a % of Total Revenues column

g. Balance sheet as of 1/31/08 with a % column

h. Statement of cash flow for the month of January 2008 with no YTD column

i. Inventory profitability report for the month of January 2008

j. Items sold to customers report for the month of January 2008 in summary format without Customer ID

k. Items purchased from vendors report for the month of January 2008 in summary format without Vendor ID

l. Collection aging report as of 1/31/08

m. Payment aging report as of 1/31/08

n. Business summary report as of 1/31/08

o. Key balances report as of 1/31/08

p. Inventory valuation report as of 1/31/08 without Item ID, Item Class, Cost Method, and Stocking U/M

q. Export the inventory profitability report you created to Excel and then print the Excel spreadsheet from Excel with row and column headers and gridlines in landscape orientation

r. Prepare a summary reconciliation to explain any differences between the supporting schedules and the financial statements you just created like the one created in the chapter

merchandising

Comprehensive Problem 3: SUNSET SPAS INC.

Restore the backup you made for Sunset Spas Inc. in Chapter 7 into a new company folder. (Do not restore this backup into an existing folder.) Change the company name to include Ch 11 at the end so that the new company name is **Sunset Spas Ch 11**. Change the system date to **1/1/07** and the accounting period to **Period 1 — 1/1/07 — 1/31/07**. Add the following business events:

Chronological List of Business Transactions

Date	Transaction
1/17	Paid $18,000 in liability insurance for the year to Hartford Insurance (new vendor with ID = HI) using Check No. 110. (*Hint:* Record this as Prepaid Expenses.)
1/17	Received invoice A4900 from Staples (new vendor with ID = ST) for $500 in office supplies purchased on account which are expected to be consumed in this month. Terms are net 30.
1/17	Received net 30 terms from Cal Spas, changed the default shipper for this vendor to Cust. Pickup, and increased Sunset's credit limit with Cal Spas to $50,000.
1/17	Using Purchase Order No. 5003, ordered one each of Items 301, 302, and 303 for immediate delivery, terms: net 30, from Cal Spas.
1/18	Created a new customer: Landmark Landscaping, ID = LL, address = 8500 Ridgefield Place, San Diego, CA 92129, shipping = Cust. Pickup, payment terms net 15, Sales Tax = Tax, and a credit limit of $25,000.
1/18	Sold two of Item 302 to Landmark Landscaping with six hours of installation on invoice 10001.
1/19	Granted terms of net 15 to customer Marriott Hotels, changed the default shipper for this customer to Cust. Pickup, and changed Sunset's credit limit with Marriott to $50,000.
1/19	Sold two of Item 202 and one of Item 302 to Marriott Hotels with 15 hours of installation on invoice 10002 payment terms net 15.
1/19	Applied the Marriott Hotels prepayment received on 1/16/07 to invoice 10002.
1/20	Hired a new employee, Walton Perez, ID = WP, 530 Miramar Rd. Apt 230, San Diego, CA 92145, a single man, Social Security number 323-99-2394. He will earn an hourly wage of $9.00, is paid semimonthly, and is subject to all payroll taxes. He will start work 2/1/07.
1/22	Purchased equipment for installation and support of spa services from Outlet Tool Supply (a new vendor with ID OTS, shipper = Cust. Pickup, terms net 30, credit limit $30,000) for $25,000. Received Outlet's invoice 92378 with 30-day terms. (Record as Equipment.)
1/22	Received and deposited (Deposit Ticket ID = 906) a $3,500 check (Check No. 9098) from a new customer, Kristen's Spa Resort (ID KSR and shipper — Cust. Pickup), for work to be performed next month.
1/23	Received a $23,000 invoice 982223 from the City of San Diego (ID = SD) for licenses payable with terms net 15.
1/24	Changed terms for Pam's Designs (a customer) to net 15 with a credit limit of $70,000 and shipper = Cust. Pickup.
1/24	Sold six of Item 203 to Pam's Designs with 18 hours of installation on invoice 10003, payment terms net 15.
1/25	Received a $1,400 bill (invoice 309) from Verizon (new vendor with ID = V) for telephone installation services terms net 15.
1/26	Took delivery of a shipment from Cal Spas (Sunset's Purchase Order No. 5003, Cal Spas' invoice 2987). All items were received. (Terms are net 30.)
1/29	Received $5,000 payment (Landmark's Check No. 3098) on account from Landmark Landscaping, which was deposited into the checking account with Deposit Ticket 907.
1/30	Paid two bills in full: City of San Diego and Verizon using Check Nos. 111 and 112, respectively.

1/31	Paid employees. Sanchez worked 84 hours, and Lee worked 67 hours during the period. Start with Check No. 113. See tax information in the table on the next page.
1/31	Accrued $3,000 in additional telephone services provided by Verizon to accounts payable for which a bill had not yet been received. Set up for reversal next month. (Use journal entry 3.)
1/31	Recorded the expiration of one month's prepaid insurance. (Use journal entry 4.)
1/31	Reclassified Kristen's Spa Resort prepayment of $3,500 and Landmark's prepayment of $5,000 as customer deposits for reversal next month. (Use journal entry 5.)
1/31	Recorded depreciation expense of $1,750 ($1,500 on equipment, $250 on furniture). (Use journal entry 6.)
1/31	Accrued interest expense on note payable for $1,000 to a liability account called accrued expenses for reversal next month. (Use journal entry 7.)
1/31	Accrued interest income to short-term investments for $75 for reversal next month. (Use journal entry 8.)
1/31	Accrued revenue and related cost of goods sold for a shipment which took place 1/31/07 but was invoiced in February. The sale was to Pam's Design and represented two Item 201 spas which were sold for $7,000 each, sales tax of $1,085, and which cost Sunset $5,000 each. (Use journal entry 9.)
1/31	Reconciled the bank account. There were no bank service charges. The bank statement balance was $34,793.43 at 1/31/07. Check Nos. 104, 113, 114, and 115 had not been paid according to the bank statement. One deposit, made on 1/27/07 for $5,000, was not reflected on the bank statement.
1/31	Income and expense budget information for January through March is as follows: Merchandise sales of $170,000 are expected in January, increasing $10,000 per month thereafter. Service sales of $10,000 are expected in January, increasing $1,000 per month thereafter. Cost of goods sold is expected to be 75% of merchandise sales. Depreciation, insurance, interest, supplies, rent, and telephone are expected to remain constant at $1,800, $1,500, $1,000, $500, $3,000, and $1,500, respectively. A one-time license fee of $20,000 was expected for January. Salaries expenses are estimated at $10,000 per month.
1/31	Asset, liability, and equity budget information for January is as follows:

Checking	$ 31,850
Accounts Receivable	100,000
Inventory	150,000
Prepaid Expenses	15,000
Short-Term Investments	30,000
Furniture	4,500
Equipment	37,400
Acc. Depreciation Furniture	250
Acc. Depreciation Equipment	1,500
Deposits	3,000
Accounts Payable	29,800
Sales Tax Payable	15,000
Fed. Pay. Tax Payable	2,500
State Pay. Tax Payable	500
Customer Deposits	9,000
Notes Payable	200,000
Common Stock	100,000

Pay/Tax/Withholding	Christopher	Sanchez	Lee
Hours	n/a	84	67
Check Number	113	114	115
Rate	60,000.00	13.00	12.00
Gross Pay	2,500.00	1,092.00	804.00
Federal Withholding	−342.50	−149.60	−110.15
Social Security Employee	−155.00	−67.70	−49.85
Medicare Employee	−36.25	−15.83	−11.66
CA—Withholding	−137.50	−60.06	−44.22
CA—Disability	−12.50	−5.46	−4.02
CA—Employment Training Tax	2.50	1.09	0.80
Social Security Employer	155.00	67.70	49.85
Medicare Company	36.25	15.83	11.66
Federal Unemployment	20.00	8.74	6.43
CA—Unemployment	6.25	2.73	2.01
Check Amount	1,816.25	793.35	584.10

Create and print the following reports with no page numbers and without zero balance accounts (like you did in this and previous chapters):

a. Bank reconciliation report for January 2007

b. Budgeted income statement accounts for January through March 2007 with a YTD column

c. Budgeted versus actual income statement for the month of January 2007

d. Budgeted balance sheet accounts for January through March 2007 with a YTD column

e. Budgeted versus actual balance sheet for the month ended January 2007 with Budget, Variance, and % Variance columns

f. Statement of income and retained earnings for the month of January 2007 with a % of Total Revenues column

g. Balance sheet as of 1/31/07 with a % column

h. Statement of cash flow for the month of January 2007 with no YTD column

i. Inventory profitability report for the month of January 2007

j. Items sold to customers report for the month of January 2007 in detail format without Customer ID

k. Items purchased from vendors report for the month of January 2007 in summary format without Vendor ID

l. Collection aging report as of 1/31/07

m. Payment aging report as of 1/31/07

n. Business summary report as of 1/31/07

o. Key balances report as of 1/31/07

p. Inventory valuation report as of 1/31/07 without Item ID, Item Class, Cost Method, and Stocking U/M

q. Export the inventory profitability report you created to Excel and then print the Excel spreadsheet from Excel with row and column headers and gridlines in landscape orientation

r. Prepare a summary reconciliation to explain any differences between the supporting schedules and the financial statements you just created like the one created in the chapter

Payroll Taxes

- Calculate federal income tax withholding.
- Calculate Social Security and Medicare taxes.
- Calculate federal unemployment taxes.
- Learn about state income and unemployment taxes.

Overview

Throughout this text, you have been provided information for employee payroll tax withholding and employer payroll tax expenses. Peachtree has the ability to calculate each of these for you; however, they charge you an annual fee to do so. Some businesses will find this service very valuable and worth the cost, and some will not. Payroll tax computations are not straightforward. They are, in fact, quite convoluted and dependent on all sorts of exceptions and rules. For example, federal income tax withholding is dependent on an employee's income; whether they are being paid weekly, biweekly, semimonthly, monthly, etc.; the number of exemptions they claim; and their filing status: married, single, head of household, etc.

This appendix is designed to provide you a basic overview of the payroll tax conundrum and is focused on federal taxes only, as each state has its own rules for income tax withholding, unemployment, etc.

Federal Income Tax Withholding

As previously mentioned, federal income tax withholding is dependent on an employee's income; whether they are being paid weekly, biweekly, semimonthly, monthly, etc.; the number of exemptions they claim; and their filing status: married, single, head of household, etc. Guiding employers in this regard is Circular E (Employer's Tax Guide), which can be found online at the Internal Revenue Service Web site at **http://www.irs.gov/pub/irs-pdf/ p15.pdf**.

The IRS provides tables in this document to compute the specific amount to be withheld from each employee. It also provides a percentage method, which is much easier to produce for our purposes. Employees must supply employers with payroll tax information each year such as their filing status: married, single, head of household, and the number of exemptions they are claiming.

The steps necessary for computation of an employee's federal income tax withholding are as follows:

1 Determine the frequency of wage payments: weekly, biweekly, semimonthly, monthly, etc.

2 Determine the employee's filing status.

3 Based on the above, choose the appropriate table for Percentage Method of Withholding found in Figure A1.1.

Figure A1.1

Tables for Percentage Method of Withholding

Tables for Percentage Method of Withholding
(For Wages Paid in 2006)

TABLE 1—WEEKLY Payroll Period

(a) SINGLE person (including head of household)—

If the amount of wages (after subtracting withholding allowances) is: Not over $51 . . . . . $0

Over—	But not over—	The amount of income tax to withhold is:	of excess over—
$51	—$192	10%	—$51
$192	—$620	$14.10 plus 15%	—$192
$620	—$1,409	$78.30 plus 25%	—$620
$1,409	—$3,013	$275.55 plus 28%	—$1,409
$3,013	—$6,508	$724.67 plus 33%	—$3,013
$6,508	. . . . . .	$1,878.02 plus 35%	—$6,508

(b) MARRIED person—

If the amount of wages (after subtracting withholding allowances) is: Not over $154 . . . . . $0

Over—	But not over—	The amount of income tax to withhold is:	of excess over—
$154	—$440	10%	—$154
$440	—$1,308	$28.60 plus 15%	—$440
$1,308	—$2,440	$158.80 plus 25%	—$1,308
$2,440	—$3,759	$441.80 plus 28%	—$2,440
$3,759	—$6,607	$811.12 plus 33%	—$3,759
$6,607	. . . . . .	$1,750.96 plus 35%	—$6,607

TABLE 2—BIWEEKLY Payroll Period

(a) SINGLE person (including head of household)—

If the amount of wages (after subtracting withholding allowances) is: Not over $102 . . . . . $0

Over—	But not over—	The amount of income tax to withhold is:	of excess over—
$102	—$385	10%	—$102
$385	—$1,240	$28.30 plus 15%	—$385
$1,240	—$2,817	$156.55 plus 25%	—$1,240
$2,817	—$6,025	$550.80 plus 28%	—$2,817
$6,025	—$13,015	$1,449.04 plus 33%	—$6,025
$13,015	. . . . . .	$3,755.74 plus 35%	—$13,015

(b) MARRIED person—

If the amount of wages (after subtracting withholding allowances) is: Not over $308 . . . . . $0

Over—	But not over—	The amount of income tax to withhold is:	of excess over—
$308	—$881	10%	—$308
$881	—$2,617	$57.30 plus 15%	—$881
$2,617	—$4,881	$317.70 plus 25%	—$2,617
$4,881	—$7,517	$883.70 plus 28%	—$4,881
$7,517	—$13,213	$1,621.78 plus 33%	—$7,517
$13,213	. . . . . .	$3,501.46 plus 35%	—$13,213

TABLE 3—SEMIMONTHLY Payroll Period

(a) SINGLE person (including head of household)—

If the amount of wages (after subtracting withholding allowances) is: Not over $110 . . . . . $0

Over—	But not over—	The amount of income tax to withhold is:	of excess over—
$110	—$417	10%	—$110
$417	—$1,343	$30.70 plus 15%	—$417
$1,343	—$3,052	$169.60 plus 25%	—$1,343
$3,052	—$6,527	$596.85 plus 28%	—$3,052
$6,527	—$14,100	$1,569.85 plus 33%	—$6,527
$14,100	. . . . . .	$4,068.94 plus 35%	—$14,100

(b) MARRIED person—

If the amount of wages (after subtracting withholding allowances) is: Not over $333 . . . . . $0

Over—	But not over—	The amount of income tax to withhold is:	of excess over—
$333	—$954	10%	—$333
$954	—$2,835	$62.10 plus 15%	—$954
$2,835	—$5,288	$344.25 plus 25%	—$2,835
$5,288	—$8,144	$957.50 plus 28%	—$5,288
$8,144	—$14,315	$1,757.18 plus 33%	—$8,144
$14,315	. . . . . .	$3,793.61 plus 35%	—$14,315

TABLE 4—MONTHLY Payroll Period

(a) SINGLE person (including head of household)—

If the amount of wages (after subtracting withholding allowances) is: Not over $221 . . . . . $0

Over—	But not over—	The amount of income tax to withhold is:	of excess over—
$221	—$833	10%	—$221
$833	—$2,687	$61.20 plus 15%	—$833
$2,687	—$6,104	$339.30 plus 25%	—$2,687
$6,104	—$13,054	$1,193.55 plus 28%	—$6,104
$13,054	—$28,200	$3,139.55 plus 33%	—$13,054
$28,200	. . . . . .	$8,137.73 plus 35%	—$28,200

(b) MARRIED person—

If the amount of wages (after subtracting withholding allowances) is: Not over $667 . . . . . $0

Over—	But not over—	The amount of income tax to withhold is:	of excess over—
$667	—$1,908	10%	—$667
$1,908	—$5,670	$124.10 plus 15%	—$1,908
$5,670	—$10,575	$688.40 plus 25%	—$5,670
$10,575	—$16,288	$1,914.65 plus 28%	—$10,575
$16,288	—$28,629	$3,514.29 plus 33%	—$16,288
$28,629	. . . . . .	$7,586.82 plus 35%	—$28,629

4   Determine the amount of wage payment.

5   Determine the number of employee withholding allowances.

6   Use Figure A1.2 to calculate the value of one withholding allowance.

Payroll Period	One Withholding Allowance
Weekly...	$ 63.46
Biweekly..	126.92
Semimonthly..	137.50
Monthly..	275.00
Quarterly..	825.00
Semiannualy...	1,650.00
Annually...	3,300.00
Daily or miscellaneous (each day of the payroll period).............	12.69

Figure A1.2

One Withholding Allowance

7   Compute the employee's withholding amount by multiplying the employee's withholding allowances by the value of one withholding allowance determined above.

8   Calculate the net wages by subtracting the employee's withholding amount determined above from his or her wage payment.

9   Using net wages determined above, calculate the required federal income tax withholding using the table you selected found in Figure A1.1.

For example, a single employee, claiming two withholding allowances, is paid $600 weekly.

To calculate the federal income tax withholding:

1   Frequency of wage payments: **weekly**.

2   Employee's filing status: **single**.

3   Appropriate table for Percentage Method of Withholding: **Table 1(a)**.

4   Amount of wage payment: **600**.

5   Number of employee withholding allowances: **2**.

6   Value of one withholding allowance: **63.46**.

7   Employee's withholding amount: 2 × 63.46 = **126.92**.

8   Net wages: 600.00 − 126.92 = **473.08**.

9   Required federal income tax withholding: 14.10 + [15% × (473.08 − 192.00)] = **56.26**.

A second example, a married employee, claiming three withholding allowances, is paid $1,500 semimonthly.

To calculate the federal income tax withholding:

1 Frequency of wage payments: **semimonthly**.

2 Employee's filing status: **married**.

3 Appropriate table for Percentage Method of Withholding: **Table 3(b)**.

4 Amount of wage payment: **1,500**.

5 Number of employee withholding allowances: **3**.

6 Value of one withholding allowance: **137.50**.

7 Employee's withholding amount: 3 × 137.50 = **412.50**.

8 Net wages: 1,500.00 − 412.50 = **1,087.50**.

9 Required federal income tax withholding: 62.10 + [15% × (1.087.50 − 954.00)] = **82.13**.

A third example, a married employee, claiming five withholding allowances, is paid $8,000 monthly.

To calculate the federal income tax withholding:

1 Frequency of wage payments: **monthly**.

2 Employee's filing status: **married**.

3 Appropriate table for Percentage Method of Withholding: **Table 4(b)**.

4 Amount of wage payment: **8,000**.

5 Number of employee withholding allowances: **5**.

6 Value of one withholding allowance: **275**.

7 Employee's withholding amount: 5 × 275 = **1,375**.

8 Net wages: 8,000 − 1,375 = **6,625**.

9 Required federal income tax withholding: 688.40 + [25% × (6,625 − 5,670)] = **927.15**.

Social Security and Medicare Taxes

The Federal Insurance Contributions Act (FICA) provides for a federal system of old-age, survivors, disability, and hospital insurance. The old-age, survivors, and disability insurance part is financed by the Social Security tax. The hospital insurance part is financed by the Medicare tax. Each of these taxes is reported separately. Generally, you are required to withhold Social Security and Medicare taxes from your employees' wages, and you must also pay a matching amount of these taxes. Certain types of wages and compensation are not subject to Social Security taxes. Generally, employee wages are subject to Social Security and Medicare taxes regardless of the employee's age or whether he or she is receiving Social Security benefits.

Social Security and Medicare taxes have different rates, and only the Social Security tax has a wage base limit. The wage base limit is the maximum wage that is subject to the tax for the year. Determine the amount of withholding for Social Security and Medicare taxes by multiplying each payment by the employee tax rate. There are no withholding allowances for Social Security and Medicare taxes. The current employee tax rate for Social Security is 6.2% (amount withheld). The employer tax rate for Social Security is also 6.2% (12.4% total). The 2005 wage base limit was $90,000. For 2006, the wage base limit is $94,200. The current employee tax rate for Medicare is 1.45% (amount withheld). The employer tax rate for Medicare tax is also 1.45% (2.9% total). There is no wage base limit for Medicare tax; all covered wages are subject to Medicare tax. Guiding employers in this regard is Circular E (Employer's Tax Guide), which can be found online at the Internal Revenue Service Web site at **http://www.irs. gov/pub/irs-pdf/p15.pdf**.

The steps necessary for computation of an employee's withholding and employer's computation of Social Security and Medicare taxes are as follows:

1 Determine the employee's cumulative earnings year-to-date prior to this paycheck.

2 Determine the amount of wage payment for the current period.

3 Determine if the employee's cumulative earnings exceed or are close to the Social Security wage base limit.

4 Calculate the Social Security tax by multiplying the appropriate wage payment by 6.2%.

5 Calculate the appropriate Medicare tax by multiplying the wage payment by 1.45%.

For example, in 2006, a single employee, claiming two withholding allowances, is paid $600 in the current week. Cumulative earnings to date are $3,000.

> ## To calculate the Social Security and Medicare tax:
>
> **1** Cumulative earnings year-to-date: **3,000**.
>
> **2** Wage payment: **600**.
>
> **3** Cumulative earnings compared to the Social Security wage base limit: **3,000 is less than 94,200**.
>
> **4** Social Security tax: 600 × 6.2% = **37.20**.
>
> **5** Medicare tax: 600 × 1.45% = **8.70**.

A second example, in 2006, a married employee, claiming three withholding allowances, is paid $1,500 semimonthly. Cumulative earnings to date are $6,000.

> ## To calculate the Social Security and Medicare tax:
>
> **1** Cumulative earnings year-to-date: **6,000**.
>
> **2** Wage payment: **1,500**.
>
> **3** Cumulative earnings compared to the Social Security wage base limit: **6,000 is less than 94,200**.
>
> **4** Social Security tax: 1,500 × 6.2% = **93.00**.
>
> **5** Medicare tax: 1,500 × 1.45% = **21.75**.

A third example, in 2006, a married employee, claiming five withholding allowances, is paid $8,000 monthly. Cumulative earnings to date are $88,000.

> ## To calculate the Social Security and Medicare tax:
>
> **1** Cumulative earnings year-to-date: **88,000**.
>
> **2** Wage payment: **8,000**.
>
> **3** Cumulative earnings compared to the Social Security wage base limit: **88,000 is less than 94,200 but close. Difference is 6,200**.
>
> **4** Social Security tax: 6,200 × 6.2% = **384.40** (since this will bring the employee up to the wage limit).
>
> **5** Medicare tax: 8,000 × 1.45% = **116.00**.

Federal Unemployment Taxes

Use Form 940 (or Form 940-EZ) to report your annual Federal Unemployment Tax Act (FUTA) tax. FUTA tax, together with state unemployment systems, provides for payments of unemployment compensation to workers who have lost their jobs. Most employers pay both federal and state unemployment taxes. Only the employer pays FUTA tax. Do not collect or deduct it from your employees' wages. The tax, currently at 0.8%, applies to the first $7,000 you pay each employee in a year after subtracting any exempt payments. The $7,000 amount is the federal wage base. Your state wage base may be different. Instructions can currently be found at **http://www.irs.gov/pub/irs-pdf/i940.pdf**.

The steps necessary for computation of an employee's federal income tax withholding are as follows:

1   Determine the employee's cumulative earnings year-to-date prior to this paycheck.

2   Determine the amount of wage payment for the current period.

3   Determine if the employee's cumulative earnings exceed or are close to the FUTA wage base limit.

4   Calculate the FUTA tax by multiplying the appropriate wage payment by 0.8%.

For example, in 2006, a single employee, claiming two withholding allowances, is paid $600 in the current week. Cumulative earnings to date are $3,000.

To calculate the FUTA tax:

1   Cumulative earnings year-to-date: **3,000**.

2   Wage payment: **600**.

3   Cumulative earnings compared to the FUTA wage base limit: **3,000 is less than 7,000**.

4   FUTA tax: 600 × 0.8% = **4.80**.

A second example, in 2006, a married employee, claiming three withholding allowances, is paid $1,500 semimonthly. Cumulative earnings to date are $6,000.

To calculate the FUTA tax:

1 Cumulative earnings year-to-date: **6,000.**

2 Wage payment: **1,500.**

3 Cumulative earnings compared to the FUTA wage base limit: **6,000 is less than 7,000 but close. Difference is 1,000.**

4 FUTA tax: 1,000 × 0.8% = **8.00.**

A third example, in 2006, a married employee, claiming five withholding allowances, is paid $8,000 monthly. Cumulative earnings to date are $88,000.

To calculate the FUTA tax:

1 Cumulative earnings year-to-date: **88,000.**

2 Wage payment: **8,000.**

3 Cumulative earnings compared to the FUTA wage base limit: **88,000 is more than 7,000.**

4 FUTA tax: 0 × 0.8% = **0.00.**

State Income Tax Withholding and Unemployment Taxes

Each state, of course, has its own rules for withholding state income taxes and computing the employer's cost for unemployment. Some states, Florida and Nevada for instance, do not have a state income tax. Other states, such as California and Hawaii, not only have state income taxes but also have training taxes.

Most of the state income tax computations are similar to the federal computations in that they have different tables for different filing status: single, married, etc., and they have tables for exemption allowances. Rather than explain how to calculate taxes for each and every state in the union, I suggest you visit your local state tax agency to determine income tax and unemployment tax rates and requirements. Some Web site references follow: (Remember, these sites worked when this text was published. They may no longer work if the state moved them or reconfigured their Web site.)

California   **http://www.edd.ca.gov/taxrep/taxrte9x.htm**
Florida   **http://www.myflorida.com/dor/taxes/**
Hawaii   **http://www.hawaii.gov/tax/a1_3tax_address.htm**

Appendix 1 Questions

1 What factors affect an employee's federal income tax withholding?

2 Where can employers get guidance on federal income tax withholding?

3 What do withholding allowances do to the computation of federal income tax withholding?

4 What does the Social Security tax finance?

5 What does the Medicare tax finance?

6 What is the Social Security tax rate?

7 Is there a wage base limit to the Social Security tax? If so, what is it for 2006?

8 What is the Medicare tax rate?

9 Is there a wage base limit to the Medicare tax? If so, what is it for 2006?

10 Who pays FUTA, and what is the current rate and computational structure?

Appendix 1 Assignments

1 In 2006, a married employee, claiming one withholding allowance, is paid $800 in the current week. Cumulative earnings to date are $4,000. Calculate the following:

   a. Federal income tax withholding

   b. Employee Social Security taxes to be withheld

   c. Employee Medicare taxes to be withheld

   d. Employer Social Security tax

   e. Employer Medicare tax

   f. FUTA

2 In 2006, a single employee, claiming three withholding allowances, is paid $2,000 semimonthly. Cumulative earnings to date are $6,500. Calculate the following:

   a. Federal income tax withholding

   b. Employee Social Security taxes to be withheld

c.   Employee Medicare taxes to be withheld

d.   Employer Social Security tax

e.   Employer Medicare tax

f.   FUTA

3   In 2006, a single employee, claiming zero withholding allowances, is paid $10,000 monthly. Cumulative earnings to date are $90,000. Calculate the following:

a.   Federal income tax withholding

b.   Employee Social Security taxes to be withheld

c.   Employee Medicare taxes to be withheld

d.   Employer Social Security tax

e.   Employer Medicare tax

f.   FUTA

index

Records windows, Peachtree, 13–14
Reports, 10
    create a budget vs. actual,
       304–306
    for analysis of sales and
       purchases, creating additional,
       322–326
    guided tour on, 23
Restore
    a file using Peachtree's backup
       procedure to an external disk,
       133–135
    a Peachtree file, 16
    and open company file, 16
    Peachtree backup files from CD,
       5–6, 314–322
Retained earnings, creating a
    statement of, 49–52, 314–316
Revenues
    accruing, 270–272
    adjusting for unearned, 275–278
    budgeting, 292–293
    investigate, 63–65
Reverse transaction, 268
Reviewing the business status center,
    85–89

S

Sales
    adjust for sales occurring but not
       invoiced, 271
    recording of, 169–173
Sales order, create, 155–159

Sales tax and payroll tax amounts,
    verify record, 245–247
Sara Duncan, CPA, 207–210
Service items, set up, 118–123
Set up
    beginning balances, 129–133
    customers, 109–116
    inventory items, 118–123
    new accounts, 129–133
    payroll, 123–129
    service items, 118–123
    vendors, 116–118
Shortcuts, Peachtree's, 17
Short-term investment activity,
    recording of, 225–226
Social Security taxes, 353–354
Sports City, 339–341
State income tax withholding, 356
State unemployment taxes, 356
Statement of cash flows
    creating, 71–73, 320–322
    investigating, 79–81
Stockholders' equity, create budget
    for liabilities and, 301–302
Sunset Spas, 214–217, 344–348
System date, 13

T

Tasks, 8
    windows, Peachtree, 13–14
Time sheet information, 200
Time sheets, complete weekly,
    180–184

Title bar, 11
Transaction list, prepare, 194

U

Unearned revenue, adjusting for,
    275–278
Unemployment taxes
    federal, 355–356
    state, 356
Update
    customer terms and address, 230
    customer's information,
       155–159
    vendor records for changes in
       terms, 226–227

V

Vendor records, update for changes
    in terms, 226–227
Vendors
    add new, 150–152
    setting up, 116–118
View effects of interest accrual and
    related reversal, 269

W

Weekly time sheets, 180–184
Wild Water Sports, Inc., 105–106,
    147–148, 198–202, 219–220, 265,
    291–292, 313–314